DEFIANT FAILED STATE

ALSO BY BRUCE E. BECHTOL, JR.

Red Rogue: The Persistent Challenge of North Korea

RELATED TITLES FROM POTOMAC BOOKS, INC.

Crisis on the Korean Peninsula
—Christoph Bluth

Korea on the Brink: A Memoir of Political Intrigue and Military Crisis
—John A. Wickham

DEFIANT FAILED STATE

THE NORTH KOREAN THREAT TO
INTERNATIONAL SECURITY

BRUCE E. BECHTOL, JR.

Potomac Books, Inc.
Washington, D.C.

Library of Congress Cataloging-in-Publication Data
Bechtol, Bruce E., 1959–
  Defiant failed state : the North Korean threat to international security / Bruce E. Bechtol, Jr. — 1st ed.
    p. cm.
  Includes bibliographical references and index.
  ISBN 978-1-59797-531-5 (hardcover : acid-free paper)
  1. Korea (North)—Foreign relations. 2. Korea (North)—Military policy. 3. Korea (North)—Foreign relations—United States. 4. United States—Foreign relations—Korea (North) 5. Security, International. I. Title.
  DS935.65.B43 2010
  355'.03305193—dc22

                                                                    2010023322

Printed in the United States of America on acid-free paper that meets the American National Standards Institute Z39-48 Standard.

Potomac Books, Inc.
22841 Quicksilver Drive
Dulles, Virginia 20166

First Edition

10 9 8 7 6 5 4 3 2 1

CONTENTS

ILLUSTRATIONS

PREFACE

For the past twenty years, American presidential administrations have had a variety of priorities when it came to both domestic and foreign policy, but addressing the North Korean threat to American national security has rarely, if ever, been at the top of the list. Since the end of the Cold War and the demise of the Soviet Union, North Korea has been struggling to maintain its existence, hanging on by its fingernails, as a donor state that simply could not feed a large portion of its people without foreign aid. Images of poverty and desperate food and energy needs are what visitors to the last vestiges of the "Hermit Kingdom" often report back to the West. But North Korea is a far more complicated and threatening nation-state than it appears on the surface. President Bill Clinton found this out during the nuclear crises of 1994. President George W. Bush discovered it as his administration experienced a nuclear confrontation that lasted from the fall of 2002 until the end of his presidency (among many other issues and challenges from a diverse North Korean threat). And President Barack Obama (who no doubt wanted to focus on other foreign policy issues) encountered this reality as the North Koreans tested a long-range ballistic missile during the first hundred days of his administration. Thus, while many analysts often categorize North Korea as a failing or failed state, it is the multifaceted set of threats from Pyongyang that I will address in this book.

In this book I will discuss what I consider to be the main threats that North Korea presents to the national security of the United States and its allies. I will also cover why North Korea, a country policy makers in Washington would like to "put on the back burner," continues to present various challenges that constitute immediate or impending threats to U.S. national interests in key regions of the world. Is North Korea truly a failing or failed state? Or is it a state that has cleverly adjusted to economic and geopolitical realities and is capable of surviving indefinitely? Why does a state that has so many economic and political challenges present such a wide variety of threats to the United States and key players in the region? And finally, how do the North Koreans do it? This book will answer all of these questions and give the reader food for thought regarding the future of the Korean Peninsula.

I have written this book primarily for policy analysts, functional and regional specialists, military and security specialists, scholars, and anyone who has a desire to understand the issues that make North Korea a continuing threat to the United States and its key allies in the region. It presents evidence and assessments that will be of interest to analysts on both sides of the Pacific. As such, it is not my goal in this book to produce an analysis that is overly focused on political science or international relations jargon, or a work that is built on theory. It is my hope that my analysis will be of interest to those who have a practical as well as a theoretical interest in the region and in solving the complicated issues presented by the diverse (and unrelenting) North Korean threat.

Many of my colleagues have been helpful as I conducted the research and writing of this book. Dr. Doug Streusand has been a thoughtful and patient adviser who read excerpts from my manuscript and made suggestions to make it more readable for a mainstream audience. Dr. Mark Moyar is a fellow scholar who has been helpful in making practical and scholarly suggestions about my writing and research throughout this process. I simply cannot mention these colleagues without also acknowledging Ms. Carol-Anne Parker, who was quite valuable in helping me get through all the numerous software issues that I encountered. All of these helpful individuals are my good friends and worked with me at the Marine Corps University. Without their help and encouragement this book would not have been possible. Finally, I am truly indebted to Maj. Gen. Don Gardner, USMC (Ret.). He served as the president of the Marine Corps University for my first four years there. His leadership and dedication to the faculty's scholarly achievements at the Marine Corps University will be truly missed as he moves into the "easy life" of his second retirement.

It is important that I acknowledge the Korean studies specialists and practitioners who have been invaluable in my research for this work. Col. David Maxwell (USA) is a longtime and well-known soldier-scholar among Korean specialists, and his collaboration has often proven useful. Another important individual who has offered advice throughout this process is Park Syung-je of the Military Analyst Association of the Republic of Korea. Dr. Chun Seong Whun of the Korea Institute for National Unification is a specialist who has provided advice and support, as well as key analysis, that have greatly benefited my research. Dr. Nicholas Eberstadt of the American Enterprise Institute has been a steady and balanced adviser and has always offered views that have been extremely useful. Chuck Downs, the author of *Over the Line: North Korea's Negotiating Strategy* has been an inspirational friend and an outstanding source for analysis and clear-headed, practical views. Finally, the specialist to whom I owe the most is Robert Collins, a retired senior staff officer in the Combined Forces Command and an individual who has mentored dozens of action officers and foreign area officers for many years. His insights and perspectives regarding the inner workings of the North Korean government, its motivations, and its intent were quite simply invaluable to my research for this book.

A number of other specialists have provided important insights and perspectives for my research. Though I cannot acknowledge all of them here, I would like to thank L. Gordon Flake, executive director of the Mansfield Foundation; Dr. Hugo Kim, president of the East-West Research Institute; Dr. Marcus Noland of the Peterson Institute for International Economics; Dr. Stephan Haggard of the University of California at San Diego; Lt. Gen. Ray Ayres, USMC (Ret.); Gen. John Tilleli, USA (Ret.); Dr. Patrick Morgan of the University of California–Irvine; author and analyst Joseph S. Bermudez, Jr.; independent researchers John McCreary and Merrily Baird; journalist Don Kirk; FOX News reporter James Rosen; Dr. Richard Bush, director of the Center for Northeast Asian Policy Studies at the Brookings Institution; Charles (Jack) L. Pritchard, Nicole Finnemann, and Greg Scarlatoiu of the Korea Economic Institute; Dr. Larry Niksch of Congressional Research Service; and Dr. Lee Choong-mook of the Institute of Korean Studies. All of these individuals are experts who provided background, context, and insights that were useful for my research.

I would like to briefly comment on the transliteration of the Korean language that occurs throughout my book. The written form of the Korean language (Hangul) has never been transliterated in a truly straightforward manner. The form that was used until recently (the McCune-Reischauer system) has typically been the one used by both Western and Korean publications. The South Korean government changed to its own system in 2002, but many publications—even some in South Korea—still tend to use the old system. Thus, any sources that were written before 2002 will be under the old system, and some, but not all, publications now use a completely different system for transliteration of the Korean language. Because the McCune-Reischauer system is the one that I have been trained in, I will use it throughout the book whenever possible. When quoting sources that use the new system, I will quote them exactly as written. Because of this, it may appear that I use a different spelling for some of the names in this book. In the interest of consistency, I believe that the methodology described above will be the most practical for the reader. In addition, I also used the Korean practice of placing family names first, not last, when quoting Korean individuals unless they have specifically requested otherwise or the sources from which their quotations or information are otherwise articulated. The reader will notice that sometimes I refer to South Korea as the Republic of Korea, the official name of the country. Most scholars and writers accept both terms when referring to this nation; in fact, what Americans would usually refer to as South Korea is often referred to as simply Korea by the people who live there. While I will usually refer to the Democratic People's Republic of Korea as North Korea, some sources refer to it as the DPRK; thus when using these sources, I too will refer to it in that manner.

Responsibility for the writing and research of this book is solely my own. Thus the views that I express here do not necessarily reflect the policy or position of the Marine Corps Command and Staff College, the Marine Corps University, or the U.S. government. References to Internet sites were accurate at the time of writing. Neither the author nor Potomac Books, Inc., is responsible for websites that have expired or changed since this book was prepared.

CHAPTER ONE

Introduction

Northern Korea is a nation-state that has been a thorn in the side of the United States and its foreign policy since the beginning of the Cold War. As a regime that unapologetically existed within the Soviet sphere of influence, North Korea continued to cause trouble for Washington's national security interests long after the Korean conflict had ended with such provocations as the capture of the USS *Pueblo*, the attempted assassination of the commander of U.S. Forces Korea (USFK), and the terrorist bombing of high-ranking South Korean officials on a visit to Burma.[1] These blatant acts of rogue state behavior are just a few examples of the many acts of brinkmanship and provocation that the Kim Il-sung regime carried out throughout the Cold War. His regime also began the early nuclear weaponization and ballistic missile programs for which North Korea is now noted.

In the Kim Chong-il era (beginning in 1994), North Korea's threatening state behavior continues as of the writing of this book. And yet, many analysts still believe that North Korea is a weak—perhaps a failed—state that can be "brought in from the cold" if only the right engagement strategy is utilized.[2] In fact, North Korea meets the annual Failing States Index criteria in several important categories, as reported by *Foreign Policy* journal, and has done so for several years.[3] While the Failing States Index is accurate—based on excellent analysis—and useful, North Korea as a nation-state simply does not meet the paradigms associated with most countries in the world that would bring about collapse. Thus I titled this book *Defiant Failed State*, for while North Korea may be a state that seems economically weak, politically unstable, and socially bizarre, it has truly remained defiant despite facing a variety of challenges that would bring down most other nations. In fact, North Korea remains defiant toward the Republic of Korea (ROK), its neighbor to the south; other nations in the region; and particularly the United States.

According to a Rasmussen poll conducted during August 2009, 75 percent of Americans describe North Korea as an enemy of the United States, and only Iran topped the Democratic People's Republic of Korea (DPRK) in the poll of America's potential enemies.[4] "The National Intelligence Strategy of the United States," dated August 2009, stated, "North Korea continues to threaten peace and security in East Asia because of its sustained pursuit of nuclear and ballistic missile capabilities, its transfer of these capabilities to third parties, its erratic behavior, and its large conventional military capability."[5]

The objective of this book is to show how a defiant government in North Korea has adapted to the post–Cold War environment and thus continues to pose a multifaceted threat to the national security of the United States and several of its key allies. Despite overwhelming economic odds and a lack of suppliers for its conventional weapons needs, the North Korean military still presents an immediate and constant threat to the security of its neighbors. North Korea's own arms industry has become highly proficient at distributing not only conventional weapons but also weapons of mass destruction (WMDs, or nuclear and chemical programs) and the platforms that carry them (missiles and artillery) to unstable regions of the world. Pyongyang has also shown no hesitation in supporting non-state actors that choose to engage in acts of terrorism as part of their policy. Pyongyang continues to maintain and expand its nuclear weaponization program and shows no real signs of transparent dismantlement in its future plans. Of course, the succession process in North Korea—determining who will follow Kim Chong-il should he die or become incapacitated—presents a wide variety of national security issues not only for South Korea and the United States but also for every country that has an interest in the region. Dealing with all these threats—none of which have subsided, and some of which have grown in recent years—is the most important responsibility of the ROK-U.S. alliance.

FRAMEWORK OF ANALYSIS

This volume analyzes the primary North Korean threats to U.S. national interests and those of its allies. It also examines important challenges facing the ROK-U.S. alliance as it transforms and modernizes in response to the changing needs of both nations. While I do not intend to focus on complicated international relations theory or to build a political science model for my framework of analysis, I believe that while reading this book, the reader can use the important prism of the "instruments of national power" (IOP) framework that the U.S. Department of Defense has often used for conducting its analysis of an adversary's use of the instruments of policy (read: power) from which it gains power on the international stage.[6]

The IOP framework of analysis considers a nation-state's IOPs and analyzes how effective they are while at the same time addressing how the United States can best utilize its own IOPs to deal with an enemy or peer competitor. In essence, it examines "all of the means available to the government in its pursuit of national objectives." The U.S. Department of Defense defines the four main IOPs as diplomatic, informational, military, and economic.[7] These four key instruments are widely referred to as the DIME. As the reader goes through this work, I ask that he or she analyze each chapter from this perspective. How does North Korea use diplomacy? How does a nation with almost no Internet connections and a fledgling cell phone network utilize its informational instrument of power effectively? How much of a threat does the North Korean military remain to the United States and its allies? How stable is the North Korean government and what will happen when Kim Chong-il dies? And finally, how does the North Korean economy survive, and what are its key (legal and illegal) features? I address all of these important questions in the book as I examine key threats from Pyongyang and then summarize them using the DIME framework of analysis.

RESEARCH STRATEGIES AND SOURCES

A great deal of scholarship in recent years—both in Korea and in the United States—has focused on issues relating to the Korean Peninsula. A variety of approaches were used to analyze important issues relating to the two Koreas and particularly North Korea. To date, some key examples of these approaches have included:[8]

1. analyzing the challenges from North Korea's nuclear program (most studies have been from a political science perspective)
2. examining North Korean internal politics
3. discussing North Korean foreign policy
4. studying North Korea from an economic perspective
5. evaluating the ROK-U.S. alliance (largely from a nonmilitary perspective)
6. exploring the past, present, and future North Korean–South Korean relationship

The issues articulated above are all relevant to both the contemporary and historical context that adds to the scholarship on North Korea. That said, most works that focus on either the Korean Peninsula or specifically North Korea do not address issues in the particular context of how they are a threat to the security of the United States (and its allies). Thus, it is relevant to discuss the ongoing yet seldom discussed (except for Pyongyang's nuclear program or to a lesser extent its missile program) and evolving yet dangerous North Korean military capabilities, including its large, forward-deployed conventional forces. Looking at North Korea while using the DIME methodology, it is also important to address Pyongyang's proliferation activities, not only from the perspective of how it gains badly needed cash for the regime, but also in the context of how it enables other rogue states' programs and promotes instability in volatile regions of the world as well as in Northeast Asia. This work not only studies both North Korea's military capabilities and its proliferation but also presents a case study of North Korea's diplomacy as it relates to its nuclear program and all of the other issues associated with this program during the Bush administration (2001–9). Finally, when it comes to threats to the security of the region and specifically to U.S. interests there, the issue of Kim Chong-il's health, the succession process in the North Korean government, and the potential instability that can ensue because of these complicated and often confusing issues are challenges that confront Washington and its key allies in Asia. An aging leader with poor health in Pyongyang is likely to only exacerbate these issues. Thus, I analyze and assess how the Kim Chong-il succession process has developed and what it holds for the future of North Korea and the region.

As the United States looks to important economic, security, and diplomatic challenges in Northeast Asia in the twenty-first century, it is clear that Washington cannot do it alone. The ROK-U.S. military alliance has stood as a deterrent against aggression on the Korean Peninsula and a stabilizing force in East Asia since the end of the Korean conflict in 1953. Yet this alliance has been in a state of flux since roughly 2003. Ensuring that Washington and Seoul are both capable of securing stability on the Korean Peninsula and in concurrence about how that security and stability will be achieved as both nations move through the twenty-first century has been a challenge for policy makers on both sides of the Pacific. Both governments have gone through many changes in their vision for maintaining security and stability in Asia, but one thing is clear: the North Korean threat has not subsided. Thus changes must be made with this fact in mind while planning for future contingencies.

This book is unique because it specifically addresses North Korea (and its relationship with South Korea) from a national security perspective. It is the first study to combine all the issues discussed in this chapter with an analysis of how they can be addressed now and in the future through the ROK-U.S. military alliance. There has been very little written about North Korea's conventional military forces. Indeed, relatively few published studies address North Korea's proliferation and support to terrorist groups. Inevitably, these issues are linked to North Korea's nuclear and ballistic missile programs and to the security and stability of the government in Pyongyang. By tying these issues together and addressing how they have been and potentially can be addressed by the United States and its key allies in the region (particularly South Korea), this work presents a unique analysis of the security threats posed by the reclusive communist state of North Korea and provides a strategic picture of how these threats continue to evolve, how they can be contained, and their potential for drastic change in coming years.

The research involved in writing this book comes from diverse sources. The sources used in this work include but are not limited to interviews with academics, policy makers, and military experts on both sides of the Pacific; scholarship and books by and from experts on both sides of the political spectrum regarding North and South Korean security; papers and presentations from conferences and symposia; analysis of speeches, press releases, press reports, and press conferences; U.S. and South Korean government reports, white papers, and legislative testimony; declassified defector reports; speeches and statements by policy makers in the

United States and East Asia; and papers, reports, and special releases by important think tanks, government agencies, public policy institutes, and universities. To provide insight on the diverse sources used in this book, the endnotes are augmented by a selected bibliography.

OUTLINE OF CHAPTERS

In chapter 2, I address the North Korean military threat to the security of the Korean Peninsula and Northeast Asia. During 2006, former secretary of defense Donald Rumsfeld stated that he did not see North Korea as an immediate military threat to South Korea.[9] But is this assertion true, or did he simply make the statement because of overwhelming U.S. military obligations all over the globe? Indeed, when this statement was made, and when then-president Roh Moo-hyun expressed the same assessment, it became a great matter of contention for the South Korean people, many of whom expressed disagreement, including a great majority of retired generals and high-ranking officials.[10] In order to truly analyze the threat that North Korea poses to its neighbor to the south and the region, it is important to analyze much more than just North Korea's nuclear program (though it is a significant threat) or even its proliferation of WMDs and related materials to rogue nations in the Middle East and South Asia. Korean scholar Park Hyeong-jung differentiates the North Korean threat into five categories: the conventional military threat, WMDs, ideological contamination, threats related to North Korea as a failing country, and threats to the welfare of the North Korean people.[11] For the purposes of this chapter, I focus on an analysis of North Korea's military—its entire military—and the challenges that it poses to the stability and security of the modern and democratic states in the region. Because the North Korean nuclear threat is in many ways a separate and complicated issue, it is dealt with in a separate chapter.

Chapter 3 examines North Korea's diverse and widespread proliferation to rogue states in the Middle East and South Asia, as well as Pyongyang's support to terrorist groups. While much of the talk circulating among pundits and academics has centered around such issues as North Korea's nuclear program and the ensuing talks with the United States or Kim Chong-il's health issues, the threat to U.S. interests abroad because of North Korean proliferation has often been overlooked. This oversight is unfortunate because North Korea has actively participated in the proliferation of WMD programs and technology and the weapons platforms used to launch them (ballistic missiles) to some of the most unstable regions in the world. Even as the six-party talks (the international diplomatic initiative meant to dismantle North Korea's nuclear program) with the United States and other key players were under way during 2007 and 2008, North Korea showed no signs of either ceasing or slowing its proliferation of WMD and conventional weapons to rogue states such as Syria and Iran and its support to terrorist groups such as Hezbollah.[12] In fact, North Korea continues to maintain its close relationships with state and non-state actors in the Middle East whose goals have put them in direct conflict with U.S. interests and those of its allies (such as Israel). I examine this important phenomenon and other related issues in detail.

In chapter 4, I analyze the six-party talks and the process that surrounded them during the Bush administration. In order to truly comprehend the nuances associated with the six-party talks, one must first understand the basic background on North Korea's plutonium and highly enriched uranium (HEU) programs and how they have developed. Thus, I lead off my analysis with an introduction to this material. I also provide some background to gain important perspective on the North Koreans' and Americans' actions that led to the six-party talks. Further, I cover the events that occurred during the talks between 2003 and 2005 and that led to the breakthrough that seemed to occur in 2005 as well as the activities that essentially put this framework into limbo during 2005–6. North Korea upped the ante in 2006 with two key provocative initiatives. I describe the fallout from these events in detail and analyze them, leading the reader to the real breakthrough agreement of 2007. Finally, I close with events that have occurred during and around the talks since 2007 and wrap up with my conclusion about the outlook for the six-party talks, North Korea's nuclear program, and possible implications for the future.

Chapter 5 covers the Kim Chong-il succession process and all the questions and controversy that surround it. To understand the succession process, why it is such an issue in North Korea, and when it first became an issue, it is necessary to first review some background on the Byzantine web of activities that have occurred in recent years. In addition, information on the Kim family circle, the party, and the military is useful as I examine how it ties into the government in North Korea, how it operates, and who holds the key positions of power. Because concern about

Kim's health during 2008 and beyond brought such focus on the succession process, I explore this reporting and the confusing details surrounding news about his health in detail. Directly related to Kim's health are the apparent moves that either he or the DPRK government made to prove to the world that he was healthy by reporting a flurry of appearances during November and December 2008. This rather complicated yet interesting aspect of the control of information in North Korea deserves examination in this chapter.

With the plethora of rumors surrounding Kim Chong-il's health, there have also been many rumors and reports about who is running the show in North Korea, including a possible shift in the power circle that surrounds the "Dear Leader." Directly tied to this investigation are my analysis of who could take over in the event of Kim's death and how he would do so plus my assessment of the power circles and the base of power in North Korea. Thus, I link these issues and how they are tied into the succession process (as well as the power process) in North Korea.

Scholars and pundits have recently discussed the role of China (if any) in the event of instability or, worse, a collapsed government in North Korea. It is my belief that the Chinese have a better look into North Korea than most, and thus it rates an examination. Of course, one would not expect North Korea to stand idly as its government seems to fray around the edges with a weakened or incapacitated leader. I review how the North Koreans have "circled the wagons," cracked down on their own citizens, and put relations with their neighbor to the south in a deep freeze as questions about their leader's health remain prevalent in the world view. Finally, I examine any cracks in the system that seem to be occurring or coming close to it, and I make some final assessments on what is happening on the ground in North Korea today and what could happen in the future.

Chapter 6 discusses the issue of preparing for the North Korean threat, specifically in the ROK-U.S. military alliance and the Lee Myung-bak presidency. South Korea has a difficult task. The government—along with its key military ally, the United States—must plan for a force-on-force conflict with North Korea and maintain capabilities that effectively deter the DPRK while at the same time preparing for a possible collapse of that threat. It must also plan for the huge challenges that will exist if either one of these scenarios occurs. To do so, South Korea must be able to actually either pay for the additional capabilities needed or ensure that a strong alliance exists with the United States, which can supplement the gaps until the fiscal and military readiness challenges are met.

This matter leads to the question of wartime operational control (OPCON) and the scheduled dismantlement of the Combined Forces Command (CFC) in 2012. Was this a realistic time frame? Finally, several other issues need to be addressed in the near term as South Korea looks at its military alliance with the United States, not the least of these is the cost of maintaining American troops on the Korean Peninsula (and cost sharing) and the move of U.S. troops out of Seoul and bases in the Uijongbu-Tongducheon corridor. I address these and other issues and make some suggestions for planning and policy that will be important as the ROK-U.S. military alliance continues to evolve and improve to meet the challenges for security and stability on the Korean Peninsula in the coming years.

Chapter 7 wraps up the book with concluding thoughts and summarizes the analysis conducted in this work using the DIME framework. As the United States moves into a new era of foreign policy beset by dire economic woes worldwide (including in East Asia), the many threats that North Korea presents to Washington's interests abroad remain daunting. To exacerbate this, North Korea also presents direct, real, and growing threats through its military to both South Korea and Japan—two of the closest trading partners of the United States. Through proliferation to rogue nations in the Middle East, North Korea also poses a threat to America's closest ally there, Israel. And, of course, the many questions about the Kim Chong-il succession process and the many scenarios (most of them negative) that can occur should it not go smoothly have implications for every single nation-state with a stake in what happens in Northeast Asia. I conduct an evaluation and final assessment on all of these issues as I offer final thoughts in the concluding chapter.

CHAPTER TWO

Understanding the North Korean Military Threat

to the Security of the Korean Peninsula and Northeast Asia[1]

Recent questions about the health of the Dear Leader Kim Chong-il, the stability of the government in North Korea, and the continued rhetoric and brinkmanship Pyongyang has engaged in with its neighbors and the United States have renewed a discussion about the North Korean threat to the security and stability of the Northeast Asia region. As a nation-state that has nuclear weapons, has tested them, and shows no signs of giving them up or even revealing transparently its entire capability, North Korea has certainly shown the world in recent years that it will use its WMD arsenal to promote its own national security interests.[2] But with all the attention that North Korea's nuclear program has received, it is easy to forget that this nation still maintains a huge standing army for such a small country (more than a million men in a country of less than 23 million people); has built, deployed, and tested ballistic missiles capable of carrying a chemical or even a nuclear warhead; and continues to engage in bluster, rhetoric, brinkmanship, and provocations against its neighbor to the south, other nations in the region, and the United States.[3] This chapter addresses all aspects of the North Korean military threat (except for the nuclear threat, which is addressed in chapter 4).

In order to truly understand the North Korean military threat, one must first conduct an analysis of the command and control of the North Korean military and the role that the military plays in the government. In addition, it is important to understand the disposition of Pyongyang's military forces—specifically, how are they deployed, and how does this arrangement pose a threat to South Korea? It will also be important to have knowledge of the DPRK's ground, air, naval, and missile forces, particularly their capabilities and training.

But there is more to the North Korean threat than simply conducting an analysis of the country's forces' capabilities, training, and disposition. A common definition of threat used in intelligence analysis is "capability + intent = threat."[4] Thus it is extremely important to assess North Korea's intent by examining the reorganization that its military forces underwent during the mid- to late 1990s and moving into 2000 (smaller changes occurred through 2008). This reorganization of its armed forces involved a focus on the maintenance and capabilities of Pyongyang's asymmetric threat, so I examine this evolving menace in depth in this chapter as well. Finally, I offer some conclusions that will hopefully be useful for those who conduct planning and analysis regarding deterrence and defense against the North Korean threat.

NORTH KOREAN MILITARY COMMAND AND CONTROL

North Korea is a unique case even among communist states because the leader of the nation, Kim Chong-il, exercises his authority to rule his country through the military as well as the party. In Pyongyang, though, there is perhaps more focus on the military source of power than on the Korean Workers' Party (KWP). In fact, many analysts believe that the military's influence has risen dramatically since Kim Chong-il came to power following his father's death in 1994.[5] Thus, in North Korea, the leader of the state exercises his control through the military in two key ways: he uses the military to control the country and controls the military through an elaborate command and control network that begins with the National Defense Commission (NDC) and works its way down.

As shown in figure 1 (from 2006), the NDC chairman exercises ultimate authority over the North Korean armed forces. Kim Chong-il was officially "elected" the chairman of the NDC in 1998 and was previously elected the general secretary of the Workers' Party of Korea (WPK) in 1997. Thus, Kim is officially in charge of both the party and the military.[6] But the NDC is the de facto highest political body in North Korea and a key source of the real decision-making authority in the country.

As the holder of unchallenged power as chairman of the NDC, Kim has control over "political, legislative, judicial, and economic affairs."[7] Kim's decision

FIGURE 1. *North Korean Armed Forces Command and Control*

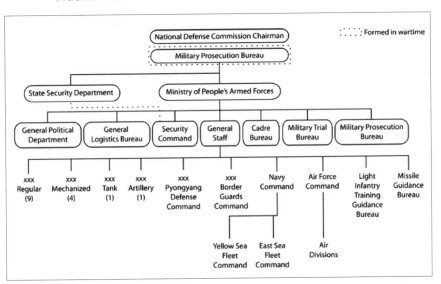

Source: Ken E. Gause, "North Korean Civil-Military Trends: Military-First Politics to a Point," Strategic Studies Institute Monograph (Carlisle, PA: U.S. Army War College, September 2006), http://www.strategicstudiesinstitute.army.mil/pdffiles/pub728.pdf.

to turn the NDC into the most important decision-making body in the country by elevating its status in 1998 shows a conscious effort to use the power base that his father helped build for him in the years when a planned succession process was in effect. Thus, the NDC and its members—all of whom have a power base in the military—have effectively made the military in North Korea not only an effective and threatening force when it comes to dealing with its neighbors but also the country's most important political entity. Other members of the NDC are placed among the highest positions of authority within the country, including foreign policy circles.[8] This scheme is the ultimate carrying out of the "Military First" policy.

While Kim Chong-il is on the NDC and in charge of the NDC, he also controls a murkier power-holding body (in the KWP) that receives much less attention by most analysts: the Organization and Guidance Department (OGD). The OGD oversees both the party and the military and has members who also sit in the NDC. Within the OGD, Department 13 and Department 4 are the two entities that monitor the military to ensure it follows the Dear Leader's ideology and

FIGURE 2. *Relationship of Organization and Guidance Department to the Military*

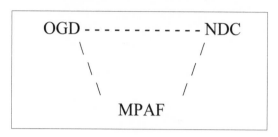

leadership. Department 13 is the most involved in ensuring ideological cooperation from the military while Department 4 has final approval authority over personnel issues involving high-ranking officers. Any rank higher than brigadier general must be approved through the OGD (see figure 2). These promotions, of course, are granted through orders of the supreme commander of the Peoples' Army, or Kim Chong-il. The supreme commander's orders are issued through the OGD.[9] These entities within the OGD do not run the military but are heavily involved in monitoring it, indoctrinating it, overseeing personnel matters at high levels, and ensuring the loyalty of its high-ranking officers to Kim Chong-il.[10]

The Central Military Committee (CMC) is subordinate to the KWP (and thus also comes directly under Kim Chong-il). While it is responsible for the day-to-day operations of the military, it has declined significantly in real power since the increased role of the NDC and is reportedly not heavily involved in military policy.[11] The Ministry of People's Armed Forces (MPAF) comes directly under the NDC and is responsible for the management and operations of the armed forces, but it is not a policy-making body. Instead, issues such as training, procurement, intelligence, and so forth come under the auspices of the MPAF, but ultimately the high-level decisions are still made at the NDC level and then passed down to the MPAF.[12] There are also two secondary ways that Kim Chong-il controls the armed forces—politically and through monitoring (spying). Kim manages the former from the KWP down to the CMC and to the General Political Bureau (as shown in figure 3), which then extends a separate chain of command down to the lowest levels of the North Korean People's Army (NKPA). The second (as seen in figure 1) goes directly from the NDC to the State Security Department (SSD). The Security Command comes directly under the SSD and has representatives

FIGURE 3. *North Korea's Command Organization Chart*

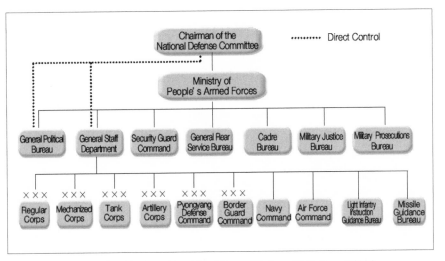

Source: Ministry of National Defense, Republic of Korea, "Defense White Paper," 2006.

monitoring activities in almost every military unit in North Korea.[13] It should be noted that the order of battle as reflected in figures 1 and 3 had changed by 2008, with some corps converting to divisions. I will explain this change in detail later in the chapter.

NORTH KOREAN MILITARY DISPOSITION OF FORCES

The disposition of North Korea's armed forces is perhaps more important than that of other nations and a focus of discussion among analysts and pundits because of the debate over whether the DPRK uses its military to deploy for possible offensive operations against South Korea or whether it is a purely a defensive force to serve against an attack from the ROK-U.S. alliance. Indeed, this debate has a profound impact on defense budgets in both the United States and South Korea, the presence of U.S. troops on the Korean Peninsula, and the foreign policies of both Washington and Seoul as well as that of other key allies that have important interests in the region.[14]

The North Korean armed forces currently number more than a million men. The majority of the armed forces are in the army, which has 950,000 men. The army is organized by corps and includes one armored (converted to a division by

2008), four mechanized (some converted to divisions by 2008), twelve infantry, one artillery (converted to division by 2008), and one capital-defense corps. There are also 85,000 personnel in the air force and 46,000 men in the navy.[15] The NK-PA's major combat units reportedly consist of at least 153 divisions and brigades, including 60 infantry divisions and brigades, 25 mechanized infantry brigades, 13 tank brigades, 25 Special Operations Forces (SOF) brigades, and 30 artillery brigades. The organization of the ground forces includes more than 20 corps-level commands.[16] Of interest, all of North Korea's missile forces are also organized into a corps, known as the Missile Training Guidance Bureau, the Missile Command, or simply "Missile Corps."[17]

The map shown in figure 4 is based entirely on unclassified sources. Thus, some of the unit designations or exact deployment locations may be slightly different from actual assessments held in classified channels by intelligence organizations or defense planning cells in the United States or South Korea. Nevertheless, it accurately reflects the scope, focus, and in general, the locations of North Korean military units. Of particular importance is the number of units located within seventy to a hundred kilometers of the demilitarized zone (DMZ). North Korea is believed to have deployed more than 70 percent of its active forces within ninety miles of the DMZ (see figure 5).[18] This number has increased significantly since the mid-1980s.[19] The disposition of forces in North Korea is an important factor in measuring the effectiveness of what remains one of the largest armies on earth. While North Korea's military equipment is undoubtedly antiquated compared to U.S. capabilities and, to a lesser extent, South Korea's capabilities, its sheer size makes it an extremely formidable threat. North Korea's aging military equipment, compared to that of its adversaries, may have been an important factor in its decision to move such a large portion of its forces so close to the DMZ, which would be near the forward edge of the battle area in the early hours of any war. By deploying its significant forces as far forward as they currently sit, Pyongyang has guaranteed a shorter warning time for ROK-U.S. intelligence and also reduced DPRK lines of communication and logistical support during what would be any large-scale combat operation.

During the mid-1990s and into 2000, the North Korean military went through a reorganization that enhanced its ability to threaten the south. (I will examine this in detail later in this chapter.) But as the disposition of forces shows, the NKPA is a

FIGURE 4. *North Korean Disposition of Forces*

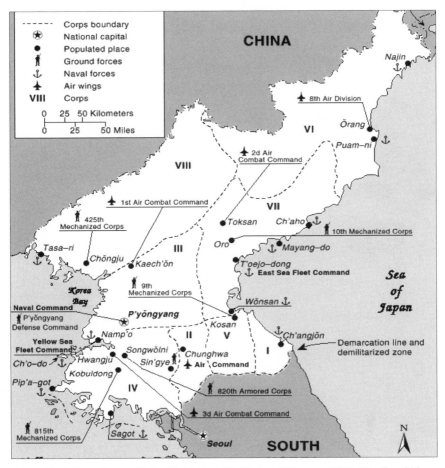

Source: North Korea Country Study (Washington, DC: Library of Congress, 2005), http://lcweb2.loc. gov/frd/cs/korea_north/kp05_03a.pdf.

complicated force, struggling to maintain its capabilities. Thus, an examination of each of the key elements of the armed forces is in order.

NORTH KOREAN GROUND FORCES

As discussed earlier, the ground forces are the heart and soul of the North Korean army. More than 950,000 active duty personnel make up the majority of units that are deployed all over the country, but as shown earlier, the majority are in the forward corps areas and second-echelon areas that are within seventy kilometers of

FIGURE 5. *Percentage of North Korean Forces Deployed near DMZ*

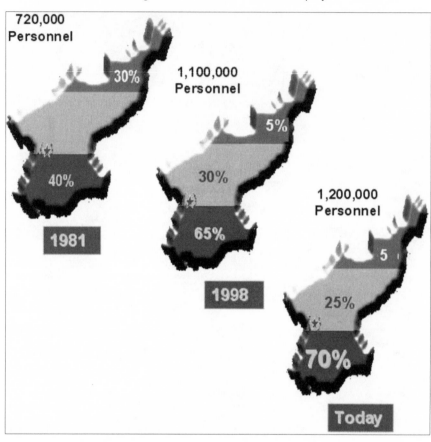

Sources: USFK Story Brief, 2005, and Andrew Scobell and John M. Sanford, North Korea's Military Threat: Pyongyang's Conventional Forces, Weapons of Mass Destruction, and Ballistic Missiles, Strategic Studies Institute Monograph (Carlisle, PA: U.S. Army War College, April 2007).

the DMZ. Because of the ground forces' sheer size, they remain a hugely important element of the North Korean military threat, despite the rise of missile forces, the threat of nuclear weapons, and the bluster raised by North Korean propaganda. Thus, the ground forces rate close analysis and discussion relating to their capabilities, deployment, readiness, and place within North Korean strategy.

The three most important categories for the North Korean ground forces as they relate to combat operations and readiness are the forward forces, the exploitation forces, and the SOF. The focus of the forward forces are the four geographical corps located in the front line along the DMZ, located from west to east as the IV,

II, V, and I "geographical" Corps. These corps are organized by geography, and the corps commanders are responsible for those military forces (with some exceptions, discussed later) that fall directly in their geographical area of command (see figure 4). The forces located in these forward corps are organized into infantry divisions that have subordinate regiments and battalions.[20]

The two most important of these forward corps, and the corps with the most forces, are II and V Corps. These corps sit on the key invasion routes of the Kaesong-Munsan corridor and the Chorwon Valley corridor. Throughout time, when invaders have needed to attack the heart of Korea—and thus Seoul—these two corridors have been the routes where large numbers of troops could traverse through the mountains.[21] A third corridor (in the I Corps' area of responsibility) is much narrower and much less capable of providing lines of communication to large numbers of troops. (For a map of the invasion corridors, see figure 6.) These corps consist largely of infantry forces supported by armor and a great deal of artillery; thus they would be among the first forces to flow into North Korea following a large-scale artillery barrage. The majority of engineer river-crossing units are located in the II Corps, which sits astride the Kaesong-Munsan corridor.[22]

The forward corps are extremely important to any force-on-force conflict that North Korea will fight with the ROK-U.S. alliance. But within the forward corps, and sitting right on the DMZ, is one of the greatest threats that the ground forces of North Korea pose to the security and stability of South Korea—long-range artillery systems. The North Korean army has more than thirteen thousand artillery and multiple rocket launcher (MRL) systems. Perhaps close to a thousand of these systems are long-range 170mm self-propelled guns and 240mm multiple rocket launchers. These systems have the ability to target Seoul from what is known as hardened artillery sites (HARTS), which are all constructed in close proximity (often within five kilometers) to the DMZ. Estimates state that as many as five hundred HARTS are located in the II and V Corps' geographical areas. According to defector reports and known North Korean doctrine, an estimated 5 to 20 percent of rounds provided to forward artillery units would be equipped with chemical munitions.[23]

In 1995, the U.S. Defense Intelligence Agency (DIA) stated that the "most significant" deployment of the North Korean armed forces since 1991 was that of the 240mm and 170mm long-range systems.[24] Since the DIA report, the number of long-range systems—both 240mm and 170mm—deployed in close proximity to

FIGURE 6. *Korean Invasion Routes*

KAESONG-MUNSAN	CHORWON VALLEY	EAST COAST
Kaesong-Munsan North	Kumwha Valley Chorwon West (MSR 3)	Taedong Mountains

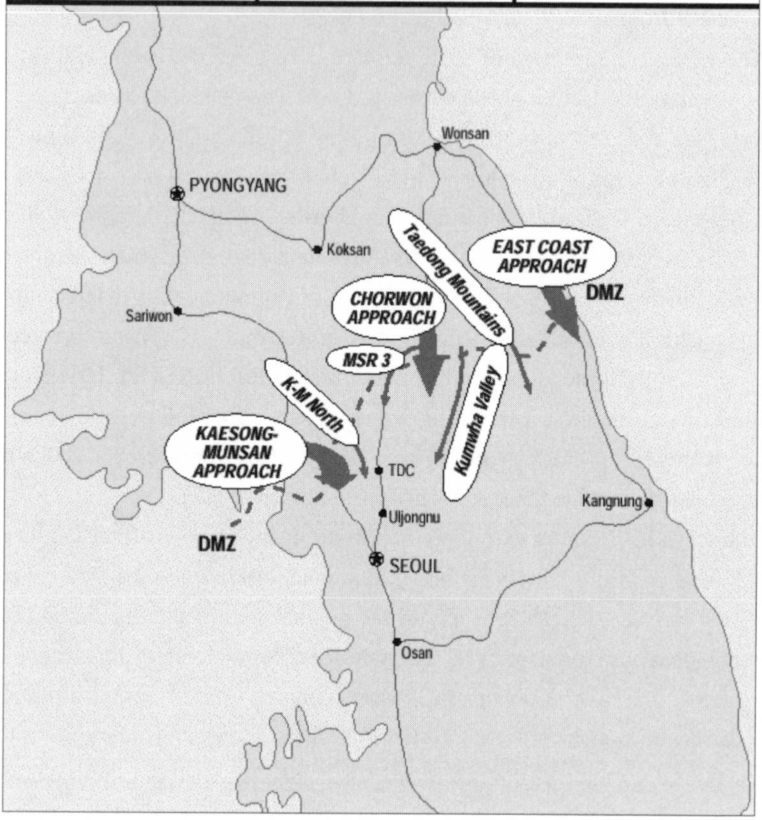

Source: U.S. Department of Defense, North Korean Country Handbook (Washington, DC: Defense Department, May 1997), http://www.dia.mil/publicaffairs/foia/nkor.pdf.

the DMZ has significantly increased. This escalation was likely part of a military reorganization, which I will discuss in detail later. Command and control of the 170mm and 240mm systems are not clear, but they likely fall under separate, independent brigades that may answer directly to a functional corps and/or a higher authority in Pyongyang (perhaps because of the chemical munitions capability).[25] Thus, these systems pose one of the major offensive capabilities in Pyongyang's ground arsenal. Estimates by the Combined Forces Command and U.S. Forces Korea state that at least 250 of these long-range systems can target Seoul.[26]

Exploitation forces (shown in highlighted areas in figure 7) are the units that would conduct an attack once vulnerabilities have been opened up in the south's defenses by massive artillery (augmented by SOF deep attacks) and initial attacks by forward corps' forces. To quote former USFK commander Gen. Robert W. RisCassi, "It would be a firepower-intensive assault with the north employing its large artillery forces to attempt to pulverize the south's defense, its frontal corps to develop a breach and, then, its exploitation forces to exploit the penetration."[27] Exploitation forces are focused around four mechanized corps, one armor corps, and one artillery corps (some of these corps were recently redesignated as divisions). These forces would be tasked with making the "big push" once initial front-line assaults have opened up gaps for them. They would be obliged to move from their positions in garrisons located farther back from the DMZ (some exploitation forces are located farther back than others) into the invasion corridors shown in figure 6. Exploitation forces also likely have a counter-amphibious mission.

SOF also comprise a large portion of the ground units in North Korea. There are several types of units that may be classified as Special Operations Forces. Depending on their type and mission, units (usually at the brigade, battalion, or company level) fall under the Light Infantry Training Guidance Bureau, Reconnaissance Bureau, army corps and divisions, or Korean People's Navy and Air Force. While reports vary, most estimates place the number of SOF at around twenty-five brigades and five independent reconnaissance battalions.[28] Their methods of insertion into South Korea vary from airlift by the more than three hundred AN-2s in North Korea's air inventory, to maritime insertion, to entering the south via tunnels dug under the DMZ.[29] One of the newest possible insertion methods is by simply crossing into South Korea disguised as civilians via one of the two transportation corridors opened up for roads and rail lines (see figure 8). According to a former North Korean military officer who defected to the south, the DPRK has built at least eight hundred underground bunkers on or near the DMZ, including a number of decoys. Construction began in 2004 and continued through 2007. Each bunker (except the decoys) contains enough military equipment to arm between fifteen hundred to two thousand men. The bunkers also contain 60mm mortar shells, various other types of ammunition, and South Korean military uniforms and name tags so that the North Korean troops can disguise themselves.[30]

FIGURE 7. *Exploitation Forces*

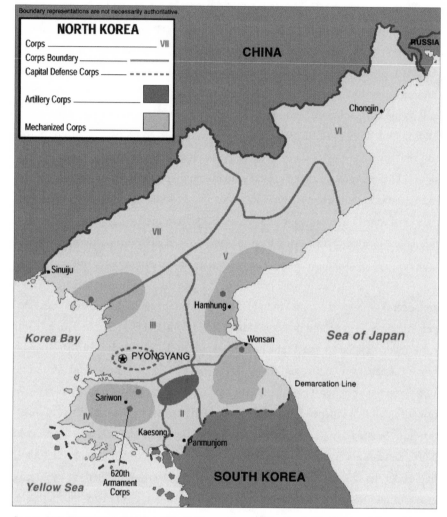

Source: U.S. Department of Defense, North Korean Country Handbook (Washington, DC: Defense Department, May 1997), http://www.dia.mil/publicaffairs/foia/nkor.pdf.

North Korean SOF are probably among the best trained, best fed, and most motivated of all the forces in the military. Three primary missions for SOF include infiltrating into rear areas to carry out subversive acts, exploring routes of maneuver for attacking forces, and occupying key tactical and strategic nodes.[31] There are reportedly roughly 70,000–100,000 SOF troops (assessments by South Korea's Ministry of National Defense placed the number even higher in 2008)

FIGURE 8. *Inter-Korean Transportation Corridors*

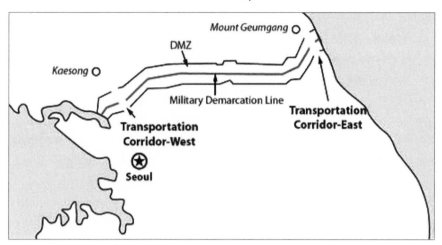

Source: Gen. Leon J. LaPorte, commander, United Nations Command; commander, Republic of Korea–U.S. Combined Forces Command; and commander, U.S. Forces Korea, statement before the House Armed Services Committee, 108th Cong., http://armedservices.house.gov/ openingstatementsa ndpressreleases/108thcongress/03-03-12laporte.pdf.

that routinely undergo intense training, including carrying fifty pounds of sand for ten kilometers in one hour, hiking in extreme cold, mastering martial arts method-ologies that include fighting with three to fifteen opponents, and even using spoons and forks as weapons. Troops also engage in intense marksmanship training and daily knife-throwing training.[32] According to press reports from 2008, North Korea may have increased the number and scope of some of these units. A South Korean military source reportedly said that "the North Korean military recently activated several light infantry divisions that are affiliated with frontline and rear corps. . . ." The source further stated that the move did not involve a massive troop redeploy-ment.[33] This reference apparently means that several divisions—most important, in the forward corps—were converted from standard, conventional, heavy infantry divisions to light infantry divisions (and thus SOF units). This conversion vice "switch" is significant because it shows that Pyongyang has recently "robbed Peter to pay Paul." It has beefed up the number of light infantry units in the forward area, yet sacrificed the heavy punch that a standard infantry division brings. Such a move enables assets that can support North Korea's asymmetric capabilities yet takes away from some of the conventional ground-taking forces, and that change is of particular importance in the forward areas. It also means newly converted

SOF units would not be limited to narrow invasion corridors and could move south through infiltration routes.

North Korea is also reportedly adjusting the training, tactics, and techniques of its SOF and possibly placing them in as high a priority as the effort to develop nuclear weapons and missiles. Officials in South Korea's military intelligence office (during a parliamentary inspection) were quoted as saying, "In addition to placing a large amount of effort into developing nuclear weapons and missiles, North Korea is increasing its special warfare capabilities based on lessons from the war in Iraq."[34] North Korean SOF have reportedly stepped up their capabilities to stage guerrilla warfare and have developed tactics that include planting roadside bombs, or improvised explosive devices (IEDs). According to American military officers, these tactics could be used against U.S. and South Korean forces stationed in the rear during any large-scale conflict.[35] According to press reports, Representative Hong Joon-pyo of the South Korean National Assembly (citing a Ministry of National Defense report) disclosed that about a third of North Korea's SOF (South Korea recently assessed the overall number at 180,000 men) operate under the direct control of the NKPA General Staff and carry out strategic missions.[36]

North Korea's SOF also deploy aboard submarines, and these units are not subordinate to the North Korean navy. Instead, they are directly subordinate to the Reconnaissance Bureau. Their inventory reportedly includes Yeoneo-class, Yugo-class, and Sango-class submarines—all of which are categorized by U.S. and South Korean military analysts as "mini-submarines." These units are highly effective in infiltrating into South Korean waters for intelligence and even attack missions. On March 26, 2010, a Yeoneo-class, Reconnaissance Bureau subordinate submarine is assessed to have sunk the South Korean Corvette *Cheonan* while it was sailing in South Korean waters south of the Northern Limit Line (NLL). The South Korean ship was split in half by a North Korean–fired, acoustic, wake-homing torpedo. Forty-six South Korean sailors were killed in the attack, and of course Pyongyang denied any involvement.[37]

THE NORTH KOREAN AIR FORCE

The North Korean Air Force (NKAF) numbers 1,562 aircraft.[38] There are 700 jets, 82 bombers, 480 transports, and 300 helicopters in the NKAF. Many, if not most, are older 1950s and 1960s models, such as the 310 MiG-15/17 aircraft, the 160 (or more) MiG-19s, the 160+ MiG-21s, 46 MiG-23s, 14 MiG-29s, 20 or more SU25s, 82 IL-28s, and up to 300 or more AN-2s (all figures are estimates). Only the SU-25s and MiG-29s can be considered up-to-date fighter or attack aircraft.[39] The NKAF in many ways has been surpassed by South Korean acquisitions since the end of the Cold War, during which the Soviet Union regularly supplied (largely for free) Pyongyang with updated military equipment. Since then Pyongyang has made some attempts to maintain its air force with smaller purchases such as 30 MiG-21s from Kazakhstan in 1999.[40] Unfortunately for the DPRK, purchases of advanced aircraft have been tough to come by since the fall of the Soviet Union.

Despite the stall in acquiring modern aircraft, the DPRK has shown remarkable resilience in being able to use its air force for brinkmanship and provocations both with the United States and with South Korea. On March 2, 2003, an RC-135S Cobra Ball aircraft–a U.S. Air Force intelligence collection platform—was intercepted by four armed North Korean MiG-29 and MiG-23 fighter aircraft over the Sea of Japan more than 150 miles off the coast of North Korea. The North Korean aircraft turned on their targeting radar and locked on the unarmed American aircraft, at one point closing to within fifty feet.[41] On ten separate occasions during February and March 2008—probably in reaction to conservative president Lee Myung-bak taking power in South Korea—North Korean Air Force fighters approached the skies near the demilitarized zone and the Northern Limit Line (NLL), the de facto border in the West Sea. South Korean military sources stated that these North Korean fighters (including MiG-21s) took off from North Korean air bases, crossed the Tactical Action Line (TAL) set by South Korea, and flew dangerously close to the DMZ and the NLL. The TAL is an imaginary line set by the south (and well known to North Korea) that runs twenty to thirty kilometers north of the DMZ and the NLL. Once North Korean fighter planes have crossed the line, they can reach skies over the Seoul metropolitan area in three to five minutes. Crossing the line, however, triggers an alert that scrambles South Korean fighters to take off from Suwon Air Base and other bases.[42]

But fighter aircraft are certainly not the only airframe that North Korea can use effectively against its more peaceful neighbor to the south. The AN-2 is a perfect example of how Pyongyang can take a primitive weapons system and turn it to the DPRK's advantage. A biplane, the AN-2 is capable of carrying eight to ten troops.

It can take off from dirt strips and fly "nap of the earth" missions when inserting SOF either during war operations or during a more limited infiltration operation. It can also fly at speeds as slow as 35 knots and use valleys to shield itself from radar.[43] The North Koreans can also effectively use the older Soviet-era IL-28 bomber airframe. They reportedly may have used this aircraft to launch air-to-ship missiles during training in 2008.[44] When it comes to defending against allied air attacks, North Korea has one of the densest air defense networks in the world, relying largely on SA-2/3/5 surface-to-air missile systems and air defense artillery. While the system is extremely dense, it is also vulnerable to a modern electronic warfare (EW) capability that the ROK-U.S. alliance possesses. Thus it is likely to be destroyed fairly quickly in a war, but it could inflict heavy casualties in the process.[45] North Korea also has strengthened the defenses for its aircraft by building underground bases beneath mountains, where aircraft can take off at high speeds from the mouth of a tunnel. At one base, the 6,000-foot runway is just minutes' flying time from the front line of the DMZ.[46] North Korea has reportedly constructed three of these bases.[47]

THE NORTH KOREAN NAVY

The North Korean navy is primarily a coastal defense force, but it can still present a threat to allied forces during a war or is capable of being used for brinkmanship and provocations. While the north has a high number of naval craft (between six hundred and eight hundred craft), most are of older Soviet or Chinese design.[48] In fact, despite what may seem a high number of craft on paper, the largest ships it possesses are the Soho and Najin class light frigates, which are 1,845 and 1,500 tons, respectively. The majority of craft in the navy's inventory are smaller torpedo boat–sized hulls that range from 60 to 220 tons. The navy also has at least eighty-eight submarines that can be used to interdict allied shipping, lay mines, and insert SOF into South Korea.[49] Another key capability of the navy is that it has two amphibious brigades (one on each coast) that would be deployed in wartime via amphibious craft or aboard one of the more than 150 hovercraft in its naval inventory.[50] Finally, the North Korean navy is a threat to allied shipping because of the many land-based land-to-sea missiles in its inventory that are deployed on both coasts. Several versions of these missiles, including the Styx and Silkworm antiship missiles, have been upgraded and tested in recent years.[51]

But the North Korean navy can do more with its navy, namely provocations. On June 29, 2002, two North Korean navy ships crossed the NLL and split so that they were going in opposite directions. One of the DPRK ships maneuvered so that it was then "side to side," facing the engine room of a ROK patrol craft (which had attempted to warn it away) and opened fire. Four South Korean troops were killed in the battle (see figure 9), and the ROK vessel later sank while being towed back to port.[52]

The ROK government, and the populace, was appalled at the incident, and it was obvious from the evidence compiled afterward that it was a well-planned and deliberate provocation designed to inflict casualties and probably to sink a South Korean naval craft. At a briefing conducted for the South Korean press, the Ministry of National Defense and Joint Chiefs of Staff (JCS) stated that the maritime clash with the North Korean vessels was an intentional provocation by the north's warships and that the north started the incident by first shooting at a South Korean patrol boat.[53] It appears that the provocation may have been planned and carried out as revenge for a naval battle in 1999 when the South Korean navy sank a North Korean ship. It may have also been carried out to bring the NLL "to the world's attention," as the World Cup games were going on in South Korea at the time.[54]

NORTH KOREAN MISSILE FORCES

The North Korean military has a variety of ballistic missiles, but when it comes to the missiles that are most threatening to the south, Pyongyang's short-range ballistic missiles (SRBMs) present the biggest threat. North Korea has been developing its missile capability since the late 1960s when it received some help from both the Soviets (FROG, or free rocket over ground acquisitions) and the Chinese (DF-61 development that was cut short before it reached fruition). While neither the Chinese nor the Soviet acquisitions resulted in ballistic missiles, sometime between 1979 and 1981 North Korea actually did receive its first ballistic missile, the Scud B (some analysts assess North Korea received the first Scuds from Egypt as early as 1976).[55] Thus began what has become a national security nightmare for South Korea and a counterproliferation dilemma for the United States, Japan, and Washington's most important ally in the Middle East, Israel.

Since first acquiring its ballistic missile program, Pyongyang has built on technology from the Scud B to develop the Scud C and later the Scud D (the

FIGURE 9. *Site of 2002 Naval Clash*

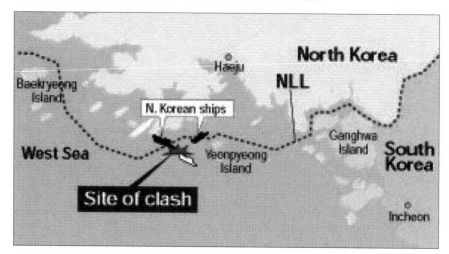

Source: Map courtesy of the Republic of Korea, Ministry of National Defense, 2002, http://www.mnd.go.kr/.

Scud D has a range of more than 700 kilometers).[56] Based on data compiled from missile tests the North Koreans conducted in 2006, they now apparently have an extended-range (ER) Scud with a range of 850 kilometers.[57] Using Scud technology, the North Koreans were also able to develop the No Dong missile. This missile has been successfully tested at least twice in North Korea and has a range of 1,300–1,500 kilometers (and can hit Japan).[58] When it comes to missiles that can specifically target nations in the region, one must also mention a missile the North Koreans have built based on SS-N-6 technology (an old Soviet submarine-launched ballistic missile). Pyongyang has found the technology to launch this missile (sometimes referred to as the Taepo Dong X or the Musudan) from both fixed and mobile land-based launchers, and it has the range (4,000 kilometers) to hit Guam.[59] A map showing potential ranges of several North Korean missiles (shown in figure 10) illustrates how far the Musudan (Taepo Dong X) could fly if it was fired from a southern azimuth in North Korea, and the U.S. territory of Guam is within its range. (The missile on the map listed as IRBM [intermediate-range ballistic missile] is identified in the press as the Musudan or Taepo Dong X.) The Iranians have already successfully tested the Musudan (Taepo Dong X) (which they apparently call the Shahab-4) in 2006. The North Koreans have ostensibly built, fielded, and deployed so many Musudan missiles that they have now formed a new independent missile division to accommodate them.[60] In fact, the fielding and deployment of these missiles have changed the South Koreans' assessment of the number of North Korean ballistic missiles. South Korea's defense minister informed the press in March 2010 that North Korea now has about a thousand ballistic missiles.[61]

Meanwhile, North Korea continues to develop the capabilities of short-range missiles that can target the south. North Korea reportedly acquired the SS-21 system (a short-range, tactical missile) from Syria in 1996. Pyongyang almost immediately began to develop and manufacture its own version of the system (identified as the KN-02), which has the range (at least 120 kilometers) to target U.S. bases south of Seoul.[62] The missile is "road mobile" and uses solid fuel, making it a system that can be deployed faster and loaded and fired more rapidly than other less modern systems.[63] In recent years Pyongyang conducted test firings of this missile that appeared successful.[64] Former commander of USFK Gen. B. B. Bell expressed concern about the KN-02, stating, "They've again tested short-range ballistic missiles that are in fact a quantum leap forward from the kinds of missiles that they've produced in the past."[65] According to South Korean government sources reported in the press, North Korea is also developing another variant called the KN-06, which may have a longer range and better accuracy than those of the KN-02. The KN-06 is reported to have a better "circular error probable" (CEP) than previous variants of short-range missiles.[66] (CEP is the radius around a target that a missile is projected to achieve, and goes to the accuracy of the system being fired.)

All of the missiles I have discussed thus far in this section can be launched from mobile transporter-erector-launchers (TELs). According to reports released to the public by both the U.S. National Air and Space Intelligence Center and the ROK Ministry of National Defense, the North Koreans have around a hundred TELs.[67] The high number of TELs in North Korea's inventory means that it could launch a significant volley in any first punch of a large-scale war that involved its neighbor to the south. The range of the missiles that can be put on TELs also means that from mobile sites, North Korea could potentially launch missiles at South Korea, Japan, and Guam simultaneously. North Korea's large numbers of mobile launchers are also augmented by the fixed sites from which No Dong and Musudan (Taepo Dong X) missiles can be launched.[68]

FIGURE 10. *Ranges of North Korea's Most Well-known Missiles*

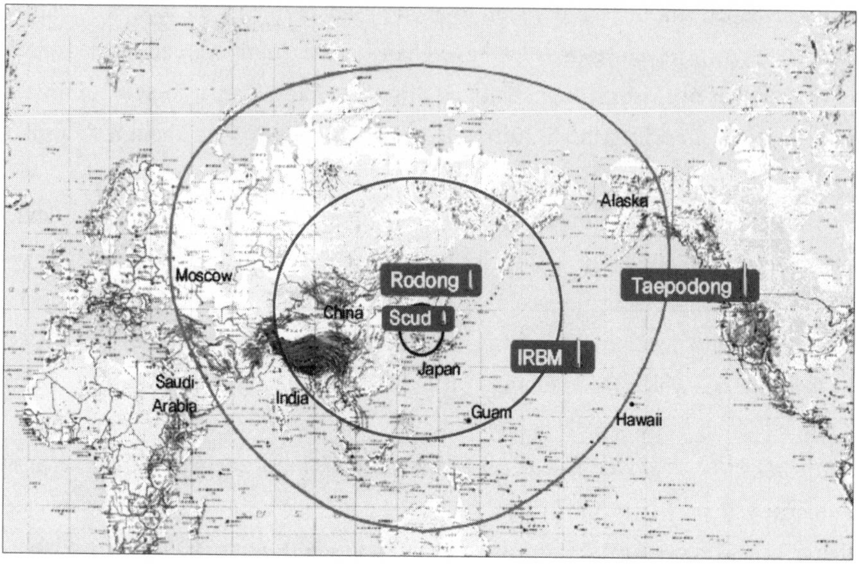

Source: Ministry of National Defense, Republic of Korea, "Defense White Paper," 2008, http://www.mnd.go.kr/.

The second missile map (see figure 11) displays the ranges of some of North Korea's well-known and often-tested systems: the Scud B, the Scud C, and the No Dong. For the purposes of this chapter, I will also briefly cover the ranges and capabilities of North Korea's long-range ballistic missile IRBM and ICBM systems. While these systems are not an immediate threat to regional security, they could potentially threaten the United States.

The Taepo Dong I was tested (unsuccessfully) in 1998.[69] The Taepo Dong II was also tested unsuccessfully during the summer of 2006. On both occasions, the missiles failed before they entered their third stage.[70] The Taepo Dong I and II appear to have been developed from Scud technology that of course was later applied to the development of the No Dong.[71] For potential ranges of these missiles, should they ever prove successful, see figure 12.

North Korea once again conducted a test launch of the Taepo Dong II system in 2009. By February 4 of that year, a train carrying components of the missile was sighted near the missile launch facility at Musudan-ri. The train had previously departed from a weapons plant known for building long-range missiles.[72] A few days

FIGURE 11. *North Korean Short- and Medium-range Missile Capabilities*

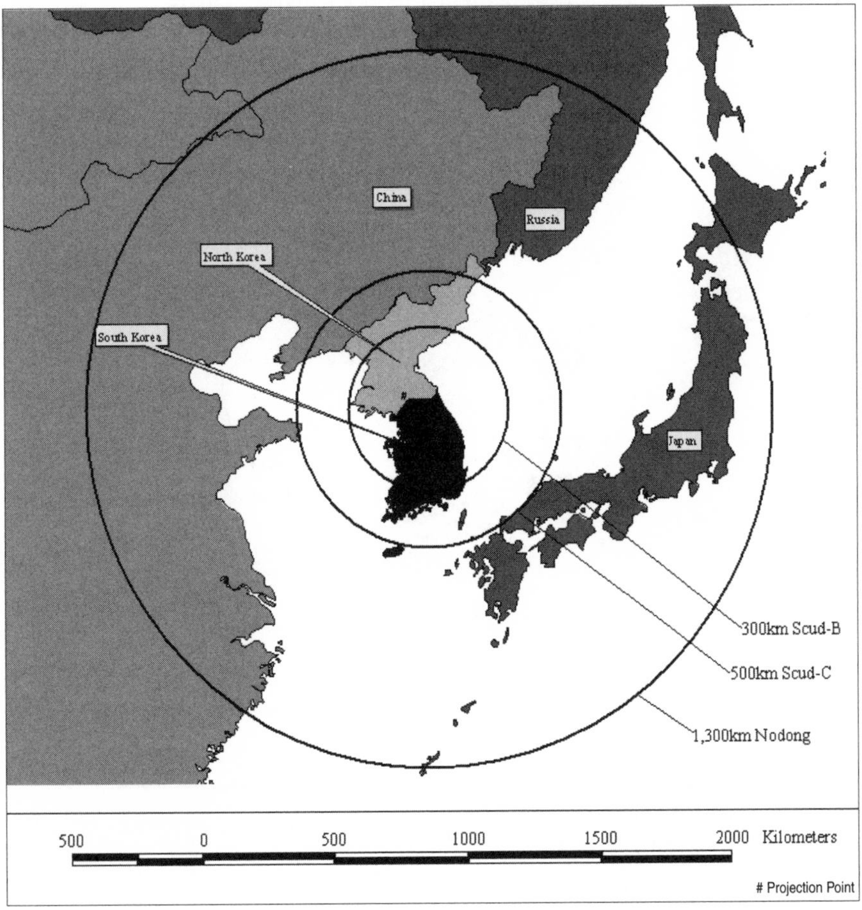
China
Russia
North Korea
South Korea
Japan
300km Scud-B
500km Scud-C
1,300km Nodong
500
0
500
1000
1500
2000 Kilometers
Projection Point

Library of Congress. Geography and Map Division. October 1999

later, in a statement obviously designed for foreign consumption, North Korea's state-run propaganda arm (*Rodong Sinmun*) declared its nation's right to develop "space technology."[73] By February 10, the U.S. military had reportedly stepped up its monitoring of North Korean activities at Musudan-ri by moving assets (including naval craft) into position in the Pacific.[74] By February 11, reports indicated that the North Koreans had transferred missile-related cargo to their missile launch site, and vehicles needed for missile launches were traveling to the missile base.[75] In addition, press reports on the same day indicated that imagery showed sophisticated telemetry equipment (needed for a missile launch) being assembled at the

FIGURE 12. *Potential North Korean Long-range Missile Capabilities*

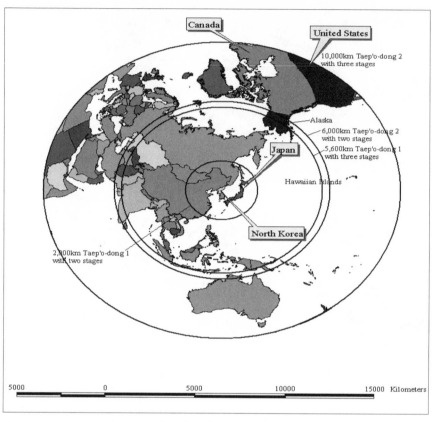

Library of Congress. Geography and Map Division. October 1999

launch site.[76] Components for the missile were transported to the site on a forty-meter-long special trailer that is reportedly capable of carrying the first and second stages of the three-stage Taepo Dong II missile.[77] Soon thereafter, the North Korean state-run press again declared Pyongyang's right to launch a satellite, proclaiming, "Space development is the independent right of the DPRK and the requirement of the developing reality."[78] The North Koreans claimed they would be launching a satellite called the Kwang Myong Song-2.[79]

On March 12, 2009, the International Civil Aviation Organization (ICAO) reported that the DPRK had officially advised it "of its intention to proceed with the launch of a communications satellite, under the terms of the DPRK's long-term plan for space development." The ICAO reported that the North Korean letter indicated the launch would take place between April 4 and 8 and identified two specific danger areas where possible debris might fall from the vehicle. If one is to plot the areas on a map, the first was off Japan's northeastern coast (approximately 373 kilometers from the launch site), and the second was in the middle of the Pacific Ocean, approximately 3,600 kilometers from the launch site in North Korea. The areas indicated are below.[80]

Area one
1) N404140 E1353445
2) N402722 E1383040
3) N401634 E1383022
4) N403052 E1353426

Area two
1) N343542 E1644042
2) N312222 E1721836
3) N295553 E1721347
4) N330916 E1643542

Many in the international community questioned the validity of North Korea's declaration of the planned test launch as a "satellite launch." Officials in both Seoul and Washington reportedly believed the real purpose of the launch was to test the Taepo Dong II system. In fact, the two are so similar that it is difficult to tell them apart until the satellite is actually launched. The vehicle (or missile, if you will) that is used to carry a dummy warhead (what a test launch would likely consist of) would be almost exactly the same as the vehicle used to launch a satellite. The major difference would only be the equipment mounted on top of the fuselage, or the missile's tip. If the vehicle was indeed intended to launch a satellite, then a bulb-like contraption would be on the tip; otherwise, a more pyramid-like device would be on top of the fuselage.

If the missile system the North Koreans claimed was being used to launch a satellite instead turned out to be a missile with a warhead, or (and this scenario could happen almost as easily) if it strayed off course and headed toward U.S. territory, the U.S. ballistic missile defense (BMD) system was prepared to both track it and shoot it down. Reportedly, air and space assets were capable of monitoring the system from takeoff until landing. Sensors and satellites located in the United States, Japan, South Korea, and the waters of the Pacific Ocean were (and are) tied into a worldwide BMD system capable of matching up with weapons systems that could take the missile out at various stages in its flight. American weapons systems located on ships at sea and on land in Alaska, Hawaii, and Japan were (and are) also tied into Japanese BMD weapons systems (SM-3 and PAC-3) that are also located on both land and ships (see figure 13).[81]

In early March 2009, the Japanese navy announced that it planned to deploy an Aegis-equipped destroyer outfitted with the SM-3 BMD system in the Sea of Japan and prepare for possible action involving the North Korean test launch.[82] Given the launch elevation of the Taepo Dong system, it would be difficult for the SM-3 to intercept a launch. (The SM-3 is designed for medium-range ballistic missile [MRBM] system defense and not against an intercontinental ballistic missile [ICBM] like the Taepo Dong.) But the system could be used if debris from the system was going to fall on the Japanese landmass.[83] Approximately 90 percent of the "danger zone" that North Korea indicated when it announced the test launch was in the Sea of Japan near Akita Prefecture.[84] In another rather ominous move, North Korea announced on March 21 that it would close two routes in its airspace during April 4–8, 2009. Flights transiting between North Korea and Russia or Japan normally used these routes.[85]

By the end of March, satellite imagery had reportedly photographed the nose cone of the Taepo Dong II, which was now sitting on its launch pad and undergoing final preparations, though it still remained partially covered.[86] But an even more interesting issue came to light on March 29, when the Japanese press disclosed that a fifteen-man Iranian delegation (including several missile experts) was in North Korea, probably to observe the imminent test launch.[87] By March 29, there were also reports that the United States was going to deploy missile interceptor ships from South Korea (other ships deployed from other areas as well), and the Japanese government began moving its PAC-3 BMD systems (and the associated seaborne SM-3 systems) into areas of northeastern Japan and prepared for the possibility of the missile falling into Japanese territory in case the North Korean launch malfunctioned.[88]

By March 30, 2009, the Taepo Dong II missile system was reportedly not only on the launch pad but also free of any covering and casting a thick shadow.[89] By April 1, press accounts citing a senior U.S. military official confirmed that the North Koreans had begun fueling the missile.[90] U.S. defense officials reportedly disclosed that imagery of the missile showed that it had a bulb-shaped nose cone

FIGURE 13. *Currently Fielded Ballistic Missile Defense System*

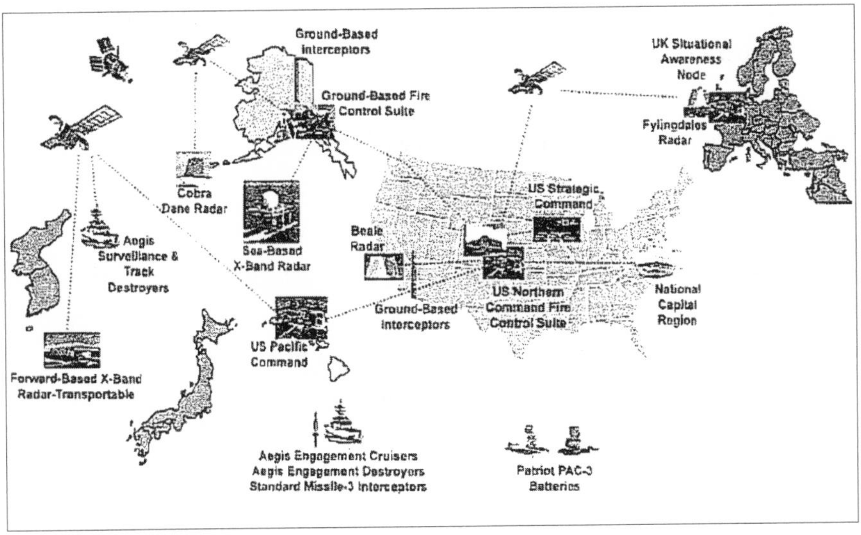

Source: Charles E. McQueary, "Ballistic Missile Defense Systems," FY 2008 Annual Report (Washington, DC: Department of Defense, Operational Test and Evaluation, December 2008), http://www.cdi.org/pdfs/fy08doteannualreport.pdf.

consistent with a satellite payload, though Institute for Science and International Security (ISIS) senior analyst Paul Brannan also told reporters, "They probably are launching a satellite. But the issue is that the steps they're going through to do that run parallel to them being able to have other capabilities."[91] Responding to reports that a satellite payload was spotted on top of the missile nearing launch, South Korean defense minister Lee Sang-hee told the South Korean National Assembly in a hearing, "Whether it is a satellite or a missile, the technology is the same." He further stated, "We understand they are equally threats to the Korean Peninsula and our surrounding region, and will respond accordingly."[92] By April 4, the North Koreans appeared ready to launch their missile in a matter of hours, as camera equipment had been set up around the launch pad to record the launch.[93]

On April 5, 2009, at 11:30 in the morning, the North Koreans launched the Taepo Dong II missile in their second launch of the system (the first being in July 2006). According to reports the press attributed to members of the South Korean National Assembly, North Korea had notified the United States, China, and Russia in advance of its plan to launch the missile (satellite) on April 5. If true, this communication was an unprecedented move by the North Koreans.[94] The North Koreans called the missile the Unha 2 Space Launch Vehicle. Iranian officials and missile experts were reportedly present to observe the launch. After launching, the spent first stage fell into the Sea of Japan (East Sea) about 580 kilometers from the launch site. The missile successfully went into its second stage before passing over Japan. The system apparently suffered some kind of sequencing complication, and the second stage failed to separate, causing both the second stage and the third stage to tumble into the Pacific Ocean.[95] According to Russian and American expert analysis that was released in the Russian and South Korean press, the missile may have impacted as far as 2,390 miles from its launch site (in the Pacific Ocean). The information indicates that the missile's second stage fired normally, but the third stage failed to separate from the second stage when it was supposed to. After burnout, the second stage briefly coasted upward into space. The third stage was then supposed to separate and fire, but it failed to do so. Thus, according to the reports, Japanese and U.S. defense officials believe the first and second stages worked as planned, and only the third stage failed. The spent first and second stages apparently fell into the danger areas the North Koreans had planned for and had reported to international authorities earlier.[96]

Following the test launch, despite the third-stage failure of the system, U.S. analysts and government officials reportedly said that the test raised new concerns about advancements in North Korean long-range missile technology. Many also said that the launch was a test of the Taepo Dong II and merely a cover for what in reality was a long-range missile test.[97] In South Korea the reaction was similar. A government official, speaking on condition of anonymity, said, "It is our assessment that North Korea's missile capabilities have advanced because its abilities to launch the rocket can be converted into long-rang missile technology."[98] Professor Yun Duk-min of the Institute for Foreign Affairs and Trade in Seoul told the South Korean press in part, "It is one of the steps that the North will take to keep improving its missile capability. The North will test again at some point."[99] North Korea obviously understood the military applications of the test launch and took elaborate steps to protect its assets. Pyongyang deployed both fighter jets and bombers near the launch area and one of its warships at sea near the site. The aircraft flew past the midway point between Japan and North Korea, and a destroyer also reportedly sailed closer to Japan than to its homeport, an unusual move. One of the aircraft conducting the patrols, a MiG-23, crashed into the sea the day before the launch.[100]

After several days of wrangling over the wording, the United Nations Security Council (UNSC) finally issued a statement unanimously condemning North Korea's test launch. The statement (and the actions taken in the resolution) was considerably watered down from what both the United States and Japan had wanted. China and Russia opposed making the resolution too harsh in what their diplomats felt would have been an overreaction. The result was a compromise that did not carry the weight Washington and Tokyo had hoped for.[101] North Korea's response to the UN resolution was quick and harsh. Pyongyang ordered UN inspectors at its Yongbyon site to leave. It also ordered them to remove both the seals on the equipment and their cameras. In addition, North Korea renounced the six-party talks, saying in an official statement that it "will never participate in the talks any longer nor . . . be bound to any agreement." Finally, the North Koreans stated that they would restart operations at their plutonium nuclear reactor. An official statement in the state-run press said that Pyongyang would "bolster its nuclear deterrent for self-defense in every way."[102] By May 7, 2009, South Korean officials reportedly had spotted increased activity at North Korea's known nuclear test site in the northeastern area of the country.[103] North Korea then conducted its second nuclear test on May 25, 2009.[104]

The implications of the Taepo Dong II launch are important, yet analysts disagree about the reasons for its timing. Why April 2009? Some have assessed that the launch was for internal North Korean consumption in order to strengthen Kim Chong-il's status after the stroke he suffered in 2008. Others have opined that the launch was likely conducted to continue raising the stakes with the Lee Myung-bak administration in South Korea. Of course, many have asserted that the launch was conducted to test the new Barack Obama administration in Washington.[105] In my view, all of these reasons are important, but they are also ancillary. The main reasons that the North Koreans tested the Taepo Dong II system were because they felt it was ready and they plan to proliferate the technology to Iran. The North Koreans likely believed they had worked out most of the issues associated with the missile launch of 2006. They were partially right, of course, as the launch was more successful than the launch of 2006 but still short of being a complete ICBM launch of a three-stage missile. Selling this missile to Iran likely means revenues in the hundreds of millions of dollars (perhaps more) as well as energy aid. According to press reports, Iranian specialists and high-ranking officials were present at the launch, just as they also were in 2006, 1998, and 1993.[106]

North Korea has proliferated nearly every kind of missile in its inventory to Iran since the 1980s. To recap, this stock includes the Scud B, C, and probably D systems; the No Dong; and the Taepo Dong X (also known as the Musudan, based on Soviet SS-N-6 technology). Iran is North Korea's oldest and most profitable client of ballistic missiles and ballistic missile technology.[107] This fact highlights the real threat from the April 2009 missile launch. While a successful three-stage launch would mean North Korea had an ICBM that could hit Alaska or Hawaii, it would also almost undoubtedly mean that Iran would end up with the technology in the near future. Thus, any missile test by North Korea should be assessed not only for its potential when launched from the North Korean landmass but also for what it would mean if such a missile were launched from the Middle East and who it would threaten. No matter what was going on with the six-party talks, relations with their neighbor to the south, or internally within the government of the DPRK, the North Koreans felt this missile system was ready, and they were going to launch it. The potential gains from proliferation were simply far too important for any significant delay. For future reference, those who have an interest in the region should consider this point, because future test launches are not only likely but also imminent in coming years, as the North Koreans further develop long-range missile technology.

North Korea followed up its long-range test launch in April with a launch of more ballistic missiles on July 4, 2009. This time they were shorter-range ballistic missiles that could threaten Japan and South Korea. Seven missiles in total were launched, and all are believed to have been launched from TELs. According to press sources, three extended-range Scuds (Scud-ER) were fired—two Scud C missiles and two No Dongs. The impact area for the missiles shows that the Scuds are apparently improving in their accuracy, as five of the seven missiles are said to have landed in the same area. The U.S. BMD system reportedly worked well during the launches, as facilities in place at Alaska, Japan, California, and Hawaii; aboard Navy ships; and in space worked together in providing accurate and timely data on the launches. Close coordination with the Japanese Self-Defense Forces continued with data shared from a combined command center at Yokota Air Base near Tokyo.[108] The timing and locations of the test launches suggest the North Koreans are working to perfect a volley effect when firing their missiles, a rather chilling capability if perfected as it could cause extensive damage to specifically targeted nodes during a conflict.

Of interest, North Korea also continues to develop new launch facilities for its missiles. A site was announced in the press that, according to Jane's Information Group senior analyst Joseph Bermudez, has been operational (for emergencies) since 2005 but has not yet been used. The site is larger and more versatile than the launching facility on the east coast, where previous launchings of the Taepo Dong missiles have occurred. Reportedly, intelligence officials have been aware of the site for several years. South Korean defense minister Lee Sang-hee recently remarked, "About 80 percent of the work has been completed and we're watching it closely." The site is located in northwestern North Korea, and the facilities are rather impressive, including a ten-story-tall tower capable of supporting any missile in North Korea's inventory.[109] While the launch pad could be the site of Taepo Dong launches, it could also be used to launch the missile that North Korea has built based on Soviet SS-N-6 technology, Taepo Dong X, and be pointed toward Japan or Guam. By June 2009, the South Korean government assessed the launch site was complete. A Taepo Dong II system had been moved to the site and was being assembled in a building there. In addition, another Taepo Dong II system was moved to the site at Musudan (where all previous launches of long-range ballistic missiles had occurred) and was also apparently being assembled.[110] This second site now gives the North Koreans the capability to launch long-range missiles simultaneously, on the same day, or even perhaps on radically different azimuths.

THE REORGANIZATION OF THE NORTH KOREAN MILITARY

The North Korean military is one of the world's largest (especially for such a small country) and, as previously discussed, continues to hone its capabilities, training, tactics, and techniques in order to maintain its readiness. But some analysts have said that because of overwhelming economic difficulties and resource constraints the North Korean military is in a state of decline.[111] Anecdotal reports as recently as 2005 state that in some units soldiers were suffering from malnutrition.[112] It is also true that key resources such as fuel and food have been in short supply in North Korea since the crisis of the mid-1990s.[113] According to an Intelligence Community Assessment released by the National Intelligence Council in December 2008, "Poor health is weakening military readiness because capable new recruits are in short supply. Loyalty may also erode over time, according to the Eurasia Group; even when soldiers are well fed, they may be concerned about their malnourished family members."[114]

According to a report based on defectors' testimonies in 2007, female soldiers are increasingly joining North Korea's armed forces, including some frontline units. Reportedly, women now guard most tunnels and bridges and even serve in exploitation forces such as mechanized units. Women are replacing male soldiers who starved to death or abandoned their posts during the food crisis of the 1990s.[115] There are also reports that some soldiers were pulled from exercises in order to support farming during 2008.[116] According to a paper Dr. David Von Hippel presented at Stanford University in 2006, ground forces' training during 2000–2005 was 13–20 percent less than estimated 1990 levels owing to shortages of fuel and parts. By 2000–2005 annual air force flight hours were at an estimated 50–60 percent of estimated 1990 levels.[117] Because of the food shortages seen in some units and the dip in training in others, does it mean the DPRK has thrown in the towel? How has the military adjusted? And perhaps most importantly, how much of a threat is the military to the security and stability of South Korea and Northeast Asia at large?

It is true that definitive studies have clearly shown a dip in the training levels of conventional military forces in North Korea since the early 1990s. But before one comes to the conclusion that this data means the offensive (and defensive) effectiveness of the military has declined, one must first examine a military reorganization that occurred in North Korea beginning in the mid- to late 1990s and continuing into 2000. While the North Korean military has always adjusted and improved its capabilities (depending on resources available) both before and since, this time period was key for evaluating the North Koreans' combat forces and how they have cleverly adjusted because of resource constraints.

During 1999, it became apparent to analysts that North Korea had made a concerted, well-organized effort to arrest what had been a decline in readiness and to improve the military capability of its armed forces. The most important enhancements in this ambitious program occurred in the ground forces. Perhaps the most critical component of this initiative was the deployment of large numbers of long-range 240mm MRL systems and 170mm self-propelled guns to hardened sites located near the DMZ. This move significantly beefed up the numbers of long-range guns that could target Seoul and other key areas of Kyonggi Province. Other force improvements made during this time included emplacing antitank barriers in the forward area and establishing new combat positions along major routes between Pyongyang and the DMZ. Of note, particularly when it comes to mechanized infantry units that make up the core of North Korea's exploitation forces, Pyongyang repositioned key units for more effective pre-deployment for combat operations while also beefing up coastal defense forces in the forward area (preventing an allied counterattack). Pyongyang also procured extra fighter aircraft in 1999. Finally, the North Koreans modified key facility defenses and dispersed forces to modify their attack locations.[118]

While the changes in the ground forces were important and compelling (the ground forces are easily and overwhelmingly the largest of the services), and smaller modifications in the air force were also interesting, another major change occurred: many of the long-range systems deployed forward probably came from an artillery corps that the North Koreans disbanded. A new corps known as North Korea's Missile Training Guidance Bureau (also known as Missile Command or Missile Corps) was formed using the staff from the former artillery corps. This reorganization points to the assessment that the North Koreans consider ballistic missiles as artillery systems and follow artillery doctrine as directed by the officers who have an artillery background.[119] This initiative may have been made because North Korea had large, diverse, and widely dispersed missile forces that needed an extensive and proficient command and control system.[120] The major reorganization of artillery and missile forces not only streamlined and improved command and control of missile and artillery forces, but it also allowed the North Koreans to engage in a more threatening posture toward their neighbor to the south. It is also important to note that the reorganization of standard infantry divisions into light infantry divisions reported in 2008 points to a focus on supporting an asymmetric capability for North Korea.

RESULTS OF MILITARY REORGANIZATION:
FOCUS ON ASYMMETRIC FORCES

The reorganization of the North Korean armed forces proves two profound points: the military is willing to make large-scale adjustments in order to maintain a credible offensive capability while also protecting itself from attack, and the new focus for North Korea's military has shifted from armored and mechanized (exploitation) forces to asymmetric forces. These asymmetric forces can legitimately be called SOF, missile forces, and long-range artillery (equipped with chemical munitions). They now can provide the punch that in the critical early days of any war would cause massive casualties and create vulnerabilities in ROK and U.S. military defenses that would hinder their capability to defend key nodes and to counterattack into North Korea. As former USFK commander Gen. Thomas Schwartz said regarding North Korea's asymmetric capability, "The result of these efforts has been to increase the survivability of North Korean combat power, and to complicate our ability to generate the forces and sorties required to defeat a North Korean attack."[121]

When it comes to asymmetric capabilities, Pyongyang's long-range artillery deployed along the DMZ can fire not only rounds that can hit Seoul, but when equipped with chemical munitions, it can also present a WMD threat that leaves almost none of Seoul safe during a sudden attack and that, with its shorter-range systems, can target other areas of Kyonggi Province with chemical munitions as well.[122] What makes this development even more disturbing is a revelation in the South Korean Ministry of National Defense's 2004 White Paper: even though its armored vehicles and tanks were proving difficult to maintain and had gone down slightly in numbers, North Korea had increased the number of artillery pieces in its arsenal by a thousand since 2000—a significant improvement.[123] Thus, while one capability declined, another improved. The missile forces discussed earlier follow artillery doctrine, are commanded by artillery officers, and would be used simultaneously with the long-range artillery in any full-scale war. Thus, a North Korean artillery attack would really involve guns, rockets, and ballistic missiles. As part of the focus on asymmetric forces, ground that it would have been taken by armored and mechanized forces can now simply be targeted by missiles and artillery. The Scud-ER is now assessed to have a range of 850 kilometers or more. Thus, Pyongyang could literally target nodes in almost the entire geographical landmass of South Korea in the early stages of any war.[124]

The North Korean SOF are the final—and arguably most vital—component of the North Korean (nonnuclear) asymmetric threat. The SOF have seen no drop in training or resources despite the tough economic times (which were worse during the mid- to late 1990s) North Korea has experienced. Perhaps as much as anything, this continued support is due to the very nature of the SOF missions and the types of training required. SOF can (routinely) practice para-drop training from towers in lieu of aircraft; thus they are not limited by either the restricted amount of fuel or flight time that their potential aircraft platforms would have when addressing training issues. During a war, SOF would likely be used simultaneously or immediately before artillery and missile attacks and would target key command and control nodes, air bases, or any other high-value targets in South Korea.[125] But those are not their only targets. They also have the capability of conducting "unconventional operations," or even terrorist acts, and in fact are expected to do so.[126] These operations would be an effective "first punch" to severely disrupt morale and alter public opinion in both South Korea and the United States.

The South Korean Ministry of National Defense's White Paper for 2008 offered some compelling and disturbing assessments regarding the way that North Korea has realigned its forces in recent years and adjusted its strategy. The document states, "North Korea's developing and reinforcing of conventional weaponry, as well as the weapons of mass destruction like nuclear and missiles, and the front-line deployment of military power are a direct and serious threat to our security." The paper also discusses (among many other things I will address) North Korea's assessed stockpile of 2,500–5,000 tons of chemical weapons (CW). Speaking on the paper, Baek Seung-joo of the Korea Institute for Defense Analyses stated, "The special warfare forces, if combined with North Korea's chemical weapons, could not only inflict substantial damage on us but also drive South Korea into panic quickly."[127]

The 2008 White Paper also offers several specific assessments regarding North Korea's evolving military force structure and weaponry. The document states that the total number of North Korean active duty troops has increased to 1.19 million men, or an addition of 20,000 troops since 2006. Regarding SOF forces, the paper states that their number has grown by 50 percent to 180,000 men. Their training has reportedly also expanded and focused on helping soldiers to quickly infiltrate cities and mountains. Shin Won-sik, the deputy of policy planning in the ROK Ministry of National Defense, stated, "After examining the wars in Iraq and Afghanistan, North Korea appears to have developed strategies that can compliment its shortfalls while reinforcing its strengths." According to the White Paper, the North Koreans have also gained 300 more MRLs, amassing 5,100 in their inventory. It also stated that North Korea is increasingly "deploying missile equipment that can move around." This development, of course, will complicate the counter-fire and missile defense missions for U.S. and ROK ground and air forces. Finally, of interest to U.S. forces that would deploy to the Korean Peninsula in the case of conflict or crisis, the paper states that the North Koreans have recently deployed new ballistic missiles that could threaten U.S. bases on Guam (from which many of the American aircraft would depart in a conflict). The ballistic missiles the paper refers to are likely the North Korean version of the old Soviet SS-N-6 missile system, the Taepo Dong X or Musudan.[128]

Of interest, another recent change that the North Korean military has made to its ground force units is to re-designate some of its functional corps as divisions. For example, the 820th Armored Corps has apparently been redesignated the Guard Seoul Ryu Kyong Su Tank Division 105. The unit is now named after the tank division that inflicted heavy casualties on ROK and U.S. forces in the early stages of the Korean War (the 105th Tank Division) and one of its early commanders.[129] According to the South Korean Defense Ministry's 2008 White Paper, between 2006 and 2008, "two mechanized corps became two mechanized divisions, one tank corps became one armored division and one artillery corps became one artillery division. But in the aspect of war potential, there is no significant change." The paper also states, "Recently, the Army reorganized unit structures by reinforcing the fire power of the first echelon in the frontline area, thereby attaining a surprise effect with overwhelming combat power in the initial engagement."[130] The North Korean military has reportedly downsized several corps-level ground units to achieve better combat flexibility in the changing balance of forces on the Korean Peninsula.[131] For an exact picture of the changes in organization that important North Korean ground units have experienced in recent years, see figure

14. Of course, these changes are also augmented by the reported conversion of seven conventional divisions to light infantry divisions, effectively rendering them SOF units. With 7,000 men or more in each of these divisions, it now means that North Korea has an additional 50,000 SOF troops deployed along its border with South Korea.[132] These modifications have apparently not changed the overall numbers of ground forces in either personnel strength (though personnel strength is up slightly) or equipment; rather, they have been implemented to adjust to changing force-on-force matchups with South Korean and U.S. forces on the peninsula.

Military reorganizations do not occur in a vacuum. The reorganization of the North Korean military that occurred at the end of the 1990s, and then was again adjusted between 2006 and 2008, was obviously designed to deal with its main enemy (the ROK-U.S. alliance) and amend the way that North Korean forces would attack in wartime. In fact, according to military sources reported in the South Korean press, Pyongyang now has a new invasion strategy. The revised strategy now focuses on attacking Seoul, and because Seoul is the capital and center of South Korea's social and economic infrastructure, this plan is centered on the destruction of the capital and the areas around it—with the hope that a cease-fire could then be negotiated from an advantageous position. The plan is said to have evolved because of the lessons learned from watching how U.S. forces operated in Iraq in 1991 and 2003. The change in plan is believed to have been made to adjust to the upgraded weapons systems in the ROK-U.S. alliance's arsenal. When one looks at this newly reported (2010) plan, the bolstering of frontline units and the conversion of some divisions to light infantry makes sense.[133]

CONCLUSIONS

North Korea has gone through a series of enormous economic challenges and crises since Kim Chong-il assumed power in 1994.[134] But the big question here is, have these experiences severely degraded the readiness and capabilities of the North Korean military and its ability to offensively threaten the south and the region? In my view, and based on the evidence presented here, the answer is that North Korea has cleverly adjusted to overwhelming economic challenges by reorganizing its military and refocusing its forces around units that can replace what was a very threatening first punch by armored and mechanized forces (a threat posed during

FIGURE 14. *North Korea's Military Command Organization, 2008*

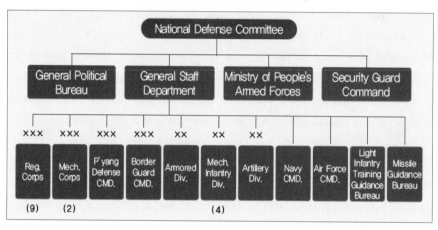

Source: Ministry of National Defense, Republic of Korea, "Defense White Paper," 2008.

the 1980s) with an asymmetric capability built around SOF, long-range artillery, and ballistic missiles. In fact, the Kim regime continues to focus on supporting its military as its highest priority. A report based on defectors' testimonies in 2008 stated that the DPRK may be diverting as much as 90 percent of its international food aid to the military.[135]

Kwon Young-se, a member of the South Korean National Assembly, quoted documents submitted by intelligence officials that said North Korea has spent $65 million purchasing foreign weapons systems since 2003. During the same period, North Korea also added Scud and No Dong missiles, artillery, and submarines to its inventory (to name a few) that were indigenously produced and likely did not contribute to the figure quoted above.[136] In fact, obtaining indigenously produced weapons and maintaining the huge resources required to keep the world's fifth-largest military running reportedly uses up half of the North Korean government's budget every year, according to high-ranking defector Hwang Jang-yop.[137] Of course, at the same time, the army continues to use brutal tactics to maintain control over the North Korean populace and prevent individuals from fleeing the country.[138]

An analysis of North Korea's military capability reveals a careful, well-planned policy of revamping the military in order to pursue a strategy toward eventual reunification through violent or threatening means despite facing challenges that would cripple such a program for most nation-states. It has been done at the expense of providing for even the basic needs of much of the North Korean populace. There are two important things to keep in mind here. The first is the sheer mass of North Korea's forces and their close proximity to the DMZ (which limits warning time). The second is that North Korea has built up its asymmetric forces' capability since the early 1990s to open up vulnerabilities in ROK-U.S. defenses that could turn the tide in the all-important early days of any war but would undoubtedly inflict hundreds of thousand of casualties (many of them civilians). As a press piece from 2003 reflects, "An invasion of South Korea would probably involve the use of commando forces, chemical weapons and massed, mobile artillery fire. Preventing such an attack could involve a decision by the United States and South Korea to launch a pre-emptive assault."[139] Former South Korean minister of national defense Kim Jang-soo supported the assumption that the North Korean asymmetric threat is a serious challenge to the security of the Korean Peninsula in November 2007 when he stated that there was no clear intelligence that North Korea had halted its pursuit of "asymmetrical weapons."[140] In the fall of 2008, Gen. Walter Sharp (commander of USFK), when referring to the North Korean military threat, said it "is still a very huge capability." He also stated that the main threat is Pyongyang's thirteen thousand artillery systems and eight hundred short- and medium-range ballistic missiles.[141]

In my view, the argument over whether North Korea has deployed and trained its forces for the defense or for the offense is a moot one. Based on the evidence presented here, it appears Pyongyang has prepared and continues to prepare for both. It is also apparent that as long as the DPRK exists as a nation-state, it will continue to develop, support, maintain, and hone these capabilities. Finally, despite the primitive state of many of North Korea's systems compared to those of the United States and South Korea, Pyongyang has adjusted by developing asymmetric capabilities and by massing key forces in forward positions from which they could be launched with little or no warning. Thus, the importance of a strong, well-equipped, and transparently led ROK-U.S. military alliance remains critical in deterring North Korea from attack and in containing Pyongyang's coercive behavior and brinkmanship.

CHAPTER THREE

Creating Instability in Dangerous Global Regions

North Korean Proliferation and Support to Terrorism in the Middle East and South Asia

In 2008 an Israeli delegate to the UN accused North Korea of engaging in proliferation of various weapons (particularly nuclear technology and conventional arms) throughout the Middle East, once again bringing to light the serious national security concern that North Korea's rogue state behavior has created for the United States and its allies. In October 2008, Israeli delegate David Danieli stated at a meeting of the International Atomic Energy Agency (IAEA) that "the Middle East remains on the receiving end of the DPRK's reckless activities." He went further, saying, "At least half a dozen countries in the region . . . have become eager recipients . . . through black market and covert network channels."[1]

With all the news reports circulating about North Korea's domestic nuclear program, the six-party talks, and Kim Chong-il's recent health problems, the DPRK's proliferation of nuclear, biological, and chemical programs and technology (hereinafter referred to as WMD) and the platforms used to launch them (ballistic missiles) to unstable regions of the world has fallen below the radar for most of those who analyze security issues on the Korean Peninsula.[2] In my view, this oversight is unfortunate. Despite the fact that North Korea previously engaged in six-party talks with the United States and key players in the region since February 2007, Pyongyang has showed no signs of ceasing or slowing its proliferation of WMDs, conventional weapons, and military training programs to anyone who is willing to purchase them, including rogue states and terrorist groups.[3] Indeed, North Korea has continued to maintain close relationships with key players in the

Middle East and elsewhere whose state behavior is a danger to Washington's national interests. The Independent Working Group at the Institute for Foreign Policy Analysis estimated in its 2009 report that "missile exports, which net North Korea around $1.5 billion a year, constitute one of its largest sources of revenue."[4] In fact, during the fall of 2008, the commander of U.S. Forces Korea, Gen. Walter Sharp, remarked that he "is worried every day by the threat of North Korea selling WMD or missile technology to other people that could use it against us or other countries."[5]

SYRIA

There certainly is no doubt that Syria has been and continues to be a supporter of terrorism and organizations that carry out terrorist acts. Thus, this section will likely be troubling to those who study the Middle East, as North Korea's long-standing relationship with Syria dates back at least twenty years. I will first address what many consider the most important of Syria's programs that has resulted from collaboration with North Korea, namely, Syria's nuclear program.

North Korea and Syria have been collaborating in the nuclear field since the late 1990s, according to Michael Hayden, the former director of the Central Intelligence Agency (CIA). When speaking to the World Affairs Council of Los Angeles in September 2008, Hayden remarked, "The depth of that relationship was revealed in the spring of last year." Hayden was referring to a plutonium nuclear reactor, which the North Koreans helped the Syrians build, that an Israeli air strike destroyed in 2007. He also stated that the facility was "similar to Yongbyon in North Korea, but with its outer structure heavily disguised." Hayden's compelling remarks showed that there was overwhelming evidence that the North Koreans built the facility in Syria: "Virtually every form of intelligence—imagery, signals, human source, you name it—informed their assessments, so that they were never completely dependent on any single channel."[6]

A great deal more evidence can be gleaned about North Korean–Syrian nuclear cooperation from a CIA background briefing given to the press on April 24, 2008. According to the briefing, the Syrians constructed a plutonium nuclear facility in the eastern Syrian Desert with the North Koreans' help. The American intelligence community began to suspect that something was going on during the late 1990s, and increasing evidence piled up from information gathered in 2000, 2001, 2003, and 2006. In 2001, intelligence was acquired tying North Korean nuclear entities to high-level Syrian officials. This material helped analysts trace their cooperation back to as early as 1997. In 2003, evidence was compiled that tied North Koreans to work sites in Syria, but the exact location could not be determined. In 2005, analysts received indications that the Syrians and North Koreans were involved in a project in the Dayr az Zawr region of eastern Syria but again without an exact location. By late 2006, an actual facility had been identified. By the spring of 2007, photographs of the facility's interior and exterior were obtained that revealed it was in fact a nuclear reactor. It is important to note that the facility was not con-figured to produce electricity; there were no power lines coming out of it. The facility used North Korean–type technology and closely resembled the facility at Yongbyon. Internal photographs revealed a gas-cooled, graphite-moderated reactor whose technology and configuration were similar to those of the Yongbyon reactor in North Korea.[7]

As the Syrians rushed to dismantle and bulldoze the facilities following the bombing by the Israeli Air Force, more evidence became obvious. For example, a light tin roof and thin curtain walls had been added to the facility after it was constructed. They were intended to alter the building's outline, which otherwise would have closely resembled the profile of the North Korea's facility at Yong-byon. Evidence presented during the briefing also pointed to a number of North Korean nuclear experts who were in the area as the project was under way. In addi-tion, analysts obtained photographs of North Korean nuclear officials meeting with Syrian officials. North Koreans made multiple visits to Syria before construction of the facility began in 2001 and also helped procure materials that were likely meant for the facility. One of the key North Koreans involved in the operation was nuclear scientist Chon Chi-bu, who was photographed and linked directly to the facility's setup. North Korean advisers also apparently assisted in damage assessment fol-lowing the facility's bombing. In short, to quote one of the senior intelligence of-ficials who conducted the briefing, "Our information shows that Syria was building a gas-cooled, graphite-moderated reactor that was nearing operational capability in August 2007. The reactor would have been capable of producing plutonium for nuclear weapons. It was not configured to produce electricity and was ill-suited for research." The official further remarked, "Only North Korea has built this type of reactor in the past 35 years."[8]

Reportedly, Israeli intelligence monitored a Syrian port where a North Korean cargo ship had docked and tracked the cargo to the nuclear facility site.[9] Originally, it was unclear if the materials carried on the North Korean ship were of the sort that would have made the Syrian facility operational or close to operational, but clearly the cargo's arrival from North Korea had something to do with the Israeli government's decision to destroy the nuclear site. Syrian ports have also regularly served as a conduit in the North Korean–Syrian–Iranian triangle of proliferation and military-WMD cooperation. Reports indicate that the Syrian port of Tartus is the initial point of land entry for North Korean missile components and technology that are sent by sea to Iran.[10] In a later account it became clear that the shipment was probably forty-five tons of yellowcake, or uranium. The ship carrying the yellowcake departed Nampo, North Korea, and hit two ports in China before reaching Tartus on September 2, 2007.[11] News reports quoting unnamed officials allege that the North Koreans later moved the yellowcake to Iran.[12]

In what is perhaps an even more disturbing aspect of the North Korean–Syrian–Iranian triangle, according to reports in the German and Israeli press, Iranian defector Ali Reza Asghari, a former general in the Iranian Revolutionary Guards and a deputy defense minister, stated that Iran had financed the plutonium facility that the North Koreans built for the Syrians. Israeli estimates reportedly figure the Iranians spent somewhere between $1 billion and $2 billion for the North Korean–Syrian nuclear project.[13]

While the nuclear cooperation between North Korea and Syria is troubling, to say the least—and both nations refuse to acknowledge that it even exists—there is much more to the relationship.[14] Perhaps the next most troubling aspect of North Korean proliferation to Syria is that of missiles. North Korea and Syria have had a long and useful collaboration on ballistic missiles since the early 1990s, and this ongoing relationship is worrisome to those who are concerned about the security of Israel and of the Middle East. In fact, U.S. congressman Bob Inglis witnessed evidence of North Korea's relationship with Syria when he was on a trip to Syria in 2009. The congressman spotted several North Koreans shopping in a Damascus bazaar. Inglis told reporters in part,

Seeing the North Koreans literally on the street in Damascus brings all this to a fine point for me. I mean, what a deal, at this point in time, for the president to be cutting missile defense, when I see with my own eyes people in North Korean outfits on the streets of Damascus, knowing that they're up to—they've got to be up to no good because of the plant that was built there and destroyed subsequently by the Israelis.[15]

By the late 1980s, Syria's relationship with the Soviet Union had deteriorated. Damascus began to look elsewhere to acquire its ballistic missiles. On March 20, 1990, a senior North Korean official named Yi Chong-ok traveled to Syria, presumably to lay the groundwork for a missile deal. Later that year, the two nations had come close to reaching a deal. Syria reportedly financed the transaction with the money ($2 billion) Saudi Arabia gave it for participating in the Gulf War coalition. The initial deal was for the purchase of 150 Scud C missiles for $500 million with long-term deliveries to continue. A key part of the arrangement was that North Korea would build two missile assembly facilities in Syria. It is believed these facilities were completed by either 1993 or 1994 and have since been producing thirty to fifty missiles a year. Syria conducted its first test of the Scud C during the summer of 1992. It has since conducted several more test launches.[16]

North Korea and Syria probably began talks regarding the transfer of the Scud D ballistic missile from North Korea to Syria during the late 1990s. In May 2000, Syria reportedly received up to fifty Scud D systems and, on September 23 of that year, conducted its first successful test flight of the Scud D.[17] During a test firing of the Scud D during 2005, the missile inadvertently landed in Turkey. Specialists from American intelligence and others examined the missile and realized that it had components not in the original model. This improved Scud D now is assessed to have a range of seven hundred kilometers and a separating warhead. The missile also had a warhead capable of delivering a chemical payload, including VX gas.[18] It can be assumed that this advanced capability was developed for the Syrians by the North Koreans, who also undoubtedly have this capability.

The North Koreans have also transferred chemical and biological weapons programs to Syria.[19] Syria may have the largest stockpile of chemical weapons in the Middle East.[20] Dozens of Iranian engineers and Syrians were reportedly killed on July 23, 2007, when they were attempting to load a chemical warhead containing VX and Sarin onto a Scud missile at a facility in Syria. The Scud and its warhead—and perhaps the manufacture—were all North Korean.[21] An accident involving missiles also occurred in 2009 in Syria when a Scud D being test launched veered off course and landed in a village market place, killing at least twenty people and injuring sixty others. The missile launch involved the participation of North Korean engineers and Iranian experts (including members of the Iranian Revolutionary Guards).[22]

But missiles are not the only way that Syria could launch chemical weapons. Multiple rocket launchers or tubed artillery could also be (and is likely to be) used to launch chemical munitions.[23] This method is also closely tied to the North Koreans because they are assessed to have perfected the capability to equip their artillery with chemical munitions.[24] Some or all of the long-range North Korean artillery systems that currently sit in range of Seoul are believed to be equipped or are capable of being equipped with this capability. It is likely that given the level of cooperation between Damascus and Pyongyang, a chemical weapons capability also exists for Syrian artillery. It is also likely that the North Koreans have equipped and trained the associated forces.

IRAN

There has been a great deal of talk both in the press and among analysts about North Korean nuclear proliferation since Israeli air strikes took out Syria's plutonium facility in 2007. Most of the focus, though, has been on Syria. Until recently, there was very little talk of North Korean nuclear cooperation or collaboration with any other country in the region. This has recently changed.

A 2008 report from the National Council of Resistance of Iran (NCRI) says that the Iranian government had set up a facility in Tehran, where dozens of North Korean experts are helping to design nuclear warheads for ballistic missiles. (Of interest, the NCRI was the group that disclosed details about Tehran's nuclear program in 2002.) The group also claims that the North Koreans are building the nuclear warhead designs for the Iranians' Shahab-3 ballistic missile, the Iranian version of the North Koreans' No Dong ballistic missile. U.S. officials reportedly believe that the design for a highly enriched uranium (HEU) warhead, built small enough to fit on a No Dong, which was found when inspectors went through Libya's nuclear program components, is the same design that the Pakistanis (through the A. Q. Khan network) gave to the Iranians and the North Koreans. Thus the nuclear connection between Iran and North Korea originally began with the help of Pakistan.[25] The collaboration between Pyongyang and Tehran reportedly started around 2003 when DPRK nuclear specialists made increased visits to Iran. These visits appear to have either accelerated or initiated work between Iranian and North Korean specialists to develop a nuclear warhead for the No Dong missile (Shahab-3 in Iran).[26] According to press reports citing people living inside Iran and foreign intelligence officials, during this time frame so many North Koreans were working on nuclear and missile projects there that the Iranians actually set aside a resort on the Caspian coast for their exclusive use.[27]

The assertion that North Korea has developed technology to fit a small nuclear warhead on a No Dong missile is also supported by statements made by former senior U.S. intelligence official Arthur Brown. Addressing the Foreign Correspondents' Club in Japan, Brown stated, "The fact that they have a warhead that's fitable to the Nodong (ballistic missile) is pretty much given."[28] Brown's remark was further supported by testimony from Gen. Kim Tae-young, the chairman of the South Korean JCS, who told members of the National Assembly in 2008 that "North Korea has been pushing to develop a small warhead to be mounted on a missile."[29] If this information is true, it is possible that the warhead is of an HEU design, as a plutonium warhead may be too big to fit on a missile. All of this recently disclosed evidence points to two key issues. First, North Korea is likely involved in a collaborative nuclear program with Iran, and they are working together to perfect a warhead for a No Dong (Shahab-3) missile. Next, their work further supports indications that North Korea has an active HEU program and may be proliferating it. North Korea, until recently, continued to publicly deny the existence of an HEU program.[30]

North Korea has reportedly also collaborated with Iran on another form of technology that is key to Tehran's nuclear weaponization program: its underground bunkers and tunnels. In a project estimated to have cost hundreds of millions of dollars, the North Koreans helped the Iranians plan and build ten thousand meters of underground facilities with reinforced concrete ceilings, walls, and doors that can withstand bunker-busting munitions.[31] In June 2005, Lyu-Do Myong, one of the North Korean government's experts on underground construction, led a delegation to Tehran. Its mission was to collaborate in the design and construction of the Iranian underground tunnel network for its nuclear facilities.[32] A Congressional Research Service report from 2009, citing sources in the Japanese press, states that high-level Iranian officials visited North Korea in February and May 2008. The Iranian delegation included members of the Atomic Energy Commission and the National Security Council. According to the report, the reason for these visits was to ensure North Korea did not reveal its collaboration with Iran's nuclear program in what were then ongoing talks with U.S. State Department negotiator Christopher Hill.[33]

When it comes to missiles, no nation has bought as many different kinds of missiles and missile technology from North Korea, or had a longer relationship of acquisition with North Korea, than Iran. North Korea had successfully tested its own indigenously produced, reverse-engineered version of the Scud B ballistic missile during 1984, after getting its first Scud from Egypt sometime during the late 1970s.[34] During the early 1980s, Pyongyang entered into an agreement with Iran, which received North Korean missiles in exchange for hard currency. The Iranians almost instantly made good use of the newly acquired missiles from North Korea and fired them at Iraq in the now infamous "War of the Cities."[35] Meanwhile, North Korea was already working on increasing the range of its Scud missiles. Pyongyang successfully produced and tested its own version of the Scud C during 1986 and then again in 1990. Soon thereafter, the Scud C missile was also sold to Iran.[36]

North Korea conducted a successful test of the No Dong missile in 1993.[37] Iranians were reportedly present at the test launch.[38] Iran began acquiring No Dong missiles almost immediately during the mid-1990s and was able to provide the North Koreans with something in return that they needed very badly—oil. Based on various sources, it appears that the No Dong/Shahab-3 missiles were purchased at least partially with Iranian oil instead of cash.[39] Apparently the Iranians are not only working with the North Koreans to build a nuclear warhead for the No Dong/Shahab-3, but they also have flight tested the missile several times and as recently as July 2008.[40]

During the 1990s, the North Koreans built a missile system based on the old Soviet SS-N-6 submarine-launched ballistic missile. They converted this system to a land-based, road-mobile missile system with an estimated range of four thousand kilometers.[41] The North Koreans reportedly sold eighteen of these systems to Iran in the fall of 2005.[42] The Iranians did not wait long to test this missile (named Shahab-4) and conducted their first test launch on January 17, 2006. The missile flew a full three thousand kilometers, and the Iranians intentionally destroyed it in mid-flight.[43] Performance data recovered from the test flight revealed a range capability of four thousand kilometers for the missile. North Koreans were likely present at the launch.[44] The missile is probably what is referred to in the South Korean press either as the Taepo Dong X or the Musudan. It is also deployed in North Korea, though it has only ever been flight-tested in Iran. All of the missiles on the map in figure 15 were acquired from North Korea. Clearly these missiles can now hit targets not only all over the Middle East but also points in Europe.[45]

North Korea is also collaborating with Iran on its long-range Taepo Dong I and II systems. This work reportedly began in the late 1990s, as Pyongyang helped the Iranians develop their own versions of Taepo-Dongs and Taepo-Dong variants, known in Iran as the Shahab-5 and possibly the Shahab-6. None of these missiles appear to be operational yet. Tests of both systems—the Taepo Dong in 1998 and the Taepo Dong II in 2006 and 2009—failed.[46] Reportedly, in 2006 an Iranian delegation of engineers was on hand for North Korea's missile test launches, which included Scud, No Dong, and the Taepo Dong II systems. Ten engineers from the Iranian Revolutionary Guards were at the launches, according to Japanese and South Korean press sources, and were involved in the preparation for the Taepo Dong II launch. Perhaps more important (and more likely), the Iranians were also said to have been on hand to arrange for their possible procurement of the technology associated with the missile.[47] Iranian military officials and scientists also reportedly were in North Korea for the April 5, 2009, Taepo Dong II test launch (which was more successful than the 2006 launch but did not enter its third stage); and a group of more than fifty North Korean nuclear and missile engineers visited Iran soon after the test.[48]

Finally, Iran has a long history of acquiring conventional weapons from North Korea. During the Iran-Iraq War, Tehran acquired long-range artillery systems

FIGURE 15. *Ranges of Iran's Missiles*

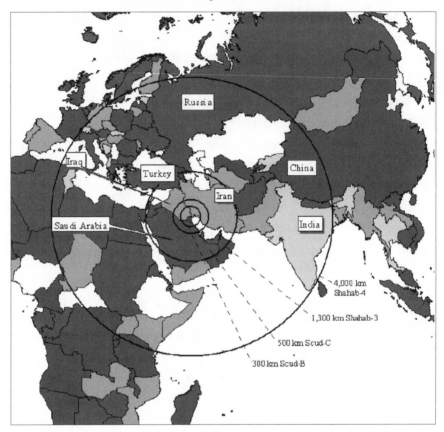

Source: U.S. House of Representatives, Permanent Select Committee on Intelligence, "Recognizing Iran as a Strategic Threat: An Intelligence Challenge for the United States," Staff Report (Washington, DC: House Permanent Select Committee on Intelligence, Subcommittee on Intelligence Policy, August 23, 2006), http://intelligence.house.gov/Media/PDFS/IranReport082206v2.pdf#search=%22Recognizing%20Iran%20as%20a%20Strategic%20Threat%3A%20An%20Intelligence%20Challenge%20for%20the%20United%20States%22.

from North Korea. Of note, they were of the same type (a 170mm self-propelled artillery system) that North Korea currently has deployed near the DMZ—many of which are pointed at Seoul—and are thought to be capable of delivering chemical munitions.[49] North Korea has also reportedly sold a variety of naval craft to Iran, including mini-submarines, which would be able to function with relative ease in the shallow waters off the Iranian coast.[50] The North Koreans likely sold other weapons systems to the Iranians as well. Such systems would probably include small arms, other types of naval craft, and components for radar and air defenses.

North Korea's long and profitable relationship of proliferation with Iran is probably the largest moneymaker of all the deals that Pyongyang has with both state and non-state actors. Congressional Research Service analyst Larry Niksch estimates the North Koreans earn between $1.5 billion and $2 billion annually from their proliferation of weapons and technology to Iran. According to Dr. Niksch, these figures are "based on North Korea's gains from all of its collaborative endeavors with Iran: development of missiles, development of nuclear warheads for at least the Nodong (Shahab) missile, North Korean arms and training for Hezbollah, and North Korea's assistance to Iran in constructing deep, underground facilities to house parts of Iran's nuclear infrastructure."[51] Conventional weapons sales to Iran may make the figure even higher.

LIBYA

North Korea had a relationship with Libya that purportedly began sometime during the early 1990s. While rumors of conventional arms sales are probably true, one of the most important deals that Libya and North Korea made was for the delivery of Scud C missile systems. Libya reportedly also was looking to acquire the No Dong missile during the late 1990s, but apparently it never did.[52] When Libya agreed to completely disclose the details of its WMD programs and dismantle them under the eyes of international inspectors, several Scud Cs from North Korea were included in its stockpile of weapons that were handed over.[53] But the inspections of Libya's weapons program detailed much more than just missiles. It also showed both the ties between the North Korean and Libyan nuclear programs and the connections those two countries had with Pakistan.

According to an article released in the American press in 2005, U.S. government scientists conducted scientific tests and concluded with 90 percent certainty that North Korea sold processed uranium to Libya, as the two nations were both working to bring their HEU programs to fruition. During 2004, international inspectors found the evidence that North Korea provided Libya with nearly two tons of uranium hexafluoride when Libya submitted its program to inspectors in the midst of its agreed dismantlement and provided the toxic material to the United States. After extensive testing conducted at the Oak Ridge National Laboratory in Tennessee in 2004, intelligence officials revealed to the press that scientists determined that the material originated in North Korea, not Pakistan.[54]

Still more was discovered about Libya's nuclear program as it went through inspection and dismantlement. According to reports released to the press, Pakistan had supplied it with Chinese blueprints and plans for designing a nuclear warhead for delivery by a missile (China had provided a great deal of assistance to Pakistan for its nuclear weaponization program). Intelligence officials believe the plans were also provided to both the Iranians and North Koreans. The discovered documents had detailed technical instructions for manufacturing components for the device and fitting it atop a ballistic missile (in all likelihood a No Dong). Among the many documents examined were important and specific descriptions (sometimes in Chinese) of a warhead design. The documents showed detailed designs of what analysts reportedly assess to be a 500-kilogram warhead.[55] This revelation is extremely crucial because it shows that while Libya and North Korea were cooperating, they were also likely sharing designs the A. Q. Khan network in Pakistan had given them. It also points to what may be the basis for the current, collaborative development of a nuclear warhead project reportedly under way in Iran between North Korean and Iranian engineers and scientists.

OTHER NATIONS IN THE MIDDLE EAST

North Korea has had a long and troubling relationship involving proliferation of WMDs, the platforms to carry WMDs, and even conventional weapons deals with Iran, Syria, and, until 2004, Libya. But these are not the only nations in the Middle East with which North Korea has had weapons transactions in recent years. To a lesser extent, Pyongyang has also engaged in deals with at least three other nations in the region. This information, of course, adds further credibility to the assessment that North Korea will sell anything to anybody who has the cash (or something useful to barter) to pay for it.

It is fairly well known among analysts who study North Korea that Pyongyang was able to kick off its Scud missile program because of a deal with Egypt. Cairo sent Scud B missiles, which were originally acquired from the Soviet Union, to North Korea in the late 1970s. As part of the agreement between Egypt and North Korea, Pyongyang also reportedly helped the Egyptians build a Scud B production facility during the 1980s and 1990s and supplied components and other materials for their Scud C system, including perhaps actual Scud C missiles. Unconfirmed reports have stated Egypt was also attempting to acquire the No Dong missile system from the North Koreans as well, but to date these reports have not been proven.[56] According to accounts from the 1990s, Egypt received numerous shipments of Scud C components from North Korea and possibly missiles and was working to enhance their range. The Egyptians have probably (with the help of the North Koreans) begun indigenous production of the Scud C.[57]

But Egypt is not the only U.S. ally to acquire missile systems from North Korea. During 2002, North Atlantic Treaty Organization (NATO) forces (from the Spanish navy) intercepted a shipment of fifteen Scud missile systems on board the merchant ship *So San* bound for Yemen. The missiles were hidden under thousands of bags of cement (which is what the ship's crew falsely declared on its manifest). Reportedly, NATO naval forces were acting on U.S. intelligence when they intercepted the ship. Embarrassing the United States, Yemen asked that the missiles be released as they were part of what the Yemeni government described as a legal arms deal. The Bush administration granted the Yemeni government's request, allowing Yemen to receive the North Korean missiles even though it had violated an agreement not to purchase missiles and parts from North Korea.[58] Another nation friendly to the United States, the United Arab Emirates (UAE), also is reported to have purchased twenty-five Scud B missiles from North Korea, as well as artillery and MRLs.[59]

ARMS DEALS WITH PAKISTAN

The focus of this chapter is on the Middle East, but it is important to include information about Pakistan (and South Asia) because it too has been tied into WMD proliferation in the Middle East and closely connected to North Korean proliferation activities.

In 2002, following an accusation by the United States that North Korea was developing an HEU program in collaboration with Pakistan, Pakistani scientist A. Q. Khan confessed that he had run a network that sold HEU technology to Pyongyang, among others. According to numerous sources, Khan admitted that he had supplied the North Koreans with centrifuge prototypes and blueprints that had enabled Pyongyang to begin its centrifuge enrichment program.[60] At the time, and even now, the Pakistani government denied knowledge of the operation, but a great deal of evidence shows that the government in Islamabad not only sanctioned and enabled the operation, but it also profited from it. Dr. Khan confirmed this information himself. In 2008 he revealed that the planes carrying the uranium enrichment materials to North Korea and elsewhere were loaded under the supervision of Pakistani security officials. He also stated that he had originally taken sole responsibility for the nuclear proliferation because his friends had persuaded him that it was in the national interest.[61] Khan also denied his early confession in whole, saying that he had not meant a word of it. In fact (and as many suspected), Khan stated that it was forced on him by then-president Pervez Musharraf.[62] Thus, the evidence is clear that the Pakistani military—and the government—was involved in collaboration with North Korea and others for an HEU nuclear weaponization program.

In an interview with the Japanese press, former Pakistani leader Benazir Bhutto stated that in 1993 she had been able to "obtain technology from a long-range missile" from North Korea. The missile was the No Dong, and the payment for the missile was uranium enrichment technology. A. Q. Khan escorted Bhutto to North Korea, thus beginning the two countries' nuclear cooperation in the mid-1990s.[63]

While the Pakistani collaboration program began in the mid-1990s, by 2000–2001 it had kicked into high gear. The agreement, apparently originated under Bhutto and continued under Khan's supervision after Bhutto fell from power, was a "nukes-for-missiles" barter deal between Islamabad and Pyongyang, two regimes that were both strapped for cash. Pakistan provided technology, equipment, and blueprints to North Korea, while North Korea provided missiles (primarily the No Dong) to Pakistan (which already had North Korean Scud missiles).[64] According to press reports, the missiles and nuclear technology were shuttled between North Korea and Pakistan on American-built C-130s.[65] Also of interest, these long-range "shuttle" trips made by C-130s carrying nuclear materials, technology, and scientists to North Korea and No Dong missiles back to Pakistan reportedly flew through Chinese airspace.[66] On one of the trips, the Pakistan Air Force C-130 used to transport the weapons and technology reportedly broke down in North Korea and was temporarily unable to return to Pakistan. It is said to have created quite a dilemma in North Korea, which had no spare parts for the American-made aircraft.[67]

The nukes-for-missiles deal ended after A. Q. Khan's "confession" (now completely disowned) and probably because of pressure put on Pakistan by the United States, which began supplying foreign aid to Pakistan when Islamabad joined Washington in prosecuting the war on terror.[68] Unfortunately, the damage was already largely complete. Khan's nuclear "bazaar"—financed, endorsed, and enabled by the Pakistani military and government—had already provided nuclear plans, components, centrifuges, blueprints, technology, and scientific support to North Korea, Iran, and Libya. Of note, the design for an HEU warhead that originated in Pakistan, with the A. Q. Khan network, and that can be fitted aboard a ballistic missile (presumably the No Dong) is now reportedly being modified and perfected in Iran in a collaboration between Iranian and North Korean specialists. Thus, Pakistan was the conduit in the North Korean–Iranian collaboration and possibly in other related activities. But North Korean proliferation goes beyond arms deals with nation-states in the Middle East and South Asia. Pyongyang also has enabled terrorist groups.

PROLIFERATION TO TERRORIST GROUPS

HEZBOLLAH

North Korea is well known as a nation-state that will sell anything to any nation that will pay for it. But it does not limit its deals to the state actors in the Middle East. It also has a relationship with Hezbollah that, according to some reports, goes back to the late 1980s. During this period, Hezbollah operatives received several months of training in North Korea. Among the key players in Hezbollah who spent time in North Korea were Hassan Nasrallah, the secretary-general; Ibrahim Akil, the security and intelligence chief; and Mustapha Badreddine, head of counterespionage operations. Their training in guerrilla operations occurred at the behest of Iran and appears to be yet another result of Tehran's close relationship with North Korea. According to several reports, North Korean instructors also supervised all of the building of Hezbollah's underground facilities in southern Lebanon during the 2003–4. These facilities included dispensaries for the wounded, food stocks, and arms dumps.[69] Thus, the North Koreans clearly provided assistance to Hezbollah, through Iran, for extensive operations that could be run from underground facilities.[70]

It is likely that the Hezbollah's underground facilities served as a major factor in the difficulties the Israeli military encountered during combat operations against

Hezbollah in 2006. In fact, as Israeli reporter Lenny Ben-David has articulated, "Hizbullah's military bases, armories, bunkers and communications networks were much more extensive than Israel's intelligence services estimated on the eve of the 2006 war." Ben-David asserts that the tunnel-building operations were conducted under the auspices of the North Korea Mining Development Trading Corporation, a company that has been officially subject to sanctions by the United States for its activities.[71]

Hezbollah also has reportedly received shipments of important arms that have been used to inflict casualties on Israeli troops and civilians. According to sources in the South Korean press, the Mossad has discovered that Hezbollah was able to hit the outskirts of Tel Aviv with short-range missiles containing components supplied by North Korea. According to the report, the missile components were shipped from North Korea to Iran, where they were then assembled (presumably by Iranians) and transported to Hezbollah via Syria.[72] The connections that the North Koreans have with Hezbollah through both Iran and Syria are clear.[73] A North Korean arms shipment confiscated in the UAE in 2009 had components and detonators for 122mm rockets that Israeli officials reportedly believe were eventually bound for Hezbollah.[74] There are reports that Hezbollah has also received other shipments of arms with the potential to cause serious damage to Israel as well. According to the opposition group the Reform Party of Syria (RPS), Hezbollah acquired CW agents from North Korea during the summer of 2008. RPS, which reportedly has ties to the Lebanese intelligence community, states the recently acquired mustard and nerve gas were received with Syria's help and can be mounted on Hezbollah's short-range missiles that target Israel.[75] If true, this development would significantly change the threat to Israel's security.

On April 8, 2009, thirty individuals holding dual citizenship in both the United States and Israel filed suit in U.S. Federal District Court against North Korea for the injuries that they received during the 2006 Lebanon war between Hezbollah and Israel's military forces. The lawsuit totaled more than $100 million. The plaintiffs alleged North Korea trained leaders of the Hezbollah movement and built arms and storage bunkers and other (underground) structures that enabled Hezbollah to conduct warfare against Israel in 2006. Finally, the plaintiffs claim the North Koreans provided training that helped Hezbollah operatives evade fighter jets while still being able to fire rockets at civilian areas of Israel. The suit also cites a May 2008 congressional memo that describes a huge facility the North Koreans built for Hezbollah: a fifteen-mile-long tunnel Hezbollah used to reportedly mass its troops for the attack.[76]

THE TAMIL TIGERS

Hezbollah is not the only terrorist group that has had connections to the North Koreans in recent years. A video of an attack during 2000 by the Liberation Tigers of Tamil Eelam (LTTE), or Tamil Tigers, on a Sri Lankan navy ship reveals they were piloting speedboats of North Korean origin. The video also showed the rebel group using what appeared to be a North Korean variant of a Russian (and later Chinese) 107mm Katyusha rocket launcher.[77] An analysis of the video in *Jane's Intelligence Review* concludes that there can be little doubt that the armaments the LTTE used were of North Korean origin:

> In the video, LTTE Sea Tigers can be seen using a variant of the 107mm Katyusha rocket, fired from a lightweight tripod, in pairs. This is believed to be a variant of the Chinese Type 63 107mm launcher. The Chinese produce a single tube version called a Type 85 fired from a man-portable tripod, but the North Koreans produce a double version. This is quite a rare weapon. . . .[78]

The LTTE also was supposed to receive a shipment of 152mm and 130mm artillery shells and 120mm mortars from the North Koreans during 2007, but the Sri Lankan navy thwarted the shipment. The seizure of an LTTE boat mounted with a 14.5mm machine gun is also said to be connected with the North Koreans.[79] The Sri Lankan navy is known to have intercepted and attacked North Korean merchant ships carrying arms to the LTTE on three different occasions in recent years: October 2006, February 2007, and March 2007. It reportedly was able to sink two of the North Korean ships. Of interest, on several occasions, the North Korean merchant ships fired on the Sri Lankan vessels (which likely led to the eventual sinking of two of the belligerent ships). According to a Congressional Research Service report that cites the *Sankei Shimbun* in Japan, the Sri Lankan government filed an official protest with the North Koreans.[80]

CONCLUSIONS

North Korea's activities in the Middle East and South Asia and with terrorist groups have been both disruptive to regional security and the national security interests of the United States and its allies. Thus, it is rather surprising that these activities have received relatively little attention as the United States and other parties seek to persuade North Korea to transparently dismantle its nuclear programs through diplomacy. While the United States has reportedly brought up the issues of nuclear proliferation, North Korea continues to publicly deny its involvement, and there has been no mention of North Korea's support to terrorist organizations.[81] As the evidence indicates, Pyongyang has shown no signs of slowing down its arms deals, its collaboration on WMD initiatives, or its support to terrorism in what is arguably the most volatile region on earth.

Given that the evidence points to North Korea's participation in proliferation programs to rogue nations and to its support of terrorist groups, it is likely that many in the United States were disturbed when on October 11, 2008, the Bush administration announced it would remove North Korea from the list of state sponsors of terrorism (SST).[82] Soon after the deal was declared, many conservatives expressed dismay, with some voicing concern that it also sends a very bad message to Iran. Representative Ileana Ros-Lehtinen of Florida remarked, "By rewarding North Korea before the regime has carried out its commitments, we are encouraging this regime to continue its illicit nuclear program and violate its pledge to no longer provide nuclear assistance to extremist regimes."[83] Many conservative lawmakers in South Korea's National Assembly who had been largely supportive of Bush's policies previously were also outspoken about their concern regarding the delisting.[84] Former deputy negotiator for the U.S. delegation to the six-party talks and current director of Asian studies at Georgetown University Victor Cha admits, "Pyongyang's uranium-based nuclear activities and its proliferation connections with Syria are said to be covered by the scope of the agreement, though ambiguities remain. Moreover, none of this is set in stone until the six parties codify the understandings reached in Pyongyang—and even then, who is to say the North won't welsh again in the future?" Cha does believe that the delisting agreement is "another yard gained in a slow ground game."[85] At the time of North Korea's delisting, Barack Obama also reportedly hailed the Bush administration's decision to take Pyongyang off of the terrorism list as an "appropriate response."[86] Thus, it is likely to remain a fixture in the Obama presidency.

Despite removing Pyongyang from the State Department's SST list, the December 2008 round of six-party talks resulted in none of the formal agreements the Bush administration had hoped for. In fact, North Korea dismissed one of the key oral agreements discussed earlier among the six parties concerning the removal of nuclear samples from North Korea for analysis and verification. The North Koreans claimed in December 2008 that this testing would violate their sovereignty. Then U.S. State Department spokesman Sean McCormack told reporters that the United States would not rethink its removal of North Korea from the list.[87] Former senior adviser for Asian issues at the National Security Council Michael J. Green was quoted in the South Korean press as saying, "The Bush administration erred in removing North Korea from the list without extracting a more concrete step on verification. We now know the North Koreans tricked us."[88]

Despite the optimism of Bush administration officials and former officials (as well as the man who would become the next president of the United States), many questions remain. Does this compact in fact mean that if nuclear weaponization programs are simply frozen (because the program most certainly has not been dismantled, and the North Koreans have not even admitted the locations or numbers of their plutonium weapons or their HEU facilities), the U.S. government will forgive other acts of irresponsible state behavior such as proliferation and support to terrorism by delisting a state that agrees to some initial (and these agreements are certainly far from being anything but initial) moves in the right direction? In the interest of not inciting the North Koreans, will the U.S. government now ignore their other acts that disrupt stability in the Middle East in the interest of pursuing the six-party talks? North Korea resorted to brinkmanship during the fall of 2008 by initiating activity at a nuclear test site, leading to the assessment that a possible test could occur again.[89] North Korea also apparently began preparations for another long-range missile test at its missile testing facility on the east coast.[90] Did these brinkmanship moves (and North Korean threats to restart their reactor) create a flurry of activity that resulted in Washington letting it off the hook? And if so, does this behavior set a precedent for Washington's dealings with other states that engage in rogue behavior such as Iran?

Certainly these questions are troubling. But perhaps the most vexing question is, how can the United States and its allies put enough pressure on North Korea to end activities that disrupt stability and security in the Middle East? The Proliferation Security Initiative (PSI) is one method that the United States and many allies have used (with mixed results at best) in an attempt to disrupt North Korea's proliferation activities, although the program has been aimed primarily at maritime means of proliferation in the past. Perhaps increased ROK participation in PSI will now enhance its effectiveness.[91] In fact, only nine weeks before President Bush removed North Korea from Washington's SST list, India—responding to a U.S. request—blocked a North Korean cargo plane from delivering its cargo to Iran by denying the pilot permission to fly from Myanmar (Burma) to Iran through Indian airspace.[92] The aircraft was an IL-62 owned by the North Korean "airline." A senior U.S. official reportedly stated, "It was frankly a success that we stopped North Korea from doing this."[93] According to several press sources, the Americans believed the aircraft was carrying gyroscopes for missile guidance systems.[94]

The passage of UNSC Resolution 1874, initiated after North Korea's ballistic missile and nuclear tests in 2009, is another example of the international community undertaking PSI-like initiatives. UNSC 1874 has led to sanctions being carried out that have probably forced a change in tactics, techniques, and procedures in the North Korean proliferation system. The U.S.-led initiative has involved many nations, including South Korea, and shows a resolve that needs to be maintained if the international community truly wants to demonstrate firmness regarding North Korea's proliferation activities.[95]

The interesting example of a North Korean aircraft flying out of Burma and carrying components of weapons systems that will enhance Iran's missile capability also brings us to the subject of North Korean proliferation to Burma. A variety of reports now indicate North Korea is helping Burma with a fledgling nuclear weaponization program. Burma has a small reactor that it claims is for peaceful purposes, but reportedly the government sent thirty officers to study reactor technology in North Korea during 2003 and in 2006 started buying machinery required for reactor construction.[96] According to an essay written in *Foreign Affairs* by Michael Green and Derek Mitchell, "Western intelligence officials have suspected for several years that the regime has had an interest in following the model of

North Korea and achieving military autarky by developing ballistic missiles and nuclear weapons."[97]

Reports from exiles say that the North Koreans are engaged in tunneling and constructing water-cooling systems for the Burmese in an isolated area of the country.[98] Workers who have been in the area describe the underground facility as "quite huge" and say that the Burmese are working in collaboration with North Korean technicians. The facility is surrounded by tight security.[99] Recent reports and actual photos smuggled out of Burma now confirm that North Korean experts have been helping the Burmese with tunneling systems since at least 2006.[100] In January 2009, a North Korean believed to be a weapons specialist working on a secret project at the facility died from undisclosed causes. His body was quickly cremated, and his remains were shipped back to North Korea.[101] According to the Japanese press, three individuals were arrested in June 2009 for attempting to illegally export a magnetic measuring device for developing missile systems to Burma. Police discovered that the content of the order originated with a Hong Kong–based North Korean firm.[102] In 2010 Assistant Secretary of State for East Asian and Pacific Affairs Kurt Campbell warned Burmese officials about collaboration with North Korea. And Sen. James Webb of Virginia reportedly cancelled a trip to Burma because of its ties to North Korean proliferation.[103] Details of the secret North Korean–Burmese project remain sketchy but are disturbing to those who follow Pyongyang's proliferation of technology and weapons.

Despite efforts that have often proven to be extremely frustrating at times to disrupt the North Koreans' proliferation and support of illicit activities, it appears that Pyongyang has always been able to come up with new strategies and techniques to get past them and continue initiatives that have gained it both cash and resources. Thus, only continued vigilance and close collaboration by the United States and its allies will be able to contain the rogue state behavior of a North Korea that shows no signs of halting its association and cooperation with dangerous state and non-state actors in the Middle East and South Asia.

CHAPTER FOUR

Running in Place

North Korea's Nuclear Program and the Six-party Talks during the Bush Administration[1]

N orth Korea has developed a nuclear program that is both dangerous and potentially destabilizing to the region. Despite the best efforts of three different American presidents, North Korea's program has now produced weapons that have been proliferated to other rogue states and tested at least partially successfully in 2006 and 2009. Because North Korea brutalizes its own people, maintains a hostile attitude toward its neighbors, and continues to have a basket case economy, its nuclear program is of great concern not only to other nations in the region and those who have interests in the region but also to nations that exist in other volatile regions such as the Middle East and South Asia, where proliferation has created difficult and complicated security dilemmas.

While I believe the specific details of North Korea's nuclear program are extremely important (and I will provide background on both the plutonium and HEU programs), they are not the focus of this chapter. Indeed, while the nuclear program was in existence during the entire Clinton administration, it also will not be the focus of this chapter. There is a great deal of literature on both these subjects. Instead, this chapter will focus on the six-party talks and how they evolved during the Bush administration. My reasons for this approach are simple. The events that led to the six-party process and the various steps that the process went through from 2003 through the end of the Bush administration in 2009 will have an effect on the security and stability of the Korean Peninsula well into the Obama presidency in the United States and the Lee Myung-bak administration in South Korea. Since their very inception the six-party talks, its activity during the Bush administration, and the many events that occurred as the diplomatic progression occurred have been the focus of a great deal of debate and criticism for various reasons from both those on the Left and those on the Right. Thus, my goal is to sort through the evidence and present a clear picture of why the process was initiated, what its goals were, how successful it was during the Bush years, and what the chances of success for this process are during the Obama administration.

BACKGROUND ON NORTH KOREA'S PLUTONIUM AND HEU PROGRAMS

Kim Il-sung is said to have planned for a nuclear program as early as the 1960s. North Korean scientists trained in the Soviet Union during this time frame and reportedly were schooled by the Soviets in how to process plutonium. A small, experimental plutonium reactor was completed in a facility at Yongbyon sometime between 1980 and 1987.[2] Once the reactor and associated facilities were done, they were almost impossible to hide. A plutonium facility of the type at Yongbyon is typically rather large, difficult to conceal, and easily photographed by outside collection methods.

During the early 1990s, rumors began to circulate that North Korea was developing nuclear weapons at the facility. In the post–Cold War environment, these reports may have created enough pressure for North Korea to sign an International Atomic Energy Agency safeguards agreement on January 30, 1992.[3] Inspectors from the IAEA conducted six separate inspections in North Korea, the last of which occurred in February 1993. Based on these inspections, it appeared that the North Koreans had reprocessed plutonium on three separate occasions in 1989, 1990, and 1991. What had appeared originally to be a spirit of cooperation ended when inspectors were denied access to two suspect nuclear waste sites that Pyongyang declared to be military sites and off-limits.[4] This standoff with the IAEA resulted in the first North Korean nuclear crises. It looked as if North Korea and the United States may have actually been on the brink of war until talks between Jimmy Carter and Kim Il-sung brought about an end to the impasse. President Carter's visit with the North Koreans led to what would eventually be called the Agreed Framework, which froze North Korea's facilities at Yongbyon in exchange for annual heavy fuel oil shipments (HFO) and the building of light water reactors (for the peaceful use of nuclear technology) by the United States.[5]

As a result of the terms of the Agreed Framework, the North Koreans agreed to freeze—but not dismantle—their nuclear program. Facilities were sealed but not torn down, and nuclear components were not dismantled or removed.[6] In addition, the North Koreans delayed returning to the worldwide Nuclear Non-Proliferation Treaty (NPT) as various elements of the framework were implemented under the Clinton administration.[7] North Korea did not have to dismantle any facilities as a result of the agreement, and this condition would lead to numerous problems in later years during the Bush administration. In addition, North Korea's use of the NPT—choosing to return or walk away from it—would also be an issue that would arise in later years.

The nuclear confrontation between the United States and North Korea that continued throughout the Bush administration and into the Obama administration is generally agreed to have begun during bilateral U.S.–North Korean talks on October 3, 2002. At that time Assistant Secretary of State for East Asian Affairs James Kelly confronted two North Korean negotiators—Kim Kye-kwan and Kang Sok-ju—with the fact that the United States had knowledge and strong evidence of North Korea's clandestine HEU weaponization program, which was a violation of the Agreed Framework. Kelly called for the North Koreans to dismantle the program. North Korea's first foreign minister, Kang Sok-ju, reportedly admitted to the program and made several demands that Washington would be unlikely to meet, not the least of which was a nonaggression treaty.[8] Several days after the meeting, Bush officials made the decision to publicly release the details of the North Koreans' stunning admission of a clandestine nuclear weaponization program, and the North Koreans promptly and publicly denied ever admitting to it.[9]

North Korea took quick and hostile action in response to the public disclosure of its clandestine HEU nuclear weaponization program by the United States. Pyongyang expelled the IAEA inspectors who had been present at Yongbyon on December 27, 2002, and on January 10, 2003, North Korea announced that it was withdrawing from the NPT—again.[10] These moves reflected the weakness of the Agreed Framework, which had been in existence since 1994; moreover, the plutonium facilities at Yongbyon were only frozen, not dismantled. Thus, they could be reactivated at any time, for any reason. This option is exactly what the North Koreans chose to do. Second, by walking away from the NPT again, the North Koreans showed that its value to them was not even worth the paper it was written on.

According to Siegfried S. Hecker of Stanford University's Center for International Security and Cooperation, by 2005 the North Koreans had made great use of the time available since IAEA inspectors were expelled in December 2002. According to a paper he presented in Washington, D.C., the North Koreans unloaded the reactor at Yongbyon in April 2005 to extract the plutonium. They then reloaded the reactor and resumed operations during June 2005. Hecker has suggested (then and on other occasions) that the North Koreans had extracted enough plutonium and developed enough fissile material to build about six to eight nuclear weapons. In his paper he acknowledged, "Given demonstrated technical capabilities, we must assume they have produced at least a few, simple, primitive nuclear devices."[11] I will talk more about the plutonium program at length later, but suffice to say, based on the reports from those who have visited North Korea (including Hecker) and the nuclear test conducted in 2006, there is no doubt that North Korea has developed and manufactured plutonium nuclear weapons. The questions that some have raised are about the HEU program. How did North Korea acquire this program and how far along is it? In fact, some have even said that the program does not exist and was a political tool that the Bush administration used as an excuse to walk away from the Agreed Framework.

The debate about North Korea's clandestine HEU nuclear weaponization program began almost as soon as the crisis erupted in 2002. In fact, some even dispute the translation of what the North Koreans actually said to James Kelly in October 2002.[12] One of the most outspoken of those who has said (since almost the outset of its public disclosure) that the assertion of a North Korean clandestine HEU program was false has been noted journalist Selig Harrison. In fact, in congressional testimony given on February 13, 2009, Harrison stated in part, "The assumption of any kind of weapons grade uranium program has been exaggerated, was used as an excuse to abrogate the Agreed Framework in 2002, and has had disastrous consequences. . . ."[13] Throughout the Bush administration, many scholars concurred with Harrison's assertions. For example, during 2003 Leon Sigal of the Northeast Asia Cooperative Security Program reportedly told the press, "There is no agreed estimate of anything. As with Iraq, there is significant disagreement in the intelligence community about pieces of this."[14] In his statements Harrison also made comparisons to Iraq that have tended to muddy the waters, particularly since the evidence chain is far different; that did not stop many scholars and pundits during the Bush administration from bringing them up as a reason why the vast array of evidence regarding North Korea's HEU program must be in doubt.[15]

While Selig Harrison's claims are interesting, they appear to be based entirely on what the North Koreans have told him. In order to make a true assessment regarding North Korea's HEU program, one must look at the evidence purely at its face value and throw out all the biases on both sides of the political spectrum. Thus, it is particularly important to note statements by others who also have in-depth knowledge of the evidence. Robert L. Gallucci, a former Clinton administration official who had access to highly classified data on North Korea's nuclear program (and who is anything but a George Bush supporter), declared in 2004 that there is "no doubt" that North Korea had the HEU technology. He further said, "I think the North would like to keep its enrichment program as insurance against U.S. actions. This is not something we cannot allow them to do." Gallucci also remarked, "We should be aware that A. Q. Khan, the Pakistan father of the enrichment program, and sometimes called the father of the bomb in Pakistan, has admitted to transferring centrifuge technology, selling it to North Korea. I do not know why the North Koreans insist refusing to admit this."[16] In congressional testimony, Charles L. (Jack) Pritchard, president of the Korea Economic Institute, addressed the fact that future talks should cover North Korea's HEU program during the Obama administration. He stated in part, "In revamping the Six Party agenda, a path to resolving our concerns over HEU and Syria-related proliferation activities must be found."[17]

Because the debate has now lasted for several years—often driven by from what end of the political spectrum one analyzes geopolitics—about the very existence of North Korea's HEU weaponization program, I believe it is important to examine the available evidence on this issue. It is my belief that several governments, investigative reporting in the press, and "smoking guns" coming out of Pakistan, Libya, and Iran have presented overwhelming evidence that shows North Korea has been building an HEU program since at least the late 1990s. Thus, a presentation of this evidence is in order.

In chapter 3, I discussed Benazir Bhutto's and A. Q. Khan's compelling statements admitting that they had proliferated important HEU weaponization technology, blueprints, plans, and even scientists to North Korea throughout the 1990s on behalf of the Pakistani government.[18] But high-level Pakistani officials were not the only ones to disclose the active and large-scale proliferation of HEU technology from Pakistan to North Korea. High-ranking North Korean defector Hwang Jang-yop spoke to the South Korean press about the issue during 2004. He said that during the peak of the restrictions placed on North Korea's plutonium reactor during 1996, he had voiced his concerns to a high-ranking official, and "before the fall of 1996, he said we've solved the problem. We don't need Plutonium this time. Due to an agreement with Pakistan, we will use uranium."[19]

The evidence trail that leads to North Korea from Pakistan is quite compelling. Whether it is the evidence that Pakistan used American-made C-130s to transport the centrifuges, plans, and scientists to North Korea for the burgeoning HEU program (flying through Chinese airspace) or the fact that in exchange, North Korea provided No Dong missiles that were capable of providing a platform for Pakistan to launch nuclear weapons at India, the many issues that have come out point to a nuclear bazaar run by Pakistan's A. Q. Khan for North Korea (among others).[20] In fact, there are even rumors that Pakistani scientists may have taken up residence in North Korea to help the Koreans with their HEU program. South Korean scholar Cheon Sung-hun of the Korea Institute for National Unification told the South Korean press in 2004 that "nine Pakistani nuclear scientists have been missing since they left their country six years ago, and we cannot rule out the possibility that some of them are in North Korea."[21]

The public disclosure that North Korea was also probably collaborating with Libya during its HEU development period (Libya and Iran were also cooperating with Pakistan at the time as well) is troubling and represents another piece of the puzzle. As then–vice president Dick Cheney remarked in a speech given at Fudan University in China, "The Libyans acquired their technical expertise, weapons design and so forth from Mr. A.Q. Khan, Pakistan. . . . Mr. Khan also provided similar capabilities to the North Koreans. So we're confident that the North Koreans do, in fact, have a program to enrich uranium to produce nuclear weapons."[22] Equally disturbing are the many reports that came out of Iran in 2003 and have continued as of the writing of this book. According to dissident groups, press reports, and scholars who focus on the region, North Korea is collaborating with Iran on building a 500-kilogram HEU warhead for a missile (reportedly the No Dong, which is called the Shahab-3 in Iran).[23] The original design for the warhead probably came from the Pakistanis, who also gave the same design to the Libyans.[24]

The dilemma of detecting an HEU facility is that it can be much smaller than a plutonium-processing facility, could even be built underground, and is far less vulnerable to technical intelligence collection means than the very large facility the North Koreans have at Yongbyon.[25] In dealing with such an opaque government and society as North Korea's, it has been difficult since the crisis started in 2002 to get the North Koreans to even admit that they have the program. But after several years of denials from the North Koreans and as many pundits and scholars both in the United States and South Korea (almost exclusively on the Left) supported these denials, the evidence regarding its existence once again began to seep out to the public in late 2008. In 2009 in an interview with the press, outgoing U.S. secretary of state Condoleezza Rice reportedly said, "I think the intelligence community now believes that there is an undisclosed either imported or manufactured weapons-grade HEU in North Korea."[26] During her confirmation hearings in January 2009, incoming secretary of state Hillary Clinton also voiced concern about North Korea's HEU program: "Our goal is to end the North Korean nuclear programs—both the Plutonium processing program and the highly enriched uranium program, which there is reason to believe exists, although never quite verified."[27] Meanwhile, according to a senior South Korean official (who declined to be identified), U.S. and South Korean intelligence had discovered a North Korean secret HEU facility by February 2009. The facility is said to be underground and located in Sowi-ri, North Korea, in the same province where the Yongbyon facilities are located. The facility reportedly can produce small amounts of highly enriched uranium.[28]

According to an account written by A. Q. Khan and publicized in late 2009, North Korea had already possibly enriched small amounts of uranium by 2002. Khan toured a plant there that he says had three thousand centrifuges or more. He also said that Pakistan helped the North Koreans with drawings, vital machinery, and technical advice for at least six years. Khan also visited a plant that made uranium hexafluoride, a gas required for the uranium enrichment process, during 2002. In return for the vital equipment and software that Pakistan supplied, North Korean technicians taught the Pakistanis how to make Krytron electrical switches used in nuclear detonations. Khan also asserted that top Pakistani political and military officials assisted and approved of the collaboration.[29]

Ultimately one of the more compelling aspects of the evidence dealing with Pyongyang's HEU weaponization program came from the North Koreans themselves. As I described earlier, after Kang Sok-ju admitted to James Kelly in 2002 that North Korea had an active HEU weaponization program, days later Pyongyang denied ever having made the statement and continued to deny the program's existence for several years thereafter. In June 2009 this stance changed. The state-run Korean Central News Agency formally admitted to the existence of an HEU weaponization program when it announced, "The process of uranium enrichment will be commenced."[30] Of interest, after North Korea's public disclosure, some analysts continued to downplay even North Korea's formal acknowledgment of its HEU weaponization program. In congressional testimony on June 17, 2009, Selig Harrison stated, "The prospects for capping the arsenal at its present level have improved as a result of Pyongyang's June 13 announcement admitting that it has an R and D [research and development] program for uranium enrichment. Since this program is in its early stages, and it not yet actually enriching uranium, there is time for the United States to negotiate inspection safeguards."[31]

Harrison's testimony did not address evidence regarding North Korea's long-running nukes-for-missiles deal with Pakistan, the facilities at Sowi-ri, and the collaboration with Iran since at least 2003. But following the initial announcement (June 2009), the North Koreans made another admission on September 4, 2009. This time, the DPRK's permanent representative to the UN sent a letter to the UNSC president that stated, "Experimental uranium enrichment has successfully been conducted to enter into completion phase."[32] The South Korean minister of unification disclosed in June 2009 that North Korea was believed to have had an HEU program before the United States raised the accusation in 2002 and that the north had no intent of terminating it.[33] In fact, according to an unclassified CIA point paper distributed to Congress in 2002, the CIA had "recently learned that the North is constructing a plant that could produce enough weapons grade uranium for two or more nuclear weapons per year when fully operational—which could be by mid-decade."[34] Experts in South Korea have reported that a completed HEU facility (such as the one at Sowi-ri) could produce one or two nuclear devices per year.[35] Based on the evidence presented, this program is far beyond the R & D stage and may be close to (if not already) producing HEU weapons. In fact, it is my assessment that North Korea is likely to conduct a test of an HEU device when the leadership there feels the geopolitical situation warrants it. Such a test will put to rest the statements of the many naysayers in the United States and South Korea who have denied its existence since it was first disclosed publicly in 2002.

While it appears the big issues that remained unresolved as the Bush administration left office were North Korea's HEU programs, its weapons, and its proliferation to other rogue states, a great many twists and turns in the six-party talks occurred from 2003 until the Obama administration assumed power in 2009. Many lessons can be learned from these important developments. Thus, it will be my goal for the remainder of this chapter to assess what happened, why it happened, and what the results (if any) meant for the United States, North Korea, and the region.

ACTIONS THAT LED TO THE SIX-PARTY TALKS

While the George W. Bush administration was subjected to a great deal of criticism for ending the Agreed Framework process, many difficult circumstances led to the confrontation between James Kelly and the two senior North Korean negotiators, Kim Kye-kwan and Kang Sok-ju, in December 2002. These factors are important and, in my view, should be part of any analysis that addresses the history of the six-party talks. As the Clinton administration came to a close and the presidential election results remained in doubt at the end of 2000, the ongoing sensitive talks with the North Koreans were suspended. In fact, a scheduled trip by envoy Wendy Sherman was cancelled.[36] In addition, it was very well known (including to the North Koreans) that the incoming Bush administration planned to take a different approach to Pyongyang.[37] Because of the delayed transition period for the Bush administration (as a result of contested presidential election results), it was several months before key personnel could be put into position. These delays during a highly sensitive and important period of talks with the North Koreans likely made an already edgy government in Pyongyang even more tentative about dealing with the new American government. These differences in the U.S. government's approach to North Korea also caused problems with Washington's allies in Seoul.[38] Finally, talks originally scheduled for July 2002 were delayed because of a North Korean–initiated sea battle with the South Koreans that summer.[39]

During his bid for the presidency, Bush had campaigned for a harder line with the North Koreans and had been critical of Clinton administration policies that had only frozen (not dismantled) the facilities at Yongbyon, failed to keep Pyongyang from test launching a long-range ballistic missile in 1998, and engaged in talks with the DPRK that most conservatives in the United States thought were unwise.[40] The North Koreans were reportedly very apprehensive about dealing with the Bush administration. In a speech at the Young Korea Academy Forum for Unification in Seoul during June 2004, Lim Dong-won, the head of the National Intelligence Service in South Korea during the Kim Dae-jung administration, stated that Kim Chong-il told him that he had cancelled his planned visit to South Korea in 2001—in fact, saying that he "had no choice"—because of the outcome of the U.S. elections. Kim Chong-il revealed to Lim that his advisers thought Bush's polices would "threaten the North Korean regime."[41] Thus, walking into talks with the North Koreans, the Bush administration was confronted with inherited policies it disagreed with, a North Korean government that was hostile to negotiating with a new American administration it did not trust (and actually feared, if one is to believe Lim's statements), and an ally in South Korea that was even softer in its policy toward Pyongyang than the Clinton administration had been.

THE SIX-PARTY TALKS BEGIN, 2003–5

As a result of the 2002 confrontation between James Kelly and the North Korean negotiators, there was a brief impasse of several months in the talks between the DPRK and Washington. The United States at the time no longer wanted to deal with the North Koreans on a bilateral basis, largely as a result of the North Koreans' lack of transparency. For their part, the North Koreans declared the Agreed Framework was "null and void."[42] Diplomats within the Bush administration and from the region developed a new framework for negotiations on North Korea's nuclear program and called it the six-party talks. The six parties in the talks included the United States, South Korea, North Korea, the Russian Federation, Japan, and China.[43] The negotiations involved a multilateral approach to resolving the issues surrounding North Korea's nuclear program. The first of these talks was held during April 2003,[44] and five sessions occurred between April 2003 and the fall of 2005.

During the first two years of the six-party talks, most analysts agree that there were few if any consequential results. The talks were typically hosted in Beijing by the Chinese government. Many, including some in the U.S. government, perceived China as being a positive influence on the talks. China is well known as being North Korea's lone remaining real ally. In fact, during these early stages of the six-party talks, China worked closely with South Korea, where the government hoped a steady engagement policy would persuade Pyongyang to move forward in ridding the Korean Peninsula of nuclear weapons.[45] While China and South Korea did improve their relationship during this early period of the talks, there was no significant change in North Korea's behavior. American hopes that the Chinese would be able to exert influence or even pressure on the North Koreans regarding their nuclear program proved to be disappointingly false.

The first ray of light in the six-party talks occurred on September 19, 2005. At that time, Pyongyang pledged in principle that it would eventually abandon its nuclear weapons programs in exchange for economic assistance and security pledges from Washington. The United States also pledged to eventually build a light water reactor for the North Koreans (nuclear power for peaceful purposes). The agreement's details were very hazy and light on specifics.[46] The South Korean minister of unification at the time, Chung Dong-young, announced to the press that the breakthrough was largely a result of his efforts. He claimed to have had numerous meetings with both American and North Korean officials that led to this move in what had been a standstill in negotiations between Pyongyang and the other parties (particularly the United States).[47]

Immediately following the breakthrough in the talks, a reporter asked a South Korean official if "enriched uranium will be included in the nuclear programs scrapped by North Korea." The official replied, "It says all nuclear weapons and existing nuclear programs in the agreement."[48] The key concern of American conservatives and those who watch North Korea on a daily basis was verification. Throughout the history of its nuclear program North Korea has failed to live up to inspection agreements. As Henry Sokolski, executive director of the Nonproliferation Policy Education Center, said at the time, "There's no good way to locate Kim's nukes using special technology. Inspectors will have to ask the regime to learn more, and Kim is sure to demand that the U.S. make concessions for every answer. In this game, Pyongyang's deck will always be larger than ours."[49] Nevertheless, despite its lack of clarity, details, or formalization, North Korea's agreement in principle to dismantle its nuclear program sparked hopes in 2005 that a successful end was in sight for talks that had dragged on, accomplishing almost nothing, for more than two years.

NORTH KOREA'S ILLICIT ACTIVITIES CAUSE AN IMPASSE, 2005–6

While the agreement reached between the North Koreans and the other five parties in the talks was potentially a landmark event, it left many unanswered questions regarding specifics, verification, and obligations by all parties. Because the agreement was so lacking in details, had it actually been the nexus to get North Korea to dismantle its nuclear weapons program, diplomats would have had to hammer out a great many issues. But this work did not happen. The reason why is simple. On September 15, 2005, the U.S. Treasury Department took action under section 311 of the USA PATRIOT Act and designated Banco Delta Asia (BDA) in Macao as a "primary money laundering concern." Treasury's undersecretary for terrorism and financial intelligence, Stuart Levey, stated, "Banco Delta Asia has been a willing pawn for the North Korean government to engage in corrupt financial activities through Macau, a region that needs significant improvement in its money laundering controls." Levey further commented, "By invoking our USA PATRIOT Act authorities, we are working to protect U.S. financial institutions while warning the global community of the illicit financial threat posed by Banco Delta Asia." The comments, stated in a Treasury Department press release, highlighted illegal and illicit activities the bank had conducted for the North Koreans and prohibited U.S. banks from doing business there.[50]

The reaction from the North Koreans was to demand that the United States immediately release the bank's frozen funds and drop sanctions on eight of their companies accused of being fronts for illicit activities and proliferation of WMDs. When the six parties met again during November 2005, the talks went nowhere, and the issue of North Korea's nuclear program apparently took a backseat to the concerns relating to Pyongyang's illicit activities and the front companies that supported them. These activities consisted of (and still do) illegal drugs, primarily methamphetamines and heroin; counterfeit money, primarily American hundred-dollar bills; counterfeit cigarettes; and arms sales that included WMDs and missiles.[51] The U.S. Treasury Department's action and the corresponding fallout in the international financial world as it related to North Korea produced a stalemate in the talks that the North Koreans had likely not anticipated. But to understand why the Americans had taken these measures, it is also important to know just how widespread the North Koreans' illicit and illegal activities— centered at the time around Banco Delta Asia in Macao—are in Asia.

According to State Department official William Bach (in congressional testimony given in 2003), the North Korean government has been actively involved in illicit activities for more than thirty years. According to Bach, "For some 30 years, officials of the Democratic People's Republic of Korea have been apprehended for trafficking in narcotics and other criminal activity, including passing counterfeit U.S. notes." He further specifically addressed illegal drugs when he said, "More recently, there have been very clear indications, especially from a series of methamphetamine seizures in Japan, that North Koreans traffic in, and probably manufacture, methamphetamine drugs."[52] Perhaps just as important, North Korea's illegal and illicit programs became an important way for the regime to fund the elaborate lifestyle of its elite and various other programs, including the nuclear program.[53]

Pyongyang apparently began this enterprise in earnest when subsidies from the Soviet Union ended in 1990. The illicit programs are run out of an office within the Korean Workers' Party known as Bureau Number 39 (also known as Office Number 39), which sits near the Koryo Hotel in Pyongyang (where many foreign visitors stay). Front companies such as Daesung Chongguk (with offices in Austria) and Zokwang Trading Company (which operated out of Macao) are controlled by Bureau Number 39, which answers directly to Kim Chong-il.[54] According to interviews conducted by *Wall Street Journal* reporters, Bureau Number 39 generated a hard-currency slush fund that amounted to approximately $5 billion.[55] For many of the years that North Korea's illicit programs were in operation, Zokwang Trading Company was located in an office building close to Banco Delta Asia, which held $25 million of the North Korean government's money, much of which was found to be from illegal activities.[56] Macao was the center of much of North Korea's money laundering for its activities until the international law enforcement light began shining on the small former Portuguese colony in 2005. Of course, North Korea, then and now, also diversified its slush funds in such places as Luxembourg and Singapore.[57]

North Korean drug operations are known to involve the manufacture and sale of both heroin and methamphetamines. Australian Federal Police seized a shipment of heroin in Australia from the North Korean merchant ship *Pong-su* that had a reported street value of $221 million.[58] While heroin sales are likely important to the coffers of Bureau Number 39, methamphetamines are said to be a bigger moneymaker. Japanese police estimated in 2003 that North Korean methamphetamines accounted for 43 percent of the illegal market there.[59] To distribute their illegal drugs, North Korean government operatives also reportedly have connections with the Yakuza in Japan and with organized crime syndicates in both China and Taiwan.[60] Even the military in North Korea has a history of supporting drug distribution and playing a role in drug drops, with its personnel said to have often been used in this capacity.[61]

Trafficking counterfeit cigarettes has not been discussed nearly as much as the illicit drug operations or the counterfeit currency operation, but their manufacture and illegal sale apparently picked up during the 1990s when North Korea began to feel a strong economic pinch. The North Koreans reportedly manufacture their counterfeit cigarettes in two factories that are obviously off-limits to foreigners and illegally sell them under such brand names as Marlboro and Seven throughout Asia and even in the United States.[62] In congressional testimony, U.S. State Department official Peter Prahar stated that between 2002 and 2005, counterfeit Marlboro cigarettes were identified in thirteen hundred incidents in the United States. Prahar also reported that federal indictments were filed alleging that over a period of several years criminal gangs had arranged for a forty-foot container of DPRK-originated counterfeit cigarettes to enter the United States at the rate of one per month. He also said that the fake cigarettes from North Korea were sold on a large scale all over Asia, including such places as Japan, the Philippines, and Singapore. As with all North Korean illegal operations, Pyongyang's government networks also dealt with organized crime syndicates in China, among other places, to sell the cigarettes.[63] Also, as with North Korea's other illicit operations, the funds were likely often laundered through front companies and banks in Macao and elsewhere.

Counterfeit currency was a particular concern of the Bush administration because the currency being counterfeited was (and probably still is) U.S. hundred-dollar bills. The U.S. Secret Service cited the North Korean–produced counterfeit currency as among the most sophisticated in the world.[64] The bank in Macao was reportedly used to launder the fake bills, but as with their drug operations, the North Koreans were also heavily involved with international organized crime.

Pyongyang's partners included Asian organized crime syndicates, possibly the Russian Mafiya, and even members of the Irish Republican Army.[65] The North Korean government is unique because since the Nazi era, it is the only sovereign nation-state government known to be actively involved in the manufacture and distribution of counterfeit currency.[66] But, as a result of American law enforcement efforts, other countries—including important Asian economic powers such as China and Japan— also began to crack down on North Korean accounts in their banks because of fears of North Korean government–sponsored organized crime.[67]

The effects of the crackdown on Banco Delta Asia were cascading, almost immediate, and had devastating economic ramifications on North Korea's ability to generate badly needed hard currency. Thus, the North Koreans' reaction was obviously a negative one; in fact, it led to a stalemate in the six-party talks. But there was a result from the U.S. crackdown on North Korea's illicit activities that even American policy makers were unlikely to have predicted: because the ill-gotten gains proved a large-scale benefit for North Korea's elite, Kim Chong-il's slush fund, and even the military, the suppression of their illicit activities actually began to squeeze them where it hurt the most—in their wallets. The United States had been looking for a way to leverage the North Koreans since the beginning of the six-party talks in 2003. It now appeared that it had a chance to do so, because North Korea's illegal and illicit financial networks were being forced out into the light of day. As Rachel L. Loeffler, former deputy director of global affairs at the U.S. Treasury Department, stated in 2009,

> In short, the mere announcement of a possible regulatory measure that would apply only to U.S. institutions caused banks around the world to refrain from dealing with BDA and North Korea. By March 2007, when Washington actually made it illegal for U.S. banks to maintain relationships with BDA, many in the global financial community had already cut ties with BDA on their own.[68]

NORTH KOREA TAKES ACTION: THE MISSILE AND NUCLEAR TESTS OF 2006

As the six-party talks proceeded into 2006, North Korea decided to make an issue about the building of a light water reactor by the United States. Previously, both President Bush of the United States and President Roh of South Korea had publicly stated that North Korea must first take verifiable steps to dismantle its nuclear program.[69] But the North Koreans were certainly not without leverage of their own. During the summer of 2006, they made preparations for a long-range ballistic missile test. On July 4 and 5, North Korea test launched seven ballistic missiles, including one Taepo Dong 2 (which failed to successfully reach its second stage) and several Scud and No Dong systems. The missile launches were met with outrage by the international community.[70]

As the North Koreans prepared to launch the eye-opening test, respected analysts in both the United States and South Korea assessed that it was being used to get the United States to ease its stranglehold on the North Korean economy after cracking down on the north's illicit activities and the banks that supported them. Kim Tae-woo of the Korea Institute for Defense Analyses said, "The U.S. is now strangling North Korea economically . . . their immediate objective is to make the U.S. step back."[71] Former Pentagon official Chuck Downs commented, "Pyongyang has created an opportunity to break out of the negotiating deadlock that has stymied the regime for years, dissolve the international consensus on how to deal with the regime's illicit smuggling and counterfeiting activities, and change politics in South Korea and the U.S."[72]

As the six-party talks remained mired in disagreement over Pyongyang's illicit programs and details of what the agreement to dismantle should include, North Korea effectively ended any debate about whether it actually had nuclear weapons. On October 9, 2006, the North Koreans conducted their first underground nuclear test. Most analysts agreed that the test appeared to have been a partially successful detonation of a plutonium nuclear device.[73] Siegfried Hecker visited North Korea following the test and stated, "The DPRK aimed for 4 kilotons [kt] and got 1 kiloton. That is not bad for the first test. We call it successful but not perfect."[74] Hui Zhang, a research associate at the Belfer Center for Science and International Affairs of the John F. Kennedy School of Government at Harvard University estimated, "If North Korea planned the yield of 4 kt (as reported), the test could be not a failure. It could show that Pyongyang already has confidence to explode a larger nuclear device and is pursuing a much more compact warhead for its missiles."[75] Following the test, North Korea reiterated its demand that the United States stop the financial restrictions that were at the time strangling North Korea's access to banks in the international arena as a condition to return to the six-party talks. Kim Chong-il reportedly told Chinese officials, "If the U.S. makes a concession to some degree, we will also make a concession to some degree, whether it be bilateral talks or six-party talks."[76]

The chess game continued through the end of 2006. The United States had been successful in putting the North Korean economy under considerable pressure by initiating financial restrictions on banks that dealt with Pyongyang's widespread and lucrative illicit activities as well as by working with international law enforcement to inform institutions and governments about these activities. For their part, the North Koreans had not blinked. Instead, they responded defiantly by first testing several ballistic missiles during the summer of 2006 and then taking the even more drastic step of testing a nuclear device in October 2006. The question was, who would blink first? The United States was under considerable pressure from its allies in the six-party talks (particularly the government of South Korea) to ease law enforcement and financial actions that had put North Korea "under the gun."[77] The North Koreans were adamant about funds being released in Banco Delta Asia, largely because the repercussions in the international banking community made it extremely difficult for them to run their money (much of it from illegal or illicit activities) through banks throughout Asia and elsewhere. Had the United States kept up the pressure on North Korea's ability to operate its financial networks, there is no telling what steps Pyongyang would have taken next. But it did not happen.

THE SIX-PARTY TALKS MOVE FORWARD: THE AGREEMENT OF 2007

In the chess game that began after North Korea's reported admission of an HEU program to the United States during late 2002, Pyongyang had shown it would not hesitate to play hardball. It certainly proved it by conducting missile and nuclear tests that gained worldwide attention. Of course, the United States also played a tough game and put real pressure on North Korea's fragile, and largely illegal, economy. But the United States was the first to make the concessions necessary to restart the six-party talks and prompt what policy makers at the time hoped would be the beginning of North Korea's dismantlement of its nuclear program.

In an accord reached by all six parties and released on February 13, 2007, they agreed the following issues would be addressed in the "initial phase":

1)   The DPRK will shut down and seal for the purpose of eventual abandon-
ment the Yongbyon nuclear facility, including the reprocessing facility and
invite back IAEA personnel to conduct all necessary monitoring and verifica-
tions as agreed between IAEA and the DPRK.

2)   The DPRK will discuss with other parties a list of all its nuclear programs
as described in the Joint Statement, including plutonium extracted from used
fuel rods, that would be abandoned pursuant to the Joint Statement.

3)   The DPRK and the US will start bilateral talks aimed at resolving pend-
ing bilateral issues and moving toward full diplomatic relations. The US will
begin the process of removing the designation of the DPRK as a state-sponsor
of terrorism and advance the process of terminating the application of the
Trading with the Enemy Act with respect to the DPRK.

4)   The DPRK and Japan will start bilateral talks aimed at taking steps to
normalize their relations in accordance with the Pyongyang Declaration, on
the basis of the settlement of unfortunate past and the outstanding issues of
concern.

5)   Recalling Section 1 and 3 of the Joint Statement of 19 September 2005,
the Parties agreed to cooperate in economic, energy and humanitarian assistance to the DPRK. In this regard, the Parties agreed to the provision of emergency energy assistance to the DPRK in the initial phase. The initial shipment
of emergency energy assistance equivalent to 50,000 tons of heavy fuel oil
(HFO) will commence within next 60 days.[78]

Also, the six parties formally agreed to establish the following working groups
to carry out the actions of the initial phase:

- Denuclearization of the Korean Peninsula
- Normalization of DPRK-US relations
- Normalization of DPRK-Japan relations
- Economy and Energy Cooperation
- Northeast Asia Peace and Security Mechanism[79]

Senior U.S. officials' statements to the press regarding the actual details of
the deal reached with the North Koreans disappointed many analysts. When asked

about the ambiguity of the February 13 statement, Condoleezza Rice remarked in part, "This is the first step, but there's a step in the follow-on phase which is the complete declaration." When she was asked about the fact that the North Koreans continued to deny the existence of their HEU program (which had caused the crisis in the first place), Rice remarked, ". . . As I said, we are in the first quarter, not the fourth, and we are going to pursue the issue of the highly enriched uranium program. We've made that clear." During the same briefing, a member of the press asked Rice a difficult two-part question: how far along was North Korea's HEU program and was it true "that the North Koreans expect that the issue of the Macao bank will be resolved shortly and that within 30 days they will see some of their funds released. . . ?" The frozen funds in the Macao bank and related crackdowns all over Asia had set the North Koreans back on their heels and had caused the talks to stall since 2005. Rice responded in part, "We've been having good discussion with all of the parties involved in that and we'll look to what kind of remediation needs to take place to resolve our concerns. But that's a legal channel. . . . In terms of the HEU program, . . . I can't go much farther beyond saying that we have concerns about the highly enriched uranium program."[80]

The chief negotiator to the six-party talks, Christopher Hill, had brokered the new deal with the North Koreans. Hill had strongly advised Rice (who, in turn, was able to convince President Bush) to take the terms of the deal despite the advice of many others in the Bush administration who were against it because it eased the constraints on North Korea's illicit programs and put no real pressure on Pyongyang to disclose details of its HEU program.[81] Hill defended the terms of the agreement in a speech he gave on February 22, 2007:

It is unlikely that the North Koreans will roll out of bed in the morning and say we are going to make a strategic decision to get out of all of this. More likely, they are going to make decisions to move on a step-by-step basis, and as they move one step, they will look back and say, this is a better place than we were yesterday, and that will encourage them to take still another step. . . . By no means have we achieved the final step.[82]

In the minds of some—on both ends of the political spectrum—the key issue (which was not addressed) was still the HEU program. Yet, even as the ink was drying on the agreement, the North Koreans continued to deny the very existence of the program.[83] Despite what many considered a poorly conceived deal that gave all the advantages to Pyongyang, the United States pushed forward. The North Koreans were adamant about not accepting any of the initiatives of the February 13 agreement unless the United States released their funds in Banco Delta Asia in Macao.[84] Unlike the ambiguity in Condoleezza Rice's statement about easing up on North Korea's illicit and illegal activities, the United States made a clear move to back off any pressure that it had been applying to Pyongyang's lucrative support funds for its military and the elite. In June 2007, the funds were released from Banco Delta Asia in Macao.[85] This move effectively ended a policy that had been successful in pressuring North Korea. As Undersecretary Stuart Levey told the American Bar Association in 2008, "Many private financial institutions worldwide responded by terminating their business relationships not only with [BDA], but with North Korean clients altogether."[86] It appears the Treasury Department was forced to back off as U.S. policy took a decided turn in a different direction.[87]

STONEWALLING AND DENIALS: THE EVENTS OF 2007–9

The talks reached a new phase after all six parties reached the agreement in early 2007. But the agreement was notably vague in many ways and left many questions unanswered about verification, the existence of North Korea's HEU program, and the speed with which North Korea would dismantle its facility at Yongbyon. During 2007 all talks seemed to focus only on the facility at Yongbyon and not on the actual fissile material that was—and probably still is—located elsewhere. As the talks continued in 2007, another issue arose: proliferation. In September 2007 the Israeli Air Force bombed and destroyed a facility in Syria that was a (now-confirmed) plutonium nuclear weaponization facility built for Damascus using North Korean technology and assistance.[88] The occurrence in the Middle East brought up fresh concerns regarding North Korea's nuclear program. At the time Pyongyang had disclosed nothing about its fissile material, its weapons, or its HEU program. But now that its proliferation to rogue states was visible for all to see, apprehensions about the impact of Pyongyang's nuclear weaponization program on other volatile regions outside Northeast Asia increased.

During April 2008, North Korea and the United States seemed to be on the verge of reaching a deal where the former would turn over documents that would fully disclose its nuclear program. Some worried that the accord was yet another U.S. concession (depending on what the documents revealed), but Washington pushed on. Calls for revelations about North Korean proliferation to Syria and its covert HEU program seemed to go unheeded. State Department spokesman Sean McCormack claimed on April 18 that the deal would allow inspectors access to all of North Korea's facilities.[89] North Korea's reluctance to reveal these activities reportedly held up the documents' release for several months.[90] The deal that was unfolding that April seemed to offer some movement on reducing North Korea's plutonium activities, and Washington seemed focused on this aspect of the talks.[91] In return for turning over documents and blowing up its cooling tower at the Yongbyon nuclear facility, North Korea insisted that the United States remove it from the State Department's list of state sponsors of terrorism.[92]

Finally, in May 2008, North Korea handed over more than eighteen thousand pages of documents relating to its nuclear program. However, the documents reportedly did not contain information about Pyongyang's proliferation to Syria or its HEU program.[93] Reportedly, the North Koreans "acknowledged" U.S. concerns over their HEU program and proliferation, and that was the extent of their disclosure of these two key details. About the Syrian proliferation question, Robert Gallucci (former lead negotiator on nuclear issues during the Clinton administration) stated, "That is a huge undropped shoe and it must be dealt with."[94] Following North Korea's release of the documents, which cannot be legitimately called anything close to a complete disclosure, the U.S. Senate earmarked $15 million in economic aid for North Korea and another $53 million to provide for 1 million tons of fuel in exchange for progress in the six-party talks. The bill passed with seventy votes for and twenty-six opposed.[95]

Despite disturbing North Korean actions that were revealed in late 2007 and in full detail in 2008 and despite its failure to share details of its covert HEU program, the six-party talks continued into the summer of 2008.[96] In a frank statement that was very revealing about North Korean intentions, the Korea Economic Institute's Charles Pritchard told the press that the North Koreans he met while on a trip in April 22–26, 2008, said that they would destroy their nuclear facilities but not necessarily their weapons and materials already manufactured. State Department officials responded to the press that North Korea "often takes a tougher stance in conversations with private-sector analysts to enhance its negotiating position." Mr. Pritchard also stated that North Korean officials he spoke with continued to deny their proliferation activities.[97] Despite the concerns and analyses of many in both the United States and allied nations, in a major show that Washington hailed as a profound step in the right direction, North Korea televised its demolition of the cooling tower at the Yongbyon plutonium facility in late June 2008.[98]

As June moved into July, 2008 proved to be a frustrating year for many in both the Bush administration and others in the six-party talks who were hoping to oversee the transparent dismantlement of North Korea's nuclear program. During this period, a blueprint was laid out for verifying Pyongyang's nuclear disarmament. Unfortunately, it did not call for North Korea to give details of either its HEU program or its proliferation to Syria.[99] Nevertheless, on June 26, 2008, President Bush "announced the lifting of the Trading with the Enemy Act (TWEA) with respect to the Democratic People's Republic of Korea (DPRK, or North Korea), and notified Congress of his intent to rescind North Korea's designation as a State Sponsor of Terrorism (SST)."[100] The U.S. government's announcement was based on North Korea handing over the long-awaited "declaration" of its nuclear programs. The declaration, however, not only lacked details of its HEU program or proliferation, but it also failed to provide any information on North Korea's nuclear weapons arsenal (including numbers of bombs or where they are stored).[101] To further exacerbate concerns many had about North Korea's HEU program, fresh traces of HEU were reportedly discovered among the more than eighteen thousand pages of documents that the North Koreans turned over to the United States. Condoleezza Rice told the American press, "As we've gotten deeper into the process, we've been troubled by additional information about North Korea's uranium-enrichment capability. . . ."[102]

By July 17, 2008, North Korea had pulled half of its eight thousand fuel rods from the nuclear reactor at Yongbyon as it slowly met its obligations to dismantle its nuclear program, according to sources in the multilateral negotiations.[103] Talks on July 12, 2008, had produced an agreement for verification of North Korea's nuclear facilities, but the talks failed to produce details of when and how it would take place.[104] By July 22, the United States had proposed a specific mechanism to the North Koreans for verifying their nuclear dismantlement, but the proposal received a lukewarm reception in Pyongyang.[105] As the North Koreans continued to stonewall on verification, on July 31, President Bush made a statement to the press that he would not remove them from the SST list unless they agreed to a protocol for verification of their uranium-based nuclear program and their weapons proliferation.[106] By September 2008, the issue of verification and complete disclosure was still at an impasse. North Korea began to up the ante by apparently breaking the seals at its Yongbyon nuclear facilities and hinting that it would begin to restore the facilities there.[107] The North Koreans' actions were in response to Washington's request that verification would involve "full access to any site, facility or location," and it would allow inspectors to take both still photos and videos and to stay at suspected sites as long as necessary. The U.S. proposal also stipulated that inspectors should be able to make repeated visits to sites and to take samples (which could of course be analyzed in the United States).[108]

By October 2008, Bush administration officials had admitted to the press that the fragile agreement could collapse if the Washington and Pyongyang did not come to a consensus very quickly.[109] But the situation seemed to be saved when, despite North Korea's lack of cooperation, the United States did in fact remove North Korea from its SST list. In response, the North Koreans reportedly again resumed their agonizingly slow disabling of the facilities at Yongbyon.[110] As former Bush official Victor Cha stated in an opinion piece, "A McCain or Obama administration will have to contend with the problems of dismantlement, uranium, and Syria, and other nuclear issues which undeniably will come up during the verification of Yongbyon."[111] Soon after being dropped from the list of states supporting terrorism, North Korea demanded a subsistence allowance for the ten thousand people it claimed earned their living from the Yongbyon operation.[112] Pyongyang also demanded that the other members of the six-party talks set a specific timetable, in writing, for providing energy assistance in return for its nuclear disablement.[113]

The verification agreement that the United States and North Korea reached during the fall of 2008 was troubling to many who felt that Washington had given in to North Korean demands that did not adequately address much of Pyongyang's nuclear program. As Bruce Klingner of the Heritage Foundation stated, "Some verification measures are tenuously based on side letters or oral agreements with North Korea." Klingner further stated, "U.S. officials privately acknowledged that the verification protocol will not provide access to inspect the nuclear test site, plutonium waste site, or facilities involved in the weaponization of plutonium. Experts will have access only to Yongbyon and some academic institutions."[114] In what many analysts considered to be troubling, North Korea's HEU program and proliferation were reportedly to be referred to in an "appendix to the main document" and were to be dealt with separately.[115] Thus, in essence, when it came to any verification of either of these essential items, Washington agreed to "kick the can down the road." Since the appendix was reportedly less binding than the adopted main document, what was contained in it would likely be addressed in future talks; thus, the issues that Washington had originally pushed so hard for became almost ancillary in the verification process.[116]

Finally, in November 2008, North Korea announced that it would not allow inspectors to take samples to verify its nuclear capabilities. Pyongyang announced that inspectors could not remove samples from its facility at Yongbyon, meaning they could not be taken out of the country.[117] The announcement rendered what had already been a weak agreement even weaker. Now inspectors were not only limited in the facilities that they could verify but also in the way that they could conduct their inspections. Being unable to remove samples from North Korea made it much more difficult to verify where the samples came from, how they affected the nuclear weaponization program, and other important technical issues that would have been vital for ensuring Pyongyang was transparent in the dismantlement and disclosure process.

What made the verification agreement even weaker was the fact that the United States had accepted many verbal agreements with North Korea. For example, according to press reports, the only written documentation regarding sampling was a "memorandum of conversation" written by Christopher Hill to Condoleezza Rice. An unnamed senior State Department official conceded that no other evidence of North Korea's commitment to sampling existed.[118] North Korea's agreement to a verification protocol was probably one of the key reasons that the communist state was taken off of the State Department's SST list, yet Pyongyang later claimed it never made a promise to allow sampling and accepted a document with no specific enforcement measures.[119] In an interview with the South Korean press, the Bush administration's top State Department official on nuclear verification said that sampling should be guaranteed as a way to assess North Korea's nuclear capability. Assistant Secretary of State for Verification, Compliance, and Implementation Paula DeSutter said, "Sampling is a very normal part of many arms control agreements. . . .". She further stated, "Analysis happens, not on site but back at laboratories specifically designed to do the work."[120]

In late November 2008, the U.S. State Department announced that it expected North Korea to commit, in writing, to allowing its inspectors to take samples from nuclear sites in the reclusive state. The announcement was made in reference to talks that were to occur the next month.[121] After four days of talks held during December 2008, North Korea refused to agree to a system of verification that would satisfy the United States. Of significant importance, the North Koreans refused to allow soil and air samples to be taken from the nuclear facilities to locations outside their country where proper scientific analysis could occur. The impasse effectively extinguished any chance the Bush administration may have had to end the confrontation before its term expired.[122] Christopher Hill told the press at the Beijing airport, "Ultimately, the DPRK (North Korea) was not ready, really, to reach a verification protocol with all of the standards that are required."[123] At a White House press briefing, Press Secretary Dana Perino stated, "There was an open door, and all they had to do was walk through it because five of the members of the Six-Party talks had all agreed to a verification protocol."[124] Thus, after delisting North Korea from the list of nations supporting terrorism based on what were essentially verbal agreements, the United States was now faced with a nation that once again in reality was refusing to transparently and verifiably dismantle its nuclear weapons program.

The events of that December showed that despite an engagement policy the Bush administration had followed since February 2007 (a complete turnaround from its policies in 2001), the North Koreans had no real intention of giving up all aspects of their nuclear weaponization program. More information followed in later weeks that was even more troubling. In an essay he wrote for *Foreign Affairs* in February 2009, Defense Secretary Robert Gates admitted that the United States believed North Korea had produced several nuclear bombs: "North Korea has built several bombs, and Iran seeks to join the nuclear club."[125] Of course, in a move that President Bush said was the North Koreans "trying to test the process," the North Koreans hinted that they would (again) slow the process of disablement at their Yongbyon nuclear facility. The DPRK's nuclear envoy, Kim Kye-kwan, was quoted in the Japanese press as saying the North Koreans would "probably adjust the pace of disablement at nuclear facilities if aid is suspended." He likely made the threat in response to an announcement by Washington that energy aid to the impoverished state had been suspended because of the failure of the talks. Many experts now believe, however, the North Koreans held out on discussions about a verification protocol until the Obama administration assumed office.[126]

As the Bush administration prepared to leave office, relationships also began to fall apart among the other nations involved in the six-party talks. Both Russia and China openly disagreed with Washington over stopping fuel aid to North Korea because of the failure to reach a verification protocol during December 2008. Both nations stated that they planned to continue the aid to Pyongyang, further exacerbating the lack of leverage the United States had over North Korea.[127] In January, White House officials urged North Korea to return to the talks,[128] but they also voiced legitimate concerns about North Korea's HEU program.[129] Later in the month, senior U.S. officials disclosed to the Japanese press that particles of HEU had been detected on aluminum pipe the North Koreans had previously submitted to the Americans as a sample.[130] Condoleezza Rice confirmed these suspicions when she stated, "I think the intelligence community now believes that there is an undisclosed either imported or manufactured weapons-grade HEU in North Korea." She continued, "But that's why the verification protocol becomes even more important to establishing what the nature and status of the HEU program is and what they've done with it and what they might do in the future."[131] As the Bush administration left office, issues still remained about North Korean proliferation, its HEU program, and the verification of all of its programs, including the locations and numbers of its plutonium weapons. Indeed, even the dismantlement of the Yongbyon facility remained in limbo.

CONCLUSIONS

When the Bush administration left office, North Korea still possessed its nuclear weapons. Pyongyang also had neither made a proper accounting of its HEU program and its proliferation to Syria (or any other state) nor fully dismantled the reactor at Yongbyon. Ultimately, the Bush administration's failure to accomplish any of its goals in dealing with the North Koreans can be blamed on Washington at least as much as on Pyongyang. From the beginning, the Bush administration seemed to be split in the interagency process about what policy to follow. And the potentially strong leverage Washington had after squeezing North Korea's illicit financial networks was abandoned when the talks took a new direction in February 2007. As Nicholas Eberstadt of the American Enterprise Institute has stated, "Adrift without a strategic compass, Bush's North Korea team ended up clinging like shipwreck victims to the desperate prospects of their negotiating sessions with North Korean officials, sacrificing substance so that the process might continue."[132] Dr. Eberstadt highlights an important fact: the Bush administration had trouble settling on a focused policy in its first years, but by 2005 it had finally found a way (perhaps to their surprise) to put pressure on North Korea. But despite this success, disagreement in the interagency process once again led to a definitive policy shift and a sea change (in 2007) that brought about a complete dependence on the six-party process and effectively took the pressure off North Korea.

I believe that the focus on North Korea's illicit activities cannot be stressed enough. If one looks all the way to the beginning of the North Korean nuclear confrontation, which has been ongoing in some form or another through two full presidential administrations, incentives have never worked in getting the Koreans to be transparent about their nuclear weaponization activities. Only pressure has worked, and that was only for a short time (as the Bush administration changed direction in 2007). The pressure applied beginning in 2005 was effective, though it is likely the missile tests and the nuclear test of 2006 were enough to intimidate Washington into relenting to Pyongyang's demands. As Marcus Noland has noted, ". . . A 2005 U.S. Treasury action against a small Macau bank where North Korean accounts were associated with missile proliferation, unrecorded gold sales, and allegedly North Korean leader Kim Chong-il's political slush fund, tanked the black market value of North Korean currency, disrupted legitimate commerce, and reportedly necessitated a scaling back of festivities associated with the Dear Leader's birthday."[133]

North Korea is a complicated, isolated country. Dealing with the reclusive communist state requires a comprehensive, focused, and consistent policy. The lessons that can be learned from an examination of the six-party process and North Korean policy as a whole during the Bush administration are important. Setting a policy and sticking with it are extremely important for dealing with North Korea and to prevent miscommunication with the power brokers in Pyongyang. In addition, an interagency process that involves infighting and prevents decisions from being permanent and transparent can completely unravel any gains. The potential pressure points for leveraging North Korea remain.

North Korea challenged the Obama administration almost immediately after taking office. Pyongyang tested a long-range ballistic missile in April 2009 (as described in chapter 2) and followed with a nuclear test on May 25, 2009, after the reaction to the missile test caused a unified negative reaction from the UN.[134] Preparations for the nuclear test were first noted by May 7, 2009.[135] Most analysts assessed that the power of the underground nuclear test was significantly higher than the test conducted during 2006 (which was about a kiloton). Estimates have varied, but most agree that the power of the explosion was two to six kilotons , with around four kilotons as the best guess. Experts have also determined that a device the size of the one tested in 2009 could kill tens of thousands of people if detonated over a major city and that the North Koreans are likely to test another device in the future.[136] The U.S. Office of the Director of National Intelligence made the following statement regarding the 2009 North Korean nuclear test: "The U.S. Intelligence Community assesses that North Korea probably conducted an underground nuclear explosion in the vicinity of P'unggye on May 25, 2009. The explosion yield was approximately a few kilotons. Analysis of the event continues."[137] In my view, the nuclear test of 2009 and the missile test a month before show that North Korea is using the testing of its WMD systems to gain political and economic concessions from the United States.

Actions taken by the UN and the world following North Korea's 2009 nuclear test were more forceful than those taken in the past. The UNSC Resolution 1874 from June 2009 calls on all states to take action against North Korean arms transfers, calls on states to help with inspections on the high seas of suspected proliferation merchant ships, and calls on all member states to inspect suspected North Korean arms-carrying ships (mostly focusing on WMD-related materials). The UN resolution also directs states to take financial measures, including the freezing of assets, where such assets "could contribute to prohibited DPRK programs."[138] The sanctions relating to North Korean merchant ships carrying arms may have worked early on: in June and July 2009, a merchant ship named the *Kang Nam*, suspected of carrying arms to Burma, turned around and reentered port in North Korea after being tailed by a U.S. Navy ship for several days and after receiving notification from several nations that it would be searched when it entered port.[139] According to unnamed U.S. officials (as reported in the press), at least three ports denied the ship entry, which may have been what forced it to turn back.[140] The UN further focused sanctions on North Korea in July 2009, when several more specific companies (North Korean "front companies") were named as being subject to previous resolutions. In fact, the document even named particular North Korean government officials who would now be "subject to the provisions of the measures imposed. . . ."[141]

Regarding the all-important actions that can be taken against North Korea's illegal and illicit financial activities, during the summer of 2009, the United States reportedly formed an interagency team to focus on the sanctions imposed on North Korea and to ensure that they were enforced. The team is said to consist of representatives from the State Department, the White House, the National Security Agency, the Treasury Department, and others. The goal is to help to shine the light on North Korea's proliferation and illicit activities. As of the summer of 2009, key members of the team, including Ambassador Philip Goldberg and Treasury Department official Stuart Levey, had visited banks and government officials in such places as Hong Kong, Japan, South Korea, and Malaysia.[142] An advisory released by the U.S. Department of the Treasury on June 18, 2009, stated in part that "the UN Security Council's adoption of specific financial measures to address this conduct reinforces long-standing Treasury Department concerns regarding North Korea's involvement, through government agencies and associated front companies, in financial activities in furtherance of a wide range of illicit activities. These activities include currency counterfeiting, drug trafficking, and the laundering of related proceeds." The advisory further states, "The Treasury Department encourages financial institutions worldwide to take similar precautions."[143] The move, reminiscent of the actions taken in 2005 and 2006 (and abandoned in 2007), has the potential to once again squeeze North Korea's financial assets throughout Asia and elsewhere.

One of the key banking institutions designated by the U.S. Treasury Department was the Korea Kwangson Banking Corporation (KKBC).[144] By October 2009, according to reports in the Japanese press, the KKBC branch located in Dandong, China, had either closed completely or was close to shutting down.[145] As time progressed, other nations actively joined the United States in enforcing the sanctions against North Korean proliferation that were brought about because of Pyongyang's nuclear test. In August 2009, UAE authorities seized a ship carrying North Korean weapons—rocket-propelled grenades and fuses and ammunition marked as oil-drilling equipment—to Iran.[146] In September 2009, Indian authorities seized a North Korean ship that was suspected of carrying arms but later released the vessel.[147] In October 2009, it was confirmed that South Korean authorities seized a cargo ship carrying North Korean chemical and biological weapons–related equipment bound for Syria.[148] In December 2009, Thai officials confiscated an aircraft carrying nearly forty tons of North Korean military equipment bound for Iran. The confiscated equipment included missile components, rocket-propelled grenades, and long-range multiple rocket launchers. Companies in five different countries were involved in the cargo laundering, showing the complexity of North Korean proliferation operations.[149]

Should the UN sanctions be fully initiated, including by international banking institutions and port authorities throughout Asia where North Korean merchant ships may call, Washington should be prepared to stand its ground, follow through, and ensure the North Koreans concede to important issues that will lead to dismantlement. How this matter plays out will be important for the security of the region and of the states that have interests in it. Of course, prematurely abandoning sanctions (if they are truly enforced) could once again lead to disaster, for North Korea has proven skillful in getting around sanctions over a period of many years. Ultimately, a policy that is focused more on engagement than on putting any pressure on North Korea is likely to lead to North Korea's continued existence as a nuclear state that engages in proliferation to fund its elite and military. Thus, the Clinton and Bush administrations' failure to successfully disarm North Korea's nuclear program leaves the current government in Washington with many difficult decisions to make—and few viable options.

CHAPTER FIVE

Maintaining a Rogue Regime

*Kim Chong-il and the North Korean
Regime Succession Process*

During the later months of 2008 there was a great deal of attention paid to Kim Chong-il's health in both Northeast Asia and the United States. Rumors of a stroke, possible partial incapacitation, and even coma were rampant in both policy and press circles.[1] The issue of Kim's health is extremely important because Pyongyang's reclusive leader has ruled the country since 1994 with a unique blend of Confucian "divide and conquer," a reliance on the military, and a larger-than-life persona among his people that can reasonably be called contrived hero worship.[2] This style of rule has thus far left no definitive succession process in place for who will rule the country when Kim passes from the scene. The future of North Korea has thus become a matter of concern for analysts and policy makers in both the United States and key nations in Northeast Asia. Thus, this chapter provides background on how much of the controversy surrounding Kim's family began, reviews key events that occurred during 2008 and 2009, analyzes the North Korean government and how it will affect the succession process, and outlines some possible scenarios that may occur in the future.

THE KIM REGIME IN RECENT YEARS: QUESTIONS AND INTRIGUE

Questions regarding the Kim regime and the succession process began to arise in 2004. By that time, Kim Chong-il had been in power for ten years, following the death of Kim Il-sung and the peaceful transition of power from father to son.[3] The power succession of father to son had begun in 1974 when the elder Kim was at the peak of his power (at the age of sixty-two). By laying the foundation of power for his son by gradually elevating him to important positions within the party and the government and by building a network of trust for his son among key players in the army, the party, the security services, and the Kim family's inner circle, Kim Il-sung was assured that Kim Chong-il would have a strong power base by the time he assumed power in 1994.[4] The elder Kim also decreed that his son be called the Dear Leader.[5] Prior to assuming power, Kim Chong-il ranked second in the hierarchy in the North Korean government. He was a member of the Korean Workers' Party Political Bureau, had a seat on the Central Military Commission, and was in charge of the KWP Secretariat. Many of Kim's classmates from the Mangyongdae Revolutionary School were placed in key government posts. In 1991, Kim was named supreme commander of the North Korean military, and in 1992, he was awarded the title of marshal.[6] Thus, a detailed, all-encompassing, and complete power base was laid for Kim Chong-il well before his father's death that essentially made him the only one who could assume all the reins of power.

Ten years after assuming power, Kim Chong-il had still not officially named a successor (nor does it appear a power base had been laid for one), and rumors regarding who would follow him after his death began to arise.[7] Unusual events that caused some to question the stability of the Kim regime began to publicly surface in 2004.[8] Rumors began circulating that portraits of Kim Chong-il had been removed in several spots in Pyongyang.[9] Press reports in both Korea and Japan indicated that the term "Dear Leader" was at least temporarily dropped when referring to Kim Chong-il in North Korea's official media.[10] Perhaps just as disturbing, international press reports indicated that according to Chinese officials, up to 130 generals and an unknown number of government officials had defected to China.[11] North Korean Foreign Ministry officials vehemently denied both the removal of Kim's portraits from public places in North Korea and the reports that generals and government officials had defected to China.[12] In an interesting note, soon after these reports surfaced, the top officers in the North Korean military pledged their support to the Dear Leader at a public event in Pyongyang.[13]

That same year, Kim Chong-il's government also engaged in purges, some within the power circle around Kim himself. The most important official purged during this time was Chang Sung-taek, Kim's brother-in-law, who at the time was not only in the Kim family's inner circle but was also a high-ranking party member.[14] According to reports trickling out of North Korea, Kim purged several of his relatives (and, of course, their families) for trying to seize power. As if things had not already fallen into the category of truly weird intrigue, in 2004 Chang Sung-taek's wife (Kim Chong-il's sister), Kim Kyong-hee, was injured in an auto accident in what many presumed to be a possible (though uncorroborated) assassination attempt.[15] Kim Kyong-hee was reported to be in deep depression at the time and had been undergoing medical treatment for alcohol abuse in France.[16] She reportedly was again listed in critical condition due to alcohol abuse in early 2009.[17] Kim Chong-nam, Kim Chong-il's oldest son, also was reported to have narrowly avoided an attempt on his life while traveling in Austria. According to press reports at the time, it may have been because of infighting within factions in Kim's inner circle that were struggling to gain supremacy while establishing the Dear Leader's successor.[18] While the oldest son would traditionally be the heir to power in a Confucian society, Kim Chong-nam has had problems gaining his father's approval over the years. He is widely known as a heavy spender and drinker, and his tumultuous 2001 trip to Japan (trying to sneak into Tokyo Disneyland on a fake passport) did not garner him any goodwill.[19]

Kim Chong-il has three sons. There were signs during 2005 that he was leaning in favor of naming his second son, Kim Chong-chol, as successor to the regime. At that time Kim Chong-chol was given a KWP post that was apparently designed to prepare him for further leadership positions within the North Korean government.[20] Kim Chong-chol may have dined with his father and Hu Jintao in October 2005, and his portrait has reportedly been hung in the Central Committee building in Pyongyang.[21] There are also conflicting reports, though, regarding Kim Chong-chol. According to Kim Chong-il's former Japanese chef, the elder Kim regards his second son as "too girly" to assume the reins of power in North Korea, and Lee Kyo-duk of the Korean Institute for National Unification reports that the second son may be suffering from excessive female hormones.[22] But an important aspect of Kim Chong-chol's status may have been revealed in 2006 when it was reported that some North Korean officials were wearing lapel pins bearing his likeness, a significant factor in DPRK internal politics.[23] While the third and youngest son, Kim Chong-un, was less conspicuous during this time frame, the Japanese press reported that senior members of the Korean Workers' Party were wearing badges with his likeness during 2006.[24]

The list of Kim Chong-il's descendants reveals a man who has enjoyed the talents of many women. The oldest son is descended from Kim's deceased mistress Sung Hae-rim. The two younger sons are from another former mistress (possibly his wife, but her status is not confirmed), Ko Young-hee, who died of cancer in 2004.[25] According to reports in the South Korean press, Kim Chong-il married yet another mistress, Kim Ok (the marriage is said to have occurred in 2006). She is described as a powerful member of his inner circle now, though he is apparently maintaining other mistresses as well.[26] The intrigue surrounding Kim's family continued into 2006 when he apparently "un-purged" his brother-in-law Chang Sung-taek.[27] Chang's tribulations and those of his wife (Kim's sister) did not end there, though. Their daughter died of an apparent suicide in Paris in July 2006.[28] Kim Chong-il's complicated and diverse family is one based both on marriage and mistresses, although the status of his relationships is often intentionally left murky (see figure 16).

Chang Sung-taek's return in 2006 may have marked the resurgence of his career and been an important sign that Kim Chong-il placed extreme trust in him. By 2007 he had been given a powerful post within the KWP's Organization and Guidance Department, its most powerful bureau. He also has had ties—albeit tenuous—to the military through his two brothers (one of whom is now dead), both high-ranking generals and one eventually a vice marshall.[29] Chang was reportedly sent to Beijing during February 2008 to purge corruption among North Korean corporations doing business in China.[30] He is said to be favored by the Chinese (which may be part of what got him into trouble with the Dear Leader in the first place), and some analysts have said he, in turn, favors Kim Chong-il's oldest son, Kim Chong-nam. From his position in the OGD, Chang is also now in charge of two important security services—the State Security Department and the Ministry of People's Security (MPS).[31] Chang has been an important player in the Kim family circle since his reemergence in 2006, and I will discuss his role at length later.

Since assuming more of the limelight in 2006, Kim Chong-il's most recent cohort, Kim Ok, has reportedly favored Kim Chong-il's youngest son, Kim Chong-un. Kim Ok is also said to be deeply involved in running Office Number 39, which

FIGURE 16. *Kim Chong-il's Family Tree (Major Confirmed Relationships)*

A. Hong Il-chon - Kim Hye-Kyong 1st Daughter of KCI	1st wife/Divorced, Married 1960s Still living
B. Sung Hae-rim - Kim Chong-nam 1st Son of KCI	Deceased—Long-time consort
C. Kim Yong-suk - Kim Sol-song 2nd Daughter of KCI	2nd wife, Married 1970s Current status unknown

D. Ko Young-hee
- Kim Chong-Chol
  2nd Son of KCI
- Kim Chong-un
  3rd Son of KCI
- Kim Yo-Chon
  3rd Daughter of KCI
	Deceased—unknown if ever
	married

E. Kim Ok	Identified in 2006 as "First Lady" Of North Korea Marriage is unconfirmed

Source: Based on Merrily Baird, "North Korea: Challenges for the Succession Ahead," presented at the Korea: Challenges for the 21st Century conference, Sam Nunn School of International Affairs and the Center for International Strategy, Technology, and Policy, Georgia Institute of Technology, November 1–2, 2006.

is in charge of North Korea's weapons proliferation and illicit economic activities. She may be close to one of Kim's three daughters, Kim Sol-song, who reportedly has a high post in the KWP and, while limited by her gender, is trusted by her father.[32] She was also said to be close to Ri Che-kang, who occupied a powerful position within the OGD.[33]

Ri Che-kang was rumored to be a rival of Chang Sung-taek's and a military hard-liner who had wielded significant power within the government since 2004.[34] Another military hard-liner and key figure who wielded power within the OGD was Ri Yong-chol. He was considered to be at the same level as Chang Sung-taek and held power within the military apparatus. Both Ri Che-Kang and Ri Yong-chol were younger than longtime trusted Vice Marshal Cho Myong-rok, who is nominally in charge of the General Political Bureau (GPB) and thus can watch and control many of the politics within the military from his post.[35] Yet another key figure is Kim Kyong-ok, who also sits within the OGD and was reportedly recently promoted to first vice department director. Kim Kyong-ok is associated with military affairs in his post and during the fall of 2008 was reported to have assumed many of the duties of Ri Yong-chol, who was in poor health.[36] Another KWP member rumored to wield a great deal of power is Ri Pyong-sam, a military officer who is in charge of monitoring ministers and department heads from his MPS post.[37] Finally, another key figure is Hyon Chol-hae, who has sometimes been linked with Kim Chong-il's second son, Kim Chong-chol. Hyon holds the title of deputy director of the General Political Bureau of the North Korean People's Army and as such is one of Cho Myong-rok's three key deputies.[38] When Cho's health deteriorated, Hyon was assigned the title of standing deputy chief of the GPB.[39] Hyon has been described as Kim Chong-il's closest aide. In fact, Hyon accompanied Kim Chong-il on at least thirty-two of his guided tours during 2008 and thirty tours during 2007, more than any other official.[40]

The complicated and often confusing picture of who is in key positions within Kim's family (and who is favored by the father), who has come to the fore within the political-military apparatus, and who is wielding the real power in the party is an interesting one and has undergone many changes since 2004. But before one can get into the succession process and who is running the show (and how), it will be important to understand the state of Kim Chong-il's health and the propaganda surrounding him.

KIM CHONG-IL'S HEALTH ISSUES: WHAT HAPPENED
AND HOW WELL DID HE RECOVER?

In September 2008, rumors regarding Kim Chong-il's health began to circulate widely. Kim by then had been out of public view since early August 2008. Exacerbating the rumors were reports of five Chinese physicians entering North Korea for an extended period.[41] Nearly a week later, Kim's close cohort (and reported wife) was said to be at the Dear Leader's sickbed.[42] It was probably not the first major medical problem that Kim Chong-il had experienced in recent years, as the Japanese press reported he had undergone heart surgery by a team of German doctors during 2007.[43] The 2008 reports began to take shape as it became apparent that

Kim Chong-il had in fact suffered a probable stroke. The condition may have been coming on for months as he may have begun losing consciousness at work as early as April 2008.[44] Soon other reports began to trickle out of North Korea that lent a positive light to Kim's health. In fact, by September 14, 2008, he was supposedly able to brush his own teeth.[45] Nevertheless, the long stay by the Chinese doctors— all said to be neurosurgeons—supported the theory that Kim had suffered a serious setback in his health.[46]

Despite the many reports and rumors running rampant about Kim Chong-il's health, South Korean military sources reported no unusual movement in the North Korean military.[47] To put a finer point on it, North Korean experts documented no signs (during September 2008) of internal instability in North Korea.[48] On October 2, 2008, the official organ of the KWP, the *Rodong Sinmun*, stated that Kim Chong-il had been working nonstop and remarked on how "tired he must be" in the first mention of his health by the North Koreans.[49] In mid-October 2008, South Korean defense minister Lee Sang-hee confirmed that he believed Kim Chong-il was still in control of the DPRK government when he said, "Kim Jong-il has not been seen in public for a while now, but both Korean and United States intelligence services estimate that he still has control over his administration."[50] Meanwhile, more speculation occurred regarding Kim's health and its effect on the North Korean government when sources in the Japanese press reported that North Korean diplomats were told to stand by for an "important announcement." South Korean government sources claimed to have no information on the rumor that had started that October.[51] Meanwhile, the North Korean government vehemently denied the reports.[52] Most North Korean citizens likely knew next to nothing about what was happening with their leader. Defectors have recounted that they heard personal details about Kim only on the rare occasions when they could sneak listening to outside radio broadcasts.[53]

On a return trip from an official visit to Russia on October 17, 2008, North Korea's foreign minister Pak Ui-chun was reported as carrying many items back to Pyongyang that were known to be Kim Chong-il's favorite foods. The items included Russian caviar and pickled cucumbers.[54] But later in the month Kim Chong-il appeared to experience more health problems as he was moved to a hospital in Pyongyang, according to a source in China who had recently returned from North

Korea.[55] Analysts and policy makers were concerned later in the month when Kim Chong-il's oldest son was spotted (and filmed by a Japanese television crew) in Paris, apparently looking for the services of a brain surgeon (likely for his father).[56] Former Japanese prime minister Taro Aso confirmed that Kim Chong-il was likely in the hospital yet also stated that North Korea's leader appeared to be capable of making decisions.[57] According to reports at the time in the South Korean press that were attributed to Seoul's intelligence agencies, Kim Chong-il had in fact suffered a setback and was in the hospital, though the head of the South Korean National Intelligence Service told lawmakers in the National Assembly that Kim was still able to run the country.[58]

The mystery regarding Kim Chong-il's health and who was treating him continued to build into November, as the French brain surgeon François-Xavier Roux was linked to the ailing North Korean leader.[59] Roux may have entered Pyongyang via an Air China flight on October 27, 2008.[60] When members of the press asked if he had visited Pyongyang, Roux confirmed that he had.[61] Meanwhile, a lockdown on information and propaganda continued in Pyongyang. A source in Pyongyang reported, "Since the end of October, there have been People's Unit lectures two or three times a week. There, people are told not to even mention anything regarding the Dear Leader's health because all rumors about his health are lies and only those who are disloyal talk about such things."[62] On November 11, sources in the Japanese and South Korean press quoting U.S. intelligence entities said that Kim Chong-il may have suffered a second stroke in October that caused damage to his left hand and foot and affected his speech. In an interview with the South Korean press, President Lee Myung-bak maintained the assessment that Kim was still able to govern.[63]

The pieces of the puzzle about Kim Chong-il's health began to fall into place during the late November–early December time frame. Several sources had asserted that he had suffered his first stroke in August and probably his second in late October. In mid-August a medical examination had found that a blood clot in his heart had moved to his brain. Doctors were dispatched to North Korea from China and France, and a French surgeon reportedly performed surgery on him soon thereafter. An unidentified diplomatic official disclosed, "It is believed that Kim has been making decisions on running the country since a statement on nuclear arms was released on November 12. However, his health is apparently deteriorating."[64]

In December 2008, the aforementioned Dr. Roux told the French daily *Le Figaro*, "Kim Jong-il suffered a stroke but did not undergo an operation. He is now better."[65] In a rather startling turn of events, almost immediately after the report came out in the French press, Roux vehemently denied the information and said he was misquoted. Roux was blunt when he stated in a cell phone conversation, "I did not see their leader." He further remarked, "Like many other . . . doctors, I have been to Korea several times. I was never to see their leader."[66] Thus, the condition of North Korea's reclusive leader has been bleak yet murky, and the information coming out of Pyongyang has not been helpful. But there is more to this story than simple rumors regarding Kim's health. During the later part of 2008, North Korean propaganda published announcements of Kim's flurry of visits to places all over his country. The tour was quite an interesting feat for a man who was said to have suffered a stroke and an unconfirmed relapse.

KIM'S MANY TRAVELS IN THE LATER MONTHS OF 2008: REAL OR PROPAGANDA?

During the summer and fall of 2008, the North Korean government and its propaganda arms continued to act as if Kim Chong-il was both healthy and firmly in control. Kim, who is widely reported to be suffering from both diabetes and heart disease, has always been portrayed as the picture of health, but his health cannot help but be a matter of interest both to nations in the region and to those nations that have concerns about North Korea's proliferation to other rogue states and the impact of a weakened or collapsed government in Pyongyang on the security and stability of the Korean Peninsula. All these factors were important when many reports filtered out of North Korea that Kim Chong-il had been visiting military units, factories, and sporting events.[67]

Analysts of North Korean activities and even government agencies are often forced to assess the status of Kim's health based on rumors and his attendance at key events rather than on North Korean governmental information releases. Thus, the questions and rumors surrounding Kim's health truly began to blossom when he failed to appear at the sixtieth anniversary of the DPRK's founding, a significant event.[68] On October 4, 2008, the North Korean government reported that he had observed a university soccer game, his first documented public appearance since

August of that year.[69] North Korea's state-run television network released photos of Kim inspecting a women's military unit on October 11, but the pictures may have been meant to deceive. According to a South Korean government official, "Based on the color of the forest in the background, the photos seem to have been taken in July or early August at the latest, before Kim fell ill."[70] Kim's unconfirmed appearances as announced by the state-run propaganda arms spurred even more rumors, but given his lifestyle since long before his father's death, his many health woes should be no surprise. He is well known for having lived a life filled with heavy eating and drinking, womanizing, and perhaps even abusing drugs.[71]

The reports during October that Kim was again up and about and making visits to spots in his country were called into question at the end of the month when he did not make an important appearance at the funeral for a high-ranking party official named Pak Song-chol (who died at ninety-five and was one of his father's trusted confidants). Kim normally attended funerals for top-ranking officials, such as former defense minister O Jin-u in 1995 and former prime minister Yon Hyong-muk in 2005.[72] Nevertheless, as November began, Kim embarked on a flurry of visits that continued to be reported by the North Korean government.[73] Although it presented accounts of an energetic Kim Chong-il, he still had had no public contact with any foreigners at all or even been filmed live on any television broadcasts. Dennis Wilder, senior adviser for Asia on the U.S. National Security Council, addressed this discrepancy on January 14, 2009, remarking that no video footage of Kim Chong-il had been released. Wilder said, "That suggests to me that there are some physical signs of his health crisis that they are unwilling to put out there."[74] The appearances seemed designed for outside consumption. As Yang Moo-jin, a professor at the University of North Korean Studies in Seoul, stated, "I think this is a message to the United States. . . ."[75] By December 2008, Kim had made at least six public visits (since the rumored stroke), according to the North Korean government.[76] His flurry of activity included (but was not limited to) attending a soccer match on November 2 and visiting military units on November 5 and a military art festival on November 16, 2008.[77]

If the accompanying photos were real, the curious and completely unconfirmed reports, which were often called into question because of the pictures' backgrounds, also apparently revealed things about Kim Chong-il's condition. According to Japanese press sources, a common thread about all the photos North Korea released is that Kim kept his left hand in his pocket. This posture lends credence to the rumor that the stroke may have partially incapacitated Kim's left side.[78] If the reports coming out of North Korea during this time were true, Kim Chong-il may have been weakened but was able to make at least some of the visits that the state-run propaganda disseminated. The Dear Leader was shown keeping up his travels into December 2008 and then into the New Year (see figure 17).[79] U.S. and South Korean intelligence agencies reportedly believed that at least some of Kim's visits were real during this time frame and that he was recovering from his stroke. Sources in the press related that aerial reconnaissance showed Kim's personal train actually traveled to the locations where Kim was supposed to have appeared. He may have left the hospital sometime in October 2008.[80]

In the North Korean state media's 2009 New Year's address, there was no mention of Kim's health problems, only discussion of his visits and a statement that the country remained politically stable.[81] On January 23, 2009, Kim finally made his first confirmed public contact with a foreign official since July 2008, when he met with Wang Jiarui, the head of the Chinese Communist Party's International Liaison Department. Pictures of the meeting were shown in the Chinese and international press.[82] Kim reportedly drank heavily with the Chinese envoy at a lengthy lunch, perhaps wishing to show his good health.[83] That January, Kim made thirteen inspection visits of industrial centers and military bases, up eight visits from the same month in 2008.[84] In February 2009, Kim made three times the number of public visits he had that same month during the previous year.[85]

During a visit by former U.S. president Bill Clinton during the late summer of 2009, Kim Chong-il was said to look "surprisingly robust" and spent a great deal of time speaking with Clinton and his delegation.[86] The commander of U.S. Pacific Forces Command echoed this opinion: "Kim Chong-il was upright. He appears to be cozy and entertaining reasonable discussions with the former President. We were less certain of these capabilities than we are now."[87] National Security Adviser James Jones stated that Kim Chong-il appeared to be in full control of his government in an interview Jones gave on FOX News on August 9, 2009.[88] The visits and their diverse nature throughout North Korea suggest the DPRK wanted to maintain a robust image of Kim Chong-il who was in charge and healthy. But

FIGURE 17. *Kim Chong-il Visits KPA Air Force Unit 1017*

Source: Rodong Sinmun (North Korea), December 28, 2008 (released January 15, 2009).

the many questions surrounding his health and how capable he was in running his autocratic government during this time persist. The public visit with a Chinese official appeared to show a weakened but at least partially recovered Kim Chong-il, while the visit with former president Clinton seemed to show a more alert individual. While Kim appeared to have recovered well enough to resume "full" duties, as late as May, 2010, reports in the press indicated that he was still suffering from the effects of his stroke and other ailments. He was filmed on Japanese television dragging his left foot in a hotel lobby during a visit to China. His left hand looked as if it had mobility problems (likely effects of his stroke), and photos showed that he had lost a great deal of hair.[89] Thus, one cannot help but ask, if Kim is at least partially incapacitated and weakened, who has been running the show?

CONCERNS ABOUT A PHYSICALLY WEAKENED KIM CHONG-IL:
WHO FILLED THE VOID?

With the plethora of reports relating to North Korea that led to assessments of deep troubles with Kim Chong-il's health, the question that arises is, how well was he able to effectively govern his country given the obvious physical weakness a stroke would cause? That leads to the next question: who stepped in during this critical period to fill the void? According to diplomatic sources, prior to his reported stroke, Kim personally read briefs from each major organization within the government and provided detailed instructions. But beginning as early as August 2008, Kim was bedridden and unable to do so. Reportedly, from that time on, Chang Sung-taek began to receive the briefs on Kim's behalf and made decisions on all but the highest-priority issues, for which Kim was still said to be providing the final decisions.[90] If true, this situation is significant, as Kim Chong-il has been widely described in the past as a micromanager. As Joseph Bermudez of Jane's Information Group writes, "He prefers to manage everything directly, down to the most minor of details."[91] In an interview with the Japanese press on February 9, 2009, Paek Sung-chu, head of the Defense Policy Studies Division of the Korea Institute for Defense Analyses, stated, "It is believed that he delegated political powers to his close aides temporarily after he fell ill, but has recovered around mid-December and has taken these powers back. However, it is thought that it will be difficult for him to handle all the details of national administration."[92] Kim is said to have recovered by February 2009, but it is likely that the experience nevertheless left him weakened physically.[93] In 2010 stories circulated that he was undergoing regular kidney dialysis.[94]

The interesting case of Chang Sung-taek became even more interesting as details about Kim Chong-il's poor health begin to emerge. The formerly "purged" brother-in-law of Kim Chong-il was seen as a de facto stand-in for the Dear Leader by November 2008. Cheong Seong-chang, an analyst at the Sejong Institute in South Korea, remarked that the influence of Chang Sung-taek had become enhanced because of the stroke suffered by North Korea's leader. Said Cheong, "Chang is apparently in charge of receiving orders from Kim and channeling them (to state agencies)."[95] A senior South Korean intelligence official who declined to be identified said that Chang was also acting as a stand-in during daily state affairs. Baek

Seung-joo of the Korea Institute for Defense Analyses has remarked that Chang's influence is likely to grow as Kim continues to age and his health deteriorates, for relatives would limit others' access to Kim Chong-il.[96] Professor Yang Moo-jin of the University of North Korean Studies in South Korea put a slightly different spin on Chang's increased power during Kim Chong-il's recovery period, saying, "At most, Chang is being used to keep the state stable until one of Kim's sons is able to take over."[97] According to reports in the Japanese press, Chang and his wife (Kim's sister), Kim Kyong-hee, visited Kim Chong-il in the hospital almost every day following his stroke.[98] During the early months of 2010, Kim Kyong-hee accompanied her brother on field inspections and was again actively serving in the party.[99]

Analysts in both South Korea and the United States reportedly believe Chang Sung-taek would be a key player in a succession process and see him as a heavy hitter because he controls the SSD and MPS.[100] Others have suggested that when Kim Chong-il had health problems he was indirectly running North Korea through Chang along with Kim Ok, the de facto "first lady" of North Korea. Some expected this practice to continue as long as Kim Chong-il still possessed his mental faculties.[101] The South Korean press reported that an unidentified diplomat said Chang Sung-taek and Kim Ok "will take over if Kim Chong-il has only physical disabilities."[102] Because she is close to Kim, it is likely Kim Ok played a key role in carrying out government policies following his stroke. As American scholar Marcus Noland has said, "In some ways, she's the one guarding the bedroom or hospital door. She would be in a position to convey his preferences."[103] Many analysts agree, however, that in the case of Kim's death, Kim Ok's power would disappear. Koh Yu-hwan, a specialist at Dongguk University in South Korea, has said her influence comes from her personal relationship with Kim Chong-il. He states, "Should he die, she risks losing it."[104] There was a press report in 2009 (to date, unconfirmed) that Kim Ok had actually married someone else and left her job as Kim Chong-il's secretary.[105] Regardless of whether the report is true, her brother and father are both high-ranking officials in North Korea, so her status likely remains important.

While the assessment may be accurate that both Chang Sung-taek and Kim Ok filled a power vacuum that existed because of Kim Chong-il's stroke, the military's role in this power sphere cannot be discounted. Hyon Chol-hae was reported to have assumed a powerful role following the medical emergency as well. Given his closeness to Kim, this news should not come as a surprise. According to Suh Jae-jean of the Korea Institute for National Unification, "It seems that Hyon Chol-hae is currently running North Korea behind the scenes. He is expected to play a leading role in laying the foundation for the post-Kim Chong-il era according to Kim's wishes."[106] Ri Myong-su of the powerful National Defense Commission has also been mentioned. According to Ryu Dong-ryeol of the Police Science Institute in South Korea, "Hyon and Ri report directly to Kim Chong-il."[107] In an interview with the Japanese press, Arthur Brown, a former senior U.S. intelligence officer, has said that members of the KWP and the North Korean army have boosted their clout because of Kim's physical condition. In addition to Chang and Kim Ok, he singled out Hyon Chol-hae, Ri Myong-su, and Kim Yang-gon.[108] Kim Yang-gon was in charge of the United Front Department of the KWP in 2009.[109]

By December 2008, analysts in the United States and South Korea (among others) said that they had seen a significant shift in the North Korean power structure. While no fundamental differences in the Kim regime were readily apparent, those who watch North Korea reportedly indicated real changes among those supporting Kim and the North Korean government. Chang Sung-taek seemed to be involved in this development, but his role remained murky.[110] While South Korean and American officials noted that Kim's condition had somewhat improved, he still appeared to be weak. These officials also reported that some senior military and party officials in North Korea had been replaced since Kim's stroke in August, again adding to the finding that there has been a shift in the power structure.[111] While I have assessed the power of several individuals within Kim's circle, others also have concluded that the party and the military have consolidated power in the wake of Kim's health issues. Following Kim's stroke, a combination of senior military officials and party members began to fill the power vacuum, according to officials quoted in the American press. One official was quoted as saying, "He doesn't have a clear successor, and it's entirely possible that there is some infighting with the North Korean elite."[112]

On February 10, 2009, the North Korean state-run media announced Vice Marshal Kim Yong-chun would replace Vice Marshal Kim Il-chol as the minister of the People's Armed Forces, and Gen. Ri Yong-ho would replace Gen. Kim

Kyok-sik as the chief of the General Staff.[113] Kim Il-Chol was commander of the navy before assuming his post, and he had been classmate of Kim Chong-il's at the Mangyongdae Revolutionary School. Kim Il-chol had reportedly been in poor health for some time. His replacement, Kim Yong-chun, is interesting because he is the former commander of the VI Corps (which was formerly located in the northeastern section of the country). A graduate of the Soviet Frunze Military Academy, he was commander of the VI Corps when its senior officers mutinied against Kim Chong-il in early 1995. The mutiny was brutally suppressed by bringing up a crack infantry division from the Forward Corps (by train). The VI Corps was disbanded and eventually moved, and Kim Yong-chun, who informed on his senior corps staff, was rewarded for his loyalty with the job of chief of the General Staff. His senior staff escaped to China, where the men remain to this day.

Little is known of Gen. Ri Yong-ho, but he was the former commander of the Pyongyang Defense Command, which protects the city and ultimately Kim Chong-il. Both new appointees appear to have been picked because of their absolute loyalty to the Dear Leader.[114] Gen. Kim Kyok-sik was reassigned to command of the IV Corps, which sits astride the Northern Limit Line. The corps would likely provide the forces that would create a provocation with the South Koreans along the border, which Pyongyang had been raging against in its state-run propaganda. Thus, he may have been put in this position because of the faith that Kim Chong-il has in him; it might not be a demotion.[115] In fact, the evidence now supports the assessment that he was put in charge of the IV Corps because he held Kim Chong-il's trust and, perhaps just as important, because he had the skill to plan provocations in the NLL. During January 2010, North Korean artillery fired hundreds of shells into the NLL area, some of which landed within less than two kilometers of the disputed de facto sea border. The move raised tensions between the two Koreas.[116] On March 26, 2010, the South Korean corvette *Cheonan* sank from an external explosion while on patrol near the NLL. Forty-six personnel out of a crew of 104 perished in the tragedy. A torpedo that South Korean and international defense officials assess was fired by North Korean maritime Special Forces was the cause of the violent explosion that blew the ship in half, sinking it quickly.[117] A South Korean and international team of experts briefed the public that evidence definitively showed a North Korean SOF mini-submarine fired a torpedo that sank the

Cheonan.[118] Kim Kyok-sik was likely involved in planning both of these events and probably reported directly to Kim Chong-il.

On February 20, 2009, North Korea made an official announcement that Gen. O Kuk-ryol, a renowned "hawk," was being appointed vice chairman of the NDC. O is reportedly a close confidant of Kim Chong-il, who has advocated a hard-line stance against the south. O also played a role in helping the Dear Leader consolidate his power when Kim Il-sung was still alive. Finally, an unidentified defector told the South Korean press that O Kuk-ryol is a close friend of Kim's youngest son, Kim Chong-un. Professor Yang Moo-jin told the French press, "His promotion is seen as another strong message toward South Korea. It is also aimed at enhancing stability in the military by appointing Kim's trusted old guard to a key post."[119] To enhance this process, Ri-Chol, another close confidant of Kim Chong-il's, reportedly returned to North Korea from Europe in 2010. The former ambassador to Switzerland may have returned to help look after the succession process. Ri is reported to have been the individual who looked after the Dear Leader's sons when they attended school in Europe and, perhaps nearly as important, was the caretaker of Kim's secret funds in Switzerland, Luxembourg, and elsewhere in Europe.[120]

To truly understand how power works within the North Korean government, one cannot look at it from the viewpoint of a line and block organization chart. Thus the structure shown in figure 18 is probably the best illustration of the way things actually work within Pyongyang's power structure. Members of Kim's family since the founding of the DPRK have traditionally been given favorable positions within North Korea's government. Kim Chong-il also draws his power from a base that his father helped build for him in both the military and the party. Members of the National Defense Commission have been chosen from this base, and it also serves as the source for those who sit in the powerful OGD of the KWP. Finally, the security services monitor each other, the military, and the party.

Even within such institutions as the military, there are factions. For example, as Professor Toshimitsu Shigemura of Waseda University in Japan articulates, "North Korean military personnel are divided into two groups: field soldiers that engage in combat operations and political soldiers that supervise field soldiers. Political soldiers are tasked with providing ideological education to field soldiers as well as detecting a planned coup d'etat."[121] Cheong Seong-chang adds, "Military

FIGURE 18. *Kim's Power Circle*

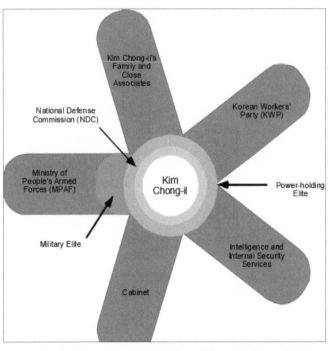

Source: Joseph S. Bermudez, Jr., "North Korea's Strategic Culture," Defense Threat Reduction Agency, Advanced Systems and Concepts Office, Fort Belvoir, Virginia, October 31, 2006.

commanders are not even allowed to congregate in small numbers of threes or fours, lest they plan for factional power."[122]

The military is arguably the most powerful entity in the country, but the conditions of distrust under which it operates are also present in all North Korean institutions. In North Korea, even high-level officials are under surveillance and in fear of their job security. As Korean scholar Hwee Rhak Park writes, "North Korean policymakers could be strongly constrained by a mutual surveillance system in the name of ideology . . . or regime survival. When some are considered too liberal or too flexible they may be replaced."[123] Within North Korea, there is no system of checks and balances except Kim Chong-il. Thus, without a clear path of succession, which was established for him under his father in 1974, there is no system in place for any one man or even a junta of individuals to rule the country effectively.

Given the assessments that Kim's failing health has brought about a real change in the power structure of North Korea (though no one seems to be able to say exactly how that change has occurred or the extent to which it has been implemented), several plausible scenarios may have already transpired. Leonid A. Petrov, a research associate at the Research School of Pacific and Asian Studies at the Australian National University, figures that following Kim's stroke in August 2008, a more hard-line stance was taken. He states, "Since then, a group of North Korean top brass, who are ready to turn the clock back, rules the country collectively."[124] While Petrov's assertion is interesting and may be at least partly accurate, there are other possibilities as well. One is that a more hard-line stance has been taken (and approved by Kim) to keep the regime from collapsing. Another is that the regime has tightened internal control. Yet another is that there may be an ongoing internal power struggle because of Kim's weakened condition. Finally, the possibility is that there will be more reliance on China.[125] I will discuss more on these issues later, but clearly some type of change has occurred.

To judge whether change has occurred—and if more change is likely—one only has to read a revealing statement that came from North Korea's state media during December 2008: "The inalterability of comradeship is clearly shown at the time of radical transition in political status. Whenever we faced critical or unfavorable moments during our revolution days, people who cherished their faithfulness to comrades won fame as revolutionaries, but those who failed to do so fell onto the path of treachery."[126] This mention is the first time the term "transition in political status" has been used since Kim Chong-il assumed the leadership of the DPRK. The wording, designed for North Korean citizens' consumption, makes one wonder what the "transition" was that the country's leadership was preparing the people to embrace.

THE CHINA CARD: RESPONSE TO KIM'S HEALTH ISSUES AND POTENTIAL FOR THE FUTURE

China is North Korea's only real remaining ally; thus, the expectation that Beijing would have grave concerns about Kim's stroke makes sense and raises obvious questions regarding the stability of the North Korean government. According to reports in the Chinese press, North Korea and China planned to take their relations to a "higher level" in 2009. Yang Hyong-sop, vice president of the DPRK's Presidium of the Supreme People's Assembly, said at the time that Kim Chong-il attached great importance to his nation's relationship with China. The DPRK hosted several events during what was called the 2009 Friendship Year, and Liu Xiaoming, the Chinese ambassador to North Korea, stated that China will "push forward bilateral exchanges and cooperation with the DPRK in every field."[127] Some experts have said the two communist states showed signs of strengthening ties in order to secure a better position in the diplomatic dialogue that would occur with the new U.S. administration under Barack Obama.[128] Meanwhile, the Chinese leadership reportedly instructed its intelligence agencies to intensify their monitoring of activities in North Korea, a special group under Xi Jinping was formed to look into the North Korean succession issue, and Hu Jintao ordered the state media to refrain from commentaries on Kim Chong-il's health and what would occur in the DPRK if he was to become incapacitated.[129]

The Chinese military's reaction to questions and concerns regarding Kim Chong-il's health was swift and compelling. By October 2008, the Chinese People's Liberation Army (PLA) was reportedly deploying more than 100,000 troops from several regions in China near the Chinese–North Korean border.[130] The troops were stationed near the border in anticipation of any instability or regime change that might occur in North Korea and cause a flood of refugees across the border.[131] In related activity, Chinese forces conducted large-scale and unusual military exercises in the Liaodong and Shandong peninsulas near North Korea. The exercises involved a wide range of combat units, and many analysts at the time saw them as China's message that it was ready for military action if need be.[132] According to a source in the Japanese press attributed to a Chinese military attaché, Beijing's military has made plans to build five new bridges across the Yalu River, which separates the two nations.[133] If true, they would enable the Chinese to better handle a flood of refugees in the case of a severe North Korean crisis. Conversely, it would also allow vehicles and troops to access North Korea if China planned to interfere in Pyongyang's internal affairs.

China's economic weight in North Korea probably had reached an unprecedented apex by the fall of 2008 as well. A combination of the north's troubled relations with its neighbor to the south, continuing global sanctions, and bad economic times may have helped push North Korea closer to its powerful ally in Beijing.[134] Despite this alliance, China reportedly reduced crude oil shipments to North Korea and stepped up customs inspections along the border following North Korea's launch of a Taepo Dong II missile in April 2009.[135] Both the economic and military factors suggest China wants to continue to use North Korea as a buffer state against foreign powers, particularly the United States, on its border.[136] It is likely the reason that Beijing maintains both a strategic and a military treaty with North Korea.[137] According to numerous reports, ideally the Chinese would not want to see the North Korean government collapse if Kim Chong-il were to die or were incapacitated, for it is in the Chinese national interest to have a stable North Korea to the south. The Chinese are said to be close to both Kim Chong-nam (Kim Chong-il's oldest son) and Chang Sung-taek.[138] The question that remains unanswered is how far the Chinese would go to try and achieve their strategic aims in North Korea.

NOBODY—NOBODY—CIRCLES THE WAGONS
LIKE THE NORTH KOREANS

In the wake of reports that Kim Chong-il suffered a stroke in August 2008 and the resulting rumors that began to surface even in North Korea's closed society, Pyongyang decidedly began to take several measures. As North Korea has always done in times of possible internal instability or turmoil, it cracked down on the populace. Since Kim's reported stroke, those fleeing the country have undergone stiffer punishments as new measures have apparently been put into effect. As Tim Peters, director of the Christian aid group Helping Hands, put it, "The penalties are getting stronger and they have increased after Kim Chong-il's stroke."[139] UN official Vitit Muntabhorn told the international press in December 2008 that fewer North Koreans seem to be escaping across the border into China.[140]

After stories regarding Kim's health began to circulate, North Korea stopped issuing passports to those wishing to visit relatives outside the country and even made it more difficult for those conducting business, according to a North Korean businessman interviewed in China. The country mobilized "inquisition squads," women were not allowed to ride bicycles, and "ideology sessions" were stepped up. Since September 2008, these measures were apparently increased. Japanese reporter Jiro Ishimaru opines, "The storm of control measures blowing over that country now was started by the power people in North Korea who are doing everything they can to tighten social order because they see a crisis looming in the maintenance of the system."[141] Purges have also reportedly occurred as well. For example, Choe Sung-chol, the former vice chairman of the Asia-Pacific Peace Committee (the organization that handles inter-Korean affairs on behalf of Pyongyang), was said to be languishing on a chicken farm in early January 2009 as he underwent "revolutionary training."[142] Choe was reportedly later executed.[143] The purges continued into 2010, with high-level officials included again. The director of the KWP's powerful Office Number 39, Kim Tong-un, was relieved of his post and replaced by his deputy, Jon Il-chun. Pak Nam-ki, the director of the Planning and Finance Department, did not fare as well. Blamed for economic woes in late 2009 and early 2010 because of disastrous currency reform, Pak was publicly executed on March 12, 2010, in Pyongyang.[144] According to reports in the press attributed to sources in North Korea, around one hundred senior officials were ousted or executed in the 2010 purges. This is the fifth set of large-scale purges Kim Chong-il has initiated since assuming power.[145]

Many of the anti-dissent crackdown measures were apparently implemented at the order of Chang Sung-taek, who reportedly assumed many of the day-to-day duties of running the country as Kim Chong-il recovered from his stroke. Some North Koreans have called him "the most villainous follower" of Kim Chong-il.[146] The stringent conditions and punishments for North Korean citizens are nothing new, as North Korean prison camps are infamous for their brutality.[147] Indeed, these conditions are exactly what has led thousands of North Koreans to risk their lives and attempt to escape across the Chinese border every year.[148] But because of internal concerns, North Korea apparently made a policy decision to further repress many aspects of its society.

Perhaps one of the more telling signs that the North Korean government decided to further restrict its citizens and keep the information flow about its leader to a mere trickle was the effort taken to ensure leaflets sent from South Korea did not get distributed. South Korean nongovernmental organizations (NGOs) sent the leaflets (often articulating rumors about Kim Chong-il's health) over on balloons, and the north's elite obviously considered them an affront to their control. The government mobilized soldiers to confiscate the leaflets and sweep the countryside to ensure none reached the populace at large. Residents were ordered not to read the leaflets and to report them to the State Security offices. Failure to comply met with harsh punishment.[149] But the North Korean regime's paranoia regarding the information coming across the border went even further. Pyongyang threatened to shut down or drastically cut operations at the Kaesong Industrial Complex, a facility where South Korean firms have employed more than 33,000 North Korean workers.[150] North Korea also warned of "grave consequences," even military action against the south, if the leaflets did not stop.[151] The leaflet drops did not stop.

The regime's reaction to the South Korean NGO leaflets being distributed in North Korea during a time of stress and even potential instability was predictable, though it can accurately be described as paranoid and heavy handed. It also shows what a high value Pyongyang's inner circle places on the absolute control of information. In November 2008, Pyongyang announced that it planned to shut down a South Korean tourist operation in the city of Kaesong, selectively expel South Koreans working in the Kaesong Industrial Complex, and severely curtail the number of daily cross-border trips for the freight train between Kaesong and Seoul. The industrial complex at Kaesong, however, had employed North Koreans and generated tens of millions of dollars a year for the North Korean government. The tourist operation hosted 110,000 visits with each person paying a hundred dollars in entrance fees.[152]

Those on the Left in South Korea blamed the conservative policies of Lee Myung-bak for the North Koreans' hard-line moves.[153] But after scrutinizing events in North Korea, it seems far more likely that Pyongyang was circling the wagons to show it would take whatever measures necessary to ensure its population was protected from information from the south as much as possible. During October 2008, North Korea had already threatened to reduce Seoul to rubble unless the South Korean government forced the NGOs to stop releasing the leaflets into their country.[154]

The border restrictions North Korea imposed on visiting South Koreans were a critical and important change to the status quo. For those South Koreans crossing back and forth, the border went from being open four times a day to twice a week on the border's eastern corridor and was reduced from nineteen times a day to six on the more active western corridor. The number of individuals in groups (five hundred) crossing the border on the western corridor was cut in half. Tourist visits to the city of Kaesong were suspended as were most rail services.[155] Jang Cheol-hyeon, a former North Korean Communist Party official, discussed the move, saying, "The Kaesong Industrial Complex was designed to be a strategic tool to threaten the South when necessary, and now that is being put into action."[156]

On December 1, 2008, border crossings slowed to a trickle. All the restrictions listed above were put into effect, and on the eastern corridor of the border, only groups of 150 or less were allowed to cross. Time slots for entering North Korea were also severely restricted, and the number of South Korean employees working at another tourist complex at Kumgang Mountain were reduced from 190 to 100, according to announcements Unification Ministry officials in South Korea made to the press.[157] The most important personnel move was at the Kaesong Industrial Complex, where the number of South Korean nationals allowed was reduced from 1,700 to 880. In addition, the number of South Koreans allowed in the north per day went from 6,000 to 750. Any South Korean newspapers that criticized North Korea were banned, and anyone attempting to bring in their reporters would be expelled.[158] By January 2009, South Korean companies with interests at the complex had already reported many problems related to slowing business.[159]

Pyongyang's hostile behavior toward South Korea continued into December 2008. At a meeting held on December 17 in North Korea, Lt. Gen. Kim Yong-chul suddenly stood up and yelled, "All of the non-military officials are to leave!"[160] And in January 2009, a North Korean military representative went on the state-run television broadcast to demand that South Korea stop its "hostile posture" in the NLL area forming the de facto sea border on the west coast of the divided peninsula. The spokesman said that the north would preserve the sea border, implying possible use of military force. The South Korean military reacted by going on full alert for the first time since North Korea conducted a nuclear test in 2006.[161] North Korea threatened an "all out confrontational posture" against the south because of what it called violations of the sea border.[162]

In a rather ominous move, the Chinese suddenly pulled all their fishing boats out of the NLL area in an obvious precaution against the violence they believed could occur there. Before disappearing from the NLL area, about fifty Chinese fishing boats had been operating there and paying the North Korean government for the rights to do so. As the area is known for crabs, more boats traditionally arrive during the springtime crabbing season. The fishermen are also known for frequently intruding in South Korean waters and often have to be chased out by ROK Navy or Coast Guard vessels.[163] The Chinese government, however, issued the following statement (in part) to its fishermen on January 23, 2009:

> In view of the current tense and highly sensitive situation on the Korean Peninsula, it is very dangerous for Chinese fishing boats to cross the sea border and operate in waters bordering on the DPRK (also called off-limits waters especially the ROK). To avoid foreign-related incidents arising from this and ensure the safety of the crew and properties of Chinese fishing boats, the General Office and the Yellow Sea and Bohai Sea Fishery Administrative Bureau of the Ministry of Agriculture and the Shandong Provincial Oceanic and Fishery Administrative Department issued circulars urging all boat owners and captains to strictly implement the gist of the circulars of higher authorities, abide by the provisions of the PRC-ROK fishery agreement, and refrain from operating in the above-mentioned waters.[164]

On February 4, 2009, the Chinese government website of the Weihai Economic and Technological Development Zone in Shandong Province announced, "According to investigations, no fishing boats of our development zone were operating in the DPRK-ROK border waters."[165] China again cleared its boats from the area in May and June 2009 after tensions rose.[166]

North Korea further intensified its conflict with the south in late January 2009 when Pyongyang announced it was rendering null and void all of the agreements from a nonaggression pact signed in 1991. North Korea's Committee for the Peaceful Reunification of Korea accused Seoul of bringing the two countries "to the brink of war."[167] In February 2009, the U.S. military commander in Korea, Gen. Walter Sharp, gave a speech that received wide press attention. He remarked that the North Koreans should "stop the provocations that have been going on, whether it is declaring old agreements to be no longer valid or missile technology that they continue to develop."[168] While some analysts viewed the confrontational posture as brinkmanship designated for the incoming Obama administration (though the

FIGURE 19. *Restricted Area for Chinese Fishing Vessels during NLL Tensions, 2009*

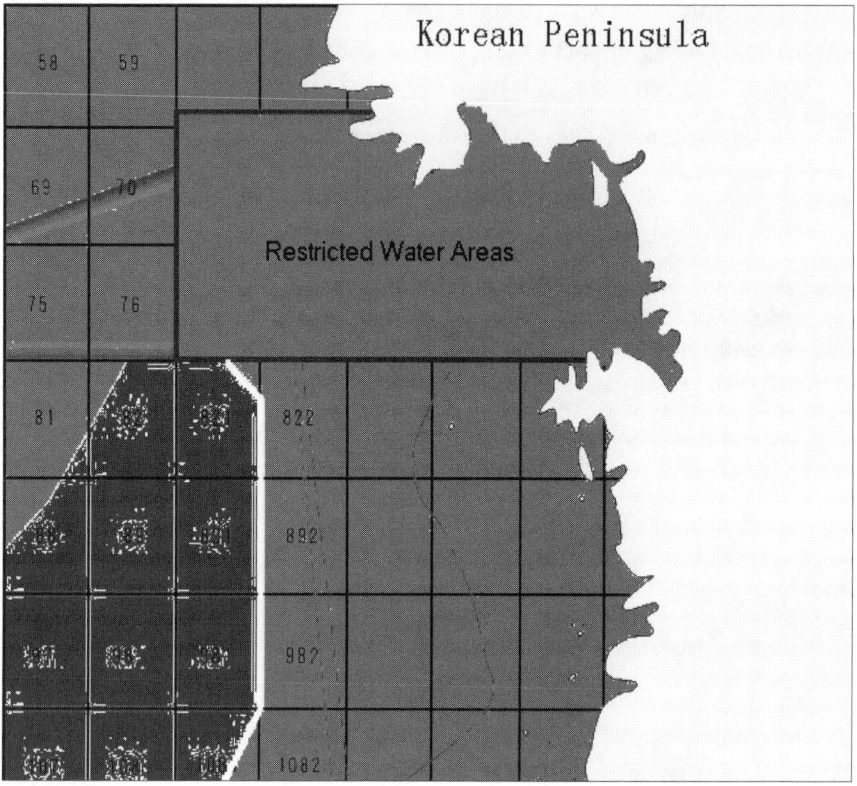

Source: Chinese Yantai Shandong Marine Fishing and Production Management Station.

rhetoric was directed at South Korea), others have assessed that given Kim Chong-il's feeble health, the government opted to further tighten the regime's control by taking an intensified confrontational stance against its neighbor to the south.[169]

North Korea continued to ratchet up tensions on the peninsula in early March 2009 when it called for general-level talks with the U.S.-led UN Command at Panmunjom for the first time in several years. Representatives from Pyongyang essentially used the talks to rant about the imminent annual ROK-U.S. military exercise.[170] In early March during the annual ROK-U.S. military exercise, the north cut its military hotline to the south. It then temporarily closed the border to workers coming to and from Kaesong on two separate occasions, leaving workers briefly stranded there.[171] The temporary border closings angered many South Koreans and may have been designed to raise the stakes as thousands of South Korean and U.S. troops (including those from many units off the peninsula) engaged in a large-scale military exercise.

The north's continued and escalating moves that affected activities at the Kaesong Industrial Complex and other destinations that South Korean visitors frequented had the potential to hurt both Koreas financially. South Korean companies had $304 million invested in production facilities and labor at the complex as of 2008. South Korea invested $443 million in building the roads, rail lines, and logistics support for the complex (and elsewhere in North Korea) and another $210 million to build the complex and its supporting power and communications facilities. It pays the North Korean government more than $32 million annually for the workers at the complex, and South Korean tourists visiting the city of Kaesong and the Mount Kumgang site generated $12 million and $18 million in revenue, respectively, for Pyongyang's coffers.[172] Thus, Pyongyang knowingly put financially lucrative operations in peril in order to raise tensions and put pressure on Lee Myung-bak's government in Seoul. As spring moved into summer in 2009, North Korea made new demands about the Kaesong Industrial Complex, including higher wages for workers, more "rent" for the facilities (built by South Korea), and other demands that some felt may force the government in Seoul to actually shut down the controversial facilities.[173]

By late May 2009, North Korea had significantly stepped up the tension not only with its southern neighbor but also with the outside world after conducting another long-range missile test in April and an underground nuclear test in May. A key South Korean response to these two provocative events was to formally join the U.S.-led Proliferation Security Initiative as a full member. North Korea immediately released a statement that said the DPRK would no longer be bound by the Korean War armistice and would respond militarily to any foreign attempt to inspect its ships, calling the South Korean move a "declaration of war."[174] North Korea also reportedly stepped up its military drills during April and May, including SOF exercises (reportedly observed by Kim Chong-il) and navy drills possibly simulating attacks in the NLL. According to South Korean military officials, Kim's air force also doubled its jet fighter missions near the NLL and the DMZ during this same period. Pyongyang also continued to raise tensions and demanded huge increases for "rent" and workers' wages at the Kaesong Industrial Complex during June and July 2009.[175] It appears stirring discord on the Korean Peninsula was a priority for Pyongyang following Kim Chong-il's stroke and recovery period. It truly circled the wagons for the region and the world to see.[176]

North Korea's circling of the wagons appears to have ebbed by September 2009. Pyongyang backtracked on its unreasonable salary increases for the workers at the Kaesong Industrial Complex (much of which, of course, always goes into the government's coffers); instead, it submitted a plan for a 5 percent hike in wages. The salary adjustment did not place a financial burden on the 112 tenant companies at Kaesong.[177] North Korea also agreed to restore the number of vehicles and personnel permitted entry to the complex to pre–December 2008 clampdown levels.[178] Pyongyang also assented to resume reunions at the Kumgang Mountain resort for relatives separated by the Korean War.[179] In an announcement made in late August, projecting changes that would occur beginning September 1, 2009, the North Korean government also guaranteed the safety of South Korean tourists visiting North Korea.[180] Yet another highlight signaling decreased tensions occurred in September when the two Koreas reopened their military hotline in a western district that had been shut down for more than a year because of "technical problems."[181]

While tensions appeared to have eased by the fall of 2009, 2010 brought in new challenges generated once again by the North Korean government. As discussed earlier, in January 2010, the North Korean military conducted provocative artillery live-fire drills close to the NLL. The March 26, 2010, sinking of the South Korean corvette *Cheonan* also showed Pyongyang's renewed emphasis on causing provocations in the NLL and raising tensions with its neighbor to the south. In April 2010, North Korea began expelling staff and sealing South Korean–owned buildings at the Kumgang Mountain tourist complex. Tours to the complex had been suspended since July 2008, when North Korean guards killed a South Korean tourist. The North Koreans had been pushing South Korea to reinstate the financially lucrative (for the DPRK) tours. Seoul, meanwhile, had been insisting on new safety agreements for visitors, a joint investigation into the fatal shooting, and a formal apology. Pyongyang did not meet these stipulations; instead, it demanded that the tours be started again "or else." The "or else" turned out to mean sealing off several buildings and expelling custodian workers.[182]

North Korea's most audacious act of ramping up tensions proved to be the sinking of the *Cheonan*, and once the investigation of the sinking was completed, South Korea took action that was important. President Lee Myung-bak announced in May 2010, that all trade and exchange programs with North Korea were suspended except for the Kaesong Industrial Complex—and companies there were told to keep their staff to a minimum. North Korean ship passage through South Korean waterways was suspended, joint exercises off the west coast with the United States were announced, and plans to reinitiate propaganda broadcasts along the DMZ (using loudspeakers) were initiated. South Korea also referred the sinking of the *Cheonan*, and the evidence associated with it, to the UN Security Council. North Korea responded to these actions by expelling some South Korean officials from the Kaesong Industrial Complex and by announcing that it was withdrawing its military safeguards with South Korea (including a hotline between the two militaries) and was threatening to "mercilessly respond" to South Korean loudspeaker broadcasts along the DMZ. Of course, North Korean also continued to deny responsibility for the sinking of the *Cheonan*.[183]

While many analysts have assessed North Korea's provocative actions were influenced by the succession intrigue, in my view, an equally important reason was that North Korea was attempting to gain economic and political concessions from South Korea, in particular, and from the United States. The South Korean government released statistics showing that its combined cash and material aid to North Korea came to $6.96 billion dollars during the ten-year period of the Kim Dae-jung and Roh Moo-hyun presidencies. According to the statistics released by Seoul and reported in the South Korean press, North Korea received roughly $2.5 billion in aid and money during the Kim administration and approximately $4.5 billion during the Roh presidency.[184] This largely unreciprocated gesture—in return, North Korea did not change its rogue nation-state behavior—ended in 2008 when the Lee Myung-bak administration took a more realistic stance toward its brethren to the north. The resumption of full-scale operations at the Kaesong Industrial Complex in 2009 and plans to resume tourist operations in 2010 were likely both designed to restart the cash flow that had become an integral part of North Korea's economy.

With all the defensive activities going on in North Korea and in its relationship with South Korea, Pyongyang surprised many when it established a mobile telephone service in the reclusive nation. The Egyptian corporation Orascom will invest $400 million there to develop the cellular network.[185] The original network was deployed in Pyongyang, but plans are in place to expand it throughout North Korea. Paik Hak-soon of the Sejong Institute told reporters that he believes only the elite will be able to use the network. Paik said, "Government, party, military people are the big beneficiaries. . . . Traders and people involved in the economy may also be allowed to use it."[186] While the new cell phone network is an obvious risk to a nation that puts a higher premium on controlling information than almost anywhere on earth, experts expect those who are not senior officials would have difficulty accessing the network anyway and that it will help speed up North Korea's economic reconstruction.[187] While North Korea has decided to build a cell phone network, all is not as it seems. According to a Chinese diplomatic source who spoke to the Japanese press, the start of the mobile phone service in Pyongyang was delayed for almost six months so that a wiretapping system could be developed. Thus, criticism of the regime or leaks of information to foreigners or the populace at large will be contained.[188] While the indigenous cell phone network is tightly controlled, the many Chinese-connected cell phones in the country are not. It is hard to suppress these phones because of the large amount of cross-border traffic with China, particularly in recent years. This phenomenon has largely caused an information explosion that truly began to expose itself during 2008. The North Koreans have reportedly purchased radio wave–detecting equipment from both Germany and China, and those caught talking to foreigners are punished severely.[189] According to a North Korean source reported in South Korea, Pyongyang has organized special police squads throughout the country (but especially in regions close to the China border) to deal with illegal cell phone usage and other banned forms of information coming into the country.[190]

NORTH KOREA'S SUCCESSION PROCESS:
WHO WILL FOLLOW KIM CHONG-IL?

The various issues and events described thus far ultimately lead to only one question: who will succeed Kim Chong-il when he dies or when he is rendered medically incapacitated? Some have suggested that a form of collective leadership could emerge perhaps with one of Kim's sons as a purely titular figurehead. Two of the primary security services, the SSD and the MPS, could keep the lid on things as they are overseen by Chang Sung-taek.[191] Other analysts have opined that a different sort of collective leadership could emerge, one that would be focused on the military with a base in the National Defense Commission and again perhaps with a member of the Kim family as a titular head of government in order to maintain legitimacy.[192] In fact, a variety of theories and scenarios predicting a collective leadership to follow the Dear Leader have been reported.[193]

Another school of thought says Kim may pick one of his sons to run the country when he steps down or dies. Kim Chong-nam, the oldest son, would be traditionally thought of as the top candidate. But while he has been given duties in the government, he spends the majority of his time out of the country and often travels by himself, sometimes even in taxis. This behavior is not what one would expect from the "crown prince."[194] As mentioned earlier, Kim Chong-nam may have hurt his chances of being the heir apparent when in 2001 he tried to enter Japan with a fake Dominican passport to visit Disneyland (with a child and two women in tow), was caught, and quickly deported. Kim Chong-il reportedly was not pleased.[195] Kim Chong-nam was educated partly in Switzerland and, according to Merrily Baird, a retired CIA analyst who now tracks North Korean politics through open sources, his time there overlapped with that of Ambassador Ri-chol.[196] Ri reportedly has managed Kim Chong-il's secret funds overseas (at least in Europe).[197] The connection to Ri may have been helpful in the oldest son's later activities working within Office Number 39, which is well known for its secret and illicit activities involving North Korea's overseas funds. During the fall of 2008, Kim Chong-nam reportedly "inspected" facilities and factories while accompanied by Chang Sung-taek.[198]

Kim Chong-chol, the second son, has been given a position within the KWP's Organization and Guidance Department. But accounts say his father thinks of him as "delicate" and that he is known for being a big Eric Clapton fan, having even followed Clapton's band around Europe on a concert tour a few years ago.[199] Kim Chong-chol has also reportedly conducted inspections within both the party and the security apparatus, though the nature and scope of these activities remain murky, as does his status within Kim's inner circle.[200] Some reports in recent years suggested that Kim Chong-chol was under consideration to be Kim Chong-il's successor. The second son's position in the party is similar to the one the elder Kim occupied as he began his grooming process.[201]

The youngest son, Kim Chong-un, has had little published about him but is thought to get along well with his father. Until the fall of 2009, he had not been reported as holding a position in the party. The youngest Kim son is said to suffer from high blood pressure and diabetes and to be the son that physically most closely resembles his father.[202] Accounts say Kim Chong-il favors Kim Chong-un over Kim Chong-chol because Kim Chong-un likes sports and is said to be more aggressive than his older brother, who is into computers and music.[203] The youngest Kim son was educated in Berne, Switzerland, where he was said to travel rarely except when in the company of the North Korean ambassador. On January 15, 2009, press reports attributed to unnamed intelligence officials stated that Kim Chong-il had picked his third and youngest son as his successor and had delivered a directive regarding his choice to the powerful OGD leadership of the party around January 8.[204]

The decision may have been driven by Kim's health issues. Kim Chong-un was twenty-five in January 2009, and his father was thirty-two when his grandfather Kim Il-sung named him as his successor. If Kim Chong-un is the chosen successor, Pyongyang would be expected to launch a propaganda campaign for his elevated standing. ROK Unification Ministry spokesman Kim Ho-nyoun responded to reports by saying, "Concerning the reported designation, we have not been able to confirm."[205] Andrei Lankov of Kookmin University told the South Korean press that given the number of false reports in the past, caution should be exercised. Lankov further said, "There have been many rumors over the years beginning in the 1990s. . . . So we don't have any reason to take this any more seriously than other previous reports."[206] Former ROK president Kim Dae-jung stated that, in his view, a possible scenario would be a coalition governing structure (party and military), with one of the sons in formal leadership.[207]

If Kim Chong-un is to be the successor (and it now appears likely that he is), it does not guarantee a smooth transition to power or even that the transition will be successful. As Baek Seung-joo said, "A successor must have a power base, personal qualities, and abilities. Despite his selection as the successor by his father, if he lacks these capabilities, he (Chong-un) is likely to be ousted when his father's political life ends."[208] Another unnamed government official in Seoul reported, "Rather than paying attention to Kim Jong-il's possible successor, we should prepare for the inevitable instability the post-Kim Jong-il regime will bring."[209]

In February 2009, a source close to the North Korean government told the Japanese press that an internal memo circulating in North Korean military headquarters said that Kim Chong-il had designated Kim Chong-un as his heir; however, the source also provided a caveat to the report: it could have been a propaganda ploy by senior military officers.[210] In May 2009, Lee Young-hwa, the head of an Osaka-based activist organization on North Korean affairs, told the Japanese press that a collaborator had passed to him information that schoolchildren in Pyongyang were singing songs praising Kim Chong-un.[211] Chang Sung-taek is said to be behind the scenes in much of the succession process.[212] Further evidence that North Korea was considering a bloodline succession came from the *Rodong Sinmun*, the state-run propaganda arm. An editorial in February 2009 stated, "In the midst of glorious inheritance of bloodline of Mount Paektu is the bright future of the Juche (self-reliance) revolution." South Korean officials said the reference to "bloodline" was unprecedented.[213] On February 18, 2009, in a speech given at a gathering of party and military officials, Pak Chae-kyong, vice minister of the Ministry of People's Armed Forces, said, "We will firmly carry on the bloodline of Mangyongdae and Mount Paektu with our guns, faithfully upholding the leadership of our supreme commander."[214] Thus, by early 2009 there were signs that Kim Chong-il was paying attention to the succession process and interested in naming a blood relative to succeed him.

On June 12, 2009, FOX News reporter James Rosen published a report that stated both military and diplomatic officials had been informed that Kim Chong-un was the heir apparent. Mr. Rosen stated, "Intelligence sources say North Korean military commanders were determined via signals intelligence on June 3 to be relaying to subordinate officers a set of six 'talking points' about the younger Kim intended to shore up support for him among the country's army and other key military institutions." Mr. Rosen further stated, "Sources also told FOX News that on the same day, U.S. intelligence intercepted congratulatory messages sent back to Pyongyang by North Korean diplomats stationed overseas, in which the officials swore allegiance to Kim Jong-un as the country's next supreme leader."[215] Also that month, the South Korean intelligence services briefed members of the National Assembly that the North Korean government had informed the army, the Presidium of the Supreme People's Assembly, the cabinet, and diplomatic missions abroad that Kim Chong-un was the designated successor to Kim Chong-il.[216] In late June, Kim Chong-il and Kim Chong-un reportedly visited one of the key intelligence–internal security services in North Korea. The Dear Leader is said to have told agency officials that they should consider "Kim Chong-un their boss and to defend him with their lives." The agency chief for this agency (and most others) is officially Kim Chong-il, but the man actually running it at the time (chief deputy director) was U Tong-chuk, a newly named member of the powerful NDC.[217] Thus, he may have been designated to play a role in mentoring the younger Kim in building a power base in the security services.

Of course, there have been predictions that Chang Sung-taek has been and will continue to be the power behind the scenes. The evidence presented earlier certainly leads one to believe that Kim Chong-il has handed over some of his power to Chang. Some have opined that this transfer indicates Chang (who is four years younger than Kim) is now a "behind the scenes leader in-waiting."[218] Technically, under the North Korean constitution, one of the generals on the National Defense Commission would be slated to take command of the country. Certainly the great argument has been that the military is the most powerful and most credible entity in the country, a source of Kim Chong-il's power, and perhaps the source behind the next leader, though one would expect a younger general would emerge and step into these shoes in such a scenario.[219] It should be noted here that Chang had a brother, Chang Song-u, who was a vice marshal in the North Korean military,[220] but he was not included on the list of 687 deputies—all considered key players in North Korea—to attend the Twelfth Supreme People's Assembly (SPA) announced during March 2009.[221] Chang Song-u's death was confirmed in August 2009, when the North Korean state-run media reported that Kim Chong-il had sent a wreath to his tomb and expressed deep condolences over his death.[222] Of note, among the members "elected," there was no major generational change, but a significant number of economic technocrats were placed in the SPA.[223] Many analysts still believe that the military apparatus remains outside Chang Sung-taek's influence.[224]

The same holds true for the NDC and the powerful generals who sit on it (outside of Kim Chong-il). They do not have control over the OGD within the KWP.

Several issues arose when North Korea held its Twelfth SPA meeting beginning April 9, 2009. First of all, North Korea expanded NDC membership from nine members to thirteen, the largest group since its inception in 1972. Also of significance regarding the NDC, Chang Sung-taek was named as a formal member, giving him a seat in both the party and the military apparatus. Chu Kyu-chang, considered one of the chief developers of North Korea's Taepo Dong programs, was also chosen as one of the new members. Three generals were also selected for the NDC: Chu Sang-son (former commander of the VI Corps), Kim Chong-kak (first vice director of the GPB, under Cho Myong-rok), and U Tong-chuk (little is referenced in the North Korean media regarding U).[225]

The results of the SPA meeting may indicate two important things. First, that Chang now has a key seat in both the party and the military means he may be one of the most important individuals that Kim wants to mentor his son. Chang could even serve as a temporary "regent" in the case of Kim Chong-il's sudden death. Of importance, Chang will still need to build a power base in the military (to date, this goal has not been accomplished). The second important development is that the increased number of NDC members likely also means that Pyongyang wishes to continue the focus on the military's power within the government. Kim's presence at the SPA also served to bolster his authority and show the nation that he was healthy, though in the film of the events he appeared thin and frail, and his left arm appeared to be stiff when he raised his hands for applause.[226] Professor Kim Yong-hyun of Dongguk University in Seoul believes the SPA's focus on the NDC was important. He writes, "The NDC has now expanded and grown stronger in terms of its members and systemic strength. A new stable foundation and chain of command has been set in place for the 'post-Kim Jong-il system.'"[227]

The same month the SPA was held in North Korea several developments became public that may shed some light on the power within Pyongyang's seat of government and ultimately the succession process. The highly secretive Operations Department, which runs clandestine operations overseas and in South Korea (and reportedly has more than two thousand agents), was transferred from its headquarters in the KWP to the NDC. Now the military controls the organization that conducts many of the most important international and South Korean clandestine and intelligence collection missions for North Korea. The Operations Department has always had both civilian and military agents, but it has also come under the party's umbrella in the past. O Kuk-ryol formerly commanded the Operations Department, and the move may have come because Kim Chong-il trusts his old friend and confidant to continue monitoring the activities of the organization that conducts important secret operations (from his new post within the NDC).[228] The scope and focus of the Operations Department's activities can probably best be described as a model that resembles a combination of the Soviet Union's Committee for State Security (KGB) and the Main Intelligence Directorate (GRU) during the Cold War.

Another important development is the disclosure that Kim Chong-un was appointed to a low-level post within the NDC.[229] In October 2009, it was confirmed that Kim Chong-un had also been given a deputy director–level post in the KWP (now giving him posts in both the party and the military).[230] This appointment may have an impact on the succession process, and if it does, both O Kuk-ryol and Chang Sung-taek would likely be among those who would mentor the youngest son in the Kim clan. Of course it should not be forgotten that Kim Chong-un's older brother Kim Chong-chol also has a low-level post in the party. Further, O and Kim Kyong-hee (Kim Chong-il's sister) are both said to be playing an important role in the succession process and reportedly appeared on a podium with Kim Chong-il at a major event during the fall of 2009.[231]

Chang Sung-taek will likely play an important role in mentoring Kim Chong-il's successor, but the moves regarding O Kuk-ryol are also significant to the process. O is an active duty general and, as such, will be able to help Kim's son build a power base within the military. Perhaps moving the secretive Operations Department into the military apparatus will also help to enable this process. From his position at the head of the Operations Department, O was noted for his involvement in a variety of clandestine activities, among them the now-infamous counterfeiting of U.S. dollars, that likely have made him a wealthy man. But O is also known for being a proponent of a strong, asymmetrically equipped North Korean military. Thus, from his new position he will not only be able to help mentor Kim's son but also assist in maintaining and honing Pyongyang's national security goals.[232] In an interview with the Japanese press, Yan Jiangfeng, the former military attaché at the Chinese Embassy in North Korea and vice chairman of the China Institute of International Strategic Studies (in 2009), stated, "National Defense Commission Vice Chairman O Kuk-ryol is popular among the military and unifying the military. It is impossible that a discord will emerge in the military under Mr. O." Yan also made an important statement about Chang Sung-taek: "He does not have military experience and it is impossible for him to have an influence on the military."[233]

Events in the spring and summer of 2010 had a significant effect on the power structure in North Korea. In April Ri Yong-chol, one of the most powerful men in the country, reportedly died of a heart attack. Ri was eighty-one years old.[234] In May Kim Il-chol, a member of the NDC and another power broker in the country, was officially relieved of his duties, with old age being cited as the reason (he was eighty at the time).[235] In early June, in what was perhaps the most shocking event to most analysts, Ri Che-kang was killed in a very mysterious car accident in Pyongyang. As the first deputy director of the OGD, Ri (who was eighty at the time of his death) was also considered one of the country's centers of power and was rumored to be on bad terms with his rival, Chang Sung-taek. Ri's death leaves the door open for Chang to consolidate still more power.[236] It appears that with Kim Chong-il's help, Chang did exactly that. In another surprise move, North Korea held a rare session of the SPA in June 2010, following Ri's death. In the session, Chang Sung-taek was promoted to a vice chairman of the NDC. Many experts believed the SPA was convened again in 2010 to focus on the succession issue. Chang and O Kuk-ryol are both seen as important mentors for Kim Chong-un, and the promotion put both of them in senior positions on the NDC, where O is also a vice chairman.[237]

An examination of those who were left wielding key elements of power in the DPRK by the summer of 2010 reveals O Kuk-ryol, who could oversee intelligence services and the military from his post in the NDC; Kim Yong-chun, who was now minister of the People's Armed Forces (and thus a military base of power); U Tong-chuk, the deputy chief of the State Security Department (under Kim Chong-il); and, of course, Chang Sung-taek, who by the spring of 2010 now had a power base in both the military and the party.[238] While others in the DPRK leadership structure held important positions, these four men appear to have been in their positions not only because of their loyalty to Kim Chong-il, but because they could play a key role in helping to mentor his son in the succession process.

Several issues need to be considered as one ponders the succession process in North Korea. First of all, Kim Chong-il does not glean his power from just the military or just the party. Further, in a country where literally everyone is being watched, he does not get his power from just the security services. He gleans his power from all three and by trusting a few close relatives who have proven absolute loyalty to him. When it comes to the party, his successor would eventually have to be put in charge of the powerful OGD within the KWP, the position Kim Chong-il currently holds.[239] When it comes to the military, Kim's successor would need to eventually also become the chairman of the National Defense Commission. If Kim's successor, or successor in waiting, were to be given both of these positions (or positions that would lead to such appointments)—as Kim Il-sung did for Kim Chong-il—this experience would prepare him for leadership of the country. The individual in these positions would also be able to control both the civilian and military security services.

The point of this discussion is that a "collective leadership" ruling the country simply could not succeed if it were led strictly by military generals for two important reasons: the military, while a powerful entity, could not run the country by itself and would need the blessing and support of powerful party members; and the generals would be unable to control a system that since 1948 has revolved around a single leader who also controlled the party and the security services. Likewise, a collective leadership of party members would be unable to control the country effectively because it would run head-on into the military, which would be unlikely to give up the powerful and elevated position it has held in the country since Kim Chong-il came to power. Thus, the potential for clashes and power grabs between these two powerful institutions is high. As Andrei Lankov articulates, "When Kim dies the fate of the country will be resolved very fast, in a matter of days. . . . If conflicts between generals and top leaders spill into the open, leading perhaps to violent clashes, the regime will face a grave if not mortal threat."[240]

The evidence, as I see it, shows that Kim Chong-il has picked his third son as his heir apparent. In February 2009, Won Sei-hoon, head of the South Korean National Intelligence Service (NIS), reportedly told a closed session of the National

Assembly that a "three generation succession appears to be possible" in North Korea, and while Kim Chong-il was still in charge, he had not fully recovered from his medical setbacks.[241] But as noted, his sons were not on the list of 687 lawmakers "elected" to the Twelfth Supreme People's Assembly announced in March 2009.[242] Kim also has not even hinted that he wants either his often-talked-about brother-in-law, Chang Sung-taek, or one of the high-ranking generals in his powerful military to take over behind the scenes or to participate in a collective leadership to support his heir. One thing has been mentioned (including by the North Korean government itself)—the year 2012. Kim Chong-il will be seventy years old then, and the year could be important for the succession process if Kim lives that long.[243] The year 2012 is also important because it is the 100th anniversary of the birth of Kim Il-sung. Some scholars have opined that Kim Chong-il likely has the goal of completing the succession process to his son by that year.[244] If Kim survives to make great pronouncements in 2012 about succession, it is likely the process would involve positions in both the party and the military, just as it did when Kim Il-sung groomed him.[245] According to sources in the Japanese press, a memo was circulated to DPRK embassies in 2009 that said in part, "We have to devote ourselves to carrying out a mission of opening the gate of a powerful state in 2012 for the time being."[246] South Korean press sources published the results of a report issued by the South Korean government–sponsored think tank, the Korea Institute for National Unification, that states in part, "The possibility of North Korean leader Kim's absence in the North after 2012 is high."[247]

More evidence that Kim Chong-un is the most likely successor to Kim Chong-il was revealed on September 25, 2009, when a Taiwanese photographer spotted a poster near a collective farm outside of Wonsan on North Korea's east coast. The poster read, "Kim Chong-eun, a young leader who succeeds the lineage of Mangyongdae and Mt. Paektu," and included the lyrics of a song related to the succession process.[248] The poster caused some controversy because it spelled the youngest son's name as Kim Chong-eun, leading to a slightly different pronunciation that the South Korean government acknowledged was correct. For the purposes of this book, I will continue to refer to the youngest son as Kim Chong-un, though it appears the name may still be roughly the same in the English transliteration.[249] Kim Chong-un's birthday was also reportedly designated a national holiday in January 2010.[250] In March 2010, a defector group in South Korea acquired a document with the very long title of "The Youth Captain, Comrade Kim Chong-un Is a Mt. Paektu Style of Captain Who Bears the Dignity and Qualifications of the Great Men in History and Carries on the Ideology and Leadership of the Great General." The document was reportedly distributed to the party's Central Committee, members of the army, and key cabinet officials.[251]

South Korean scholars have predicted a variety of possible scenarios that could occur in North Korea if Kim Chong-il were to die or be permanently incapacitated without having first officially established a successor or if a power base had not yet been established for that successor. Some have suggested a possible military coup involving either hard-liners or reformists. Others have speculated a civil war could erupt in North Korea. Still others have of course surmised that a tenuous situation would result in Chinese intervention.[252] The year 2012 is interesting (though not a definite), because some feel if Kim was able to position his son as successor, the regime could continue even after his death with a smooth transition. The consolidation of power would be difficult, though, and unlike Kim Chong-il's experience. He had twenty years to consolidate his power (with the help and guidance of his father) before Kim Il-sung's death.

Based on the evidence I have outlined, if Kim dies and his successor has not built a power base in the party, the military, and the security services, several key scenarios are possible. The first is that there would be a violent power struggle within the inner circle that surrounds him. Each side would attempt to gain the support of the military, for in a time of crisis it would be the most logical power base. It is known that certain powerful members of the military favor different members of the Kim clan. The potential for several splits with the resultant violence is high in such a scenario. Yet another scenario would see the military itself attempt to seize power. Despite my analysis and others' conjecture regarding powerful individuals in the military, no clear evidence points to what individual or group would be the most likely to attempt a power grab. Because Kim has wielded such absolute power and because North Korea's security services maintain a constant web of reporting, counter-reporting, and purges, the resultant fear (as generated by Kim's government) has made it extremely difficult for factions to form within the military, and the reporting on any factions that may exist is all guesswork. What has held the generals together since the inception of the Kim family's regime has been their absolute loyalty first to Kim Il-sung and then to his son. Without this bond, a number of factions could form very quickly or, worse, confusion within the military could ensue.

Still another plausible scenario is that following Kim's death, members of the military would overthrow Kim's named successor, seize power in the existing vacuum, and then sue for peace and unification with the south. While this scheme may seem to make no sense (and is rarely, if ever, mentioned among analysts who watch North Korea), there is reason to believe it is possible. Among scholars and NGOs who watch North Korea, rumors are that several DPRK generals are on the payroll of NIS, the largest South Korean intelligence agency. Given the well-documented corruption that exists within the North Korean government, this information should not come as a surprise. Such a scenario could be to Seoul's advantage as it would actually open a window for unifying the divided peninsula and finally bringing an end to most North Koreans' misery. Of course the scenario that many analysts have discussed and that seems as likely as any is that if the named successor is unable to hold his power base together, the party (and the OGD) cannot unite, and the army becomes factionalized, the country would fall into violent civil war. This crisis would also be a window of opportunity for the south (should circumstances permit) to step in and take over—with the ultimate goal of unifying the peninsula—perhaps even without having to take large-scale military measures.

CONCLUSIONS

Clearly, despite Kim Chong-il's apparent efforts to put forward his youngest son as his successor, no leader has yet emerged who can immediately take control of the party, the army, the security services, and Kim's family. Loyalties appear to be mixed, with the only overriding loyalty being to Kim Chong-il and no one else. Thus, if Kim lives long enough to officially name a successor and if, as Kim was able to do under his father, the successor is able to build a base of support from the important institutions in North Korea, his successor will face three key challenges. As I articulated in an earlier work,

First, it will be necessary to prevent political turbulence within the regime caused by division of loyalty between Kim Chong-il and his successor—

whoever that successor turns out to be, and whenever he is formally announced (if ever). Secondly, the goal is to ensure that the propaganda and political mythology process adequately indoctrinates the North Korean populace. Finally, it is of the utmost importance to ensure that competition between Kim family members does not impact regime security (it may have been this competition that was at least partially responsible for Chang's two-year purge). Kim will continue to be concerned with these issues as long as he remains in power.[253]

One thing is for sure, given that no succession process has been openly put into place: the potential for anarchy within North Korea following Kim's death is real. Given his health problems, one can likely expect to see continued purges, crackdowns on the populace, and renewed suspicion regarding outsiders, particularly South Koreans. The struggle for Kim's approval—or for actual power—may become intensified among members of the OGD (and those in the Kim family whom they favor) as well as the military. Indications are that some purges relating to interfamily competition between the Kim brothers have already occurred, and Kim Chong-un has risen to the forefront. Kim Chong-nam's former schoolmates and confidants who had positions within the government were reportedly purged in June 2009. And accounts say the elder brother was the victim of an attempted assassination attempt in China from aides close to Kim Chong-un.[254] According to several scholars in South Korea, the early possible purges and other activities may have caused Kim Chong-il to put pressure on his third son and to curtail Kim Chong-un's power a bit (but probably only temporarily) as the succession process continues.[255]

Should Kim Chong-il not live long enough to build a strong power base for his son, many analysts believe that the younger Kim would be vulnerable to the "old guard" of power brokers within the party and the military.[256] North Korea places great emphasis on age and experience, and the youngest Kim certainly does not have these two advantages. Any collective leadership that would emerge following Kim's rule would likely be weak and unable to hold the country together for an extended period because of the way North Korea has existed since Kim Il-sung took control. All the power has always centered around one leader, and all institutions and organizations feed into him. Attempting to radically disrupt this system in a monolithic communist government like North Korea's would likely mean confusion, power struggles, and possibly even armed conflict among factionalized members of the party, the military, and the security services. As of this writing, everybody is compelled to compete with rivals for power with few natural allies. So, lacking a clear succession process in place and a clear leader in the wings (as I stated in an earlier work), "what could easily ensue would be no-holds barred grab for power between the military, the party, and the security agencies. If so, there is no way to predict the potentiality for implosion or explosion—or both."[257]

Issues related to the succession process within the North Korean system are likely well known to its leadership, particularly Kim Chong-il. Thus, it is no surprise that in 2010 the succession process was hastened. A key sign of this was seen as the KWP political bureau scheduled its first meeting announced to the public since 1966. The meeting, set for September 2010, was likely called in order to reshuffle some of the party's official posts, mainly because of the purges and deaths to some key members earlier in 2010. But the meeting is also likely an important milestone in the ongoing process of anointing a successor to Kim Chong-il. Because of issues with Kim Chong-il's health, he is assessed to be extremely concerned—perhaps obsessed—with ensuring that the succession process of father to third son goes not only quickly but efficiently enough that his successor has a strong power base in the country's major institutions before he dies or becomes incapacitated.[258] While some analysts have said the main power base is the military, I would assess that Kim Chung-un also needs a base in the party, the security services, and, of course, within the Kim family inner circle.

If North Korea collapses, it will also mean a blow to the national security strategy of the communist government in China. Beijing's autocratic leadership probably feels that an unstable or collapsed North Korea would be a problem for its border stability. Indeed, a failed North Korea could easily lead to Korean unification, which would end China's strategic and operational depth from U.S. forces on the Korean Peninsula that began with the Korean War's armistice in 1953.[259] As Paul B. Stares and Joel S. Wit remark about China in a Council on Foreign Relations report, "Foremost would be the desire to prevent the United States from establishing military bases in the North or stationing troops, if only temporarily, near its border."[260] Likewise, Russia would not want to see North Korea founder because Moscow continues to maintain economic and political interests there as a holdover from the Cold War. It also has the potential to greatly decrease Russia's influence on the peninsula.[261]

South Korea's government would be faced with overwhelming economic difficulties as it adjusted to a unified nation with fully half of its landmass a former relic of a monolithic communist regime.[262] In the short run, Japan could be faced with either an exploding North Korea, which could lash out with weapons of mass destruction, or an imploding North Korea with economic implications that would likely affect Japan in a profound manner. In the long run, Japan would be faced with a unified Korea that would be a potential political and economic rival after the north's overwhelming task of recovering from years of communist rule. When it comes to the United States, the biggest immediate policy concern would likely be North Korea's WMDs. When asked about North Korea in 2009, JCS chairman Adm. Mike Mullen said, "The possibility of instability—and pretty severe instability—with those weapons—and certainly, if you listen to some of the rhetoric, is a big concern."[263] As I have said in the past, "There are no benign scenarios in an imploding country with a million man army, and nuclear weapons and missiles, whose control are unknown."[264]

CHAPTER SIX

Preparing for the North Korean Threat

The ROK-U.S. Military Alliance and the Lee Myung-bak Presidency[1]

P
resident Lee Myung-bak won a landslide victory in 2007. His popularity before the election was obvious, and it came as a surprise to almost no one that he won by the largest margin since democratic elections were first held in South Korea in 1987.[2] Many analysts agree that in the minds of many Koreans, the struggling economy and other issues that the Roh government had not addressed very well were key in helping conservatives return to power. But another crucial issue was Lee's strong stance on national defense and on how to handle the relationship with what remains an unpredictable and belligerent neighbor to the north, the DPRK. Indeed, as distinguished North Korean analyst Nicholas Eberstadt stated following the election of 2007,

> South Koreans winced as their government repeatedly abstained from U.N. votes criticizing North Korea for human rights abuses. They grumbled as they saw their tax-funded 'economic cooperation' projects with the North devolve into an economic lifeline for a still-hostile government in Pyongyang. And they worried as the undisguised rift with Washington over 'the North Korean threat' created unmistakable strains in the vital U.S.-South Korean alliance.[3]

Lee's presidency shows a shift to the center-right in the ROK electorate.[4]

Since Lee has assumed the presidency of South Korea, he has encountered many challenges. Indeed, many on the Left have accused Lee of being too hard

on North Korea and for bringing difficulties back into the north-south relationship (though in reality it was almost entirely a one-way relationship during Roh's
administration—when it came to compromise and transparency—almost exclusively on the part of South Korea).[5] But these criticisms have not gained nearly as
much attention as those mounted against Lee for his desire to move forward on
the free trade agreement with the United States that will give American beef imports what some critics (unfairly in my view) have called unsafe inroads into the
South Korean food market. Indeed, the "beef issue," to the surprise of many Americans, became a prominent concern in South Korea, leading to candlelight vigils,
protests in the street, and what amounted to a legitimate crisis for the Lee Myung-
bak government.[6]

While the beef issue may have been an emotional one for many Koreans, it
seems there was more to it than meets the eye. Indeed, many analysts have said it
was in reality a move by the Left designed to subvert the new government of Lee
Myung-bak. As Victor Cha, a professor at Georgetown University, recently wrote,

> While the trigger for Korea's self-paralyzing demonstrations were concerns
> about beef, it is increasingly apparent that the ideological Left in Korea,
> pushed out of power after over one decade in the seat of the presidency and
> in control of the National Legislature—and with no major election scheduled
> for another four years—have taken their politics to the streets in an effort to
> subvert the first conservative government Korean government in a decade.

Cha further cuts to the crux of the matter when he writes, "This is not about
lofty notions of a new Korean nationalism, but about the primitive struggle for political power long a part of politics on the peninsula."[7] According to press reports,
several civic groups and left-of-center activists actually planned many of the rallies
with the specific intent of bringing down Lee's government.[8]

While the beef issue drew most of the attention in South Korea in 2008, in
my view it detracted from other extremely important issues that needed to be
addressed. As it has begun to die down, the real challenges and issues that face
Lee's government and the ROK-U.S. alliance can now become the center of more
focus by policy makers and analysts in the United States and South Korea. Perhaps

most important, Lee has now stated that his policy toward North Korea is to seek eventual unification under a liberal democracy. This announcement is a significant break from the policy of his predecessors' administrations, which sought peaceful coexistence with North Korea but paid little attention to what will be a hugely expensive and problematic post-unification situation.[9] This new policy points to the important issues that will be addressed in this chapter. In order for South Korea to be able to work toward unification under a liberal, democratic government, the government in Seoul must develop its military capabilities to match the continuing North Korean threat posed by its conventional and unconventional forces. As Seoul looks to building its own capabilities, it must work closely with its most important ally, the United States. Thus, the ROK-U.S. military alliance will be the key in factor in defending the South Korean landmass, building stability for the future, and protecting Seoul's and Washington's national security interests in the region.

ROK MILITARY DEVELOPMENT: MATCHING CAPABILITIES TO THE THREAT

Many issues face the alliance between the United States and South Korea, but undoubtedly the bulwark of the relationship between these two nations is the ROK-U.S. military alliance. It has protected the stability and security of the Korean Peninsula since the end of the Korean War. The military alliance has undergone several important changes in recent years, not the least of which is the ongoing transformation of ROK military forces with an original end date of 2020 that was estimated to cost 164 trillion won. The plan, set into place under the Roh Moo-hyun administration, also was supposed to give the ROK military the independent capability to operate under separate wartime operational control from U.S. forces by 2012.[10] Evidence that the process of transitioning to two separate wartime commands, as part of what is called the Strategic Transition Plan, was going forward can be seen if one examines the Ulchi Freedom Guardian exercise held during August 2008. During the annual exercise that summer, the South Koreans and Americans simulated fighting a war under two separate operational commands—one led by the chairman of South Korea's JCS and one led by the commander of United States Korea Command (KORCOM, the future successor to USFK). The exercise was observed by several retired military officers from both the United States and South Korea and

was expected to aid in planning for the major changes that were expected to occur by 2012.[11] According to press reports, the United States and South Korea also
planned to adopt a new war plan to reflect projected changes in the military alliance
as they hold their joint-combined annual exercise in the summer of 2009 and moving through 2012.[12] But press reports attributed to a military source also revealed
in 2010, "To this end, the U.S.-led Combined Forces Command will take control,
a change of plans because the South Korean Joint Chiefs of Staff had initially been
arranged to lead the drill."[13] The report referenced the 2010 Ulchi Freedom Guardian exercise and was an interesting change of plan that likely reflected a continuing
concern over the North Korean threat.

There has been a great deal of criticism regarding the transformation plan set
into action by the Roh administration. This expensive transformation process will
not only put a huge strain on the budget of South Korea's government, but also
much of the planning put into this transformation process can legitimately be considered dangerous to South Korea's security. The plan has several key weakness: it
calls for cutting military forces by 180,000 men before acquisition of modern programs can offset the reduction in forces; the plan was not set up to counter North
Korea's nuclear and missile threats, which have proven to be significant since the
events of 2006; and it did not include enough programs or programs that are robust enough in nature or the proper security measures to meet the requirements of
Seoul's planned takeover of separate wartime operational control from the U.S.
military in 2012. There are already press reports saying that the ROK government
may push the plan back from its planned date of 2020 to 2025 because of these
reasons and because of budgetary issues.[14]

As the South Korean military continues its transformation process and pushes
ahead with the challenges it faces in the changing ROK-U.S. military alliance,
policy makers in Seoul cannot forget that the North Korean threat remains ominous
and real. North Korea continues to maintain the world's fifth-largest military, one
that is equipped with a nuclear capability, ballistic missiles, and an asymmetric capability that has evolved since the mid-1990s.[15] Pyongyang has yet to even discuss
terms for eliminating its estimated six to twelve nuclear weapons and continues
to deploy 70 percent of its ground forces within ninety miles of the DMZ. These
forces include two deployed mechanized corps, an armor corps (converted to a

division), and an artillery corps (also converted to a division) plus a missile corps that has more than six hundred Scuds and two hundred No Dong missiles capable of striking anywhere in South Korea or Japan.[16] In order for the Lee administration to make up for the mistakes made by the Roh administration's transformation program, it will need to focus on two key areas: the North Korean threat, based on the simple intelligence doctrine that a threat is defined as capability + intent = threat,[17] and a renewed focus on interoperability with U.S. forces as a ROK independent capability comes to fruition. The second key area was ignored for most of the Roh administration and will be important as the ROK and U.S. militaries make an effort to continue deterring the North Korean threat during the transitions occurring in the ROK-U.S. military alliance.

The North Korean military threat has most certainly evolved. Indeed, a drastic shortage of fuel (after losing subsidies from the Soviet Union beginning in 1990) and sometimes of food has forced a dip since the mid-1990s in the field training levels of its conventional forces as seen in its traditional infantry, mechanized, armor, and artillery units.[18] But despite these real setbacks the DPRK has adjusted quite cleverly. In fact, since the mid-1990s, North Korea has significantly increased the capabilities of its missile forces in sophistication, numbers (large increases of all types of missiles), and command and control. The North Korean army has integrated missiles into its artillery doctrine, and in any force-on-force conflict (or limited conflict, for that matter), missiles would be used as "long-range artillery systems" and able to target any node in South Korea and many in Japan.[19]

But missiles are only the beginning. Since the late 1990s, the North Koreans have significantly increased the number of long-range artillery systems (the 170mm self-propelled artillery system and the 240mm multiple rocket launcher system) deployed along the DMZ. Close to nine hundred of these systems are located within a short distance of the DMZ, and up to three hundred of them can target areas in and around Seoul.[20] The long-range artillery that can hit Seoul and other areas in Kyonggi Province is also a threat for two reasons: some or all of these systems are likely to be equipped with chemical munitions, and from their forward deployed positions, they could strike Seoul with little or no warning.[21] U.S. Department of Defense officials have estimated that in a North Korean attack on the ROK, up to 250,000 people would die in Seoul from the artillery attack alone.[22] Of course, in the asymmetric threat North Korea poses to the ROK is the DPRK's well-equipped and highly trained cadre of Special Operations Forces. These forces number more than 100,000 men (2008 estimates by the South Korean Ministry of National Defense now place the figure at up to 180,000 men) and are capable of attacking key nodes within South Korea (including American bases), disrupting command and control, and conducting acts of terrorism and assassination.[23]

Under the Roh administration, the ROK government refused to acquire anti-missile systems capable of defending the country from the north's Scud missiles that can target nodes all over South Korea. To exacerbate the situation, North Korea has now built, tested, and deployed an advanced version of the old Soviet SS-21 (known as the KN-02).[24] This development is one of the key examples where the ROK military's transformation, as directed by the Blue House under the Roh administration, failed to take into account the very threat that it was built to deter and defend against. Under the Roh administration, South Korea had agreed to purchase forty-eight secondhand PAC-2 Patriot systems from Germany, but these systems will be sadly lacking in their ability to shoot down Scuds.[25] According to sources in the South Korean press, these systems are now being deployed to some locations in the ROK.[26] In my view, it should be stressed that the PAC-2 system will be highly ineffective in either providing deterrence against a Scud missile attack or in actually shooting down the missile. The PAC-2 system destroys its target by exploding a spray of shrapnel that is meant to destroy an incoming missile. The PAC-3 uses a hit-to-kill method that is far more accurate than that of the PAC-2.[27] During the Roh administration, high-level American officials repeatedly advised the South Korean government of this fact.

Under the Lee administration, the South Koreans have taken important steps to remedy their land-based ballistic missile defense, but they are only preliminary steps. Reportedly, the South Korean government has now begun efforts to buy up to forty-eight PAC-3 fire systems, which are widely considered to be much more effective than its PAC-2 predecessor in bringing down Scud and No Dong missiles. At least some of them will be deployed by 2012.[28] Press reports also indicate the South Korean military has decided to acquire Israel's Green Pine early warning radar system for tracking cruise and ballistic missiles (to enter service by 2010 or

2011).[29] The ROK government needs to take these important initial steps toward defending against and deterring missile attacks from North Korea, but again, they are only first steps. As it stands right now, the only missile defense systems on the peninsula that are truly capable of defending against a missile attack are the sixty-four PAC-3 Patriot systems currently manned, maintained, and operated by the U.S. Army.[30]

The South Koreans can look to the Japanese model for an excellent example of how to build a missile defense system that forms a realistic deterrent and defense against possible North Korean attack. The Japanese Navy successfully conducted its first test of the SM-3 (ship-based) interceptor missile in December 2007; meanwhile, the Japanese are building a two-tier missile defense system in close cooperation with the United States. The SM-3 will be launched from Aegis class ships to intercept missiles at high altitudes, and the PAC-3 systems (deployed on land bases) will intercept missiles at lower altitudes.[31] The Japanese plan to deploy thirty-six SM-3 missiles between 2007 and 2010 on four Aegis class ships. They also plan to deploy 124 advanced-capability PAC-3 interceptor missiles by 2010 on several bases and key locations throughout their country. Finally, Japan has deployed the X-band radar early warning system.[32]

Thus far, although its threat from North Korean missiles is higher, the South Korean government plans to purchase far fewer PAC-3 missile systems than Japan operates. It has made no plans to purchase the SM-3 system for its own Aegis class ships (known as the King Sejong class destroyers) and has not agreed to join the U.S. missile defense system in a carryover from the Kim Dae-jung and Roh Moo-hyun administrations.[33] The importance of missile defense for South Korea and Japan is highlighted by press reports that indicate the United States has positioned the majority of it Aegis-equipped ships with a BMD capability in the Pacific Ocean.[34]

Japan and the United States currently man what is known as the bilateral joint operations center (BJOCC) to coordinate and share missile defense information in a timely manner. During the North Korean missile firings of July 2006 (and 2009), the United States and Japan exchanged information in a timely manner through an interim coordination facility located at Yokota Air Base.[35] Indeed, Bush administration officials have commented that having the land-borne and seaborne missile defense system ready in and around Japan during 2006 was a significant factor in allowing the president to make the decision not to destroy the Taepo Dong II before it could be launched and escalating what was already becoming a regional crisis. John Rood, acting undersecretary of state for arms control and international security, remarked on March 11, 2008, "We didn't have to seriously consider options like pre-emption or overwhelming retaliation. We had a defense, and we were content to use that defense, and it was a way of not contributing to the crisis being larger."[36]

The reason behind Seoul's failure to purchase a modern missile defense system with the capabilities necessary to truly deter the North Korean threat is most certainly not a lack of encouragement from the United States. In fact, Gen. B. B. Bell, the commander of USFK during the Roh administration, stated, "The Republic of Korea must purchase and field its own TMD system, capable of full integration with the U.S. system. The regional missile threat from North Korea requires an active ROK missile defense capability to protect its critical command capabilities and personnel."[37] The next commander of USFK, Gen. Walter Sharp, shared Bell's view. In 2009, Sharp stated in congressional testimony that South Korea should build a "layered" missile defense system (probably a reference to the same type of system that is currently being built and deployed by Japan) and look to being interoperable with the U.S. global missile defense shield (also a possible reference to the arrangement between U.S. and Japanese missile defense forces). General Sharp also stated, "In the short term, South Korea must develop a systematic missile defense solution to protect its critical civilian and military command capabilities, critical infrastructure and population centers."[38] In an interview with the South Korean press, the general said, "The ROK does not have a robust missile defense capability in place and this would likely be one of the bridging capabilities the U.S. would provide until the ROK improves this." The United States has invited Seoul to participate in its missile defense network (as Japan has already done).[39] During Lee's successful campaign for president, he reportedly stated that if elected his government may reconsider the Roh government's stance on missile defense.[40] If South Korea is to defend itself against a missile attack from the north, it must take significant steps to initiate this policy.

As North Korea prepared to test launch a Taepo Dong II ballistic missile during February 2009, the issue of South Korea participating in U.S.-led BMD initiatives again resurfaced. There was a renewed call, particularly from conservatives in South Korea, for Seoul to join the U.S. system as Japan had already done so. There is no denying that this network could serve as a significant deterrent. The south continues to develop an indigenous, independent system that will be semi-proficient at shooting down SRBMs, largely based on the outmoded PAC-2 system.[41] The South Korean military is expected to pay around $213 million for an independent defense system that will go online by 2012. An anonymous government source told the South Korean press, "When the anti-missile system is completed, we may even collaborate with the anti-theater missile team operated independently by the United States Armed Forces to defend against and shoot down theater missiles."[42] Obviously as this (in many ways lacking) ROK system goes online and as the South Koreans look to possibly (and hopefully) upgrade it, many issues will have to be worked out. In an important first step, the South Korean Aegis-equipped destroyer *King Sejong the Great* is reportedly scheduled to participate in Combat System Ship Qualifications Trials with the U.S. Navy in 2010. The drills would probably include training in engaging missile targets and could be Seoul's first move in integrating its BMD system with that of the United States.[43]

But as discussed earlier, North Korea has other threats against the south that have evolved since the mid-1990s. The biggest issue here was largely ignored or, at best, underrated during the Roh administration—that is, the necessity to acquire an independent, modern, and robust command, control, communication, computers, and intelligence (C[4]I) system capable of being fully integrated with U.S. systems and interoperable (joint) service within the ROK military. This push is very important now as the United States has reportedly completed transitioning of ten major security operations from USFK to the South Korean military. The tenth and last mission—search and rescue operations with the U.S. Air Force that will be conducted with ROK forces in the lead role—transitioned in the fall of 2008.[44] Of key importance here is that in 2005, the ground-based mission of providing counterfire against North Korean artillery (including the long-range systems) was handed over to the South Korean army. Until then, the mission had been handled by the Second U.S. Infantry Division, which was equipped with thirty multiple rocket launcher systems and thirty M109A6 Paladin self-propelled howitzers.[45] The South Korean army apparently plans to upgrade its MRLs and other advanced artillery systems—

both modernize and increase their numbers—to counter the North Korean threat, but these changes are unlikely to be fully implemented for several years.[46]

The relationship of C⁴I to this artillery mission is quite simply a matter of life or death. Integrating these systems into a modern C⁴I system means that when they are operating in a counter-battery mode, they will have a quick reaction time and be able to identify the location of North Korean artillery units with radar and to take them out just as the enemy systems have been fired or are about to be fired. Without this capability, the replacement South Korean systems are simply guns that cannot react rapidly enough to target North Korean systems and thus protect allied forces or, indeed, Seoul and the seat of government.[47] This situation becomes even more a matter of concern when integrating ROK counter-battery fire with allied airpower. Without a modern C⁴I system (which their American allies have), it is next to impossible and in fact severely degrades the South Koreans' capability to target North Korean systems and quickly destroy them. According to Representative Kim Dong-sung of the South Korean National Assembly (as reported in the South Korean press), South Korean internal communications equipment used for artillery systems near the DMZ is largely obsolete. Kim cited aging communications lines used at frontline bases and said that in some cases it could take up to ninety minutes for South Korean counter-battery systems to receive coordinates on North Korean guns.[48]

Lee Myung-bak pledged during his campaign to turn the South Korean military into an efficient, high-tech force by establishing a network-centric capability.[49] There are already signs that this process is under way. During August 2008, the United States and South Korea reached an agreement on the ROK military acquiring the Global Hawk unmanned aerial vehicle (UAV). The Global Hawk system is an advanced, long-range, long-dwell-time aircraft and can transmit its data via satellite to forces on the ground.[50] In another important initiative, the first of four ordered 737 airborne early warning and control (AEW&C) aircraft arrived in South Korea in February 2010. The E-737 aircraft will add important capabilities to the ROK military's C⁴I.[51] Seoul will also field two new signals-intelligence aircraft by 2014 and plans to eventually convert some of its KF-16s to RF-16s (among other minor upgrades to C⁴I).[52] Small UAVs for tactical use by the Army and Marine Corps are expected to be developed by 2014 as well.[53] The South Korean military also reportedly plans to increase its monitoring capability by developing more advanced drones (which may be particularly important if the Global Hawk deal falls through).[54]

ROK forces have made other efforts to upgrade C[4]I, but they have thus far proven to be too little, too late. One example is the Koreasat 5 (also dubbed Mugunghwa 5), which serves as a combined civil and military communications satellite. While it is certainly a step in the right direction, thus far this system has proven to be purely experimental, is not integrated into a national information architecture where the military is thoroughly integrated with the national command authority (such an integrated system does not exist), and is unlikely to meet even the basic needs of either an independent or an integrated C[4]I system.[55] There are also reports that the South Korean army will set up an experimental, regiment-size unit that will "adopt new organization structures, weaponry, and tactics ahead of other units" (and likely will include C[4]I).[56] Under modifications to the plan scheduled to be completed by 2020, the South Korean military plans to eventually address shortfalls in C[4]I (probably by 2020) and to focus on reinforcing its capability (currently lacking) in countering DPRK nuclear and missile attacks.[57]

To put a finer point on it, the South Korean military (and its decision makers in government) continues to depend on the United States for almost all strategic information. In fact, at least for now, ROK forces are also heavily dependent on U.S. systems for much of their tactical battlefield information.[58] South Korea holds a significant edge in integrating, interpreting, processing, and utilizing battlefield information (such as the movement of forces, activities of missile units, mechanized forces, and so on) over North Korea—especially on forces that are not fairly close to the DMZ—only because of the many high tech C[4]I systems that the United States currently mans, maintains, and deploys to the Korean Peninsula (or off the peninsula) as part of its obligations in the ROK-U.S. military alliance.[59]

To move on to the third element of the North Korean asymmetric threat, Special Operations Forces, the role of C[4]I is important for South Korea's military in defending against North Korean SOF and in working together with its American allies in order to respond and deploy in any force-on-force conflict. The recent commander of Special Operations Command Korea, Brig. Gen. Simeon Trombitas, supports this assessment. In an interview published during October 2007, Brigadier General Trombitas stated, "Constructing a bilateral C4I sharing capability with a common architecture is critical for interaction with our ROK counterparts to increase the synergy between our forces and enhance command and control."[60]

Another important factor must be addressed if one is to discuss South Korea's current capability to counter the North Korean SOF threat—namely, the airlift of South Korea's own elite Special Forces and airborne brigades. South Korea currently has seven Special Forces brigades (all airborne) in its army and five independent brigades (two infantry and three counter-infiltration). Other smaller units would also require airlift in any conflict or contingency. These units are among the ROK's most elite forces and among the best trained in the world, but they cannot reach their designated targets or conduct their vital missions without airlift. The Republic of Korea Air Force (ROKAF) transport fleet currently cannot conduct this mission with only ten C-130H cargo planes and fifteen smaller, Spanish-designed twin-engine CN-235Ms in its inventory.[61] Thus, as it stands right now, the U.S. Air Force is a major source of airlift for the ROK Special Forces and other airborne units. These C4I and airlift issues must be addressed and compensated for before the South Korean military is able to independently counter the North Korean SOF threat. Thus, as the Lee administration looks to the future, these important acquisition and integration issues will have to be addressed.

I have only addressed three key threats—or a "triad" of asymmetric threats, if you will—from North Korea. North Korea has been able to successfully integrate these capabilities into its military forces as resource constraints have limited the training and ultimately some of the readiness of its more conventional traditional ground forces. But one must keep in mind that during a full-scale force-on-force conflict, these asymmetric forces would likely be able to create gaps and vulnerabilities in ROK and U.S. military forces defending South Korea that would then enable less capable—but still deadly—DPRK forces to move into these gaps, attack key nodes, and cause significant damage in the essential early hours and days of any war. This important aspect of analyzing the threat must be (and likely is) included in any planning for conflict on the Korean Peninsula. One has only to look at the unique landmass of the Korean Peninsula along the DMZ to realize that the narrow invasion corridors into South Korea provide opportunities that can be exploited.

Although other important issues with the current ROK transformation as it deals with challenges related to both development and integration with U.S. forces exist, I will focus on one final issue, the Proliferation Security Initiative (PSI). This issue that is likely to be a source of continuing debate as the Lee administration looks to its immediate national defense and its alliance with the United States. The reason PSI is so important is because of the threat that North Korea poses to regions outside Northeast Asia through its proliferation of various weapons systems and particularly missiles. Pyongyang has shown particular proficiency in its ability to proliferate missiles, missile components, and missile technology to nations in both the Middle East and South Asia. The result is a serious threat to the status quo in these regions and often a ratcheting up of tensions.

One has only to look to the recent example of Iran to understand why PSI is so important. North Korea sold eighteen Taepo Dong X (also known as the Musudan) ballistic missile systems (based on the old Soviet SS-N-6 design) to Iran in 2005.[62] According to press reports, Iran successfully conducted a test launch of this system during 2006. The missile is said to have a range of up to four thousand kilometers.[63] Thanks to missile systems acquired from North Korea, Iran now has the capability to threaten not only Israel or other nations in its own region but also NATO forces in Europe as well.[64]

South Korea under the Roh administration refused to actively participate in PSI, and most agree that the key reason was likely a reluctance to join in activities that would hurt reconciliation efforts with North Korea.[65] In fact, Roh spoke of this issue in October 2008 when he stated, "I never accepted the (U.S.-led) Proliferation Security Initiative. I discouraged discussion of missile defense programs. I opposed OPLAN 5029 too."[66] According to press reports before Lee Myung-bak assumed the leadership of South Korea, aides stated he was reconsidering South Korea's stance on PSI and planned to take a more active role in it, particularly if North Korean nuclear provocations intensified.[67] Given the current state of affairs with North Korea's continuing nuclear program and proliferation to other rogue states such as Syria, this move appears to be practical.[68]

Following Lee's inauguration the United States renewed calls for South Korea to take an active role in PSI. At a media roundtable in 2008, Undersecretary of State for Arms Control and International Security John Rood stated, "We would certainly encourage them (South Korea) to join, and we've engaged in a number of discussions with them." He continued, "The present government in Seoul is, I think, reviewing the issue. We will await the outcome of that."[69] The Institute of Foreign Affairs and National Security (IFANS) in Seoul (a state-funded think tank) has called for more active South Korean participation in PSI in a 2009 report, saying, "South Korea needs a positive review on its role in the PSI."[70] Indeed, one of the key ways that Seoul can contribute to and strengthen the ROK-U.S. alliance would be to take a more active role in PSI. Such a move would also likely serve to hamper Pyongyang's proliferation to dangerous regions of the world. In a parliamentary hearing held in February 2009, South Korean defense minister Lee Sang-hee stated that he believed it was time for the nation to review whether to fully join PSI (South Korea had observer status at the time). Lee Seo-hang of IFANS stated, "It is right for us to declare our official and open support to PSI, and expand our participation step-by-step because countering weapons of mass destruction is a universal value we should try to uphold."[71] In March 2009, Foreign Minister Yu Myung-hwan told reporters that South Korea was considering adopting all of the PSI initiatives because of North Korea's planned missile launch.[72]

Following North Korea's long-range missile launch in 2009, South Korea (in a controversial move) formally announced that it had informed the United States and other allies of its intention to join PSI as a full member. While North Korea called the move "a declaration of war,"[73] American officials reportedly welcomed the decision.[74] On May 26, 2009, South Korea formally joined PSI as a full member. The move, which was delayed for several weeks, became inevitable after North Korea tested a nuclear device that same month.[75] Predictably, North Korea responded that it would take "immediate, strong military measures" if South Korea stopped and searched any of its ships suspected of transferring WMD-related materials.[76] In its first official act as a member of PSI, South Korea dispatched Lee Chang-geun to PSI's European Regional Operational Experts Group meeting in Poland in June 2009.[77]

CAN THE ROK GOVERNMENT PAY FOR NEEDED CAPABILITIES?

Thus far in this chapter I have addressed some of the key threats that North Korea continues to pose for planners and policy makers in Seoul as Lee Myung-bak looks ahead to challenges for national defense in coming years. But if South Korea is to truly be self-reliant in its national defense in coming years, it must also initiate the programs and policies addressed in this chapter, among others. The difficulty here is that it will be an expensive effort that is likely to put a severe strain on the South Korean economy, which is already experiencing difficulties.

President Lee has addressed two global issues that are having a profound effect on the South Korean economy—soaring oil prices and worldwide crop shortages. While on a visit to the city of Pusan during July 2008, Lee stated, "The economy is heavily dependent on exports. Therefore, these factors make it challenging for the government to find the right solutions. But we are people who tend to become strong and united when times are extremely tough."[78] The effects of rising fuel and food prices have already had an impact on the South Korean military. In fact, according to press reports in July 2008, the South Korean military was forced to reduce exercises to save energy. Flight training hours for pilots were reduced with some of the training being made up for on simulators, the army planned to decrease its field training exercises using tactical vehicles by 30 percent, and the navy planned cuts of 27 percent of its training, to include slowing down its vessels' speeds while training at sea.[79]

There is also likely to be a direct impact on another important issue for South Korea's military forces, "Defense Reform 2020," which is Seoul's transformation plan to upgrade and modernize its forces to prepare for independent national defense capabilities. According to press accounts, the transformation plan, set to be finished by 2020, may end up undergoing intense revision. Reportedly, the primary reason for the reform package's drastic overhaul is budget shortfalls, according to many military experts and defense officials in South Korea. Some experts have predicted a further decrease in the plan's defense expenditures, but there are other ramifications for the budgetary problems inherent in Seoul's current military transformation plan. First, the finish date may end up getting pushed back to 2025. Second, as discussed earlier, many authorities assess the current schedule for systems acquisition and troop cuts as inadequate to account for North Korea's asymmetric capabilities. And third (and perhaps most important), many military experts also conclude that the defense reform did not include required arms procurement plans and security measures for Seoul's transition to independent wartime operational control of its forces, originally scheduled to occur in 2012.[80]

The South Korean military has begun to unveil the basic changes to the previous government's reform plan. President Lee Myung-bak instructed a newly formed presidential security panel that "there should be changes to military operation and weapons systems," at a meeting of the Commission for National Security Review in May 2010. Lee also urged the panel to revise the Defense Reform 2020 by reassessing the existing security situation.[81] Reportedly, the military will slow down troop reductions over the next decade because of budget shortfalls and the continuing North Korean threat. The military now intends to take a more pragmatic approach by also planning to defend against the North Korean nuclear threat and to initiate troop cuts only after weapon systems have been brought on line that will make up for the decrease in manpower.[82] One only has to look at the massive troop cuts proposed under Roh administration to understand why the changes are likely to be initiated (see figure 20).

Another aspect of manpower issues under the Roh administration was the initiative to cut conscripts' military service period by six months for the army and navy by 2014. The air force service period was projected to be cut by eight months. Dubbed the Vision 2030 2+5 Strategy, Roh was warned by the state-sponsored Korea Institute for Defense Analyses that the cuts in service time were simply not feasible. Roh pushed ahead with the initiative anyway in a plan that Representative Kim Song-hoi of the National Assembly (who also reiterated the Korea Institute for Defense Analyses' warning) called a political tactic to gain support from young voters in the 2007 presidential elections. As a result, the navy and air force are reportedly already facing manpower shortages.[83]

The South Korean Military has had to overcome important budget issues in recent years. According to the South Korean press, sources in the Defense Ministry planned to cut its proposed budget for Defense Reform 2020 by 30 percent as of April 2009. The ministry planned to request procurement of more advanced Patriot missile defense systems and related early warning radars, but because of these programs' expenses, other important acquisitions, such as air tankers and UAVs, may end up being delayed. The ministry also planned to request that President Lee slow down previously planned troop reductions until acquisition efforts of high-tech systems can catch up and match the needed capabilities.[84]

FIGURE 20. *Projected Troops Cuts from Transformation 2020*

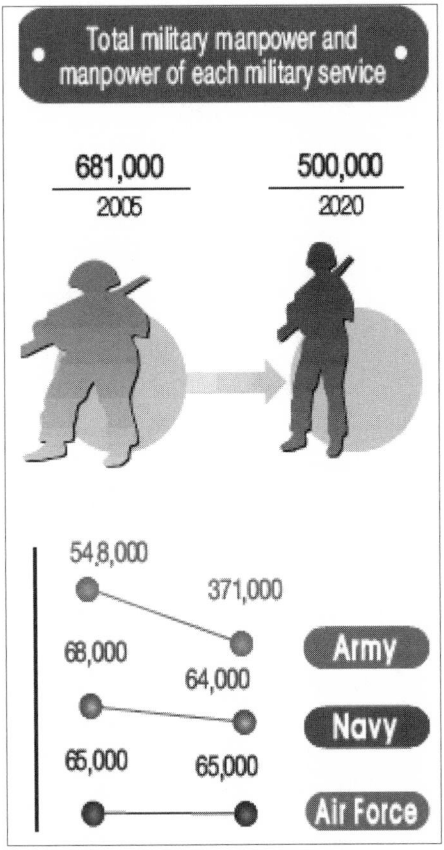

Source: Ministry of National Defense, Republic of Korea, "Defense White Paper," 2006.

The budget cuts planned caused some controversy within the government. During September 2009, the Ministry of National Defense reported that it planned to submit a 3.8 percent increase for spending the following year, or the smallest increase in defense expenditures since 1999. The surprisingly small increase in defense spending was reportedly due to economic difficulties in South Korea.[85] The Ministry of National Defense had earlier planned to submit a budget increase of 7.9 percent. In fact, the smaller budget request was said to have been suggested to the Blue House by Vice Minister Chang Soo-man, who is said to have gone over the head of the outgoing minister Lee Sang-hee. According to sources in the South

Korean press, Lee responded by writing a letter to presidential chief of staff Chung Chung-kil and others in which he urged the Blue House to accept the original version of the budget proposal (7.9 percent), saying budget cuts would dampen the ministry's efforts to strengthen defense capabilities and would send the wrong message to North Korea.[86]

To exacerbate issues related to wartime operational control and the transition of ROK and U.S. forces on the Korean Peninsula in coming years, South Korean Defense Ministry sources project an increase in the ROK-subsidized planned costs of relocating U.S. bases and American forces near the DMZ and in Seoul to a hub at Camp Humphreys (which was included in a Land Partnership Program, a trade of U.S. bases in the Western corridor for land expansion at Humphreys).[87] These important issues are related to the transformation of ROK forces, and I will discuss how the issues of defense reform and base relocation will impact the planned disestablishment of Combined Forces Command and the establishment of two separate wartime operational commands later in this chapter.

KEY FISCAL ISSUES AFFECTING THE IMMEDIATE FUTURE OF THE ROK-U.S. MILITARY ALLIANCE

Two issues are on the agenda right now that affect the immediate future of the ROK-U.S. military alliance—burden sharing and base relocation. Burden sharing has been a major source of contention since 2007, starting under the Roh Moo-hyun administration and into the Lee Myung-bak administration. The most important aspect of this issue is the non-personnel stationing costs (NPSC) for U.S. troops stationed in South Korea. In 2007, Seoul's contribution to the Special Measures Agreement (which covers these costs) represented only 41 percent of the NPSC. That year, then-commander of USFK General Bell stated that this percentage fell far short of an even cost-sharing agreement between allies, which required a 50 percent NPSC contribution from both allies.[88] These costs are typically used to pay for important alliance maintenance issues relating to the stationing of American troops in Korea such as labor costs for South Korean employees of USFK, the purchase of logistics and supplies, and the construction of military facilities. Seoul's failure to make what many consider to be a fair contribution to these costs (in an era when U.S. forces are already dangerously stretched all over the world) could lead to dangerous cuts in force and military base maintenance.[89]

During July 2008, officials from the U.S. Department of Defense and the ROK Ministry of National Defense met in Washington and held talks (called the Security Policy Initiative) to discuss a variety of issues, including burden sharing.[90] But in the end, South Korean and U.S. officials were unable to narrow their differences over how to share joint defense costs related to maintaining U.S. troops on the Korean Peninsula. During the talks, American officials again called on South Korea to pay more toward the NPSC and bring them in line with Seoul's growing economy and increased responsibility for national defense. Officials from Seoul, however, responded that their government wanted to provide military equipment and materials to the U.S. military instead of offering host nation funds in cash.[91]

As officials from the United States and South Korea prepared to meet and hold talks on cost-sharing issues in August 2008, the subject of fifty-fifty cost sharing for NPSC remained an issue of contention.[92] The meeting did not produce results that were equitable to both allies. Washington asked Seoul to pay 6.6–14.5 percent more in 2009, but South Korean officials countered that they were looking at a possible raise to a maximum 2.5 percent, equal to the 2007 domestic inflation rate. Washington also asked Seoul to increase its portion of the cost to 50 percent on a long-term basis, but South Korean officials countered to setting Seoul's share at an "adequate and reasonable" level and to change the cost-sharing method from paying one lump sum to sending materials on a case-by-case basis (once again referring to part of Seoul's offer in July 2008). Talks continued, but the issue remained difficult for the two allies to reach an agreement.[93] South Korea's share for 2008 accounted for W741.5 billion (US$1=W1,082 at the time). If boosted to a 6.6 percent raise, Seoul's share would increase to W790.4 billion, and with a 14.5 percent hike to W849 billion.[94]

During talks held in September 2008, South Korea's representative, Cho Byung-je, and his U.S. counterpart, Jackson McDonald, were still unable to reach a compromise. Seoul's position at this time was that the methodology used for computing the fiscal formula should be changed.[95] Cooperation and compromise continued between the two countries, and following the Fortieth Security Consultative Meeting between the U.S. and ROK defense chiefs, they arrived at an agreement on transfer of war reserves, which is an important military preparedness issue.[96] Talks held in October 2008, however, still failed to produce results. In these talks, the United States continued to ask for a 14.5 percent increase while the South Koreans wanted a 3 percent (or less) hike.[97]

In December, after five rounds of talks since July 2008, South Korea and the United States reached an agreement that Seoul would pay W760 billon for the cost of U.S. troops stationed in Korea. Seoul will increase its share each year, but the annual hike rate will be capped at 4 percent.[98] Seoul agreed to increase its share each year in accordance with the consumer price index until 2013 (the agreement runs from 2009–13).[99] The 2009–13 budget means that Seoul's share of funding will average out to around 47–48.5 percent during the span of the agreement. Only the 2009 number of 47 percent is reliable, with the other years fluctuating slightly because of the various factors in the formula. But the bottom line is that it still leaves South Korea paying slightly less than half of the costs. On January 15, 2009, ROK foreign minister Yu Myung-hwan and U.S. ambassador to South Korea Kathleen Stephens formally signed the deal. USFK commander General Sharp was present at the ceremony. Under the deal, South Korea will also construct 30 percent of new facilities in 2009, 60 percent in 2010, and 100 percent in 2011.[100] The W760 billion averaged out to about $691.5 million based on the 2008 average exchange rate.[101] Ambassador Stephens stated at the time that "this agreement supports the efforts of both of our nations to defend the Republic of Korea for years to come. . . ."[102]

I earlier compared South Korea's policy and acquisition of missile defense systems to that of Japan. I believe it is also useful to refer to the Japanese model when it comes to the issue of burden sharing. If one looks at NPSC costs, the percentage of what Japan pays as compared to South Korea is significantly higher.[103] Indeed, as the Japan-U.S. military alliance continues to transition, more than eight thousand of the eighteen thousand U.S. Marines currently in Okinawa will move to Guam. Tokyo has agreed to pay a significant portion of these costs.[104] The Marines are expected to relocate by 2014, and of the estimated $10.27 billion cost of the facilities and infrastructure development for the III Marine Expeditionary Force, Japan will pay $6.09 billion.[105]

Another important issue that certainly has fiscal ramifications for the United States and South Korea is that of base relocation. Under the Roh administration, the time line for consolidation of U.S. Army forces from several small bases and such large compounds as Yongsan (in Seoul) and Camp Casey (in Tongducheon) to one hub at Camp Humphreys (near Pyongtaek) was pushed back to 2012.[106] If one compares where the American bases were located in 2006 (as shown in figure 21) to their final projected locations, the U.S. troop "footprint" will be considerably smaller. Many of the small bases have been shut down already. But the relocation has run into numerous problems, not least of which is a continuing trend of cost overruns. According to press reports, the head of the U.S. base relocation office at the Ministry of National Defense, Maj. Gen. Park Byoung-hee, stated in August 2008, "The sides are working to set the target year and to determine the exact cost of the project, but there still remains a difference of opinion on several issues."[107] Unnamed officials in Seoul say the ongoing project is likely to be delayed (again) for at least a few months.[108]

The United States had reportedly asked for a delay until 2016 (for complete relocation of all bases), citing budgetary reasons.[109] It has also asked to move the Yongsan garrison to Camp Humphreys by the end of 2014 and to move the Second Infantry Division by the first half of 2016.[110] By April 2009, Washington and Seoul had come close to an agreement. It appears that the plan will be for Yongsan's U.S. Army garrison to relocate by 2014 and the Second Infantry Division by 2015 (though there are still some issues to be worked out).[111] Talks are likely to continue as these dates remain in a state of flux. In an interview with the press in March 2010, General Sharp stated that it could take five or six years before U.S. troops move to the planned consolidated military base south of the Han River.[112] This problem (along with the issue of ROK forces' transformation simply not meeting either the time lines or the capabilities requirements set during the Roh administration) will continue to have an impact on the CFC's planned disestablishment and the corresponding establishment of two separate ROK and U.S. war-fighting commands.

WARTIME OPERATIONAL CONTROL:
THE RIGHT MOVE AT THE RIGHT TIME?

The earlier issues discussed all have direct relevance to and are also directly tied in with perhaps the most sensitive question discussed in this chapter: that of wartime operational control. According to an agreement reached between Secretary Gates and Minister Kim in 2007, CFC was to be disestablished and the ROK and

FIGURE 21. *Projected Relocation of U.S. Bases in South Korea*

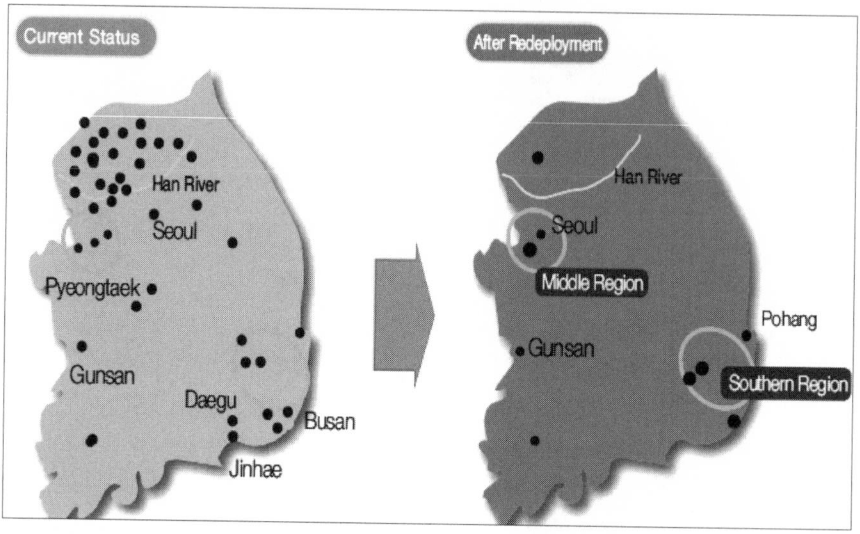

Source: Ministry of National Defense, Republic of Korea, "Defense White Paper," 2006.

U.S. militaries on the Korean Peninsula would continue to function as allies and have separate wartime operational commands effective on April 17, 2012.[113] The issue of ROK and U.S. forces fighting a conflict with North Korea under two separate military commands has been a huge source of contention, with most retired ROK military officials and generals being openly critical of the change in wartime OPCON because they believe it is both premature and dangerous to the security of South Korea.[114] Moreover, the majority of South Koreans reportedly believe that President Roh made the wrong move at the wrong time for ROK security. As Cheon Seong-whun, a scholar at the Korea Institute for National Unification, has said, "Simply because the North Korean military is most delighted to see the OP-CON transfer and the CFC dissolution, the decision is worthy of delay."[115] During the early months of 2008, U.S. officials reportedly said that ROK forces were making progress in C⁴I improvements that would be necessary in order to operate under separate wartime commands beginning in 2012. But other officials admitted that the South Korean R & D budget increased only nominally as compared to budgets of the three previous years.[116] Indeed, tough financial times ahead may mean more of the same in the future.

Other South Koreans have publicly stated that the transfer of wartime OPCON in 2012 was too soon. In February 2010, the majority party leader in the ROK National Assembly, Chung Mong-joon, stated, "A review would not be easy considering the transfer was a country-to-country pledge, but it may be possible even under the current agreement as there is a clause for assessing the transfer."[117] During the same month, Yeom Wan-kyun, the head of the U.S. policy bureau at the Ministry of National Defense, disclosed to the press that the issue of OPCON transfer was "subject to bilateral discussion over the mid to long term period."[118] And in an important statement that received a great deal of attention, Defense Minister Kim Tae-young told the ROK National Assembly that the OPCON transfer issue was being addressed at both the military level and the national level.[119]

Despite the outcry from many in South Korea, particularly now that the left-of-center government is no longer in power, several American officials have stated definitively that postponing the date for separate war-fighting commands (and ending the CFC's successful tenure) is simply not an option. The outgoing ambassador to South Korea, Alexander Vershbow, in December 2007 commented, "As I said, the strategic transition plan is already agreed upon and it is being implemented."[120] Ambassador Vershbow's words were supported in a statement from Commander of USFK General Sharp, who according to press sources said in 2009, "On the OPCON transfer, we are on track. We will be prepared for 17 April 2012. By 2012, the Republic of Korea military leadership will be ready to take over."[121] In congressional testimony he gave in March 2010, General Sharp also remarked that delaying OPCON transfer would send the wrong message to the North Koreans.[122] In my view this push was a big mistake. While complete self-reliance and its own separate wartime operational control may seem the right thing to do in the long run, it will quite simply be impossible to realistically complete all the initiatives important for assuming wartime OPCON by 2012 or to have anything close to a self-reliant military by that time. The North Koreans can interpret, and in fact would be likely to interpret, that a divided command signals a lessening of the U.S. defense commitment to South Korea. In addition, the vulnerabilities created by a change in wartime OPCON before ROK forces have needed capabilities present a lesser, not greater, deterrent to North Korea.

During his campaign for the presidency, Lee's aides hinted that he might have been considering a proposal to the United States that would push back the CFC's dismantlement for two or three years unless North Korea discarded its nuclear weapons programs.[123] Kim Tae-woo, a researcher at the Korean Institute for Defense Analyses, recently said, "Lee has been seeking to take a more cautious position on the wartime operational control transfer." He further commented, "Now we must see whether Lee can convince the U.S. to change its mind, though it seems to be a long shot at the moment."[124] The South Korean public seems to support a delay in Wartime OPCON transfer. In a poll taken during April 2010 by the Korean Institute for Defense Analyses, 48.8 percent favored delaying the transfer, while only 35.8 percent supported proceeding as planned.[125] Members of the National Assembly support pushing back the date for transferring wartime OPCON. Not the least among them is Kim Hak-song, the current chairman (2010) of the eighteenth ROK National Assembly's National Defense Committee. Kim is opposed to OP-CON transfer before North Korean denuclearization.[126]

Other important issues, in my view, must be considered before disestablishing the CFC and having the United States and South Korea assume separate wartime operational control of their forces. The first point is unity of command. The loss of a unified command (which is what exists today) is likely to curtail the high degree of coordination that currently exists between ROK and U.S. forces. It is also likely to lead to higher casualties, including among South Korean civilians. The other issue is political. The change in wartime OPCON could lead to misperceptions about the ability of the ROK military to conduct a war with the north on its own, and in the United States it could also lead to reduced congressional and public support for a large-scale presence of U.S. troops on the Korean Peninsula.[127] Any force reduction would be extremely dangerous for South Korea's security and stability and would not bode well for regional security as a whole, particularly given the fact that some U.S. senators have recently shown an impatience with the alliance, perhaps because of U.S. obligations elsewhere.[128]

If one examines the command relationship as it exists today, it shows a seamless, transparent chain of command that extends from two separate national command authorities (NCA) in Washington and Seoul. In wartime—and when the NCA in Seoul agrees to it (the South Korean president is the final authority), based on the advice of the minister of national defense and of the Joint Chiefs—desig-

FIGURE 22. *Current Wartime Command Relationships: ROK-U.S. Forces*

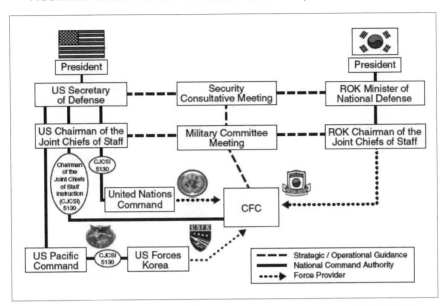

Source: Lt. Gen. Stephen G. Wood, USAF, and Maj. Christopher A. Johnson, DM, USAF, "The Transformation of Air Forces on the Korean Peninsula," *Air and Space Power Journal* 22, no. 3 (Fall 2008), http://www.airpower.maxwell.af.mil/airchronicles/apj/apj08/fal08/wood.html.
Note: CJCSI stands for "Chairman, Joint Chiefs of Staff Instruction."

nated ROK forces chop to the CFC commander. In turn, the CFC commander then answers to both the U.S. and the South Korean NCAs and carries out their strategic decisions in command of ROK and U.S. forces as they carry out war-fighting operations under a unified, combined force (see figure 22).

Examining the way command relationships are projected to change (see figure 23), during wartime ROK forces will no longer chop to CFC, for it will no longer exist. Instead, two separate war-fighting commands will exist—U.S. Korea Command (USKORCOM) for the United States and Joint Forces Command (KJFC) for South Korea (the name for the South Korean Command is likely to change). Unity of command will no longer exist, and forces will be fighting in the restricted terrain of the Korean Peninsula answering to two separate NCAs.

Figure 24 shows the current construct of CFC and its component commands. In the current framework, each component command contains both American and South Korean military forces, fighting together (and planning for future military

FIGURE 23. *Projected Wartime Command Relationships*

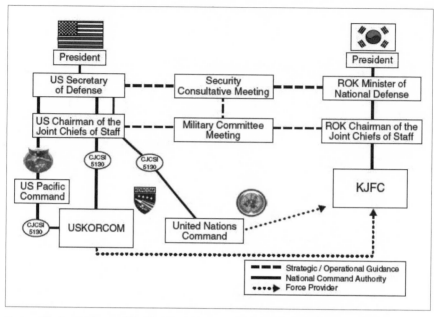

Source: Wood and Johnson, "The Transformation of Air Forces on the Korean Peninsula."

operations in a seamless, combined environment). U.S. commanders do not domi-
nate this structure. In fact, if one looks at the flags on figure 24 that identify the
country of the component commander, the majority of component commands (including the largest, the Ground Component Command) are commanded by South
Korean general officers. This structure is projected to change dramatically when
CFC is disestablished.

As shown in figure 25, both U.S. and South Korean forces will be organized to
fight separately. This arrangement will create difficulties in command and control
of forces, particularly in the case of South Korea. Its air force is not projected to
have the capabilities necessary to fight a large-scale war on its own, its C⁴I capabilities are not yet fully developed, and its navy is still building toward the maritime sealift and antimissile capabilities that it will need in a fight with North Korea.
Gen. Walter Sharp has reaffirmed that the United States plans to provide stronger
naval and air support to South Korea following the CFC's disestablishment.[129] In a
speech at the 2009 Korean-American Association, General Sharp announced that

FIGURE 24. *Current Wartime Structure of ROK-U.S. Military Forces*

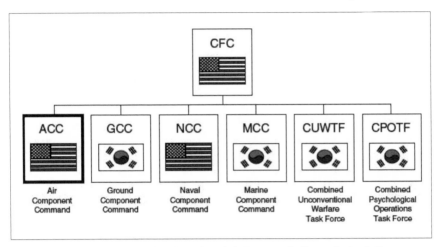

Source: Wood and Johnson, "The Transformation of Air Forces on the Korean Peninsula."

there will be a combined air force command following the CFC's dissolution. Reportedly, a plan is also being drawn up for a combined intelligence group after the CFC is terminated.[130] Sources in the South Korean press have revealed that the United States will continue to lead air operations (both ROK and U.S.) after the projected wartime OPCON change.[131] U.S. forces will also lead combined amphibious operations.[132] Command and control for these entities is likely still being coordinated as the ROK and U.S. forces will be commanded separately above the component level. As shown in figure 25, much of what is currently combined operations and planning is projected to become coordination via boards, bureaus, coordination centers, and cells. Unity of command will then vanish, and the battlefield environment will become more complicated.

According to a Ministry of National Defense press release, as the two allies build toward the disestablishment of CFC many initiatives will occur. The ROK JCS will hold quarterly reviews to assess 114 tasks in six fields: the "establishment of theater combat command systems, a ROK-U.S. military cooperation system, operational plans, command execution systems, joint exercises and basis for the transfer of OPCON." The ROK JCS plans to build a new command headquarters by 2011 and will establish a military consultation group at the Camp Humphreys garrison once U.S. forces are relocated there. Construction on the new ROK JCS command headquarters began in March 2010.[133] Consultative bodies that will replace much of the CFC infrastructure are planned for both peacetime and wartime. There will also be a joint (combined) crisis management system, though its infrastructure and makeup are unclear.

Of course, this entire system will be less streamlined than what has existed under CFC. Command and control will also be much more of a challenge. The two separate (ROK and U.S.) theater commands will be independent of each other but will work together within a joint defense system.

According to the press release, air operations and at least some intelligence operations will remain combined as they are under the CFC, though the structure and command of these extremely important elements continues to be worked out. (The Americans are likely to command these elements, as the ROK military simply will not have the capabilities to do so.)[134] Amphibious operations are also scheduled to be conducted in a combined environment—likely because the ROK Marine Corps and Navy simply lack certain capabilities—as are operations for the recovery of WMDs (both under U.S. command). Aside from these exceptions, as a press report articulates, "the Korea Command will control operations of U.S. forces in Korea, U.S. reinforcements and some United Nations troops."[135]

The USFK commander discussed many of the related key issues in a speech he gave on April 5, 2010.

> The ROK and the U.S. have agreed upon which organizations will report to the ROK Joint Chiefs of Staff and which will retain a U.S. headquarters. Some, like the Ground Operations Command will report to the ROK JCS. For some special mission capabilities, the U.S. will continue to serve as the lead headquarters in order to optimize capabilities. Additionally, appropriate boards, centers and cells will serve as coordination elements at all levels of Alliance military efforts.

General Sharp discussed the relationship of the all-important United Nations Command in the future infrastructure when he said, "There is some work left to be done on the exact command relationship of the United Nations Command, but KORCOM will be a supporting command to the ROK JCS in accordance with

FIGURE 25. *Projected Wartime Structure of ROK-U.S. Military Forces*

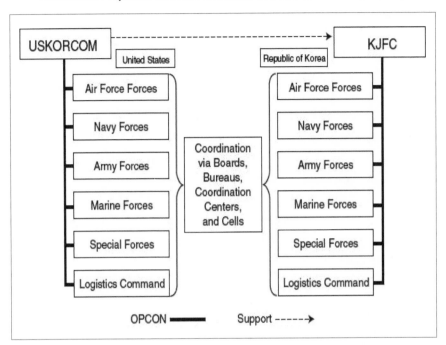

Source: Wood and Johnson, "The Transformation of Air Forces on the Korean Peninsula."
Note: ROKAF and USKORCOM air force components are scheduled to remain in a "Combined Air Component."

Joint doctrine. KORCOM will maintain OPCON over US Forces and be a force provider to the ROK JCS."[136]

Ultimately, all the issues addressed in this chapter are tied into the wartime OPCON. South Korea is facing tough economic times. Thus, its government is unlikely to be able to fund many of the important initiatives that are necessary to implement independent capabilities. These capabilities were not planned for responsibly in the previous ROK presidential administration, which unwisely downplayed the North Korean threat. The same fiscal concerns facing ROK military acquisition programs also impact Seoul's ability to complete infrastructure initiatives associated with moving U.S. forces from key locations in the ROK to the major hub at Camp Humphreys. USFK had planned to transform into Korea Command as approved by U.S. national authorities beginning in 2010 and to begin transferring units to Camp Humphreys as barracks and other facilities are built.[137] Any delays in any part of the process could cause problems. Because all of these issues are tied together and because plans simply do not seem to be moving on schedule, ideally what would happen is that the United States would sacrifice a few years of OP-CON transfer delay for completion of important initiatives. In fact, some officials in the South Korean government have suggested this compromise is what could happen.[138] It would also give the ROK military time to build up its capabilities in a more realistic, pragmatic manner and allow it to more effectively face the northern threat.

And then, of course, when one is considering wartime OPCON, the most important reason for a ROK-U.S. military alliance and a strong U.S. troop presence on the Korean Peninsula is the ongoing and menacing presence of a belligerent North Korean military with asymmetric capabilities. As Lee Jong-gu, the former head of the Korea Retired Generals and Admirals Association, said in an interview with the South Korean press,

> We must consider 'when,' not 'under what conditions,' when dealing with the transfer of wartime operational command. North Korea is highly unlikely to abandon its nuclear weapons and South Korea is not expected to equip itself with a military strong enough to deter North Korea's provocations by 2012. It is unreasonable to set a deadline for the transfer of wartime operational command, which is directly related to South Korea's security, when North Korea is heightening its nuclear threat.[139]

Following the nuclear test that North Korea conducted in May of 2009, many retired generals and conservative members of the National Assembly echoed the general's assessments and called for a review of the date of 2012 as a reasonable time frame for disestablishment of CFC.[140]

THINKING THE UNTHINKABLE: PREPARING FOR NORTH KOREAN COLLAPSE

Earlier in this chapter, I discussed some of North Korea's key military capabilities that present a significant and immediate threat to the stability and security of South Korea. But as I have also discussed in chapter 5, North Korea has the potential to collapse, implode, explode, or perhaps even fall into a state of anarchy because of concerns related to its government, economy, society, and the Kim Chong-il succession process. Planning for these various scenarios is just as important as planning for a conventional force-on-force conflict between North and South Korea.

By September 2008, after seven months in office, the Lee Myung-bak administration still had yet to formally implement its own emergency manual for contingencies. At that time it continued to use documents left over (which most agree were sadly lacking and unrealistic) from the Roh Moo-hyun administration.[141] Key in this discussion is the fact that Operations Plan (OPLAN) 5029 had been changed to a Contingency Plan (CONPLAN) during the Roh administration. Contingency plans are normally far less detailed, particularly when it comes to such important issues as the deployment of forces from the United States to the Korean Peninsula, command and control, and logistics. The original OPLAN 5029 dealt with the military action that ROK and U.S. combined forces would take should a variety of events occur. Various contingencies reportedly contained in the plan included the collapse of the North Korean regime, a mass exodus of refugees, natural disasters, a "civil" war in North Korea, a palace coup, and other events short of a force-on-force conflict.[142] In 2005 the Roh administration announced the termination of OPLAN 5029 in a statement that said in part, "We have terminated the U.S.-South Korea Combined Forces Command's efforts to map out a plan, code named 5029, because the plan could be a serious obstacle to exercising Korea's sovereignty."[143] The move was announced by the ROK National Security Council (which is very unusual) and was apparently made with little to no consultation with military officials from either South Korea or the United States. OPLAN 5029 was later converted to a CONPLAN that was much more abstract in nature and left many questions about specific details, such as troop numbers and command and control, unanswered.[144]

During September 2008, a high-ranking official from Seoul reportedly visited Washington for talks on converting CONPLAN 5029 back to an OPLAN that would be more realistic. An unnamed official in Seoul remarked, "Right after the inauguration of the Lee Myung-bak administration, the government worked on transforming Concept Plan 5029 to OPLAN 5029, which includes a military capability operation plan."[145] The Lee government was said to be working on a new version of the plan by September 2008 that included possible diplomatic measures with neighboring states.[146] Rumors about Kim Chong-il's health issues may have triggered more intense pressure for both Washington and Seoul to renew efforts at converting 5029 back to an OPLAN, though the rewrite is likely to have structural changes because of the CFC's projected disestablishment in coming years.[147] Control of North Korea's nuclear and missile facilities in the case of a collapse (or other catastrophic scenario) are reportedly among the key concerns for planning.[148] In plans being drawn up, the United States will reportedly take the lead in taking control of North Korea's WMD.[149]

Secretary of Defense Robert Gates was said to have thrown his weight behind changing CONPLAN 5029 back to an OPLAN (the designation 5029 may change as the plan evolves). Gates apparently also said that the United States would provide fighting power to South Korea in order to assist its ally in implementing the plan.[150] The United States supports setting up a detailed plan for using military forces in the case of a North Korean collapse, according to press sources, and the move came at the Military Committee Meeting between the U.S. and ROK heads of the Joint Chiefs of Staff during October 2008.[151] U.S. Forces Japan (USFJ) and Japanese Self-Defense Forces have also reviewed the plans for a joint operation in case of an emergency on the Korean Peninsula. Civilian airports and harbors that would be used, the admission and transport of wounded troops, and a study of flight restrictions are among the issues that are said to have undergone evaluation.[152]

In February 2009, Gen. Walter Sharp announced at a press conference that "we have plans that take a look at both an all-out attack from North Korea and instability in North Korea. Instability going from the entire range of humanitarian disaster and all the way up to major civil war and potential loose nuclear weapons. . . ."[153] According to an unnamed South Korean government source, President Lee Myung-bak asked the CFC to finalize OPLAN 5029 (changing it back from a CONPLAN to an OPLAN) by April 30, 2009.[154] Making military plans more realistic is an important step, but it will be a difficult road ahead as CFC's structure converts to two separate war-fighting commands in coming years. Sources in the South Korean press revealed that a group of South Korean and American officials met in Hawaii during August 2009 to address plans for all possible contingencies that could occur in North Korea. The two sides are said to have agreed on a variety of issues, including seeking cooperation from China and combining ROK and U.S.

forces to conduct operations.[155] On November 1, 2009, the South Korean press disclosed that South Korea and the United States had completed joint action plans to respond to different contingencies in North Korea, including all of those discussed (quoting an unnamed South Korean government official).[156] Other sources revealed that by early 2010, massive revisions had been made with plans for a more active role to be played by several agencies.[157]

Another key concern in the case of planning for a potential North Korean collapse is working with China. Beijing is Pyongyang's lone remaining real ally and would need to be consulted if U.S. and South Korean troops were to deploy into North Korea. According to reports citing an unnamed Bush administration official, the Chinese and Americans quietly held talks during the fall of 2008 about what to do in the case of catastrophic scenarios in North Korea. The unnamed official said that the Chinese were reluctant to admit anything about the discussions publicly because of their relationship with North Korea.[158] But other unnamed U.S. officials have said the Chinese have been reluctant to talk about specific scenarios and about how to react and work with South Korea and the U.S. in the case of a collapse in North Korea. Reportedly, the Chinese fear that planning for such events could unnerve North Korean leaders and present an image to the outside world that China is conspiring against the often paranoid regime.[159] China is likely unwilling to admit that quiet discussions have even occurred with Washington for these reasons.

According to a "Key Points Memo" released by the Center for Strategic and International Studies summarizing a conference held with Chinese scholars October 12–13, 2009, several issues are important to Beijing. Based on the discussions at the conference, it appears the Chinese may be concerned about how North Korea would perceive open discussions between China and the United States regarding DPRK regime security. One Chinese general remarked that if ROK forces crossed the thirty-eighth parallel, China would be compelled to intervene militarily. The memo also addressed the issue of mutual suspicion between South Korea and China, with Seoul fearing China would want to keep North Korea intact as a separate state (even after collapse) and the Chinese fearing that Seoul would try to seize the opportunity presented by instability to reunify the peninsula without involving the international community.[160]

Nevertheless, if Washington and Beijing have at least broached the subject of North Korea's future, it is a step in the right direction and will hopefully help to prevent regional confusion or even conflict in the event of a North Korean collapse or implosion. To date, it remains unconfirmed as to whether any formal discussions have occurred between officials. China scholar Dr. Larry Wortzel makes it clear in a 2009 Strategic Studies Institute book that based on his discussions with Chinese military officers, it appears the PLA expects to be consulted before any contingency operation is put into effect. Dr. Wortzel also concludes the PLA would be reluctant to engage in contingency planning because of the state of PRC–North Korean relations.[161]

CONCLUSIONS

Both the United States and South Korea can do important things to improve the ROK-U.S. military alliance. I will boil them down to four basic pillars of cooperation that, in my view, will enhance the current status quo and then offer some suggestions that are likely to be force-enhancing initiatives as the alliance looks to the future challenges it will be facing in coming years.

In previous work I have addressed the four basic pillars of cooperation that the South Korean government can look to both domestically and with the United States as it confronts the threat of a rogue state to the north and the tough fiscal realities it will continue to face because of challenging economic times.[162] The first pillar is closer technological cooperation, which should involve bigger, more robust, longer-range combat, communications and intelligence systems. Joint government and business ventures must be initiated that will enable quality-focused programs to upgrade defense capabilities and surpass threat systems while at the same time downplaying vulnerabilities that are likely to occur as the CFC is dissolved. The second pillar, closer intellectual cooperation, focuses on a renewed and continuing commitment to combined doctrine, training, and education. Third, South Korea will see closer ideological cooperation and a newfound commitment to democracy, human rights, and free market economies as it reaffirms its alliance with the United States after facing tough times under the previous administration in the Blue House. The final and perhaps most important pillar is a fiscal commitment to support cooperation on all the fronts listed above. It can be accomplished through defense appropriations that enable realistic, threat-based acquisition of important systems that will be needed for truly independent national defense capabilities.

As South Korea looks to improve its national defense, the United States can also play a major role as a strong supporting ally. By allowing the ROK government time to build up its capabilities and improve its forces—by delaying the implementation of a change to wartime OPCON—Washington will prove its support for its loyal military ally and seventh-largest trading partner.[163] In fact, Washington has now agreed to do just that. In June 2010, on the sidelines of the G-20 conference of world leaders held in Toronto, Canada, Presidents Lee Myung-bak and Barack Obama agreed to delay the transfer of wartime OPCON to December 1, 2015. While exact details of the new transition—including the adjustment of C⁴I, other key military systems, and upcoming exercises are to be worked out as the delay is implemented—the plan will give the South Korean military more time to prepare for roles and missions, and to conduct relevant acquisition of systems than the old date of 2012 would have allowed. Both South Korean and U.S. analysts, policymakers, and military experts have hailed the move. Predictably, only the Far Left in Korea (largely supporters of former President Roh Moo-hyun) have criticized the three-year delay.[164] To anyone who has done a thorough analysis of current correlation of forces, opposing firepower ratios, or terrain-dominated strategy, it is obvious that South Korea's military will continue to need the help of the United States in meeting the North Korean threat. The tyranny of proximity dictates that one can hardly draw any other conclusion. As Lt. Gen. Edward Rice of USFJ remarked in 2008, "North Korea continues to be a regime that is not very transparent in terms of their capabilities and their intentions."[165] Thus, these two great nations—the United States and South Korea—must reinforce an alliance that will continue to contribute to the security of the Korean Peninsula and the stability of Northeast Asia as a whole.

CHAPTER SEVEN

Conclusion

North Korea's Threats to the
United States and Its Allies

P erhaps one of the biggest challenges for those who have an interest in the security and stability of the Korean Peninsula is the simple fact that many (including some who are Korean scholars) continue to downplay the multi-faceted threat that North Korea presents. The threat from North Korea's huge military, the threat from North Korea's WMD production and deployment, the threat from the same WMD issue as is the weapons are proliferated to volatile regions of the earth, and the threat from a Kim Chong-il regime with the potential for instability because of a tenuous succession process are all issues that, in order to be solved, may involve troops from many nations and, perhaps almost as daunting, monetary costs that could run into the hundreds of billions of dollars. Despite this, many scholars and pundits minimize North Korea's military threat to the region, dismiss its ongoing proliferation to dangerous states (often states that are enemies of the United States), and fail to understand how important planning for a North Korean collapse will be as we look to a future there that shows all the signs of being very bleak. Thus, this final analysis reviews the overall threats and solutions posed by the reclusive and defiant government in Pyongyang and examines possible end states for dealing with the DPRK.

EFFECTIVE DIPLOMACY: WHO HAS SHOWN
THE BEST TALENT AT USING IT?

Looking at the North Koreans' nuclear confrontation during the Bush administration, it is easy to see that they were extremely skilled at using diplomacy to advance their foreign policy agenda. Pyongyang's adroit use of diplomacy was not new, nor was its use of brinkmanship. North Korea had been able to use bluster, brinkmanship, and threats throughout its dealings with the Clinton administration.[1] What is so important about understanding North Korea's use of diplomacy is that its modus operandi has remained virtually the same since Pyongyang began dealing with the West. It did not change when North Korea desperately needed foreign food and energy aid during the mid- to late 1990s and opened up to NGOs.[2] North Korea's use of diplomacy certainly did not change during the Bush administration. As I have outlined in previous chapters, Pyongyang still tested long-range missiles and a nuclear weapon, conducted violent provocations along the DMZ and Northern Limit Line border areas, and engaged in rhetoric that can be considered nothing short of bombastic.[3]

What did change over a period of several years involving many North Korean issues was not only the players who dealt with North Korea from the outside—those in leadership positions changed several times in the United States, South Korea, and Japan—but also the policies in which those players engaged. The Sunshine Policy of the Kim Dae-jung administration in South Korea, and what I would describe as the same policy only on steroids under his successor, Roh Moo-hyun (the policy of Peace and Prosperity), was focused almost exclusively on engagement with North Korea. In short, it offered carrots but failed to utilize any sticks.[4] This policy abruptly ended when the Roh administration left power and Lee Myung-bak entered the Blue House in 2008.[5] President Lee's strategy demanded more transparency and reciprocity from the neighbor to the north, and Pyongyang's obvious negative reactions have been described in detail in this book. Nevertheless, one hopes President Lee (and his successor) stays the course and keeps his policy toward Pyongyang consistent.

The issue of diplomacy with the United States was different. While it is true that the North Korea policy changed definitively from the Clinton administration to the Bush administration, many policy shifts within both administrations likely created confusion in their dealings with North Korea and made it easier for Pyongyang to manipulate things in their favor. Not the least of these policy shifts occurred in February 2007, when the Bush administration eased up on pressure it had been applying to North Korea's illegal and illicit international dealings and began the long process of expecting North Korea to comply with agreements that, instead, were often broken or brushed aside.[6] From 2007 until the end of its term, the Bush administration put what pressure it could on the Japanese government in the hopes that Tokyo would work toward a peaceful solution to North Korea's nuclear question. But it also did not occur because Japan also went through a policy shift from one that was looking toward a closer relationship with Pyongyang to a much more hard-line approach that was focused on no concessions until the highly emotional issue of abducted citizens could be resolved to the satisfaction of the Japanese populace and government. The disclosure that North Korea had returned to Japan fake remains of citizens who had been previously kidnapped on Pyongyang's orders set Japan on the road of complete policy reversal, cemented its stance as the most hard-line member in the six-party talks, and created a firestorm with the Japanese populace.[7]

Through all the changes in democratic governments in South Korea, Japan, and the United States; through all the policy shifts that occurred within the administrations of these governments (for various reasons); and despite the many geopolitical shifts that occurred within the Northeast Asia region, North Korea's policy remained essentially the same. In fact, the individuals who formulated and implemented North Korean policy also remained the same. Pyongyang's ability to keep the same people in place and to set a policy without having to worry about internal pressures from its populace gave the government enormous advantages in dealing with its neighbors and the United States. That said, North Korea's foreign policy is neither complicated nor difficult to understand. It is also rather simple to assess what pressure points are the most effective for leveraging Pyongyang's behavior. Despite this knowledge, the key democracies that have dealt with North Korea since the nuclear confrontation first erupted in the early 1990s continue to change policies, tactics, and goals in their dealings with North Korea. As long as this fluctuation continues, Pyongyang will have the diplomatic advantage and will continue to gain concessions, intimidate its neighbors, proliferate WMD to rogue states, and maintain its nuclear program.

I would also add that no matter what direction Washington's North Korea policy goes in coming years, those advising the White House should keep in mind that the power brokers in Pyongyang will always use coercive diplomacy to gain an advantage. The Lee Myung-bak administration that came to power in South Korea in 2008 seems to grasp this fact very well, but the jury is still out as to whether those in the Obama administration will use this understanding when making their basic judgments for their policy decisions. Certainly there is much to be gained from examining past precedent. As Moon Soon-ho, a scholar at the Sejong Institute near Seoul, Korea, has said,

> When looking at the history of the US-ROK-DPRK relations, South Korea (ROK) and the U.S. have not been able to successfully apply coercive diplomacy to achieve their objectives. North Korea (DPRK), on the other hand, has effectively coerced these two allied nations. As North Korea's recent provocative military threats indicate, North Korea will continue to use coercive diplomacy as long as it finds its foundation in Songun, or military-first, politics. South Korea and the U.S. must come up with a different approach than they did in the past to deal with North Korea.[8]

HOW EFFECTIVE IS NORTH KOREA'S INFORMATIONAL INSTRUMENT OF POWER?

Undoubtedly North Korea's ability to control the information flow to its people has been challenged since the reclusive communist state was forced to open up to NGOs and UN-sponsored aid programs beginning in the mid-1990s.[9] Despite the many challenges Pyongyang faced, the North Koreans have cleverly adjusted. After many years of operating in North Korea, NGOs continue to have little contact with everyday North Koreans and minimal impact on North Korean society. Even today, NGOs and UN organizations keep running into successful North Korean roadblocks that prevent the groups from properly monitoring where their aid goes or from interacting with members of the North Korean populace any more than is absolutely necessary in the minds of the Pyongyang government.[10]

Today in North Korea almost no one, except members of the elite, has access to the Internet. This restriction includes college and university students. Except for elite citizens sanctioned by Kim Chong-il, North Koreans do not have access to foreign television or radio broadcasts, and they are not allowed to read foreign newspapers, journals, or books, except under the supervision of designated party members. Thus, quite literally, besides the small cadre of those whom Kim Chong-il and his inner circle trust, no one is allowed access to outside information. The people only see exactly what the government wants them to see. South Korea, meanwhile, has attempted to broadcast information into North Korea, and this effort has increased in recent years largely because of defector groups. Four defector-run radio stations that broadcast to the north have been formed since 2005. Surveys among defectors indicate 20 percent or more listened to foreign broadcasts.[11]

But most North Koreans remain ignorant to happenings in the outside world, and their government wants it that way. As Joseph Bermudez of Jane's Information Group articulates, "The average citizen within the DPRK has very little opportunity to access foreign or uncensored information." Bermudez further states, "To do so, and to be found out can result in extreme prison (i.e., detention camp) sentences."[12] In fact, the Committee to Protect Journalists, a nonprofit organization located in New York, named North Korea the "most censored country in the world" in 2006.[13] As Professor Andrei Lankov of Kookmin University in Seoul says of most North Korean citizens,

> They are terrified and isolated, have none of the rudimentary self-organization required to start a resistance and to a large extent are still unaware about any alternative to their mode of life (rumors about prosperous life outside North Korean borders are spreading, but only a minority of the North Koreans understand how backward and poor their society really is in comparison with its neighbors).[14]

It is no wonder that during the fall and winter of 2008 and into the spring of 2009, the North Korean government and military reacted with such force and speed when South Korean NGOs released leaflets (by balloon) into their country. The leaflets contained information about issues such as Kim Chong-il's health, dire conditions in the north, and South Korea's welcoming of refugees. They also encouraged North Koreans to rise up against their leader.[15]

North Korea's extremely effective use of controlling information and its paranoid control of everything that goes in and out of the country do not stop with its own people. One of the issues that made the six-party talks so difficult throughout the Bush administration was North Korea's lack of transparency. The information flow of documents, access to important sites, discussions with scientists and engineers, and just about any other way of gaining a true picture of North Korea's nuclear program were severely limited.[16] North Korea has never been open about its nuclear program. Whether during the Clinton administration, when Pyongyang hid a clandestine HEU program as the facilities at Yongbyon were frozen, or during the Bush administration, when Pyongyang denied proliferation to Syria despite overwhelming evidence, North Korea has managed to control information about its nuclear activities in ways that made it exceedingly difficult to advance talks toward a meaningful end state.[17] Future negotiators and policy makers would do well to keep this important lesson in mind.

NORTH KOREA'S MILITARY INSTRUMENT OF POWER:
THE EVOLVING THREAT

While North Korea continues to make the headlines in the international press when it conducts long-range missile tests, raises the stakes with its nuclear program, or conducts belligerent (and often what nonspecialists see as bizarre) acts of provocation with its neighbors, many analysts and in fact many people in both the United States and South Korea perceive the DPRK as nothing more than a paper tiger teetering on the brink of collapse.[18] In my view, this impression is mistaken. It is true that millions have starved to death in North Korea since the early 1990s and that food and fuel conditions there continue to be abysmal. But the very reasons for those conditions stem largely from Kim Chong-il and the elite's having diverted the country's best resources into maintaining the military, building up asymmetric weapons and capabilities, and pampering the country's small, select elite that keeps the government in power. The paradigms that exist in the West are widely different in North Korea; thus, those who would draw corollaries to those communist regimes that collapsed after the Cold War do not understand the many differences that exist in the social structure and government in East Asian nation-states.

What perhaps causes the most headaches for military planners and high-ranking defense officials in South Korea and the United States but receives little attention in the press or in academic circles are the evolving capabilities of the conventional North Korean military forces. These forces do not gain the attention that a long-range missile test or an underground nuclear test draws, yet they are easily the most immediate threat to the security and stability of the Korean Peninsula. As the commander of U.S. Forces in Korea stated in a speech given to a group of business leaders in Seoul, "North Korea has an old but very large military that is positioned in a very dangerous place, very close to the Republic of Korea." The general further commented on North Korea's formidable Special Operations Forces and their vast artillery forces when he observed, "They have a very large special operating force. It has the world's largest artillery force that is positioned as far south as possible and that can rain on Seoul today."[19] South Korean generals have made similar remarks repeatedly, and this is important.[20] Not only do they recognize that North Korea has gone to great expense and sacrifice to maintain its army (equipped with vintage Soviet equipment for the most part), but perhaps just as important (as General Sharp remarked), it has positioned its conventional military units so they can deploy and attack South Korea with little warning (depending on the unit and the system) from Washington and Seoul's C⁴I systems.

While North Korea's conventional forces certainly constitute a continuing dilemma for the ROK-U.S. military alliance, one cannot discount Pyongyang's missile forces. It is important to again note that the SRBMs in North Korea's arsenal are considered systems that would be utilized as part of its military artillery doctrine. Thus, since these missiles (mostly Scuds) are considered artillery systems, they would likely be used in tandem with North Korea's thirteen thousand artillery pieces in an attack that could literally cover the entire South Korean landmass. But the missiles can do more. No Dongs can be—and are likely slated to be—used to target Japan, making the current North Korean missile threat a danger not only to its neighbor to the south but also to the region (and U.S. bases in Japan). Finally, among the systems already deployed, the missile sometimes called the Taepo Dong X or Musudan (the North Korean version of the Soviet SS-N-6), is capable of targeting Guam and poses an ominous threat to both civilian and military personnel who live there. While their long-range ICBM systems—the Taepo Dong I and II—have not yet proven capable of complete success, the test launch in 2009 shows that the North Koreans continue to make progress in their development. If and when these systems prove to be successful, they will be a threat not only to the

United States but also to regions where rogue states purchase these missiles or the technology associated with them.

Finally, North Korea's nuclear weapons constitute a threat to the region and to the international community. North Korea has already detonated a plutonium nuclear device (in 2006 and 2009). It is likely that it has several plutonium weapons and that these weapons are probably each some primitive form of a bomb. Further, growing evidence about North Korea's HEU program is at least as disturbing. A successful completion of this program (which may have happened already) would mean that North Korea had a nuclear weapon that could probably be mounted on a missile. If and when this program reaches fruition (if it has not already), the most likely missile on which such a warhead would be mounted is the No Dong. That combination would allow North Korea to threaten Japan with a nuclear attack. Of course, based on the fact that North Korea proliferates nearly every asymmetric weapons system it has to Iran, it also means that Iran would have the same capability (it already has the No Dong) and thus could threaten Israel with a nuclear attack. This scenario highlights a key aspect of the North Korean military threat—proliferation. North Korea has shown it can and will proliferate any weapons system to anybody—rogue states and terrorist groups—that can pay for it. Thus, the military threat from North Korea is two-pronged with the possibility of an attack from the unpredictable and reclusive communist state or from one of the many states and non-state actors to which Pyongyang continues to sell its many conventional and asymmetric systems.

DOES NORTH KOREA HAVE AN ECONOMIC INSTRUMENT OF POWER?

There is almost no doubt among experts and even those who have only a cursory knowledge of East Asian affairs that North Korea's economy is in dire straits and has been since the early 1990s. A Human Rights Watch assessment released April 18, 2009, says in part, "The DPRK has largely recovered from a famine in the mid-late 1990s that killed millions of people and stunted the development of many children for life, but serious food shortages persist and vulnerable members of the population, including young children, pregnant and nursing women, the disabled and elderly, still suffer."[21] While the populace continues to scrape by, the elite lives in high style, and the military (especially key units) continues to be the next highest priority (after the elite) for fuel and food in a country that is badly starved for both.[22] Because of North Korea's poverty and its obvious inability to either feed its people or provide fuel for its infrastructure, it should be clear that North Korea is now and has always been a donor state. Prior to the end of the Cold War, the North Korean economy was heavily subsidized by the Soviet Union. Today, it relies on foreign aid from NGOs, from the UN, and particularly from China. Reportedly, China was providing North Korea $1.5 billon in annual aid by 2009, quadrupling the $400 million in aid that Beijing had provided for Pyongyang in 2004.[23] Large-scale foreign food aid from South Korea ended in 2008, and China likely picked up the slack by increasing what was already a high amount of "trade."[24]

Even as UNSC sanctions from 2009 and unilateral economic sanctions from countries such as the United States, South Korea, and Japan were going into effect in 2010, North Korea was continuing to draw a variety of foreign aid packages from the UN. Despite the fact that donor fatigue has been referenced as a factor in aid that had been going to North Korea since roughly 1995, the aid from the UN continued.[25] In fact, in 2010 the UN planned to spend more than $170 million on new programs in the DPRK, according to a FOX News report. The many programs involved such things as medical aid, agricultural projects, water and sanitation initiatives, and even disaster management.[26]

As the rest of North Korea manages to subsist, its elite manages to live a lavish lifestyle, and its military continues to remain an economic priority precisely because Pyongyang allows so little transparency regarding where the aid is distributed. While this transparency issue is a concern to the UN, NGOs, and democracies such as the United States and South Korea, it remains of little concern to China. Apparently it was not a high priority for the governments of Kim Dae-jung and Roh Moo-hyun, both of which preceded the current Lee Myung-bak government in South Korea. Lee's government has demanded openness, and North Korea's refusal resulted in an immediate dropoff (and ultimately cessation) of food aid in 2008. Thus ended the era (at least temporarily) of South Korea being North Korea's second-largest supplier of food aid (China is widely believed to be the largest donor).[27]

As reports of dire food and fuel conditions persist, it cannot be forgotten that much of this situation is of the North Korean government's own making. And the aid it does get from outsiders is not enough for the country—or the government—to survive. Thus, its illicit and illegal activities, such as proliferation and various other enterprises that include but are not limited to counterfeiting U.S. currency and manufacturing and selling illegal drugs and counterfeit cigarettes (as detailed in chapters 3 and 4, respectively), serve as an important ancillary way for the government to raise money, to irritate democracies such as the United States, and to create national security dilemmas in regions such as the Middle East. David Asher, an adjunct scholar at the Institute for Defense Analysis, estimated in 2005 that the criminal sector makes up to 40 percent of the real North Korean economy.[28] Thus, while no one will mistake North Korea for an economic powerhouse, its economic activities (particularly proliferation) do pose a threat to the national security of the United States and its allies.

CAN THE ROK-U.S. MILITARY ALLIANCE MEET THE CHALLENGE?

In the age of shrinking defense budgets, Washington's allies in the Far East have good reason to worry. It is expensive both in terms of personnel and budget to maintain a large troop presence on the Korean Peninsula. But as of this writing, the Lee Myung-bak administration has made numerous changes and policy moves that show that the government of South Korea is more than willing to meet the United States halfway and has made investments in its own national defense that will help counter the North Korean military threat. In my view, the key to maintaining a strong, vibrant ROK-U.S. military alliance is ensuring that both the South Korean and American people understand the gravity of the many threats that North Korea presents to the national security of both nations.

As the United States and South Korea look to the future, working beyond a crippling world recession and realizing that the Cold War has truly ended everywhere except the Korean Peninsula, the issues of military readiness, international cooperation, and cultural understanding will be key to maintaining and adjusting an alliance that has kept peace and stability on the Korean Peninsula since 1953. By looking at North Korea through a prism of how it is—and not how we would like it to be—these two great nations will continue to adjust their forces and their planning to meet the needs of modern warfare and deterrence. Failure to do so will mean that as long as the North Korean nation-state exists, it will continue to disrupt regional cooperation and development. In this key period in Asia's development and modernization, it will be vital to maintain the ROK-U.S. alliance to meet the needs of a changing security environment.

IMPLICATIONS

The analysis in this book has focused on some of the key threats that North Korea presents to the national security of the United States and its allies. In this chapter, I have used the Department of Defense's instruments of national power (DIME) prism and provided a brief summary of how North Korea has utilized its own instruments of national power successfully to manipulate the geopolitical environ-ment in East Asia to its advantage. Despite having lost subsidies from the Soviet Union more than twenty years ago, North Korea has found ways to adjust its con-ventional and asymmetric military capabilities so that they continue to pose a threat to Pyongyang's neighbors in the region. While North Korea's economy cannot support the infrastructure, Pyongyang has also cleverly adjusted in this area as well by engaging in illicit activities and proliferation, which form a huge portion of the country's real gross domestic product. Despite the best efforts of three American presidents, North Korea's nuclear program remains a real threat, both in the region and worldwide, because of proliferation. Finally, the tenuous status of the DPRK governmental succession process means that while the government remains steady under the leadership of Kim Chong-il, his death or incapacitation would likely lead to instability or even collapse, which, in turn, would impact the national security of every nation-state that has interests in Northeast Asia.

Many of Washington's largest trading partners are in Northeast Asia. China, Taiwan, Japan, and South Korea together supply and consume a huge portion of America's imports and exports, respectively, and Northeast Asia is the fastest-growing economic region in the world. Thus, much more is at stake there than just ideology. A stable, economically prosperous region means benefits for not only those in the region itself but also for the United States as well. Thus, the presence of U.S. troops in Korea and Japan and the stability they provide are vital for the region. As long as the threat from North Korea persists, these troops will play a vital role in deterring and, if necessary, defeating that threat.

Those who downplay the multifaceted threat from North Korea to the region and to the United States would be well advised to do in-depth research on these issues before dismissing Pyongyang's capabilities. Those who believe North Korea is likely to change its system of government, end its proliferation, dismantle its large military (often used for brinkmanship and provocations), or get rid of its nuclear weaponization and ballistic missile programs would also be well advised to study past precedent. North Korea has never shown any evidence that its government will change its policies, nor would I assess that it is likely to do so in the future. Only deterrence of North Korea's large military will prevent it from disrupting the security of and stability on the Korean Peninsula. Only containment will slow North Korean proliferation to rogue states and terrorist groups. Only a well-planned, robustly manned, and combined operation will be able to someday stabilize the peninsula when the unthinkable happens and North Korea collapses. And the most practical way to accomplish all of these missions is for the United States to maintain its partnership in a strong ROK-U.S. military alliance and a steady troop presence in the region.

NOTES

ONE. **Introduction**

1. For details of the capture of the USS *Pueblo* and its crew in 1968, see Mitchell B. Lerner, *The* Pueblo *Incident: A Spy Ship and the Failure of American Foreign Policy* (Lawrence: University Press of Kansas, 2003). For details of the 1983 attempted assassination of the commander of USFK by North Korean Special Forces, see "1983: The Year in Review," Headquarters, United States Forces Korea/Eighth United States Army, 1984, http://www.nautilus.org/foia/foiachrons/ahr_eightythree.pdf. For details of the 1983 terrorist bombing attack on high-ranking South Korean officials in Burma, see "Seoul Condemns Bombing as Plot by North Korea," *New York Times*, October 11, 1983, http://www.nytimes.com/1983/10/11/world/seoul-condemns-bombing-as-plot-by-north-korea.html.

2. For an example of analysis that reflects a pro-engagement policy and that addresses North Korea's economic woes, see Esther Pan, "North Korea's Capitalist Experiment," *Backgrounder,* Council on Foreign Relations, June 8, 2006, http://www.cfr.org/publication/10858/.

3. For details on the "Failed States Index" from 2008, see Fund for Peace, "Failed States Index Scores 2008," http://www.fundforpeace.org/web/index.php?option=com_content&task=view&id=292&Itemid=452; and "The Failed States Index 2008," *Foreign Policy*, July–August 2008, http://www.foreignpolicy.com/story/cms.php?story_id=4350.

4. "North Korea, Iran, Rank One, Two on U.S. Enemies List Wednesday," *Rasmussen Reports*, August 12, 2009, http://www.rasmussenreports.com/public_content/politics/current_events/ally_enemy/north_korea_iran_rank_one_two_on_u_s_enemies_list.

5. Office of the Director of National Intelligence, "The National Intelligence Strategy of the United States of America" (Washington, DC: Office of the Director of National Intelligence, August 2009), http://www.dni.gov/reports/2009_NIS.pdf.

6. For a definition of the term "instruments of national power," see United States Joint Forces Command, "Joint Forces Command Glossary," 2006, http://www.jfcom.mil/about/glossary.htm#ONA.

7. See Joint Doctrine Division, *Joint Pub 1-02: Dictionary of Military and Associated Terms,* Joint Electronic Library, Department of Defense, October 17, 2008, http://www.dtic.mil/doctrine/dod_dictionary/.

8. Some works that address challenges to U.S. security and the region from North Korea's nuclear program are: Victor D. Cha and David C. Kang, *Nuclear North Korea: A Debate for Engagement Strategies* (New York: Columbia University Press, 2003); Gordon C. Chang, *Nuclear Showdown: North Korea Takes on the World* (New York: Random House, 2006); Michael O'Hanlon and Mike Mochizuki, *Crisis on the Korean Peninsula: How to Deal with a Nuclear North Korea* (Washington, DC: Brookings Institution Press, 2003); and James M. Minnich, *The Denuclearization of North Korea: The Agreed Framework and Alternative Options Analyzed* (Bloomington, IN: 1st Books Library, 2002). For examples of works that analyze North Korean internal politics, see Young Whan Kihl and Hong Nack Kim, eds., *North Korea: The Politics of Regime Survival* (Armonk, NY: M. E. Sharp, 2006); and Sung-chol Choi, ed., *Understanding Human Rights in North Korea* (Seoul, Korea: Center for the Advancement of North Korean Human Rights, 1997). Some works that examine North Korean foreign policy include: Tae-hwan Kwak and Seung-ho Joo, eds., *The United States and the Korean Peninsula in the 21st Century* (Aldershot, Hampshire, UK: Ashgate, 2006); Chuck Downs, *Over the Line: North Korea's Negotiating Strategy* (Washington, DC: AEI Press, 1999); and Ted Galen Carpenter and Doug Bandow, *The Korean Conundrum: America's Troubled Relationship with North and South Korea* (New York: Palgrave Macmillan, 2004). Important works that study North Korea from an economic perspective include: Robert Daniel Wallace, *Sustaining the Regime: North Korea's Quest for Financial Support* (Lanham, MD: University Press of America, 2007); and Nicholas Eberstadt, *The North Korean Economy: Between Crisis and Catastrophe* (Piscataway, NJ: Transaction Publishers, 2007). Studies that have examined the ROK-U.S. alliance include: David I. Steinberg, ed., *Korean Attitudes Toward the United States: Changing Dynamics* (Armonk, NY: M. E. Sharpe, 2004); Donald W. Boose, Jr., Balbina Y. Hwang, Patrick Morgan, and Andrew Scobell, eds., *Recalibrating the U.S.–Republic of Korea Alliance* (Carlisle, PA: Strategic Studies Institute, 2003); and Lee Suk Bok, *The Impact of U.S. Forces in Korea* (Washington, DC: National Defense University Press, 1987). Some important works that examine the past, present, and future relationships of North Korea and South Korea include: Don Oberdorfer, *The Two Koreas: A Contemporary History* (New York: Basic Books, 2001); Ho-Youn Kwon, ed., *Divided Korea: Longing for Reunification* (Chicago, IL: North Park University Press, 2004); Edward A. Olsen, *Korea: The Divided Nation* (Westport, CT: Praeger, 2005); and Roland Bleiker, *Divided Korea: Toward a Culture of Reconciliation* (Minneapolis, MN: University of Minnesota Press, 2005).
9. "Rumsfeld Says N. Korea Poses No Immediate Military Threat to South," *Voice of America News*, August 27, 2006, http://www.globalsecurity.org/wmd/library/news/dprk/2006/dprk-060827-voa01.htm.
10. Hyeong Jung Park, "Divergent Threat Perceptions on North Korea," *Mansfield Foundation Commentary*, 2007, http://www.mansfieldfdn.org/programs/program_pdfs/rok_us_park.pdf.
11. Ibid.
12. For some interesting background on Syria's WMD programs, its cooperation with Iran, support to Hezbollah, and the North Korean tie-in to many of Damascus's programs, see Amanda Moodie, "Syria: Coming in from the Cold?" *WMD Insights*, October 2008, http://www.wmdinsights.org/I27/I27_ME2_Syria.htm.

TWO. Understanding the North Korean Military Threat to the Security of the Korean Peninsula and Northeast Asia

1. An earlier and shorter version of the analysis in this chapter was originally published as Bruce E. Bechtol, Jr., "Understanding the North Korean Military Threat to the Security

of the Korean Peninsula and Northeast Asia: Declined or Evolved?" *Korea Observer* 40, no. 1 (Spring 2009): 115–54. The author would like to thank Dr. Choong-mook Lee, the managing editor of the *Korea Observer.*

2. For analysis of North Korea's nuclear weapons capability and its use of this capability to ensure its national security, see Cheon Seongwhun, "The Question President Bush Needs to Answer: Do You Really Believe Kim Jong-il Will Give up His Nuclear Weapons?" *Nautilus Institute Policy Forum Online* 08-081A, October 23, 2008, http://www.nautilus.org/fora/security/08081cheon.html.

3. For an example of recent bluster in North Korean rhetoric, see "N. Korea Threatens to Turn S Korea into 'Debris,'" AFP, October 28, 2008, http://www.usatoday.com/news/world/2008-10-28-korea-tension_N.htm.

4. Melissa Applegate, *Preparing for Asymmetry: As Seen through the Lens of Joint Vision 2020* (Carlisle, PA: Strategic Studies Institute, 2001), http://www.au.af.mil/au/awc/awcgate/ssi/preparng.pdf.

5. Yoel Sano, "Pyongyang Shuffles Its Military, Not Policies," *Asia Times*, May 5, 2007, http://www.atimes.com/atimes/korea/ie05dg01.html.

6. "10 Years of DPRK with SONGUN Policy," *People's Korea*, 2004, http://www1.korea-np.co.jp/pk/207th_issue/2004071702.htm.

7. KBS World, "NK Politics/Regime: National Defense Commission," *North Korea A to Z,* October 31, 2008, http://world.kbs.co.kr/english/event/nkorea_nuclear/general_03f.htm.

8. Lim Jae-Hyoung, "The Power Hierarchy: North Korean Foreign Policy Making Process," *East Asian Review* 14, no. 2 (Summer 2002): 89–106, http://www.ieas.or.kr/vol14_2/14_2_5.pdf.

9. Choi Choel-hee, "The Relationship between the Party and the Army under the Military-First Policy," *Daily NK*, October 21, 2008, http://www.dailynk.com/english/read.php?catald=nk00400&num=4199.

10. Kim Sung Chull, *North Korea under Kim Jong Il: From Consolidation to Systemic Dissonance* (New York: State University of New York Press, 2006), 89–91.

11. Ken E. Gause, *North Korean Civil-Military Trends: Military-First Politics to a Point,* Strategic Studies Institute Monograph (Carlisle, PA: U.S. Army War College, September 2006), http://www.strategicstudiesinstitute.army.mil/pdffiles/pub728.pdf.

12. Daniel A. Pinkston, "Domestic Politics and Stakeholders in the North Korean Missile Development Program," *Nonproliferation Review*, Summer 2003, http://cns.miis.edu/npr/pdfs/102pink.pdf.

13. Joseph S. Bermudez, Jr., "SIGINT, EW, and EIW in the Korean People's Army: An Overview of Development and Organization," in *Bytes and Bullets: Information Technology, Revolution, and National Security on the Korean Peninsula,* ed. Alexandre Y. Mansourov (Honolulu, HI: Asia Pacific Center for Security Studies, 2005), http://www.apcss.org/Publications/Edited%20Volumes/BytesAndBullets/CH13.pdf.

14. Jeffrey Robertson, "After Iraq: A Military Solution in North Korea?" *Research Note* no. 29, Department of the Parliamentary Library, March 24, 2003, http://www.aph.gov.au/library/pubs/rn/2002-03/03rn29.pdf.

15. Richard M. Bennett, "Missiles and Madness," *Asia Times*, August 18, 2006, http://www.atimes.com/atimes/korea/hh18dg02.html.

16. Andrew Scobell and John M. Sanford, *North Korea's Military Threat: Pyongyang's Conventional Forces, Weapons of Mass Destruction, and Ballistic Missiles,* Strategic Studies Institute Monograph (Carlisle, PA: U.S. Army War College, April 2007), http://www.strategicstudiesinstitute.army.mil/pdffiles/pub771.pdf.

17. Joseph S. Bermudez, Jr., "Moving Missiles," *Jane's Defence Weekly*, July 27, 2005, http://www.janes.com/defence/land_forces/news/jdw/jdw050727_1_n.shtml.

18. Linda D. Kozaryn, "Despite Progress, North Korea Poses Major Threat," American Forces Press Service, April 3, 2001, http://www.fas.org/news/dprk/2001/dprk-010403.htm.

19. Scobell and Sanford, *North Korea's Military Threat.*

20. "Korean People's Army: Introduction," GlobalSecurity.org, April 27, 2005, http://www.globalsecurity.org/military/world/dprk/army.htm.

21. Charles Scanlon, "S Korea's Shock at US Troop Cuts," BBC News, June 8, 2004, http://news.bbc.co.uk/1/hi/world/asia-pacific/3786811.stm.

22. Joseph S. Bermudez, Jr., e-mail interview conducted by the author, December 2, 2008.

23. Joseph S. Bermudez, Jr., "North Korea's Long Reach in Profile," *Jane's Intelligence Review*, November 11, 2003, http://www.janes.com/defence/land_forces/news/idr/idr031111_1_n.shtml.

24. Defense Intelligence Agency, *North Korea: The Foundations of Military Strength, Defense Intelligence Agency—Update 1995* (Washington, DC: Defense Intelligence Agency, 1995), 13.

25. Colin Robertson and Rear Adm. (Ret) Stephen H. Baker, "Stand-off with North Korea: War Scenarios and Consequences," (Washington, DC: Center for Defense Information, 2003), http://www.cdi.org/north-korea/north-korea-crisis.pdf.

26. Gen. B. B. Bell, commander, United Nations Command; commander, Republic of Korea–United States Combined Forces Command; and commander, United States Forces Korea, testimony before the House Armed Services Committee, March 12, 2008, http://www.shaps.hawaii.edu/security/us/2008/bell_031208.html.

27. Patrecia Slayden Hollis, "The Korean Theater—One-of-a-Kind: Interview with General Robert W. RisCassi," *Field Artillery*, February, 1993, http://sill-www.army.mil/famag/1993/FEB_1993/FEB_1993_PAGES_7_10.pdf.

28. Harry P. Dies, Jr., "North Korean Special Operations Forces: 1996 Kangnung Submarine Infiltration," *Military Intelligence Professional Bulletin*, October–December 2004, http://findarticles.com/p/articles/mi_m0IBS/is_4_30/ai_n13822276.

29. "North Korean Special Operations Forces and the Second Front," Special Operations.com, 2000, http://www.specialoperations.com/Foreign/North_Korea/Second_Front.htm.

30. See "North Korea's Underground Bunkers," *Radio Free Asia*, November 16, 2009, http://www.rfa.org/english/news/korea/bunkers-11162009134509.html; and "N. Korea 'Planned to Invade South Despite Sunshine Policy,'" *Chosun Ilbo*, November 18, 2009, http://english.chosun.com/site/data/html_dir/2009/11/18/2009111800451.html.

31. See Baek Seung-joo, "How to Deal With the Threat of N. Korea's Special Forces?" *Chosun Ilbo*, May 12, 2010, http://english.chosun.com/site/data/html_dir/2010/05/12/2010051201255.html.

32. North Korean Affairs Research Institute, "North Korea's Eighth Special Army Corps," *Seoul NK Focus* [in Japanese], April 18, 2008, http://www.nkfocus.jp.

33. "N. Korea Augments Special Warfare Units," *Korea Herald*, January 1, 2008, http://www.koreaherald.co.kr/.

34. "N. Korea Developing Special Warfare Capabilities: Officials," *Yonhap News*, October 29, 2008, http://www.koreancenter.or.kr/news/news_foreign_view.aspx?menu_code=02001000&news_id=aen20081029009500315.

35. Sam Kim, "N. Korea Developing Guerrilla Warfare Capabilities: U.S. Commander," *Yonhap News*, June 23, 2009, http://english.yonhapnews.co.kr/news/2009/06/23/0200000000aen20090623002600 315.html.

36. Sam Kim, "N. Korea's General Staff Runs Own Special Forces for Strategic Purposes: Lawmaker," *Yonhap News*, October 5, 2009, http://english.yonhapnews.co.kr/national/2009/10/05/0301000000aen20091005004600315.html.

37. See Shin Joo-hyun, "North Korean Submarine Helmsman Breaks 14-Year Silence," *Daily NK*, June 1, 2010, http://www.dailynk.com/english/read.php?catald= nk02500&num=6445; and Kim So-hyun, "Reconnaissance Bureau is Heart of N.K. Terrorism," *Korea Herald*, May 26, 2010, http://www.koreaherald.com/national/ Detail.jsp?newsMLId=20100526000675.

38. W. Thomas Smith, Jr., "Kim, His Nukes, and His Army: North Korea's Kim Jong Il Tests Nukes; Threatens War with the United States," *World Defense Review*, October 16, 2006, http://worlddefensereview.com/wts101606.shtml.

39. Federation of American Scientists, "North Korean Air Force," *Nuclear Forces Guide,* 2008, http://www.fas.org/nuke/guide/dprk/agency/af.htm.

40. "S. Korea Voices Concern over MiG-21 Sale to N. Korea," *Kyoto News*, August 12, 1999, http://findarticles.com/p/articles/mi_m0WDQ/is_1999_August_16/ai_55496607.

41. Eric Schmitt, "North Korean MiG's Intercept U.S. Jet," *New York Times*, March 4, 2003, http://www.nytimes.com/2003/03/04/international/asia/04KORE.html?scp =6&sq=eric%20schmitt%20march%202003&st=cse.

42. "N. Korea Steps up Provocations," *Chosun Ilbo*, March 31, 2008, http://english .chosun.com/site/data/html_dir/2008/03/31/2008033161011.html.

43. "North Korea: Special Forces," SpecWarNet, August 15, 2008, http://www .specwarnet.net/asia/NKSF.htm.

44. Ser Myo-ja and Kim Min-seok, "Missile Launch by North Seen as Negotiation Tactic," *Joongang Ilbo*, October 9, 2008, http://joongangdaily.joins.com/article/view .asp?aid=2895882.

45. Scobell and Sanford, *North Korea's Military Threat.*

46. Michael Sheridan and Uzi Mahnaimiin, "Kim Jong-il Builds 'Thunderbirds' Runway for War in North Korea," *The Sunday Times*, April 27, 2008, http://www.timesonline .co.uk/tol/news/world/asia/article3822538.ece.

47. "TV Report on DPRK's Underground Military Runway Facilities near Wonsan," MBC TV [in Korean], December 19, 2009, http://imnews.imbc.com/replay/nwdesk/ article/2525060_5780.html.

48. "Korean People's Army Navy," GlobalSecurity.org, April 27, 2005, http://www .globalsecurity.org/military/world/dprk/navy.htm.

49. "World Navies Today: North Korea," *World Navies Today: All the World's Navies*, November 3, 2001, http://www.hazegray.org/worldnav/asiapac/n_korea.htm.

50. "Combating North Korean Maritime Special Operations Forces," SpecialOperations .com, 2000, http://www.specialoperations.com/Focus/Maritime_SOF/.

51. "North Korea Conducts Short-Range Missile Test," Associated Press, May 25, 2007, http://www.iht.com/articles/ap/2007/05/25/asia/as-gen-nkorea-missiles.php.

52. Ministry of National Defense, Republic of Korea, "The Naval Clash on the Yellow Sea on 29 June 2002 between South Korea and North Korea: The Situation and ROK's Position," GlobalSecurity.org, July 1, 2002, http://www.globalsecurity.org/wmd/library/ news/rok/2002/0020704-naval.htm.

53. Yu Yong-won, "JCS Says NK Opened Fire First," *Chosun Ilbo,* June 29, 2002, http:// english.chosun.com/site/data/html_dir/2002/06/29/2002062961009.html.

54. Bruce E. Bechtol, Jr., "The Northern Limit Line of 2002: Motivations and Implications," *Pacific Focus* 19, no. 2 (Fall 2004): 233–64.

55. See Joseph S. Bermudez, Jr., *A History of Ballistic Missile Development in the DPRK*, CNS Occasional Papers: #2 (Monterey, CA: Center for Nonproliferation Studies, Monterey Institute of International Studies, 1999), http://cns.miis.edu/pubs/opapers/op2/ index.htm.

56. "Syria Improves Its SCUD D Missile with Help from North Korea," *Geostrategy-Direct*, February 22, 2006, http://www.geostrategy-direct.com/geostrategy%2Ddirect/.

57. Kim Min-seok and Brian Lee, "Pyongyang Reportedly Tests New Scud," *Joongang Ilbo*, July 19, 2006, http://joongangdaily.joins.com/200607/18/20060718213835147 9900090309031.html.

58. Wisconsin Project on Nuclear Arms Control (Wisconsin Project), "North Korea's Nuclear-Capable Missiles," *The Risk Report* 2, no. 6 (November–December 1996), http://www.wisconsinproject.org/countries/nkorea/nukemiss.html.

59. Alon Ben-David, "Iran Acquires Ballistic Missiles from DPRK," *Jane's Defence Weekly*, December 29, 2005, http://www.janes.com/security/international_security/news/jdw/jdw051229_1_n.shtml.

60. See "N. Korea Sets up Special Missile Division: Source," *Yonhap News*, March 9, 2010, http://english.yonhapnews.co.kr/national/2010/03/09/8/0301000000AEN2 0100309001600315F.HTML; Jung Sung-ki, "NK Creates Mid-Range Ballistic Missile Unit," *Korea Times*, March 9, 2010, http://www.koreatimes.co.kr/www/news/nation/2010/03/205_62096.html; and Bruce Klingner, "New North Korean Missile Unit Reflects Growing Missile Threat," *Heritage Foundation Report*, March 11, 2010, http://www.heritage.org/research/reports/2010/03/new-north-korean-missile-unit-reflects-growing-missile-threat.

61. Jack Kim, "North Korea Has 1,000 Missiles, South Says," Reuters, March 17, 2010, http://www.nytimes.com/reuters/2010/03/17/world/international-us-korea-north -missiles.html.

62. James Dunnigan, "North Korea's SS-21 Missiles," *StrategyPage*, May 12, 2005, http://www.strategypage.com/dls/articles/2005512213718.asp.

63. Paul Kerr, "North Korea Increasing Weapons Capabilities," *Arms Control Today*, December 2005, http://www.armscontrol.org/act/2005_12/dec-nkweapons.asp.

64. "NK Fired Russian Missile: Official," *Korea Times*, May 4, 2005, http://times .hankooki.com/lpage/nation/200505/kt2005050422050611990.htm.

65. Gen. B. B. Bell, commander, United Nations Command; commander, Republic of Korea–United States Combined Forces Command; and commander, United States Forces Korea, statement to the Senate Armed Services Committee, March 7, 2006, http://www.senate.gov/~armed_services/statemnt/2006/March/Bell%2003-07-06.pdf.

66. Yun Sang-ho and Ryu Won-sik, "South Korea and US Intelligence Confirmed Long-Range Missile Engine Test Last Month," *Dong-a Ilbo* [in Korean], October 6, 2009, http://www.donga.com.

67. National Air and Space Intelligence Center (NASIC), "Ballistic and Cruise Missile Threat," NASIC-1031-0985-09 (Wright-Patterson Air Force Base, OH: NASIC, 2009), http://www.fas.org/programs/ssp/nukes/NASIC2009.pdf; and Ministry of National Defense, Republic of Korea, "Defense White Paper," 2008, http://www.mnd.go.kr/.

68. See "North Korea Building New Missile Bases, Silos along East Coast: Report," *Yonhap News*, August 3, 2006, http://www.freerepublic.com/focus/f-news/1676857/posts; and "N. Korea Has Eight Medium-Range Missile Pads: NIS," *Chosun Ilbo*, July 12, 2006, http://english.chosun.com/site/data/html_dir/2006/07/12/2006071261018.html.

69. David Sanger, "North Koreans Said to Be Near a Missile Test," *New York Times*, June 18, 2006, http://www.nytimes.com/2006/06/19/world/asia/19korea.html ?_r=2&oref=slogin&oref=slogin.

70. The Taepo Dong I failed to successfully enter its third stage in 1998, and the Taepo Dong II blew apart and fell into the sea while attempting to go from its first stage to its second stage in 2006. For more details of these two launches, see "U.S. Officials: North Korea Tests Long-Range Missile," CNN.com, July 5, 2006, http://www.cnn .com/2006/WORLD/asiapcf/07/04/korea.missile/.

71. See "North Korea's Missile Programme," BBC News, July 5, 2006, http://news.bbc .co.uk/2/hi/asia-pacific/2564241.stm; and David C. Wright, "An Analysis of the North

Korean Missile Program," in *Report of the Commission to Assess the Ballistic Missile Threat to the United States*, ed. Donald Rumsfeld and others (Washington, DC: Federation of American Scientists, July 15, 1998), http://www.fas.org/irp/threat/missile/rumsfeld/pt2_wright.htm.

72. See "Advanced N. Korean Missile Last Seen on East Coast: Officials," *Yonhap News*, February 4, 2009, http://english.yonhapnews.co.kr/northkorea/2009/02/04/28/040100 0000AEN20090204005600315F.HTML; and Jung Ha-won, "Satellites Detect Possible Missile Moves in North," *Joongang Ilbo*, February 4, 2009, http://joongangdaily.joins .com/article/view.asp?aid=2900589.

73. See "*Rodong Sinmun*: DPRK Entitled to Use Space for Peaceful Purposes," *People's Daily*, February 8, 2009, http://english.people.com.cn/90001/90777/90851/6587821.html.

74. David Morgan, "U.S. Steps up Monitoring of North Korea: Official," Reuters, February 10, 2009, http://www.reuters.com/article/politicsNews/idustre51a0cc20090211.

75. "N. Korea Shipping Missile-Related Cargo to Launch Pad: Source," *Yonhap News*, February 11, 2009, http://www.koreancenter.or.kr/news/news_foreign_view.aspx?menu _code=02001000&news_id=aen20090211008100315.

76. Barbara Starr, "U.S. Official: North Korea Might Be Making Missile Preparations," CNN.com, February 10, 2009, http://www.cnn.com/2009/WORLD/asiapcf/02/10/north.korea.missile/index.html.

77. "N. Korea 'Transports Missile to Launch Site,'" *Chosun Ilbo*, February 13, 2009, http://english.chosun.com/w21data/html/news/200902/200902130001.html.

78. Kim Hyun, "N. Korea Signals Satellite Launch, Feasts on Leader's Birthday," *Yonhap News*, February 16, 2009, http://english.chosun.com/site/data/html_dir/2009/02/13/2009021361001.html.

79. See "Defiant N Korea Launches Rocket," BBC News, April 5, 2009, http://news.bbc .co.uk/2/hi/asia-pacific/7982874.stm.

80. See International Civil Aviation Organization, "ICAO Officially Advised of DPRK Plans for Rocket Launch," news release, March 12, 2009, http://www.icao.int/icao/en/nr/2009/pio200902_e.pdf.

81. For more details regarding South Korean and U.S. assessments concerning the purpose of North Korea's second Taepo Dong II test launch, the differences between a vehicle carrying a dummy warhead vice a satellite, and the capabilities of the U.S. ballistic missile defense system, see Tony Capaccio, "Pentagon Tester Lacks 'High Confidence' in U.S. Missile Defense," *Bloomberg News*, February 24, 2009, http://preview.bloomberg.com/apps/news?pid=newsarchive_en10&sid=afc4fyAJl1Tg; "North Korean Leader Says Communist Regime Strong—Agency," *Ria Novosti*, March 15, 2009, http://en.rian.ru/world/20090315/120566933.html; Martha Raddatz and Lauren Sher, "U.S. Ready to Respond to N. Korea Missile," ABC News International, February 26, 2009, http://abcnews.go.com/international/story?id=6965611; Jung Sung-ki, "Will NK Rocket Launch Be 'Wolf in Sheep's Clothing'?" *Korea Times*, March 26, 2009, http://www.koreatimes.co.kr/www/news/nation/2009/03/113_42065 .html; and Charles E. McQueary, "Ballistic Missile Defense Systems," *FY 2008 Annual Report* (Washington, DC: Department of Defense, Operational Test and Evaluation, Department of Defense, December, 2008), http://www.cdi.org/pdfs/fy08doteannual report.pdf.

82. "Japan to Deploy Interceptor in Sea of Japan to Counter N. Korea," *Kyodo News*, March 3, 2009, http://www.japantoday.com/category/national/view/japan-to-deploy -interceptor-in-sea-of-japan-to-counter-n-korea.

83. Hiroyuki Koshoji, "Analysis: North Korean Threat to Japan," *UPI*, March 16, 2009, http://www.upi.com/Top_News/Special/2009/03/16/Analysis-North-Korean-threat-to -Japan/UPI-60071237239346/.

84. "'Danger Zone' for Debris Lies in EEZ," *Yomiuri Shimbun*, March 18, 2009, http://www.yomiuri.co.jp/dy/national/20090318tdy02304.htm.

85. Bomi Lim, "North Korea to Close Air Routes for Rocket Launch," *Bloomberg News*, March 22, 2009, http://www.bloomberg.com/apps/news?pid=newsarchive&sid=aze46e_vye9a#.

86. "Spy Satellites Spot Nose Cone of N Korea Rocket," AFP, March 29, 2009, http://newsx.com/story/48860.

87. "Iran Missile Experts in North Korea 'to Help with Rocket Launch,'" *TimesOnline*, March 29, 2009, http://www.timesonline.co.uk/tol/news/world/asia/article5994905.ece.

88. See Jon Herskovitz, "U.S. Deploys Anti-Missile Ships before N. Korea Launch," Reuters, March 29, 2009, http://www.reuters.com/article/idUSTRE52T0F820090330; "Missile Units on Way to Northeast Japan ahead of N Korean Rocket Launch," *Japan Today*, March 29, 2009, http://www.japantoday.com/category/national/view/missile-units-on-way-to-northeastern-japan-ahead-of-n-korean-rocket-launch; and "Japan to Order N. Korean Rocket Destruction to Prepare for Failure," *Kyodo News*, March 27, 2009, http://www.istockanalyst.com/article/ viewistocknews/articleid/3151494.

89. Sam Kim, "N. Korean Rocket Shown Fully Mounted in Commercial Satellite Image," *Yonhap News*, March 30, 2009, http://english.yonhapnews.co.kr/northkorea/2009/03/30/3/0401000000aen20090330003100315f.html.

90. Mike Mount, "North Korea Is Fueling Rocket, U.S. Military Says," CNN.com, April 1, 2009, http://edition.cnn.com/2009/WORLD/asiapcf/04/01/north.korea.rocket/index.html.

91. David Morgan, "North Korea Missile Shows Sign of Satellite Payload—U.S.," Reuters, April 1, 2009, http://thestar.com.my/news/story.asp?file=/2009/4/1/worldupdates/2009-04-01t030602z_01_nootr_rtrmdnc_0_-388132-2&sec=worldupdates.

92. Sam Kim, "N. Korean Satellite Same Threat as Missile: S. Korean Defense Chief," *Yonhap News*, April 1, 2009, http://www.tmcnet.com/usubmit/2009/04/02/4102501.htm.

93. Sam Kim, "N. Korea Set to Launch Rocket in Hours," *Yonhap News*, April 4, 2009, http://english.siamdailynews.com/asia-news/eastern-asia-news/korea-news/north-korea-news/north-korea-set-to-launch-rocket-in-hours.html.

94. "N. Korea Notified U.S., China, Russia of Launch Time," *Chosun Ilbo*, April 7, 2009, http://english.chosun.com/w21data/html/news/200904/200904070024.html.

95. Joseph S. Bermudez, Jr., "Launch Failure Frustrates North Korea's Missile Aspirations," *Jane's Defence Weekly*, April 7, 2009, http://search.janes.com/Search/documentView.do?docID=/content1/janesdata/mags/jdw/history/jdw2009/jdw39507.htm@current&pageSelected=allJanes&keyword=joseph%20bermudez&backPath=http://search.janes.com/Search&Prod_Name=JDW&.

96. See "North Korea's Missile Flew 500 Miles Farther Than It Was Expected," *Pravda*, April 13, 2009, http://english.pravda.ru/world/asia/13-04-2009/107390-north_korea_missile-0; and "N. Korea Rocket Flew Farther Than Previously Thought," *Chosun Ilbo*, April 13, 2009, http://english.chosun.com/w21data/html/news/200904/200904130006.html.

97. Julian E. Barnes and Greg Miller, "North Korea Shows Progress in Mastering Missile Technology," *Los Angeles Times*, April 6, 2009, http://www.latimes.com/news/nationworld/world/la-fg-north-korea-missile6-2009apr06,0,4471509.story.

98. Sam Kim, "S. Korea Considers N. Korean Rocket Launch Step Forward in Missile Capability," *Yonhap News*, April 6, 2009, http://english.yonhapnews.co.kr/national/2009/04/06/97/0301000000aen20090406006900315f.html.

99. Yoo Jee-ho, "North's Rocket Shows Improved Technology," *Joongang Ilbo*, April 7, 2009, http://joongangdaily.joins.com/article/view.asp?aid=2903232.

100. See Sam Kim, "N. Korea Deployed Top Air, Naval Forces to Guard Rocket Launch," *Yonhap News*, April 8, 2009, http://english.yonhapnews.co.kr/national/2009/04/05/66/0301000000aen20090405008200315f.html; and "N. Korean Jet Crashed in East Sea before Rocket Launch, Gov't Source," *Yonhap News*, April 9, 2009, http://english.yonhapnews.co.kr/northkorea/2009/04/09/0401000000aen20090409009100320.html.

101. See "UN Security Council Condemns North Korean Rocket Launch," AFP, April 14, 2009, http://www.channelnewsasia.com/stories/afp_asiapacific/view/422132/1/.html; "No Security Council Agreement on NKorea Launch," AFP, April 5, 2009, http://rawstory.com/news/afp/no_security_council_agreement_on_nk_04052009.html; Kim Sue-young, "China, Russia Wants to Keep 6-Way Talks Alive," *Korea Times*, April 7, 2009, http://www.koreatimes.co.kr/www/news/nation/2009/04/113_42759.html; and "Full Text of U.N. Security Council's Statement on N. Korean Rocket Launch," *Yonhap News*, April 14, 2009, http://english.yonhapnews.co.kr/news/2009/04/14/0200000000aen20090414000500315.html.

102. See Jon Herskovitz, "North Korea Orders U.N. Inspectors Out," Reuters, April 14, 2009, http://www.reuters.com/article/idUSTRE53C42820090414 and "DPRK to Withdraw from Six-party Talks," *Xinhua*, April 14, 2009, http://news.xinhuanet.com/english/2009-04/14/content_11183813.htm.

103. See Jack Kim, "North Korea Seen Readying for New Nuclear Test," Reuters, May 7, 2009, http://uk.reuters.com/article/worldnews/iduktre54609q20090507?rpc=401&=undefined&sp=true.

104. See "Outrage over N Korea Nuclear Test," BBC News, May 25, 2009, http://news.bbc.co.uk/go/pr/fr/-/2/hi/asia-pacific/8066861.stm.

105. See Breffni O'Rourke, "Rocket Launch, Reelection Boost Kim Jong Il's Standing," *Radio Free Europe*, April 9, 2009, http://www.rferl.org/content/rocket_launch_boosts_supreme_leaders_standing/1605612.html; Jack Kim, "Scenarios: How Far Will North Korea Raise Tensions?" Reuters, March 26, 2009, http://www.reuters.com/article/idUSTRE52P17F20090327 and Matthew Lee, "North Korean Missile Launch Tests Obama," Associated Press, April 5, 2009, http://www.guardian.co.uk/world/feedarticle/8440034.

106. See Stephanie Griffith, "Iran Present at North Korean Missile Launch Says US," AFP, July 20, 2006, http://www.spacewar.com/reports/iran_present_at_north_korea_missile_launch_says_us_999.html; Gordon C. Chang, "A Missile Shot for Iran," *Manila Times*, April 8, 2009, http://www.manilatimes.net/national/2009/april/08/yehey/opinion/20090408opi7.html; and Jeff Stein, "U.S. Claim that Iran Attended Launch Would Be Explosive—if True," *Congressional Quarterly*, July 28, 2006, http://public.cq.com/public/20060728_homeland.html.

107. For details of North Korean proliferation of missiles to Iran, see Center for Nonproliferation Studies (CNS), "North Korea's Ballistic Missile Program," in *Chronology of North Korea's Missile Trade and Developments*, Center for Nonproliferation Studies (online), Monterey Institute of International Studies, 1980–89, http://cns.miis.edu/archive/country_north_korea/chr8089.htm; and Kevin Kane, "Iran and North Korea's Military Relations: Trading with Terrorists?" *Daily NK*, February 5, 2007, http://www.dailynk.com/english/read.php?cataid=nk00300&num=1638.

108. See "North Korean Missile Launches Aimed at Improving Accuracy: Official," *Yonhap News*, July 5, 2009, http://english.yonhapnews.co.kr/news/2009/07/05/0200000000aen2009070500160015.html; Hyung-jin Kim, "Report: N Korean Launches Maybe Included New Scud," Associated Press, July 6, 2009, http://abcnews.go.com/International/wireStory?id=8004245 and Richard Halloran, "Valuable Defense Lesson for U.S.," *Washington Times*, July 13, 2009, http://www.washingtontimes.com/news/2009/jul/13/valuable-defense-lesson-for-us/.

109. Kim Sung-jin, "North Korea's New Launch Site for Missiles," *Vantage Point* 31, no. 10 (October 2008): 22–23.

110. See "N.K. May Launch Missile in 1–2 Weeks," *Korea Herald*, June 2, 2009, http://www.koreaherald.co.kr/newkhsite/data/html_dir/2009/06/02/200906020087.asp; Yoo Jee-ho, "Ignoring Warning, North Puts Missile Near Launching Pad," *Joongang Ilbo*, June 3, 2009, http://joongangdaily.joins.com/article/view.asp?aid=2905643; "AP: N. Korea Completes ICBM Launch Site," *Dong-a Ilbo*, June 6, 2009, http://english.donga.com/srv/service.php3?bicode=060000&biid=2009060686248; and "N. Korean Missile Train on the Move," *Chosun Ilbo*, June 17, 2009, http://english.chosun.com/site/data/html_dir/2009/06/17/2009061700282.html.

111. Richard Halloran, "North Korea: In Military Decline but Definitely Dangerous," *International Herald Tribune*, December 3, 1996, http://www.iht.com/articles/1996/12/03/edhall.t.php.

112. Kurt Achin, "Video Shows N. Korean Soldier Allegedly Suffering from Malnutrition," *Voice of America,* July 28, 2005, http://www.voanews.com/english/archive/2005-07/2005-07-28-voa9.cfm.

113. Rebecca MacKinnon, "Food, Fuel and Medicine Shortages Plague North Korea," CNN.com, December 14, 1999, http://archives.cnn.com/1999/ASIANOW/east/12/14/nkorea.crisis/.

114. National Intelligence Council, "Strategic Implications of Global Health," Intelligence Community Assessment 2008-10D, December 2008, http://www.dni.gov/nic/PDF_GIF_otherprod/ICA_Global_Health_2008.pdf.

115. "North Korean Forces Increasingly Manned by Women Soldiers," *World Tribune*, January 24, 2007, http://www.worldtribune.com/worldtribune/wtarc/2007/ea_nkorea_01_25.html.

116. "N.K. Stops Drills, Sends Troops to Help Farms: Source," *Yonhap News*, May 28, 2008, http://english.yonhapnews.co.kr/northkorea/2008/05/28/30/0401000000aen20080528001000315f.html.

117. David F. Von Hippel, "Estimated DPRK Military Energy Use: Analytical Approach and Draft Updated Results," paper presented at the DPRK Energy Expert Study Group Meeting, Stanford University, California, June 26–27, 2006, http://nautilus.org/DPRKEnergyMeeting/papers/DvH_DPRK_Military.ppt#270,1,EstimatedDPRK Military Energy Use: Analytical Approach and Draft Updated Results.

118. Gen. Thomas A. Schwartz, commander, United Nations Command/Combined Forces Command; and commander, United States Forces Korea, statement for the record to the Senate Armed Services Committee, March 7, 2000, http://armed-services.senate.gov/statemnt/2000/000307ts.pdf.

119. Bermudez, "Moving Missiles."

120. For analysis on dispersal and numbers of North Korean missile systems, see Daniel Pinkston, *The North Korean Ballistic Missile Program*, Strategic Studies Institute Monograph (Carlisle, PA: U.S. Army War College, February 2008), http://www.strategicstudiesinstitute.army.mil/pdffiles/PUB842.pdf.

121. Gen. Thomas A. Schwartz, commander, United Nations Command/Combined Forces Command; and commander, United States Forces Korea, statement for the record to the Senate Armed Services Committee, March 5, 2002, http://www.shaps.hawaii.edu/security/us/schwartz_2002.html.

122. Wisconsin Project, "North Korea Chemical and Biological Weapon Update—2005," *The Risk Report* 11, no. 4 (July–August 2005), http://www.wisconsinproject.org/countries/nkorea/north-korea-chem-bioupdate2005.html.

123. Brian Lee, "Defense Paper: North Boosts Artillery but Cuts Tanks, Armor," *Joongang*

Ilbo, February 5, 2005, http://joongangdaily.joins.com/200502/04/200502042241418 509900090309031.html.

124. "Concerns Raised over Possible North Korean Scud Derivative," *Jane's Information Group*, March 10, 2005, http://www.janes.com/security/international_security/news/ jmr/jmr050310_1_n.shtml.

125. "North Korean People's Army Study Guide: Part 3—Special Operations Forces," GlobalSecurity.org, April 28, 2005, http://www.globalsecurity.org/wmd/library/ news/dprk/1996/kpa-guide/part03.htm.

126. Robert D. Kaplan, "When North Korea Falls," *Atlantic Monthly*, October 2006, http:// www.theatlantic.com/doc/200610/kaplan-korea.

127. Jun Kwanwoo, "NKorea Deploys More Missiles, Bolsters Troops: SKorea," AFP, February 23, 2009, http://news.yahoo.com/s/afp/20090223/wl_asia_afp/nkoreaskorea militarymissiles.

128. See Sam Kim, "(Lead) N. Korea Steps up Special Forces, Deploys Medium-Range Missiles: Defense Paper," *Yonhap News*, February 23, 2009, http://english.yonhap news.co.kr/northkorea/2009/02/23/51/0401000000aen20090223002700315f.html; Sam Kim, "N. Korea Ups Ante by Diversifying Missiles Targeting U.S.," *Yonhap News*, February 23, 2009, http://english.yonhapnews.co.kr/national/2009/02/23/71/03 01000000aen20090223 006700315f.html; and Sam Kim, "(3d LD) N. Korea Deploys Medium-Range Missiles, Bolsters Special Forces: Defense Report," *Yonhap News*, February 23, 2009, http://english.yonhapnews.co.kr/national/2009/02/23/85/0301000 000aen20090223004500315f.html.

129. Kim Chong-il visited the apparently newly designated 105th Tank Division (a name change from the 820th Armored Corps) during January 2009 when the name change was announced in the state-run Korean Central News Agency. See "Kim Jong-il Makes First Public Appearance in 2009," *Korea Times*, January 4, 2009, http://www .koreatimes.co.kr/www/news/nation/2009/01/113_37231.Html.

130. Ministry of National Defense, "Defense White Paper" (2008).

131. See Robert Karniol, "North Korea Rethinks War-Fighting Strategy," *Straits Times*, March 16, 2009, http://www.straitstimes.com/vgn-ext-templating/v/index.jsp?vgnex toid=88b5cad819a00210vgnvcm100000430a0a0arcrd&vgnextchannel=0162758920e 39010vgnvcm1000000a35010arcrd.

132. See "North Korea Has Deployed 50,000 Special Forces Along Frontlines: Source," *Yonhap News*, May 5, 2010, http://english.yonhapnews.co.kr/northkorea/2010/05/05/ 0401000000AEN20100505001500315.HTML.

133. Kim Min-seok and Yoo Jee-ho, "North Adopts New War Strategy: Source," *Joongang Ilbo*, April 27, 2010, http://joongangdaily.joins.com/article/view.asp?aid=2919725.

134. Marcus Noland, "North Korea: Present Status and Prospects for Survival in the Year 2000," testimony before the Subcommittee on East Asian and Pacific Affairs, United States Senate, Washington, DC, July 8, 1997, http://www.iie.com/publications/papers/ paper.cfm?ResearchID=283.

135. Heejin Koo and Jason Gale, "Kim Jong-il Diverts Food Aid to Military, Defec- tors Say," Bloomberg.com, June 3, 2008, http://preview.bloomberg.com/apps/ news?pid=newsarchive_en10&sid=aeZu7D0jt8NA.

136. Jung Sung-ki, "NK Strengthened Military during Seoul's Liberal Administra- tions," *Korea Times*, October 6, 2008, http://www.koreatimes.co.kr/www/news/ nation/2008/10/120_32250.html.

137. "Kim Jong-il 'Gets 20% of N. Korea's Budget for His Own Use,'" *Chosun Ilbo*, April 12, 2010, http://english.chosun.com/site/data/html_dir/2010/04/12/20100412005 87.html.

138. Michael Sheridan, "Refugees Shot Fleeing North Korea," *The Times*, June 29, 2008, http://www.timesonline.co.uk/tol/news/world/asia/article4232059.ece.
139. John Diamond, "N. Korea, Iraq Pose Different Threats," *USA Today*, January 2, 2003, http://www.globalsecurity.org/org/news/2003/030102-dprk01.htm.
140. Thom Shanker, "South Korean Says North Still a Threat," *New York Times*, November 8, 2007, http://www.nytimes.com/2007/11/08/world/asia/08gates.html?ex=13521780 00&en=b4b19b73713b5060&ei=5088&partner=rssnyt&emc=rss.
141. "U.S. General Concerned by Threat to Seoul Posed by N. Korea's 800-Missile Arsenal," East-Asia-Intel.com, October 17, 2008, http://www.east-asia-intel.com/eai/.

THREE. Creating Instability in Dangerous Global Regions: North Korean Proliferation and Support to Terrorism in the Middle East and South Asia

1. A shorter version of this chapter was originally published as an essay; see Bruce E. Bechtol, Jr., "Creating Instability in Dangerous Global Regions: North Korean Proliferation and Support to Terrorism in the Middle East and South Asia," *Comparative Strategy* 28, no. 2 (2009): 99–115. It is published in this volume with the express written permission of the editors. For more analysis on the statement referenced at the UN, see George Jahn, "Israel Accuses N Korea of Mideast Proliferation," *Washington Post*, October 4, 2008, http://www.washingtonpost.com/wp-dyn/content/article/2008/10/04/ar2008100400721.html.
2. For an excellent short analysis of recent events in North Korea, see Choe Sang-hun, "Kim Jong-il's Health Is Questioned," *International Herald Tribune*, September 9, 2008, http://www.iht.com/articles/2008/09/09/asia/10korea.php.
3. For details of the joint statement from February 2007, see Ministry of Foreign Affairs of Japan, "Initial Actions for the Implementation of the Joint Statement," February 13, 2007, http://www.mofa.go.jp/region/asia-paci/n_korea/6party/action0702.html.
4. Institute for Foreign Policy Analysis, "Independent Working Group on Missile Defense, the Space Relationship, & the Twenty-First Century" (Cambridge, MA: Institute for Foreign Policy Analysis, 2009), http://www.ifpa.org/pdf/IWG2009.pdf.
5. "U.S. General Concerned by Threat."
6. Michael V. Hayden, director, Central Intelligence Agency, "The CIA's Counterproliferation Efforts," address given to the Los Angeles World Affairs Council, September 16, 2008, http://www.lawac.org/speech/2008-09/hayden,michael2008.pdf.
7. Office of the Director of National Intelligence, "Background Briefing with Senior Intelligence Officials on Syria's Covert Nuclear Reactor and North Korea's Involvement," April 24, 2008, http://www.dni.gov/interviews/20080424_interview.pdf.
8. Ibid.
9. Mark Mazzetti and Helene Cooper, "Israeli Nuclear Suspicions Linked to Raid in Syria," *New York Times*, September 17, 2007, http://www.nytimes.com/2007/09/18/world/asia/18korea.html.
10. Sheridan and Mahnaimiin, "Kim Jong-il Builds 'Thunderbirds' Runway."
11. "North Korea Provided Raw Uranium to Syria in 2007: Sources," *Kyodo News*, February 28, 2010, http://www.istockanalyst.com/article/viewistocknews/articleid/3903101.
12. Kim So-hyun, "Worries Surface over N.K.-Iranian Nuclear Deals," *Korea Herald*, March 18, 2010, http://www.koreaherald.co.kr/national/detail.jsp?newsmlid =20100318000038.
13. Caroline Glick, "Column One: Israel and the Axis of Evil," *Jerusalem Post*, May 27, 2009, http://www.jpost.com/servlet/satellite?cid=1243346492707&pagename =jpost%2fjparticle%2fshowfull.
14. See Gary Samore and Bernard Gwertzman, "Samore: A Syria–North Korea Nuclear

Relationship?" Interview, Council on Foreign Relations, September 2007, http://www .cfr.org/publication/14250/.

15. Mike Lillis, "Breaking: GOP Lawmaker Spies North Koreans outside North Korea," *The Washington Independent*, April 13, 2009, http://washingtonindependent .com/38482/breaking-gop-lawmaker-spies-north-koreans-outside-north-korea.

16. "Syria Profile: Missile Capabilities: Scud C (Hwasong-6)," *Nuclear Threat Initiative*, August 2004, http://www.nti.org/e_research/profiles/syria/missile/4126_4337.html.

17. "Syria Profile: Missile Capabilities: Scud D (No-dong 1)," *Nuclear Threat Initiative*, August 2004, http://www.nti.org/e_research/profiles/syria/missile/4126_4338.html.

18. "Syria Improves Its SCUD D Missile."

19. See "Syrians with Secret CBW Material on Train that Exploded?" *Independent Media Review Analysis,* May 15, 2004, http://www/imra.org.il/story.php3?id=20828; "Source Notes Syrian Technicians Killed in Yongch'on Train Explosion," *Tokyo Sankei Shimbum,* May 7, 2004, A07.

20. Sheridan and Mahnaimiin, "Kim Jong-il Builds 'Thunderbirds' Runway."

21. James Hider and Michael Evans, "Blast at Secret Syrian Missile Site Kills Dozens," *The Times*, September 20, 2007, http://www.timesonline.co.uk/tol/news/world/ middle_east/article2489930.ece.

22. See "Test-firing of New Scud Missiles in Syria by N. Korea, Syria, Iran in May Failed Killing over 20," *Independent Media Review Analysis*, August 15, 2009, http://imra .org.il/story.php3?id=45208; and "20 Syrians Killed after Syria-Iranian-N.Korean Missile Test Fails," *Jerusalem Post*, August 15, 2009, http://www.jpost.com/Home/ Article.aspx?id=151890.

23. "Syria: Chemical Weapons," GlobalSecurity.org, April 24, 2004, http://www.global security.org/wmd/world/syria/cw.htm.

24. Wisconsin Project, "North Korea Chemical and Biological Weapon Update—2005."

25. See "North Korea Said to Work at Secret Teheran Site on Iran's Nuclear Warheads," East-Asia-Intel.com, October 3, 2008, http://www.east-asia-intel.com/eai/; and Foreign Affairs Committee, National Council of Resistance of Iran, "Nuclear Pyongyang Is Helping Iran," September 23, 2008, http://ncr-iran.org/content/view/5632/107/.

26. See Christina Y. Lin, "The King from the East: DPRK-Syria-Iran Nuclear Nexus and Strategic Implications for Israel and the ROK," Korea Economic Institute, Academic Paper Series 3, no. 7 (October 2008), http://www.keia.org/Publications/Academic PaperSeries/2008/APS-Lin.pdf.

27. Douglas Frantz, "Iran Closes in on Ability to Build Nuclear Bomb," *Los Angeles Times*, August 4, 2003, http://articles.latimes.com/2003/aug/04/world/fg-nuke4.

28. "N Korea May Already Have Nuclear Warheads: Ex-CIA Official," AFP, September 26, 2008, http://rawstory.com/news/afp/NKorea_may_already_have_nuclear _war_09262008.html.

29. "N Korea May Be Developing Small Nuclear Warhead," Associated Press, October 8, 2008, http://www.iht.com/articles/ap/2008/10/08/asia/as-nkorea-nuclear -warhead.php.

30. For more analysis on North Korea's HEU program and recent statements about it by high-ranking defector Hwang Jang-yop, see "Defector Says DPRK Piled up 'Considerable' Amount of Enriched Uranium," AFP, September 25, 2008, http://www.rushmore drive.com/news/newscluster.aspx?articleId=265093680250417033.

31. See Larry Niksch, "North Korea's Nuclear Weapons Development and Diplomacy" (Washington, DC: Congressional Research Services, Library of Congress, March 30, 2009), 14; and Mark Hosenball, "Nukes Too Deep to Hit," *Newsweek*, November 3, 2008, http://www.newsweek.com/id/165667.

32. For more details on how the North Koreans helped to design and construct Iranian bunkers and tunnels, see Robin Hughes, "Tehran Takes Steps to Protect Nuclear Facilities," *Jane's Defence Weekly*, January 23, 2006, http://www.janes.com/security/international_security/news/jdw/jdw060123_2_n.shtml.

33. Niksch, "North Korea's Nuclear Weapons Development and Diplomacy," 14.

34. Wisconsin Project, "North Korea Missile Milestones," *The Risk Report* 6, no. 5 (September–October 2000), http://www.wisconsinproject.org/countries/nkorea/missile-miles.htm.

35. Center for Nonproliferation Studies, *Chronology of North Korea's Missile Trade and Developments.*

36. Victoria Samson, "Missile Defense: North Korea's Missile Flight Tests," Center for Defense Information, November 20, 2003, http://www.cdi.org/friendlyversion/printversion.cfm?documentid=1677.

37. David C. Wright and Timur Kadyshev, "An Analysis of the North Korean Nodong Missile," *Science & Global Security* 4, no. 2 (1994), http://www.princeton.edu/~globsec/publications/pdf/4_2wright.pdf.

38. Anthony Cordesman, *Iran's Military Forces in Transition: Conventional Threats and Weapons of Mass Destruction* (Westport, CT: Praeger, 1999), 302–03.

39. See Choe Sang-hun, "Iran–North Korea Talks May Harden U.S. Stance," *International Herald Tribune*, November 27, 2005, http://www.iht.com/articles/2005/11/27/news/korea.php; "Tehran to Pyongyang: Trade Oil for Nuke Help," *WorldNet Daily*, November 27, 2005, http://www.worldnetdaily.com/news/article.asp?article_id=47597; and David Eshel, "Iran's Long-Range Missile Program: NATO's Next Challenge," *Defense Update—News Analysis*, January 19, 2005, http://www.defense-update.com/2005/01/irans-long-range-missile-program-natos.html.

40. Jonathan Karl, "Iranian Missile Hits Diplomatic Nerve: Iranian Tensions Push Price of Oil Higher," ABC News, July 9, 2008, http://abcnews.go.com/gma/story?id=5338337&page=1.

41. Joseph S. Bermudez, Jr., "North Korea Deploys New Missiles," *Jane's Defence Weekly*, August 2, 2004, http://www.janes.com/defence/news/jdw/jdw040802_1_n.shtml.

42. See Ben-David, "Iran Acquires Ballistic Missiles from DPRK"; and "Iran Bought 18 North Korean Missiles," *Taipei Times*, December 17, 2005, http://www.taipeitimes.com/news/world/archives/2005/12/17/2003284803.

43. "Iran Develops Missile with 4,000-KM Range," *Middle East Newsline*, March 2, 2006, http://www.menewsline.com/stories/2006/march/03_02_1.html.

44. Charles P. Vick, "Has the No-Dong B/Shahab-4 Finally Been Tested in Iran for North Korea?" GlobalSecurity.Org, May 2, 2006, http://www.globalsecurity.org/wmd/library/report/2006/cpvick-no-dong-b_2006.htm.

45. For the source of the map shown and other analysis on missiles Iran has acquired from North Korea, see House of Representatives, "Recognizing Iran as a Strategic Threat: An Intelligence Challenge for the United States," Washington, DC: Staff Report of the House Permanent Select Committee on Intelligence, Subcommittee on Intelligence Policy, August 23, 2006, http://intelligence.house.gov/Media/PDFS/IranReport082206v2.pdf.

46. See U.S. Senate, "Iran's Ballistic Missile and Weapons of Mass Destruction Programs," hearing before the International Security, Proliferation, and Federal Services Subcommittee of the Committee on Governmental Affairs, 106th Cong., 2nd sess., September 21, 2000, http://intelligence.house.gov/Media/PDFS/IranReport082206v2.pdf#search=%22Recognizing%20Iran%20as%20a%20Strategic%20Threat%3A%20An%20Intelligence%20Challenge%20for%20the%20United%20States%22.

47. See "Iran Military Engineers on Hand for N. Korea Missile Launch," *World Tribune*, July 12, 2006, http://www.worldtribune.com/worldtribune/06/front2453929.001388889 .html; and Barbara Demick, "N. Korea–Iran Ties Seem to Be Growing Stronger," *Los Angeles Times*, July 27, 2006, http://www.latimes.com/news/printedition/ asection/ la-fg-missile27jul27,1,6737932.story?coll=la-news-a_section&ctrack=1&cset=true.

48. See "North Korean Engineers Visited Iran," *Sankei Shimbun* [in Japanese], May 26, 2009, http://www.sankei.co.jp/; and "Media Condemn N Korea Nuclear Test," BBC News, May 26, 2009, http://news.bbc.co.uk/2/hi/asia-pacific/8067893.stm.

49. "M-1978 / M1989 (KOKSAN) 170mm Self Propelled (SP) Gun," GlobalSecurity.org, March 2005, http://www.globalsecurity.org/military/world/dprk/m-1978-170.htm.

50. "N. Korea Agrees to Supply 4 Mini-Submarines to Iran: Source," *Kyodo Press*, July 4, 2007, http://asia.news.yahoo.com/070704/kyodo/d8q5o9b00.html.

51. Larry Niksch, e-mail interview by the author, July 20, 2009.

52. Wisconsin Project, "North Korean Missile Exports," *The Risk Report* 2, no. 6 (November–December 1996), http://www.wisconsinproject.org/countries/nkorea/north-korea -missile-exports.html.

53. Sharon A. Squassoni and Andrew Feickert, "Disarming Libya: Weapons of Mass Destruction," *Congressional Research Service* (Washington, DC: CRS Report for Congress, April 22, 2004), http://www.au.af.mil/au/awc/awcgate/crs/rs21823.pdf.

54. David E. Sanger and William J. Broad, "Tests Said to Tie Deal on Uranium to North Korea," *New York Times*, February 2, 2005, http://www.nytimes.com/2005/02/02/ politics/02nukes.html?ex=1265086800&en=781422d96f3ef04f&ei=5090&partner =rssuserland.

55. See Joby Warrick and Peter Slevin, "Libyan Arms Design Traced Back to China: Pakistanis Resold Chinese-Provided Plans," *Washington Post*, February 15, 2004, http:// www.washingtonpost.com/ac2/wp-dyn/a42692-2004feb14?language=printer;   and "U.S. Intelligence Concludes Iran, N. Korea Have Chinese Nuke Warhead Design," *East-Asia-Intel*, August 9, 2006, http://www.east-asia-intel.com/eai/.

56. Center for Nonproliferation Studies, "CNS Special Report on North Korean Ballistic Missile Capabilities" (Monterey, CA: Center for Nonproliferation Studies, Monterey Institute of International Studies, March 22, 2006), http://cns.miis.edu/stories/ pdfs/060321.pdf.

57. Wisconsin Project, "North Korean Missile Exports."

58. Tony Karon, "SCUD Seizure Raises Tricky Questions," *Time,* December 11, 2002, http://www.time.com/time/world/article/0,8599,398592,00.html.

59. Bertil Lintner, "The Long Reach of North Korea's Missiles," *Asia Times*, June 21, 2006, http://www.atimes.com/atimes/korea/hf21dg02.html.

60. Mitchell B. Reiss and Robert L. Gallucci, "Red-Handed," *Foreign Affairs Online*, March–April 2005, http://www.foreignaffairs.org/20050301faresponse84214/ mitchell-b-reiss-robert-gallucci/red-handed.html.

61. Associated Press, "Pakistani Says Army Knew Atomic Parts Were Shipped," *New York Times*, July 5, 2008, http://www.nytimes.com/2008/07/05/world/asia/05pstan.html ?_r=1&partner=rssnyt&emc=rss&oref=slogin.

62. Declan Walsh, "Disgraced Atomic Scientist Disowns Confession," *The Guardian*, May 30, 2008, http://www.guardian.co.uk/world/2008/may/30/pakistan.nuclear.

63. See Yoichi Funabashi, *The Peninsula Question: A Chronicle of the Second Korean Nuclear Crisis* (Washington, DC: Brookings Institution Press, 2007), 119; and Eishiro Takeishi, "Former President of Pakistan Testified She Had Introduced Missile Technology from North Korea," *Asahi Shimbun* [in Japanese], July 18, 2004.

64. David E. Sanger and James Dao, "U.S. Says Pakistan Gave (Nuclear) Technology to

North Korea," *New York Times,* October 18, 2002, http://membres.lycos.fr/tthreat/article24.htm.

65. David E. Sanger, "In North Korea and Pakistan, Deep Roots of Nuclear Barter," *New York Times,* November 24, 2002, A02, http://www.nytimes.com/2002/11/24/international/asia/24KORE.html.

66. "High Stakes on the High Seas in Korean Blockade," *Sydney Morning Herald,* July 12, 2003, http://www.smh.com.au/articles/2003/07/11/1057783354653.html.

67. Greg Bearup, "Pakistan's Nuclear Bazaar: Dr. Khan's Shady Nuclear Family," *South China Morning Post,* February 11, 2004, http://www.worldpress.org/asia/1825.cfm.

68. "Rice: U.S. Reviewing Aid Provided to Pakistan," msnbc.com, November 4, 2007, http:// www.msnbc.msn.com/id/21613120/.

69. "Hezbollah a North Korea-Type Guerilla Force," *Intelligence Online,* no. 529 (August 25–September 7, 2006), http://www.oss.net/dynamaster/file_archive/060902/26241fe af4766b4d441a3a78917cd55c/Intelligence%20Online%20on%20Hezbolllah.pdf.

70. See Con Coughlin, "North Korea to Help Iran Build Secret Missile Bunkers," *Daily Telegraph,* December 6, 2005, http://www.telegraph.co.uk/news/main.jhtml?xml=/news/2005/06/12/wnkor12.xml&ssheet=/news/2005/06/12/ixnewstop.html; and "Report: North Korea Supervised Building of Hezbullah Underground Facilities," *East-Asia-Intel,* September 13, 2006, http://www.east-asia-intl.com/eai/2006/09_13/12.asp.

71. Lenny Ben-David, "Mining for Trouble in Lebanon," *Jerusalem Post,* October 29, 2007, http://www.jpost.com/servlet/satellite?cid=1192380684296&pagename=jpost %2fjparticle%2fprinter.

72. Moon Chung-in, "[Outlook] The Syrian Nuke Connection," *Joongang Ilbo,* November 26, 2007, http://joongangdaily.joins.com/article/view.asp?aid=2883146.

73. See Larry Niksch, "North Korea: Terrorism List Removal" (Washington, DC: CRS Report for Congress, July 10, 2008), http://www.fas.org/sgp/crs/row/RL30613.pdf.

74. Joby Warrick, "Arms Smuggling Heightens Iran Fears," *Washington Post,* December 3, 2009, http://www.washingtonpost.com/wp-dyn/content/article/2009/12/02/AR2009120203923.html.

75. "Hizballah Acquires CW," *Montreal Middle East Newsline,* July 14, 2008.

76. See David Bedein, "Israeli-Americans Sue North Korea," *The Bulletin,* April 15, 2009, http://thebulletin.us/articles/2009/04/16/news/world/doc49e4337026884764759782 .txt; and "Israelis Suing N. Korea over Failure in Lebanon, PressTV, April 11, 2009, http://www.presstv.com/detail.aspx?id=91162&sectionid=351020202.

77. Bertil Lintner, "North Korea: Coming in from the Cold," *Far Eastern Economic Review,* October 25, 2001, http://www.asiapacificms.com/articles/northkorea/.

78. Roger Davies, "Sea Tigers, Stealth Technology, and the North Korean Connection," *Jane's Intelligence Review,* March 2001, http://www.lankalibrary.com/pol/korea.htm.

79. "Tigers' North Korean Link Bared?" LankaNewspapers.com, March 5, 2007, http://www.lankanewspapers.com/news/2007/3/12823.html.

80. Niksch, "North Korea: Terrorism List Removal."

81. For an example of this, see Department of State, "Afternoon Walkthrough With Reporters at Six-Party Talks," October 30, 2007, http://www.state.gov/p/eap/rls/rm/2007/94373.htm.

82. Helene Cooper, "North Korea Is off Terror List after Deal with the U.S.," *New York Times,* October 12, 2008, http://www.nytimes.com/2008/10/12/world/asia/12terror .html?_r=3&ref=world&oref=slogin&oref=slogin&oref=slogin.

83. Matthew Lee, "N Korea off US Blacklist after Nuke Inspection Deal," Associated Press, October 11, 2008, http://news.yahoo.com/s/ap/20081011/ap_on_go_ca_st_pe/us_koreas_nuclear.

84. "S. Korean Conservatives Slam Bush's N. Korea Policy," *Chosun Ilbo*, October 23, 2008, http://english.chosun.com/site/data/html/_dir/2008/10/23/2008102361008.html.

85. Victor Cha, "Delisting North Korea," *Washington Post*, October 13, 2008, http://www.washingtonpost.com/wp-dyn/content/article/2008/10/11/AR2008101101588.html.

86. Josh Rogin, "Emerging Asian Power: A Diplomatic Challenge," *Congressional Quarterly: CQ Politics*, October 19, 2008, http://www.cqpolitics.com/wmspage.cfm?docid=weeklyreport-000002976585.

87. "US Has No Plans to Put NK Back on Terrorism List," *KBS World*, December 12, 2008, http://world.kbs.co.kr/english/event/nkorea_nuclear/news_01_detail.htm?no=5675.

88. "Nuke Talks' Collapse Strikes Blow to Bush Administration," *Dong-a Ilbo*, December 13, 2008, http://english.donga.com/srv/service.php3?bicode=050000&biid=2008121333358.

89. "Activity Spotted at North Korean Nuclear Test Site," AFP, October 1, 2008, http://www.business24-7.ae/news/asia/activity-spotted-at-north-korea—nuclear-test-site-2008-10-01-1.56438.

90. "N Korea Preparing to Test New Long-Range Missiles: Report," AFP, October 2, 2008, http:// www.spacedaily.com/reports/nkorea_preparing_to_test_new_long-range_missiles_report_999.html.

91. For more analysis of South Korea's past role in the Proliferation Security Initiative, see Myung Jin Kim, "South Korea–North Korea Relations: Influence of the PSI on North Korea," *Strategic Insights* 5, no. 7 (September 2006), http://www.nps.edu/Academics/centers/ccc/publications/OnlineJournal/2006/Sep/kimSep06.html.

92. Jay Solomon, Krishna Pokharel, and Peter Wonacott, "North Korean Plane Was Grounded at U.S. Request," *Wall Street Journal*, November 1, 2008, http://online.wsj.com/article/SB1225494 43144289535.html?mod=googlenews_wsj.

93. Glenn Kessler, "U.S. Efforts Divert Iran-Bound Cargo," *Washington Post*, November 4, 2008, http://www.washingtonpost.com/wp-dyn/content/article/2008/11/03/AR2008110302683.html.

94. Mark Hosenball and Christian Caryl, "North Korea Arms Deal Intercepted," *Newsweek*, November 22, 2008, http://www.newsweek.com/id/170322?tid=relatedcl.

95. For an example of activities that UNSC 1874 has been involved with, see "Iran Bought Masses of N. Korean Arms," *Chosun Ilbo*, December 4, 2009, http://english.chosun.com/site/data/html_dir/2009/12/04/2009120400315.html.

96. Kanbawza Win, "The 4th Burmese Empire with Nuclear Weapons," *Asian Tribune*, October 21, 2008, http://www.asiantribune.com/?q=node/13797.

97. Michael Green and Derek Mitchell, "Asia's Forgotten Crisis: A New Approach to Burma," *Foreign Affairs*, November–December 2007, http://www.foreignaffairs.org/20071101faessay86610/michael-green-derek-mitchell/asia-s-forgotten-crisis.html.

98. Bertil Lintner, "Burma's Nuclear Temptation," *Yale Global*, December 3, 2008, http://antidictatorship.wordpress.com/2008/12/19/analysis-burma's-nuclear-temptation-bertil-lintner/.

99. "Burma: Junta Said Building Armament Factory in Pinlaung with North Korean Help," *Democratic Voice of Burma* [in Burmese], January 20, 2009, http://www.dvb.no/.

100. Bertil Lintner, "Tunnels, Guns, and Kimchi: North Korea's Quest for Dollars—Part I," *Yale Global*, June 9, 2009, http://yaleglobal.yale.edu/content/NK-quest-for-dollars-part1.

101. Ahunt Phone Myat, "Democratic Voice of Burma: North Korean National Dies in Meikhtila," BurmaNet News, January 16, 2009, http://www.burmanet.org/news/2009/01/16/democratic-voice-of-burma-north-korean-national-dies-in-meikhtila-%e2%80%93-ahunt-phone-myat/.

102. "3 Held over Export Bid of DPRK Missile Know-how to Myanmar," *Yomiuri Shim-bun* [in Japanese], June 30, 2009, http://www.yomiuri.co.jp/dy/national/20090630tdy 01304.htm.

103. See Wai Moe, "Burma-North Korea Ties Resurface as Hot Issue," *The Irrawaddy*, May 12, 2010, http://irrawaddy.org/article.php?art_id=18456; Chris Green, "North Korean Weapons Trade Returns to Center Stage," *Daily NK*, May 12, 2010, http://www.dailynk .com/english/read.php?cataId=nk00100&num=6358; Hwang Doo-hyong, "U.S. Calls on Myanmar to Abide by Arms Embargo on N. Korea: State Dept.," *Yonhap News*, June 4, 2010, http://www.dailynk.com/english/read.php?cataId=nk00100&num=6358; and "Myanmar Nuclear Arms Drive Under Way: Media," AFP, June 4, 2010, http://www .google.com/hostednews/afp/article/ALeqM5hSeMkUCgvixIA-Y5rWq1334xs5Jg.

FOUR. **Running in Place: North Korea's Nuclear Program and the Six-party Talks during the Bush Administration**

1. A shorter version of this chapter was originally published as Bruce E. Bechtol, Jr., "Running in Place: North Korea's Nuclear Program and the Six-Party Talks during the Bush Administration," *International Journal of Korean Studies* 13, no. 1 (Spring–Summer 2009). The author would like to thank Dr. Hugo Wheegook Kim, the editor in chief of the *International Journal of Korean Studies*.

2. Lee Banville, "North Korea: Nuclear Standoff," *PBS Online NewsHour*, October 19, 2006, http://www.pbs.org/newshour/indepth_coverage/asia/northkorea/nuclear.html.

3. See International Atomic Energy Agency, "Agreement of 30 January 1992 between the Government of the Democratic People's Republic of Korea and the International Atomic Energy Agency for the Application of Safeguards in Connection with the Treaty on the Non-Proliferation of Nuclear Weapons," *Information Circular*, May 1992, http://www.iaea.org/Publications/Documents/Infcircs/Others/inf403.shtml.

4. See "North Korea Profile: Nuclear Overview," *The Nuclear Threat Initiative*, September 2005, http://www.nti.org/e_research/profiles/NK/Nuclear/.

5. See Joel Wit, Dan Poneman, and Robert Gallucci, "Lessons Learned: The Road Ahead from Going Critical: The First North Korean Nuclear Crisis," *Nautilus Institute Policy Forum Online*, PFO 04-24, June 24, 2004, http://www.nautilus.org/fora/ security/0424a_wit.html.

6. Daryl Kimball and Peter Crail, "Chronology of U.S.–North Korean Nuclear and Missile Diplomacy," *Arms Control Association Factsheet*, June 2008, http://www .armscontrol.org/factsheets/dprkchron.

7. Julia Choe, "Problems of Enforcement: Iran, North Korea, and the NPT," *Harvard International Review: Academy and Policy* 28, no. 2 (Summer 2006), http://www.hir .harvard.edu/index.php?page=article&id=1550&p=2.

8. Oh Young-hwan and Jeong Yong-soo, "North's Uranium Put U.S. in Policy Quandary," *Joongang Ilbo*, October 11, 2004, http://joongangdaily.joins.com/200410/200410112 231256809900092309231.html.

9. Peter Hayes, "The Multilateral Mantra and North Korea," *DPRK Briefing Book, Nautilus Institute Online*, February 20, 2004, http://www.nautilus.org/DPRKBriefingBook/ multilateralTalks/PHMultilateralMantra.html.

10. Mark Manyin, Emma Chanlett-Avery, and Helene Marchart, "North Korea: A Chronology of Events, October 2002–December 2004" (Washington, DC: Congressional Research Service, Library of Congress, January 24, 2005), http://www.fas.org/man/ crs/RL32743.pdf.

11. Siegfried S. Hecker, "Technical Summary of DPRK Nuclear Program," paper presented at the 2005 Carnegie International Non-Proliferation Conference, Washington, DC,

November 8, 2005, http://www.carnegieendowment.org/static/npp/2005conference/presentations/hecker.pdf.

12. See "North Korea's Nuclear Challenge," 2002 Carnegie International Non-Proliferation Conference, Washington, DC, November 14, 2002, http://www.ceip.org/files/projects/npp/resources/conference2002/northkorea.htm.

13. Selig Harrison, Congressional Testimony, "Smart Power: Remaking US Foreign Policy in North Korea," hearing before the House Foreign Affairs Subcommittee, February 13, 2009, http://royce.house.gov/multimedia/default.aspx?MediaID=539.

14. "Dispute Imperils North Korea Nuke Talks," Associated Press, February 19, 2004, http://www.military.com/NewsContent/0,13319,FL_korea_021904,00.html.

15. For statements by Selig Harrison that compared intelligence on North Korea's clandestine HEU weaponization program to that of Iraq, see Selig S. Harrison, "Did North Korea Cheat?" *Foreign Affairs,* January–February 2005, http://www.foreignaffairs.org/20050101faessay84109/selig-s-harrison/did-north-korea-cheat.html.

16. See Stephanie Ho, "North Korea Pursuing Two Paths toward Nuclear Weapons," *Voice of America,* June 21, 2004, http://maximpost.tripod.com/bulletin/index.blog?start=1089868702; and Robert L. Gallucci, "North Korean Nuclear Crisis: An Online Question and Answer Session," Washingtonpost.com, June 23, 2004, http://discuss.washingtonpost.com/wp-srv/zforum/04/world_gallucci062304.htm.

17. Charles L. Pritchard, president, Korea Economic Institute, "Smart Power: Remaking U.S. Foreign Policy in North Korea," statement before the House Committee on Foreign Affairs, Subcommittee on Asia, the Pacific, and the Global Environment, February 12, 2009, http://www.internationalrelations.house.gov/111/pri021209.pdf.

18. See Associated Press, "Pakistani Says Army Knew Atomic Parts Were Shipped"; Walsh, "Disgraced Atomic Scientist Disowns Confession"; Funabashi, *The Peninsula Question*; and Takeishi, "Former President of Pakistan Testified."

19. "Defector: North Korea Has Uranium Program," Associated Press, February 8, 2004, http://www.nuclearpolicy.org/newsarticleprint.cfm?newsid=1276.

20. See Sanger and Dao, "U.S. Says Pakistan Gave (Nuclear) Technology to North Korea"; Sanger, "In North Korea and Pakistan, Deep Roots of Nuclear Barter"; "High Stakes on the High Seas"; and Bearup, "Pakistan's Nuclear Bazaar."

21. "Missing Pakistani Nuclear Scientists in North Korea," AFP, June 20, 2004, http://www.pakistan-facts.com/article.php?story=20040620201344967.

22. Richard Cheney, vice president of the United States, "Vice President Speaks at China's Fudan University, April 15," speech given at Fudan University, China, April 15, 2004, http://helsinki.usembassy.gov/servlet/PageServer?Page=today2.html.

23. See "North Korea Said to Work at Secret Teheran Site"; Foreign Affairs Committee, "Nuclear Pyongyang Is Helping Iran"; Lin, "The King from the East"; and Frantz, "Iran Closes in on Ability to Build Nuclear Bomb."

24. See Warrick and Slevin, "Libyan Arms Design Traced Back to China"; and "U.S. Intelligence Concludes Iran, N. Korea Have Chinese Nuke Warhead Design."

25. "Dispute Imperils North Korea Nuke Talks."

26. "N. Korea Believed to Possess Weapons-Grade HEU," *Chosun Ilbo,* January 16, 2009, http://english.chosun.com/w21data/html/news/200901/200901160012.html.

27. "NKorea Running Secret Nuclear Plant: Report," AFP, February 18, 2009, http://www.google.com/hostednews/afp/article/ALeqM5iUMkh8pqycilFWddJSqYHe0psvcg.

28. "NK Has Built Uranium Enrichment Facilities," *Dong-a Ilbo,* February 18, 2009, http://english.donga.com/srv/service.php3?biid=2009021833768.

29. See R. Jeffrey Smith and Joby Warrick, "Pakistani Scientist Depicts More Advanced Nuclear Program in North Korea," *Washington Post,* December 28, 2009, http://www.washingtonpost.com/wp-dyn/content/article/2009/12/27/AR2009122701205.html;

and "N. Korea Had Enriched Uranium in 2002," *Chosun Ilbo*, December 29, 2009, http://english.chosun.com/site/data/html_dir/2009/12/29/2009122900357.html.

30. Kim So-hyun, "N.K. Says It Will Start Enriching Uranium," *Korea Herald*, June 15, 2009, http://www.koreaherald.co.kr/newkhsite/data/html_dir/2009/06/15/20090615 0033.asp.

31. Selig Harrison, Testimony before the U.S. Congress, House Committee on Foreign Affairs, June 17, 2009, http://foreignaffairs.house.gov/111/har061709.pdf.

32. "DPRK Permanent Representative Sends Letter to President of UNSC," Korean Central News Agency (*KCNA*), September 4, 2009, http://www.kcna.co.jp/item/2009/200909/ news04/20090904-04ee.html.

33. Kim Hyun, "N. Korea Started Uranium Enrichment before 2002: Seoul Minister," *Yonhap News*, June 15, 2009, http://english.yonhapnews.co.kr/northkorea/2009/06/17/71/ 0401000000AEN20090617006700325.HTML.

34. Central Intelligence Agency, "Untitled CIA Estimate Provided to Congress on November 19, 2002, (UNCLASSIFIED)," November 19, 2002, http://www.fas.org/nuke/ guide/dprk/nuke/cia111902.html.

35. "N. Korea Cannot Make Weapons with Enriched Uranium: Experts," *Yonhap News*, September 4, 2009, http://english.yonhapnews.co.kr/northkorea/2009/09/04/62/0401 000000AEN20090904007400320f.HTML.

36. Michael R. Gordon, "How Politics Sank Accord on Missiles with North Korea," *New York Times*, March 6, 2001, http://www.nytimes.com/2001/03/06/world/06MISS.html.

37. Alex Wagner, "Bush Puts N. Korea Negotiations on Hold, Stresses Verification," *Arms Control Today*, April 2001, http://www.armscontrol.org/act/2001_04/korea.

38. "A Visit by South Korea's Leader," *New York Times*, March 6, 2001, http://www .nytimes.com/2001/03/06/opinion/06tue3.html.

39. George Gedda, "U.S. Withdraws Offer to Hold Security Talks with North Korea Next Week," Associated Press, July 2, 2002, http://www.nautilus.org/ napsnet/dr/0207/ jul03.html#item2.

40. See Jane Perlez, "Clinton Trip to North Korea Is Mired in Transition Politics," *New York Times*, December 20, 2000, http://www.nytimes.com/2000/12/20/world/clinton-trip-to-north-korea-is-mired-in-transition-politics.html?scp=1&sq=Jane%20Perlez,%20 %93Clinton%20Trip%20to%20North%20Korea%20Is%20Mired%20&st=cse.

41. "Former NIS Head Says N.K. Leader Had Planned S.K. Visit in 2001," *Chosun Ilbo*, June 9, 2004, http://english.chosun.com/cgi-bin/printnews?id=200406090013.

42. For more details of these events, see Ivo H. Daalder and James M. Lindsay, *America Unbound: The Bush Revolution in Foreign Policy* (Washington, DC: Brookings Institution Press, 2003), 165–78.

43. Jayshree Bajoria and Carin Zissis, "The Six-Party Talks on North Korea's Nuclear Program," Council on Foreign Relations, October 14, 2008, http://www.cfr.org/ publication/13593/.

44. Edward A. Olsen, "If the United States Had 'No' Policy toward North Korea," *Strategic Insights* 4, no. 10 (October 2005), http://www.nps.edu/Academics/centers/ccc/ publications/OnlineJournal/2005/Oct/olsenOct05.html.

45. Brian Lee, "North Agrees to Give Up Its Nuclear Works," *Joongang Ilbo*, September 20, 2005, http://joongangdaily.joins.com/200509/19/200509192255503579900090209021 .html.

46. "Chung Broke Deadlock in North's Nuclear Crisis," *Joongang Ilbo*, October 4, 2005, http://service.joins.com/asp/print_article_english.asp?aid=2625262&esectcode=e _special&title=chung+broke+deadlock+in+north's+nuclear+crisis.

47. "Seoul Saved Six-Party Talks: Unification Minister," *Chosun Ilbo*, September 19, 2005, http://english.chosun.com/w21data/html/news/200509/200509190024.html.

48. Brian Lee, "Details Could Stir Controversies," *Joongang Ilbo*, September 20, 2005, http://service.joins.com/asp/.

49. Henry Sokolski, "Hide and Seek with Kim Chong-il," *Nautilus Institute Policy Forum Online* 05-80A, September 29, 2005, http://www.nautilus.org/fora/security/0580sokolski.html.

50. Department of Treasury, "Treasury Designates Banco Delta Asia as Primary Money Laundering Concern under USA PATRIOT Act," press release, September 15, 2005, http://www.treas.gov/press/releases/js2720.htm.

51. Myoung-Gun Lee, "Outlook Uncertain as Six-Party Talks End," *Dong-a Ilbo*, November 12, 2005, http://english.donga.com/srv/service.php3?bicode=050000&biid=2005111283758.

52. William Bach, Office of African, Asian, and European Affairs, Bureau for International Narcotics and Law Enforcement Affairs, Department of State, testimony, Hearing on Drugs Counterfeiting and Arms Trade, Senate Subcommittee on Financial Management, the Budget, and International Security, May 20, 2003, http://usinfo.org/wf-archive/2003/030521/epf310.htm.

53. See Seung-Ryun Kim, "North Korea's Counterfeiting Mistake," *Dong-a Ilbo*, December 24, 2005, http://english.donga.com/srv/service.php3?bicode=060000&biid=2005122473898; and Bertil Lintner, "North Korea's Missile Trade Helps Fund Its Nuclear Program," *Yale Global Online*, May 5, 2003, http://yaleglobal.yale.edu/content/north-koreas-missile-trade-helps-fund-its-nuclear-program.

54. Anthony Spaeth, "Kim's Rackets: To Fund His Lifestyle—and His Nukes—Kim Jong Il Helms a Vast Criminal Network," *Time Asia,* June 2, 2003, http://www.time.com/time/asia/covers/501030609/story.html.

55. Jay Solomon and Hae Won Choi, "Money Trail: In North Korea, Secret Cash Hoard Props up Regime," *Wall Street Journal*, July 14, 2003, A01.

56. Barbara Demick, "No More Gambling on North Korea," *Los Angeles Times*, April 6, 2006, http://www.latimes.com/news/printedition/la-fg-macao6apr06,1,7483991.story.

57. See "N. Korean Leader Moved Secret Bank Accounts to Luxembourg: Report," *Yonhap News*, December 27, 2005, http://english.yna.co.kr/engnews/20051227/4301000000 20051227194320e2.html; and "Singapore: N. Korea's New Money Haven," *Dong-a Ilbo*, August 5, 2006, http://english.donga.com/srv/service.php3?bicode=060000&biid=2006080539518.

58. "Media Release: Extra 75kg of Heroin Linked to 'Pong Su,'" *Australian Federal Police*, May 27, 2003, http://www.afp.gov.au/afp/page/media/2003/0527pongsu.htm.

59. Nick Green, "Dealing Drugs: North Korean Narcotics Trafficking," *Harvard International Review* 26, no. 1 (Spring 2004), http://hir.harvard.edu/articles/1201.

60. See Mindy L. Kotler, "Toward an 'Asian' North Korea," *Nautilus Institute Policy Forum Online* PFO 03-28, April 8, 2003, http://www.nautilus.org/fora/security/0328_Kotler.html; and Gavan McCormack, "North Korea and the US: 'Strategic Decision,'" *The Asia-Pacific Journal: Japan Focus*, December 2005, http://www.japanfocus.org/-Gavan-McCormack/1925.

61. See Association of Former Intelligence Officers, "North Korean Ship Sunk," *Intelligence Notes*, 50-01, December 24, 2001, http://www.afio.com/sections/wins/2001/2001-50.html; and Charles R. Smith, "North Korean Heroin," NewsMax.com, May 7, 2003, http://www.news max.com/archives/articles/2003/5/7/30830.shtml.

62. Park Syung-je, board member, Military Analyst Association of the Republic of Korea, Seoul, Republic of Korea, e-mail interview by author, January 22, 2006.

63. Peter A. Prahar, director, Office of African, Asia and Europe/NIS Programs, Bureau for International Narcotics and Law Enforcement Affairs, Department of State, state-

ment for hearing "North Korea: Illicit Activity Funding the Regime," Federal Financial Management, Government Information, and International Security Subcommittee, Committee on Homeland Security and Governmental Affairs, U.S. Senate, 109th Cong., 2nd sess., April 25, 2006, http://hsgac.senate.gov/_files/ 042506prahar.pdf.

64. Sheena E. Chestnut, "The 'Sopranos State'? North Korean Involvement in Criminal Activity and Implications for International Security," Center for International Security and Cooperation, Stanford University, May 20, 2005, http://www.nautilus.org/napsnet/sr/2006/0605Chestnut.pdf.

65. Josh Meyer and Barbara Demick, "Counterfeiting Cases Point to North Korea," *Los Angeles Times*, December 12, 2005, http://uniset.ca/terr/news/lat_nkor_counterfeit.html.

66. Congressman Ed Royce, "Gangster Regime: How North Korea Counterfeits United States Currency," staff report, United States House of Representatives, March 12, 2007, http://www.royce.house.gov/uploadedfiles/report.3.12.07.final.gansterregime.pdf.

67. See "Japanese Banks Match U.S. Sanctions on N. Korea," *Chosun Ilbo*, February 2, 2006, http://english.chosun.com/w21data/html/news/200602/200602020013.html; "China Cracks Down on Counterfeit Dollars," *Chosun Ilbo*, March 19, 2006, http://english.chosun.com/w21data/html/news/200603/200603190006.html; Gordon Fairclough, "North Korea Might Be Exporting Fake $100 Bills," *Wall Street Journal*, March 24, 2006, http://www.washingtonpost.com/wp-dyn/content/article/2006/03/23/AR2006032301534.html; Choi Hyung-kyu and Brian Lee, "US, China Agree to Help Attack North Counterfeiting," *Joongang Ilbo*, August 1, 2006, http://joongangdaily.joins.com/200607/31/200607312148443009900090309031.html; Lindsay Beck, "Analysis—China Grapples with North Korea's Illicit Dealings," Reuters, August 1, 2006, http://www.hses.com/n06080107.htm; Elizabeth Wishnick, "Nuclear Tension between China, N Korea," *International Relations and Security Network*, August 11, 2006, http://www.isn.ethz.ch/isn/Current-Affairs/Security-Watch/Detail/?id=52292&lng=en; and Lee Sang-il and Brian Lee, "U.S. Hails Bank of China's Freeze," *Joongang Ilbo*, July 28, 2006, http://joongangdaily.joins.com/200607/27/200607272127545339900090309031.html.

68. Rachel L. Loeffler, "Bank Shots: How the Financial System Can Isolate Rogues," *Foreign Affairs* 88, no. 2 (March–April 2009), http://www.foreignaffairs.com/articles/64822/rachel-l-loeffler/bank-shots.

69. Peter Baker and Anthony Faille, "U.S., S. Korea Find Unity against North's Nuclear Arms Program," *Washington Post*, November 17, 2005.

70. "Outrage over N Korea Missile Test."

71. See Donald Kirk, "N. Korea's Test Threat Launches Uproar," *Christian Science Monitor*, June 22, 2006, http://www.csmonitor.com/2006/0622/p06s02-woap.html; and "(2nd LD) N. Korea Trying to Shift U.S. Policy with Missile Threats: Official," *Yonhap News,* June 23, 2006, http://english.yonhapnews.co.kr/engservices/4101000000.html.

72. Chuck Downs, "Right Where He Wants Us," *Wall Street Journal*, June 21, 2006, A12.

73. Daniel Pinkston, "North Korea Conducts Nuclear Test" (Monterey, CA: Center for Nonproliferation Studies, Monterey Institute of International Studies, October 10, 2006), http://cns.miis.edu/stories/pdfs/061010_dprktest.pdf.

74. Siegfried S. Hecker, "Report on North Korean Nuclear Program," Center for International Security and Cooperation, Stanford University, November 15, 2006, http://iis-db.stanford.edu/pubs/21266/dprk-report-hecker06.pdf.

75. Hui Zhang, "North Korea's Oct. 9 Nuclear Test: Successful or Failed?" Paper presented at the Institute for Nuclear Materials Management 48th Annual Meeting, Tucson, Arizona, July 8–12, 2007, http://belfercenter.ksg.harvard.edu/files/NKtest_INMM07_Hui.pdf.

76. Burt Herman, "North Korea May Be Backing off Showdown," Associated Press, October 20, 2006, http://www.washingtonpost.com/wp-dyn/content/article/2006/10/20/AR2006102000273.html.

77. Choe Sang-Hun, "U.S. Ties with Seoul Fray over North," *International Herald Tribune*," September 13, 2006, http://www.iht.com/articles/2006/09/12/news/allies.php.

78. Department of State, "North Korea—Denuclearization Action Plan: Initial Actions for the Implementation of the Joint Statement," February 13, 2007, http://www.shaps.hawaii.edu/fp/us/2007/nk_denuclearization_action_plan_20070213.html.

79. "Initial Actions for the Implementation of the Joint Statement: Joint Statement from the Third Session of the Fifth Round of the Six-Party Talks," *Nautilus Institute Policy Forum Online Special Report*, February 13, 2007, http://www.nautilus.org/fora/security/07013statement.html.

80. Department of State, "Briefing on the Agreement Reached at the Six-Party Talks in Beijing," February 13, 2007, http://seoul.usembassy.gov/420_021407b.html.

81. For details on the reported disagreement in the Bush administration over the deal reached on February 13, 2007, see David Sanger, "Outside Pressures Snapped Korean Deadlock," *New York Times*, February 14, 2007, http://select.nytimes.com/gst/abstract.html?res=f30f13f63d5a0c778dddab0894df404482.

82. "Transcript: Update on the Six-Party Talks with Christopher R. Hill.," proceedings of Brookings Institution Center for Northeast Asian Policy Studies, Washington, DC, February 22, 2007, http://www.brook.edu/comm/events/20070228hill.pdf.

83. Brian Lee, "Seoul Aide: Uranium Is Not Forgotten," *Joongang Ilbo*, February 17, 2007, http://joongangdaily.joins.com/article/view.asp?aid=2872552.

84. Heda Bayron, "North Korea Will Not Stop Nuclear Program Unless US Releases Frozen Funds," *Voice of America*, March 18, 2007, http://www.voanews.com/burmese/archive/2007-03/2007-03-18-voa1.cfm?renderforprint=1&textonly=1&&textmode=1&cfid=127954726&cftoken=37389832&jsessionid=66302cc8eaeb5bc2083813f2f7f78513b5d4.

85. Tan Ee Lyn, "Frozen North Korean Funds Released from Macau Bank," Reuters, June 14, 2007, http://www.alertnet.org/thenews/newsdesk/T167080.htm.

86. Prepared remarks by Stuart A. Levey, undersecretary for terrorism and financial intelligence, before the American Bar Association's 22nd Annual National Institute on White Collar Crime, Press Room, U.S. Department of the Treasury, March 6, 2008, http://www.ustreas.gov/press/releases/hp863.htm.

87. For more on the apparent change in policy taken by the Bush administration in 2007, see John McGlynn, "The U.S. Declaration of War on Iran," *The Asia-Pacific Journal: Japan Focus*, March 22, 2008, http://www.japanfocus.org/products/details/2707.

88. See Uzi Mahnaimi, Sarah Baxter, and Michael Sheridan, "Israelis 'Blew apart Syrian Nuclear Cache'," *The Times*, September 16, 2007, http://www.timesonline.co.uk/tol/news/world/middle_east/ article2461421.ece; and Office of the Director of National Intelligence, "Background Briefing with Senior Intelligence Officials on Syria's Covert Nuclear Reactor and North Korea's Involvement."

89. Helene Cooper, "Past Deals by N. Korea May Face Less Study," *New York Times*, April 18, 2008, http://www.nytimes.com/2008/04/18/washington/18diplo.html?_r=1&partner=rssnyt&emc=rss.

90. See Arshad Muhammed, "Rice Says Verifying N. Korea Declaration to Take Time," Reuters, April 17, 2008, http://www.reuters.com/article/worldnews/idusn1722700420080418.

91. See Winston Lord and Leslie H. Gelb, "Yielding to N. Korea Too Often," *Washington Post*, April 26, 2008, http://www.washingtonpost.com/wp-dyn/content/article/2008/04/25/AR2008042503007.html.

92. Glenn Kessler, "N. Korea Agrees to Blow up Tower at its Nuclear Facility," *Washington Post*, May 2, 2008, http://www.washingtonpost.com/wp-dyn/content/article/2008/05/01/AR2008050103719.html.

93. See Sue Pleming, "North Korea Hands over Plutonium Documents: U.S.," Reuters, May 8, 2008, http://www.reuters.com/article/politicsnews/idusn0833667920080508; and Helene Cooper, "North Korea Gives U.S. Files on Plutonium Efforts," *New York Times*, May 9, 2008, http://www.nytimes.com/2008/05/09/world/asia/09diplo.html?partner=rssnyt&emc=rss.

94. Arshad Mohammed, "U.S. Says North Korea to Cooperate on Nuclear Checks," Reuters, May 13, 2008, http://www.reuters.com/article/politicsnews/idusn1339439320080513.

95. Kang Chan-ho and Jung Ha-won, "Washington Approves Aid Package for North," *Joongang Ilbo*, May 24, 2008, http://joongangdaily.joins.com/article/view.asp?aid=2890230.

96. For details of how the U.S. government believed the talks were progressing during this time period and what the North Koreans needed to do, see Condoleezza Rice, "Diplomacy Is Working on North Korea," Op-Ed, *Wall Street Journal*, June 26, 2008, http://online.wsj.com/article/SB121443815539505367.html?KEYWORDS=%22Diplomacy+is+working+on+north+korea%22.

97. See "North Korean Officials Share Thoughts with KEI Staff," Korea Economic Institute, May 2008, http://www.keia.org/; Glenn Kessler, "N. Korea Taking Tougher Stance, Ex-Envoy Warns," *Washington Post*, May 30, 2008, http://www.washingtonpost.com/wp-dyn/content/article/2008/05/29/AR2008052904044.html; David Gollust, "US Rejects Criticism of Former North Korea Envoy," *Voice of America*, May 30, 2008, http://www1.voanews.com/english/news/a-13-2008-05-30-voa63.html; and Helene Cooper, "In Disclosure, North Korea Contradicts U.S. Intelligence on Its Plutonium Program," *New York Times*, May 31, 2008, http://www.nytimes.com/2008/05/31/world/asia/31korea.html.

98. See Peter Walker, Jonathan Watts, and Suzanne Goldenberg, "North Korea Blows up Cooling Tower in Nuclear Concession," *The Guardian*, June 27, 2008, http://www.guardian.co.uk/world/2008/jun/27/korea.japan.

99. Art Brown, "North Korea's Stacked Deck," *New York Times*, July 15, 2008, http://www.nytimes.com/2008/07/15/opinion/15brown.html?_r=1.

100. This is a direct quote from a U.S. State Department Fact Sheet. For more details contained in the Fact Sheet on the lifting of sanctions and the intent to rescind North Korea's status as a state sponsor of terrorism, see Department of State, "North Korea: Presidential Action on State Sponsor of Terrorism (SST) and the Trading with the Enemy Act (TWEA)," *Nautilus Institute Policy Forum Online* 08-050A, June 30, 2008, http://www.nautilus.org/fora/security/08050dos.html.

101. See Peter Brookes, "Korean Nukes: Don't Get Giddy," *New York Post*, June 27, 2008, http://www.nypost.com/seven/06272008/postopinion/opedcolumnists/korean_nukes__dont_get_giddy_117426.htm.

102. Glenn Kessler, "New Data Found on North Korea's Nuclear Capacity," *Washington Post*, June 21, 2008, http://www.washingtonpost.com/wp-dyn/content/article/2008/06/20/AR2008062002499.Html.

103. "N. Korea Pulls Half of Fuel Rods from Key Reactor," *Kyodo News*, July 17, 2008, http://home.kyodo.co.jp/.

104. Yuji Anai, "Govt Anxious after Latest 6-Party Talks," *Yomiuri Shimbun*, July 13, 2008, http://www.yomiuri.co.jp/dy/world/.

105. Jae-soon Chang, "US Offers Nuclear Proposal to NKorea," Associated Press, July 22, 2008, http://www.usatoday.com/news/world/2008-07-21-2267497974_x.htm.

106. "Bush Says Not to Delist DPRK without Uranium, Proliferation Verification," AFP, July 31, 2008, http://afp.google.com/article/aleqm5ifhdwhqdfje_atvvyswaotozxarw.

107. See "N.Korea 'Upping the Pressure Piecemeal," *Chosun Ilbo*, September 24, 2008, http://english.chosun.com/w21data/html/news/200809/200809240010.html.

108. For more details of the plan for verification proposed by the United States, see Glenn Kessler, "Far-Reaching U.S. Plan Impaired N. Korea Deal," *Washington Post*, September 26, 2008, http://www.washingtonpost.com/wp-dyn/content/article/2008/09/25/AR2008092504380.html.

109. Choe Sang-hun and Helene Cooper, "U.S. Official Prolongs N. Korea Talks," *New York Times*, October 3, 2008, http://www.nytimes.com/2008/10/03/world/asia/03korea.html?_r=1&ref=world&oref=slogin.

110. Choe Sang-hun and Helene Cooper, "North Korea to Resume Disabling Nuclear Plant," *New York Times*, October 13, 2008, http://www.nytimes.com/2008/10/13/world/asia/13nkorea.html.

111. Victor Cha, "The Curse of American Reasonableness," *Chosun Ilbo*, October 20, 2008, http://english.chosun.com/w21data/html/news/200810/200810200006.html.

112. "N. Korea 'Wants Compensation for Yongbyon People,'" *Chosun Ilbo*, October 24, 2008, http://english.chosun.com/w21data/html/news/200810/200810240008.html.

113. "N. Korea Demanding Timetable for Energy Aid before 6-way Talks," *Kyodo News*, October 31, 2008, http://www.rushmoredrive.com/news/newscluster.aspx?articleid=16156002430812 324803.

114. Bruce Klingner, "North Korea Nuclear Verification: Has the U.S. Blinked?" Heritage Foundation Web Memo no. 2120, October 31, 2008, http://www.heritage.org/Research/Reports/2008/10/North-Korea-Nuclear-Verification-Has-the-US-Blinked.

115. "U.S. 'Gave Ground' to North Korea," *Yomiuri Shimbun*, November 2, 2008, http://www.yomiuri.co.jp/dy/world/20081102tdy01302.htm.

116. For more details regarding the nature of the verification protocol and the minor role that North Korea's HEU program and proliferation played in it, see "U.S. Relented over N. Korea Document," *San Diego Union Tribune,* November 2, 2008, http://www.signonsandiego.com/uniontrib/20081102/news_1n2world.html.

117. See Jon Herskovitz, "North Korea Will Not Let Nuclear Samples out of Country," Reuters, November 12, 2008, http://www.reuters.com/article/newsmaps/idustre4ab4fk20081112; and "N. Korea Refuses Nuclear Sampling," *Yonhap News*, November 12, 2008, http://english.yonhapnews.co.kr/national/2008/11/12/57/0301000000aen20081112008900315f.html.

118. See Nicholas Kralev, "U.S. Takes N. Korea's Word on Nuclear Pact," *Washington Times*, November 24, 2008, http://www.washingtontimes.com/news/2008/nov/24/us-takes-n-koreas-word-on-nuclear-pact/.

119. Jung Sung-ki, "No Document on N. Korean Pledge to Nuclear Sampling," *Korea Times*, November 25, 2008, http://www.koreatimes.co.kr/www/news/nation/2008/11/116_35065.html.

120. "(*Yonhap* Interview) Sampling Core Part of Verification Deal with N. Korea: U.S. Official," *Yonhap News*, November 26, 2008, http://english.yonhapnews.co.kr/news/2008/11/26/0200000000aen20081126002800315.html.

121. David Gollust, "US Wants North Korean Verification Commitments on Paper," *Voice of America*, November 28, 2008, http://www1.voanews.com/english/news/a-13-2008-11-28-voa52.html.

122. Steven Lee Myers, "In Setback for Bush, Korea Nuclear Talks Collapse," *New York Times*, December 12, 2008, http://www.nytimes.com/2008/12/12/world/asia/12korea.html.

123. Lee Chi-dong, "Nuclear Talks Crumble, Protracted Stalemate Looms," *Yonhap News*, December 11, 2008, http://www.koreancenter.or.kr/news/news_foreign_view .aspx?menu_code=02001000&news_id=aen20081211009700315.
124. Merle D. Kellerhals Jr., "Six-Party Talks Stall as North Korea Refuses to Sign Agreement," America.gov, December 11, 2008, http://www.america.gov/st/peacesec -english/2008/december/20081211172120dmslahrellek0.112652.html.
125. Robert M. Gates, "A Balanced Strategy: Reprogramming the Pentagon for a New Age," *Foreign Affairs*, January–February 2009, http://www.foreignaffairs.org/ articles/63717/robert-m-gates/a-balanced-strategy.
126. "North Korea's Kim Trying to Test Process—Bush," Reuters, December 15, 2008, http://africa.reuters.com/energyandoil/news/usnsp405431.html.
127. See "Six-Party Nations Disagree over Fuel Aid to North Korea," *Chosun Ilbo*, December 15, 2008, http://english.chosun.com/site/data/html_dir/2008/12/15/2008121561012 .html; "China Dismisses U.S. Bargaining on Fuel Supplies to N. Korea," *Ria Novosti*, December 16, 2008, http://en.rian.ru/world/20081216/118883866.html; and "Russia to Complete Fuel Supplies to North Korea—Envoy," *Ria Novosti*, December 12, 2008, http://en.rian.ru/russia/20081214/118850215.html.
128. Hwang Doo-hyong, "White House Urges N. Korea to Return to 6-party Talks," *Yonhap News*, January 2, 2009, http://english.yonhapnews.co.kr/news/2009/01/03/020000000 0aen20090103000100315.html.
129. Glenn Kessler, "White House Voices Concern on North Korea and Uranium," *Washington Post*, January 8, 2009, http://www.washingtonpost.com/wp-dyn/content/ article/2009/01/07/AR2009010703530.html.
130. Takeo Miyazaki, "Concentrated Uranium Detected in DPRK Samples," *Yomiuri Shimbun*, January 16, 2009, http://www.yomiuri.co.jp/dy/world/20090116tdy01302.htm.
131. "N. Korea Believed to Possess Weapons-Grade HEU."
132. Nicholas Eberstadt, "What Went Wrong? The Bush Administration's Failed North Korea Policy," *Weekly Standard*, January 26, 2009, http://www.weeklystandard.com/ Content/Public/Articles/000/000/016/024opizu.asp.
133. Marcus Noland, "North Korean Missile Test: Remedial Action," *Asia Pacific Bulletin* 33 (April 6, 2009), http://www.eastwestcenter.org/fileadmin/stored/pdfs/apb033 _1.pdf.
134. See "North Korea Conducts Nuclear Test," BBC News, May 25, 2009, http://news.bbc .co.uk/2/hi/asia-pacific/8066615.stm.
135. Jack Kim, "North Korea Seen Readying for New Nuclear Test," Reuters, May 7, 2009, http://uk.reuters.com/article/iduktre54609q20090507?rpc=401&=undefined&sp=true.
136. See Sam Kim, "N. Korean Nuclear Blast Probably Less Powerful Than Hoped For: Yale Scholar," *Yonhap News*, May 28, 2009, http://english.yonhapnews.co.kr/news/2 009/05/28/0200000000aen20090528007400315.html; and Kim Su-jeong and Yoo Jee-ho, "Expert: North's Test Not a Surprise, More to Come," *Joongang Ilbo*, June 1, 2009, http://joongangdaily.joins.com/article/view.asp?aid=2905533.
137. Office of the Director of National Intelligence, "Statement by the Office of the Director of National Intelligence on North Korea's Declared Nuclear Test on May 25, 2009," Public Affairs Office news release, Washington, DC, June 15, 2009, http://www.dni .gov/press_releases/20090615_release.pdf.
138. Department of State, "North Korea Sanctions: Resolution 1718 versus Resolution 1874," Bureau of Public Affairs, Office of the Spokesman, June 12, 2009, http://www .state.gov/r/pa/prs/ps/2009/06a/124709.htm.
139. "Rogue N. Korean Ship Returns Home," *Chosun Ilbo*, July 7, 2009, http://english .chosun.com/site/data/html_dir/2009/07/07/2009070700400.html.

140. Paul Richter, "Doubts in White House Approach to N. Korea," *Los Angeles Times*, July 14, 2009, http://www.latimes.com/news/nationworld/world/la-fg-korea-talks14 -2009jul14,0,3552905.story.

141. U.S. Department of State, "Actions Taken by the United Nations Security Council 1718 Sanctions Committee to Implement Resolution 1874," Bureau of Public Affairs, Office of the Spokesman, July 16, 2009, http://www.state.gov/r/pa/prs/ps/2009/july/126 148.htm.

142. See Michael D. Shear, "U.S. Interagency Team to Focus on Sanctions against North Korea," *Washington Post*, June 27, 2009, http://www.washingtonpost.com/wp-dyn/ content/article/2009/06/26/AR2009062604306.html; "U.S. to Coordinate with Asian Countries on N. Korea Sanctions," *Chosun Ilbo*, July 8, 2009, http://english.cho sun.com/site/data/html_dir/2009/07/08/2009070800807.html; and "U.S. Presses HK to Help Curb NKorea Bank Access," Associated Press, July 9, 2009, http://news .moneycentral.msn.com/provider/providerarticle.aspx?feed=ap&date=20090709 &id=10129918.

143. Department of the Treasury, "North Korea Government Agencies' and Front Companies' Involvement in Illicit Financial Activities," *Financial Crimes Enforcement Network*, FIN-2009-A002, June 18, 2009, http://www.fincen.gov/statutes_regs/guidance/ html/fin-2009-a002.html.

144. Department of the Treasury, "Treasury Designates Financial Institution Tied to North Korea's WMD Proliferation," press release, August 11, 2009, http://www.ustreas.gov/ press/releases/tg260.htm.

145. Toru Makinota, "Branch of North Korean Bank in Dandong, China Closed Down after Targeted by US Sanctions," *Yomiuri Shimbun* [in Japanese], October 1, 2009.

146. "UAE Seizes N. Korean Arms Bound for Iran, Diplomats Say," CNN.com, August 29, 2009, http://edition.cnn.com/2009/WORLD/asiapcf/08/28/uae.korea.ship.seized.

147. "No Radioactive Material on Korean Ship: Final Report," *Press Trust of India*, September 6, 2009, http://www.dnaindia.com/india/report_no-radioactive-material-on -korean-ship-final-report_1287997.

148. See "Reports: S Korea Seized N Korean Cargo Containers," Associated Press, October 5, 2009, http://asia.news.yahoo.com/ap/20091005/tap-as-koreas-cargo-seizure -510daa6.html; "Seized NK Containers Were Headed for Syria," *Dong-a Ilbo*, October 7, 2009, http://english.donga.com/srv/service.php3?biid=2009100756908; and "Seizure of NK Containers Conducted under UN Resolution," *Dong-a Ilbo*, October 9, 2009, http://english.donga.com/srv/service.php3?biid=2009100997628.

149. See "Firms in 5 Countries Camouflaged N. Korean Arms Deal," *Chosun Ilbo*, January 27, 2010, http://english.chosun.com/site/data/html_dir/2010/01/27/2010012700741 .html; "Missile Parts Found in N. Korean Arms Deal," *Chosun Ilbo*, December 17, 2009, http://english.chosun.com/site/data/html_dir/2009/12/17/2009121700285.html; and Brian McCartan, "Weapons Seizure Hits North Korea Hard," *Asia Times*, December 22, 2009, http://www.atimes.com/atimes/southeast_asia/kl22ae01.html.

FIVE. **Maintaining a Rogue Regime: Kim Chong-il and the North Korean Regime Succession Process**

1. See "Kim Jong-il Possibly Suffered a Stroke: US Intelligence," AFP, September 9, 2008, http://afp.google.com/article/aleqm5hi60aog6lvdvj_zbf9hguvfbqrwa; Christian Caryl and B. J. Lee, "A Prayer for the Hermit King," *Newsweek*, September 11, 2008, http://www.newsweek.com/id/158384; and "North Korean Leader Has Little Chance of Full Recovery," *Kyodo News*, September 18, 2008, http://findarticles.com/p/ articles/mi_m0wdq/is_/ai_n30895746. Some excerpts from this chapter were pub-

lished in Bruce E. Bechtol, Jr., "Maintaining a Rogue Regime: Kim Jong-il and the Regime Succession Process," Korea Economic Institute, Academic Paper Series 4, no. 7 (July 2009).

2. See Jehangir S. Pocha, "In North Korea, It's All about Kim Jong Il," *San Francisco Chronicle*, January 26, 2006, http://www.sfgate.com/cgi-bin/article.cgi?f=/c/a/2006/01/27/MNGI7GTQCL1.DTL.

3. Carol Clark, "Dear Leader or Demon?" CNN.com, 2000, http://www.cnn.com/specials/2000/korea/story/leader/kim.jong.il/.

4. See Bong-Geun Jun, "Scenarios of North Korea's Power Shift," Korean Institute of Foreign Affairs and National Security, Policy Brief no. 2008/7, November 2008, 2.

5. Terrence Henry, "After Kim Jong Il," *Atlantic Monthly*, May 2005, http://www.theatlantic.com/doc/200505/henry.

6. Paek Sung-chu, "Characteristics of the North Korean Succession System in the Post–Kim Jong-il Era and Prospects for the Adjustment of Its Policy" (Seoul: Korea Institute for Defense Analyses, April 1, 2008), 1–12.

7. See Soyoung Kwon and Glyn Ford, "Reading North Korean Ruins," *Nautilus Institute Policy Forum Online* PFO 05-18A, February 24, 2005, http://www.nautilus.org/fora/security/0518a_Ford_Kwon.html.

8. "What Do Strange Signs in North Korea Mean?" *Chosun Ilbo*, November 18, 2004, http://english.chosun.com/w21data/html/news/200411/200411180035.html.

9. James Brooke, "Monitors of North Korean News Note Dip in Reverence for Kim," *New York Times*, November 18, 2004, http:// www.nytimes.com/2004/11/18/international/asia/18korea.html.

10. "North Korean Media Drop Kim Jong-il's Dear Leader Title," *Chosun Ilbo*, November 18, 2004, http://english.chosun.com/w21data/html/news/200411/200411180014.html.

11. "North Korean Generals, Officials Defecting, but Kim Jong-il Still Strong," *AFP*, December 9, 2004, http://www.asiademocracy.org/content_view.php?section_id=1&content_id=170.

12. See "NK Foreign Ministry Denies Removal of Kim Jong-il Portraits," *Chosun Ilbo*, November 19, 2004, http://english.chosun.com/w21data/html/news/200411/200411190019.html; and "North Korea Denies Defection of Generals," *Joongang Ilbo*, December 14, 2004, http:// joongangdaily.joins.com/200412/13/200412132234036479900090209021.html.

13. "N. Korean Military Leaders Pledge Loyalty to Kim Jong-il," *Yonhap News*, February 8, 2005, http://english.yna.co.kr/engnews/20050208/3200000000200502081611 24e0.html.

14. Barbara Demick, "Kim Ousts Relative, a Potential Rival, from N. Korean Government," *Los Angeles Times,* December 9, 2004, http://www.latimes.com/news/nationworld/la-fg-purge9dec09,0,4477486.story?coll=la-headlines-world.

15. Jasper Becker, "Portrait of a Family at War: Kim Jong-il Purges Relatives after Alleged Coup Bid," *The Independent,* December 28, 2004, http://www.independent.co.uk/news/world/asia/portrait-of-a-family-at-war-kim-jong-il-purges-relatives-after-alleged-coup-bid-703873.html.

16. "N. Korean Leader's Younger Sister Alive: Source," *Yonhap News,* February 7, 2005, http://english.yna.co.kr/englishnews/20050207/3200000000200502071 75052E8.html.

17. "NK Leader's Younger Sister in Critical Condition," *Dong-a Ilbo*, March 24, 2009, http://english.donga.com/srv/service.php3?bicode=060000&biid=2009032469468.

18. "N.K. Leader's Son Avoids Assassination Plot in Austria," *Chosun Ilbo*, December 19, 2004, http://english.chosun.com/w21data/html/news/200412/200412190013.html.

19. Matthew Rusling, "Kim's Birthday No Retirement Party," *Asia Times*, February 16, 2006, http://www.atimes.com/atimes/korea/hb16dg01.html.

20. Yoo Kwang-jong, "Efforts to Hand over North's Reins," *Joongang Ilbo*, November 24, 2005, http://joongangdaily.joins.com/article/view.asp?aid=2646783.

21. Lee Young-jong, "North's Second Son Watched as Probable Heir," *Joongang Ilbo*, November 23, 2005, http://joongangdaily.joins.com/article/view.asp?aid=2646292.

22. See Aidan Foster-Carter, "Cook and Tell: Another Chef Spills the Beans," *Asia Times*, July 2, 2003, http://www.atimes.com/atimes/korea/eg02dg02.html; and Seo Dong-shin, "Speculation Rekindled over NK Power Succession," *Korea Times*, February 17, 2006, http://times.hankooki.com/.

23. See Kim Hyung-jin, "N. Korea Appears to be Ready to Anoint One of Kim's Sons as Heir: S. Korean officials," *Yonhap News*, April 5, 2006, http://english.yna.co.kr/engnews/20060405/ 4301000000200060405102217E2.html; "Lapel Pins Hint at Kim's Successor," CNN.com, April 5, 2006, http://www.cnn.com/2006/WORLD/asiapcf/04/05/nkorea.succession.ap/index.html; Rian Jensen, "On Pins and Needles over Kim Jong-il's Heir," *Asia Times*, April 28, 2006, http://www.atimes.com/atimes/korea/hd28dg01.html.

24. "Badges of Kim Jong Il 3rd Son Said 'Circulating' among DPRK Officials Since Mid-Feb," *Tokyo Sentaku*, April 1, 2006, 21.

25. "North Korea's Secretive First Family," BBC News, February 15, 2007, http://news.bbc.co.uk/2/hi/asia-pacific/3203523.stm.

26. See "Kim Jong-il Marries Former Secretary," *Chosun Ilbo*, July 24, 2006, http://english.chosun.com/w21data/html/news/200607/200607240003.html; and "N. Korean Leader Kim Has New Wife: Sources," *Seoul Times*, September 17, 2006, http://theseoultimes.com/st/?url=/st/db/read.php?idx=3725.

27. Lee Young-jong and Ser Myo-ja, "Kim Kin's Return Just as Puzzling as His 2-Year Exile," *Joongang Ilbo*, January 30, 2006, http://joongangdaily.joins.com/article/view.asp?aid=2678791.

28. See Lee Young-jong, "Kim's Niece Kills Herself in Paris," *Joongang Ilbo*, September 18, 2006, http://joongangdaily.joins.com/200609/18/2006091822294177399000903090 031.html; and "Kim Jong-il's Niece Dies of Overdose," *Chosun Ilbo*, September 15, 2006, http://joongangdaily.joins.com/article/view.asp?aid=2815190.

29. Richard Lloyd Parry, "North Korea Is Being Run by Kim Jong-il's Brother-in-Law," *The Times*, November 8, 2008, http://www.timesonline.co.uk/tol/news/world/asia/article5107960.ece.

30. Hideko Takayama, "Kim's Brother-in-Law Heads North Korea Anti-Corruption Campaign," *Bloomberg*, May 2, 2008, http://preview.bloomberg.com/apps/news?pid=newsarchive_en10&sid=aUW9JDB7tp3M.

31. "Truth about 'Collapse' of Kim Dynasty, First in Series; After All, Most Likely Successor Was Chong-nam," *Sapio* [in Japanese], October 30, 2008.

32. Richard Spencer, "Kim Jong-il's Women Banned from Planning Succession," *Daily Telegraph*, January 3, 2009, http://www.telegraph.co.uk/news/worldnews/asia/northkorea/4092859/kim-jong-ils-women-banned-from-planning-succession.html.

33. Yang Jung-a, "Kim Jong-il's Wife Kim Ok Pursues Kim Jong Woon as Successor," *Daily NK*, June 2, 2008, http://www.dailynk.com/english/read.php?cataId=nk02300&num=3672.

34. "Important Political Change in North Korea: Kim Jong-il's Brother-in-Law Comes into Power—Military Hardliners Said to Have Been Dismissed," *Zakzak* [in Japanese], October 21, 2008, http://www.zakzak.co.jp/.

35. Mark Mazzetti, Choe Sang-hun, David E. Sanger, and Mark Landler, "Analysts Try to Envision North Korea in Transition," *New York Times*, September 11, 2008, http://query.nytimes.com/gst/fullpage.html?res=9d0ce2d7143bf932a2575ac0a96e9c8b63&sec=&spon=&pagewanted=all.

36. Chang Yong-hun, "Kim Kyong-ok, Who First Appeared as Entourage of North's Kim Jong-il, Is in Charge of Military," *Yonhap News*, January 7, 2009, http://www.yonhap news.co.kr/.

37. "North Korea: Ri Pyong-sam, Beijing's Man," *Paris Intelligence Online*, March 11, 2010, http://www.intelligenceonline.com/government-intelligence/organizations/ 2010/03/11/ri-pyong-sam-beijing-s-man,82105010-art.

38. "Academics Ponder N. Korea after Kim Jong-il," *Chosun Ilbo*, September 25, 2008, http://english.chosun.com/w21data/html/news/200809/200809250001.html.

39. Ko Jae-hung, "The Status and Role of North Korea's National Defense Commission," *Vantage Point* 32, no. 2 (February 2009): 56–57.

40. "Hyon Emerges as Key Player in N. Korea during Kim's Prolonged Absence," East-Asia-Intel.com, September 24, 2008, http://www.east-asia-intel.com/eai/.

41. "S. Korean Paper Alleges Kim Jong-il Is Sick," *Taipei Times*, September 7, 2008, http://www.taipeitimes.com/news/world/archives/2008/09/07/2003422542.

42. "Kim Ok at Dear Leader's Sickbed," *Korea Times*, September 13, 2008, http://www .koreatimes.co.kr/www/news/nation/2008/09/113_31010.html.

43. "NK Leader Underwent Heart Surgery Last Year," *Korea Times*, September 13, 2008, http://www.koreatimes.co.kr/www/news/nation/2008/09/113_31009.html.

44. "Report: North Korea's Kim Began Losing Consciousness in April, Showed Im-paired Judgment," Associated Press, September 14, 2008, http://124.9.0.200/ news/2008/09/14/174677/report:-north.htm.

45. Michael Sheridan, "Who Will Succeed Kim Jong-il?" *The Times*, September 14, 2008, http://www.timesonline.co.uk/tol/news/world/asia/article4740703.ece.

46. Chae Byung-geon and Jung Ha-won, "Doctors' Long Stay May Point to Trouble for Kim," *Joongang Ilbo*, September 17, 2008, http://joongangdaily.joins.com/article/ view.asp?aid=2894965.

47. Choe Sang-hun, "Speculation on North Korean Leader Thrives in Factual Vacuum," *New York Times*, September 20, 2008, http://www.nytimes.com/2008/09/20/world/ asia/20kim.html?ref=world&pagewanted=print.

48. Michael Ha, "No Sign of Internal Instability in Pyongyang," *Korea Times*, September 27, 2008, http://www.koreatimes.co.kr/www/news/special/2010/04/242_31693.html.

49. Heejin Koo, "North Korea Says Kim Jong-il May Be 'Tired,'" *Bloomberg*, October 2, 2008, http://www.bloomberg.com/apps/news?pid=newsarchive_en10&sid=aJae VeXMt.Y4.

50. "Kim Jong-il Still in Charge of North Korea: S. Korean Minister," Associated Press, October 17, 2008, http://www.breitbart.com/article.php?id=d93skiuo0&show _article=1.

51. See Barbara Demick, "Important N. Korea News Is Expected," *Los Angeles Times*, October 19, 2008, and "Seoul Says Has No Information on N. Korea's 'Important Announcement,'" *Yonhap News*, October 19, 2008, http://english.yonhapnews.co.kr/ national/2008/10/19/47/0301000000aen20081019001900315f.html.

52. "KCNA Dismisses False Reports Released by Japanese Newspapers," *KCNA*, October 23, 2008, http://www.kcna.co.jp/item/2008/200810/news24/20081024-23ee.html.

53. "NK Intellectual Solidarity: Preparing for the Future of North Korea," *Daily NK*, Octo-ber 22, 2008, http://www.dailynk.com/english/read.php?num=4193&cataid=nk02500.

54. "Why Was DPRK Foreign Minister Pak Ui-Chun's Entourage Carrying 'Kim Jong-il Tonic Food' on Its Trip Back Home?" *Dong-a Ilbo* [in Korean], October 22, 2008, http://www.donga.com/.

55. "NK Leader Moved to Pyongyang Hospital," *KBS World*, October 23, 2008, http://rki .kbs. co.kr/english/news/news_ik_detail.htm?no=58537.

56. Leo Lewis, "Kim Jong-il Being Treated by Brain Surgeon," *The Times*, October 27, 2008, http://www.timesonline.co.uk/tol/news/world/asia/article5021218.ece.

57. "Kim Jong-il Likely in Hospital, Says Japan PM," AFP, October 28, 2008, http://www.channelnewsasia.com/stories/afp_asiapacific/view/385926/1/.html.

58. Jean H. Lee, "N. Korea's Kim Suffers Serious Setback," Associated Press, October 29, 2008, http://www.usatoday.com/news/world/2008-10-30-3230991964_x.htm.

59. John Leicester, "Mystery Deepens over Who Is Treating North Korea's Leader, as French Doctor Denies Involvement," *Minneapolis Star Tribune*, October 30, 2008, http://www.startribune.com/templates/print_this_story?sid=33582889.

60. Kim Tong-ho and Yi Yong-chong, "Who Is the Doctor Seeing Kim Jong-il?" *Joongang Ilbo* [in Korean], October 30, 2008, http://www.joins.com/.

61. "French Brain Surgeon Admits Visiting Pyongyang: Report," AFP, November 4, 2008, http://afp.google.com/article/aseqm5gbljiu2bx0wapqyorez9hybinh8g.

62. Jung Kwon-ho, "Dare Not Be Curious about Dear Leader's Health," *Daily NK*, November 4, 2008, http://www.dailynk.com/english/read.php?cataid=nk01500&num=4247.

63. "Kim Jong-il Suffered Second Stroke," *Chosun Ilbo*, November 12, 2008, http://english.chosun.com/site/data/html_dir/2008/11/12/2008111261004.html.

64. "Kim Jong-il Suffered Another Stroke Last Month," *Mainichi Daily News*, November 26, 2008, http://mdn.mainichi.jp/mdnnews/news/20081126p2a00m0na008000c.html.

65. See Georges Malbrunot, "The French Doctors Who Care for Kim Jong-il," *Le Figaro* [in French], December 11, 2008; and Steven Erlanger, "Doctor Confirms Kim Jong-il Stroke," *New York Times*, December 11, 2008, http://www.nytimes.com/2008/12/12/world/asia/12kim.html?_r=1.

66. See "Doctor Denies Comments on Kim's Health," Associated Press, December 13, 2008, http://www.chron.com/disp/story.mpl/world/6163546.html; and "French Doctor Denies Treating NK Leader," *Korea Times*, December 15, 2008, http://www.koreatimes.co.kr/www/news/nation/2008/12/113_36111.html.

67. "French Doctor Denies Treating NK Leader."

68. Tim Gjelten, "North Korean Leader's Absence Spurs Stroke Rumors," National Public Radio, September 9, 2008, http://www.npr.org/templates/story/story.php?storyId=94428411.

69. "Report: NKorean Leader Makes Public Appearance," Associated Press, October 4, 2008, http://www.breitbart.com/article.php?id=d93jo2jo0&show_article=1.

70. "Release of Kim Photos Backfires, Spurring New Speculation about His Health," EastAsia-Intel.com, October 17, 2008, http://www.east-asia-intel.com/eai/2008/10_15/list.asp.

71. Donald Kirk, "Heaven's Above! What's Up with Kim?" *Asia Times*, October 25, 2008, http://www.atimes.com/atimes/korea/jj25dg01.html.

72. "NKorean Leader Missed Funeral for Key Party Member: Seoul," AFP, October 31, 2008, http://news.id.msn.com/regional/article.aspx?cp-documentid=1759741.

73. "Kim Jong-il Makes 2nd Public Appearance in Three Days: KCNA," *Yonhap News*, November 5, 2008, http://english.yonhapnews.co.kr/.

74. Paul Eckert, "Expect Test from N.Korea, Bush Aide Advises Obama," Reuters, January 14, 2009, http://www.reuters.com/article/worldnews/idustre50d7v820090114?feedtype=rss.

75. Jae-soon Chang, "NKorea Media Reports Series of Kim Jong-il Outings," *Miami Herald*, November 6, 2008, http://www.miamiherald.com/news/world/ap/story/758820.html.

76. "North Korean Leader Makes Sixth Public Appearance," *Korea Times*, December 21, 2008, http://www.koreatimes.co.kr/www/news/nation/2008/12/113_36472.html.

77. Patrick Cockburn, "The Curious Case of the Disappearing Despot," *Independent*, November 19, 2008, http://www.independent.co.uk/news/world/asia/the-curious-case-of-the-disappearing-despot-1024596.html.

78. "Japanese TV Report: Kim Jong-il Keeps Left Hand in Pocket in All KCTV Photos," Fuji Television [in Japanese], November 27, 2008, http://www.fujitv.co.jp/index.html.

79. "Kim Jong-il Makes First Public Appearance in 2009."

80. Jon Herskovitz and Kim Junghyun, "South Korea's Kim Recovered and in Public," Reuters, December 21, 2008, http://ca.reuters.com/article/topnews/idcatre4b l03i20081222.

81. Naoko Aoki, "N. Korea Criticizes S. Korea, Mum on Leader's Health Rumor," *Kyodo News*, January 1, 2009, http://home.kyodo.co.jp/modules/fststory/index .php?storyid=416963.

82. "N. Korean Leader Says Committed to Denuclearization," *Chosun Ilbo*, January 24, 2009, http://english.chosun.com/site/data/html_dir/2009/01/24/2009012461004.html.

83. "Kim Jong-il 'Drinking Heavily,'" *Chosun Ilbo*, February 6, 2009, http://english .chosun.com/site/data/html_dir/2009/02/06/2009020661008.html.

84. "NKorean Leader's Public Activities Increase: Report," AFP, February 4, 2009, http://www.thefreelibrary.com/NKorean+leader's+public+activities+increase:+report -a01611787325.

85. "N. Korean Leader More Active This Year Than Ever," *Yonhap News*, February 27, 2009, http://english.yonhapnews.co.kr/northkorea/2009/02/27/14/0401000000AEN2 0090227007800315F.HTML.

86. Gordon G. Chang, "What's Going on in Pyongyang? North Korea Responds to Sticks, Not Carrots," *Weekly Standard*, September 21, 2009, http://www.weeklystandard.com/ content/public/articles/000/000/016/946ocfak.asp.

87. Hwang Doo-hyong, "Kim Jong-il Is Physically, Mentally Healthy: U.S. Commander," *Yonhap News*, September 15, 2009, http://english.yonhapnews.co.kr/northkorea/2009/ 09/16/65/0401000000AEN20090916003800325F.HTML.

88. "Kim Jong-il in 'Full Control' of North Korea, National Security Chief Says," FOX News, August 9, 2009, http://www.foxnews.com/politics/2009/08/09/kim-jong-il -control-north-korea-national-security-chief-says.

89. See "Kim Jong-il Still Paralyzed After Stroke," *Chosun Ilbo*, May 5, 2010, http:// english.chosun.com/site/data/html_dir/2010/05/05/2010050500400.html.

90. Shoji Nishioka, "North Korea: General Secretary Kim Jong-il Has Another Attack; Brother-in-Law Carrying out State Affairs on Behalf; Shows Power by Ascending to Party Head," *Mainichi Daily News*, November 26, 2008, http://mainichi.jp/.

91. Joseph S. Bermudez, Jr., "North Korea's Strategic Culture," Defense Threat Reduction Agency, Advanced Systems and Concepts Office, Fort Belvoir, VA, October 31, 2006, http://www.dtra.mil/documents/asco/publications/comparitive_strategic_cultures _curriculum/case%20studies/north%20korea%20(Bermudez)%20final%201%20 Nov%2006.pdf.

92. "ROK Report: North Korea Treating US Administration with Missiles; Passing on Power to Successor Possible," *Jiji Web* [in Japanese], February 9, 2009, http://jijiweb .jiji.com/.

93. Kim Min-seok, "All Signs Point to an Early Launch of Missile by North," *Joongang Ilbo*, February 16, 2009, http://joongangdaily.joins.com/article/view.asp?aid=2901087.

94. "Kim Jong-il Undergoing Regular Kidney Dialysis," *Chosun Ilbo*, January 29, 2010, http://english.chosun.com/site/data/html_dir/2010/01/29/2010012900707.html.

95. "Power Shift in North Korea Suspected," AFP, November 11, 2008, http://afp.google .com/article/ALeqM5iZEgV51ZOkUHJ7HeF3jzApaztQ6w.

96. Ibid.
97. Kim Ji-hyun, "Kim Jong-il's Health Problems Keep World Guessing," *Korea Herald*, January 1, 2009, http://kim-jong-il-news.newslib.com/story/9499-1979/.
98. "Confession of Kim Chong-nam, 37, Eldest Son: Father Jong-il's Present Condition and Successor," *Shukan Gendai* [in Japanese], November 22, 2008, 26–29.
99. Yoo Jee-ho, "Pyongyang Enacts Major Changes in Power Structure," *Joongang Ilbo*, February 18, 2010, http://joongangdaily.joins.com/article/view.asp?aid=2916768.
100. Jae-soon Chang, "North Korean Puzzle: Is a Kim Succession Emerging?" Associated Press, September 28, 2008, http://au.ibtimes.com/articles/20080928/north-korean -puzzle-is-a-kim-succession-emerging.htm.
101. "Kim's Brother-in-Law Likely to Rule NK," *Korea Times*, September 24, 2008, http:// www.koreatimes.co.kr/www/news/nation/2008/09/113_31542.html.
102. "U.S. Intelligence: N.K. Leader's Brother to Take Over," *Dong-a Ilbo*, September 24, 2008, http://english.donga.com/srv/service.php3?bicode=050000&biid =2008092472088.
103. Hyung-jin Kim, "Kim's Consort: A Key Player in North Korea?" Associated Press, September 17, 2008, http://www.msnbc.msn.com/id/26761488/.
104. Philippe Pons, "The Unsettling Eclipse of Kim Jong-il," *Le Monde* (in French), November 23, 2008, http://www.lemonde.fr/web/sequence/0,2-3210,1-0,0.html.
105. Jeong Yong-soo, "Kim Jong-il's Mistress May Have New Lover," *Joongang Ilbo*, November 23, 2009, http://joongangdaily.joins.com/article/view.asp?aid=2912916.
106. "N. Korea's Leading Apparatchiks Revealed," *Chosun Ilbo*, September 18, 2008, http://english.chosun.com/w21data/html/news/200809/200809180006.html.
107. Ibid.
108. "Ex-CIA Officer Nixes Early Recovery of N. Korean Leader Kim," *Kyodo News*, November 27, 2008, http://home.kyodo.co.jp/modules/fststory/index.php?storyid=411651.
109. "Kim Yang Gon Chosen to Spearhead N. Korea's Contacts with S. Korea," *Kyodo News*, April 9, 2007, http://findarticles.com/p/articles/mi_m0wdq/is_/ai_n18792824.
110. Kim Ji-hyun, "Allies See Shift in N.K. Power Structure," *Korea Herald*, December 27, 2008, http://media.daum.net/cplist/view.html?cateid=&cpid=22&newsid=200812270 61010561&p=koreaherald.
111. Lee Young-jong and Jung Ha-won, "Top U.S. General: Plans Made for North Change," *Joongang Ilbo*, December 26, 2008, http://joongangdaily.joins.com/article/view .asp?aid=2899077.
112. Sara A. Carter, "N. Korean Military, Party Keep Control," *Washington Times*, September 14, 2008, http://www.washingtontimes.com/news/2008/sep/14/military-party -keep-control-while-kims-ill/.
113. Kim Hyun, "N. Korea Announces Military Shake-Up," *Yonhap News*, February 11, 2009, http://www.koreancenter.or.kr/news/news_foreign_view.aspx?menu _code=02001000&news_id=aen20090211010500315.
114. John McCreary, "Nightwatch: For the Night of 11 February 2009," *AFCEA Intelligence*, February 11, 2009, http://nightwatch.afcea.org/NightWatch_20090211.htm.
115. For more about Kim Kyok-sik's background and reassignment, see "A Provocation by General Kim Kyok-sik Plotting Comeback in Pyongyang?" *Joongang Ilbo*, March 16, 2009, http://nk.joins. com/news/view.asp?aid=3335047&cont=news_polit.
116. See "N. Korea Fires Artillery near Border for Third Day," AFP, January 29, 2010, http://www.france24.com/en/20100129-nkorea-fires-artillery-near-border-third-day; and "DPRK Fires Artillery Again near Disputed Sea Border: Gov't," *Xinhua*, January 28, 2010, http://world.globaltimes.cn/asia-pacific/2010-01/501809.html.
117. Ser Myo-ja, "Stern Indicates External Explosion," *Joongang Ilbo*, April 17, 2010, http://joongangdaily.joins.com/article/view.asp?aid=2919315.

118. See "Investigation Result on the Sinking of ROKS 'Cheonan,'" *The Joint Civilian-Military Investigation Group*, May 20, 2010.

119. "NKorea's Kim Picks Hawk for Top Military Post," AFP, February 19, 2009, http://www.google.com/hostednews/afp/article/ALeqM5gGET8Vjr6rXCOUKkAbmHIP72kY_Q.

120. Kim Young-gyo, "Return of N. Korean Envoy in Geneva Enhances Jong-un's Succession: HK Daily," *Yonhap News*, April 1, 2010, http://english.yonhapnews.co.kr/north korea/2010/04/01/69/0401000000AEN20100401001300320F.HTML.

121. Toshimitsu Shigemura, "Will Chance Come for [Japan's] Diplomacy to Resolve Abduction Issue? Forecast of Future of North Korea, Shaken over Who Will Succeed Kim Jong-il," *Seiron* [in Japanese], November 30, 2008, 138–43.

122. Kim Ji-hyun, "[*Herald* Interview] Views Mixed on Post-Kim North," *Korea Herald*, January 1, 2008, http://www.koreaherald.co.kr/newkhsite/data/html_dir/2009/01/01/200901010037.asp.

123. Hwee Rhak Park, "The Self-Entrapment of Rationality in Dealing with North Korea," *Korean Journal of Defense Analysis* 20, no. 4 (December 2008): 356.

124. Leonid A. Petrov, "Conservatives Are Reasserting in N.K.," *Korea Herald*, December 17, 2008, http://www.koreaherald.co.kr/newkhsite/data/html_dir/2008/12/18/200812180004.asp.

125. See "Whither North Korea?" *Chosun Ilbo*, September 23, 2008, http://english.chosun.com/site/data/html_dir/2008/09/23/2008092361001.html.

126. Jin Dae-woong, "N.K. Media Warns People Not to Betray the Regime," *Korea Herald*, December 16, 2008, http://www.koreaherald.co.kr/newkhsite/data/html_dir/2008/12/16/200812160041.asp.

127. "DPRK Official: Relations with China to Reach Higher Level in 2009," *Xinhua*, December 26, 2008, http://news.xinhuanet.com/english/2008-12/26/content_10564589.htm.

128. Jeong Yong-soo, "China and North Korea in New Diplomatic Dance," *Joongang Ilbo*, January 3, 2009, http://joongangdaily.joins.com/article/view.asp?aid=2899376.

129. Willy Lam, "Chinese Media Go Dark on Events in N. Korea as CCP Cultivates Ties with Key Generals," East-Asia-Intel.com, September 17, 2008, http://www.east-asia-intel.com/eai/wl.html.

130. "Reports of Tension in North Korea: Chinese Deploying 100,000 Troops at PRC-DPRK Border?" *Zakzak* [in Japanese], October 22, 2008, http://www.zakzak.co.jp/.

131. Michael Ha, "China Boosts Troops on N. Korea Border," *Korea Times*, November 13, 2008, http://www.koreatimes.co.kr/www/news/nation/2008/11/116_34373.html.

132. "China Exercises in Northeast Asia Seen as Warning to Both North Korea and the U.S.," East-Asia-Intel.com, October 24, 2008, http://www.east-asia-intel.com/eai.2008.html.

133. "China May Build Military Bridges over River on Border with DPRK," *Sentaku* [in Japanese], January 2009, 99.

134. Chae Byeong-gun, "China's Influence over the North Rapidly Gaining Economic Weight," *Joongang Ilbo*, June 2, 2008, http://joongangdaily.joins.com/article/view.asp?aid=2890587.

135. "China Imposes Own 'Sanctions' on DPRK by Reducing Crude Oil Shipment, Stepping up Customs Inspections on Exports to DPRK," *Asahi Shimbun* [in Japanese], June 13, 2009, http://www.asahi.com/.

136. "China, North Korea: Preparing for Life after Kim," *Stratfor*, December 30, 2008, http://www.stratfor.com.

137. Yoji Gomi, "Demand to Delete Provision on Military Alliance," *Gendai Koria* [in Japanese], November 21, 2008, 24.

138. "Top Defector: China Will Be in the Driver's Seat Should Chaos Erupt Following Death of Kim Jong-il," East-Asia-Intel.com, September 17, 2008, http://www.east -asia-intel.com/eai/2008.html.

139. Jon Herskovitz and Kim Junghyun, "N. Korea Ups Border Punishments after Kim's Ill-ness," Reuters, December 14, 2008, http://www.reuters.com/article/idUSSEO137447.

140. Kurt Achin, "UN Envoy Says N. Korea Cracking down on Escapees," Voice of Amer-ica, October 31, 2008, http://www1.voanews.com/english/news/a-13-2008-10-31 -voa11-66793412.html?cftoken=72585323&cfid=89+645168.

141. Jiro Ishimaru, "There Are Signs of Anxieties Growing in the North Korean Regime," Sande Mainichi [in Japanese], December 7, 2008, 43.

142. "Former N.K. Pointman on Seoul Said to be Working at Chicken Farm," Yonhap News, January 11, 2009, http://english.yonhapnews.co.kr/northkorea/2009/01/11/78/040100 0000AEN20090111000600315F.HTML

143. See "N. Korea's Pointman on Inter-Korean Relations Executed: Sources," Yonhap News, May 18, 2009, http://leonidpetrov.wordpress.com/2009/05/20/n-koreas-point man-on-inter-korean-relations-executed/.

144. See Justin McCurry and Daniel Nasaw, "North Korea Sacks Kim Jong-il's Finan-cier after Sanctions," The Guardian, February 4, 2010, http://www.guardian.co.uk/ world/2010/feb/04/north-korea-sacks-kim-jong-il-banker; Kang Chol-hwan, "The Men Who Die for Kim Jong-il's Criminal Stupidity," Chosun Ilbo, March 24, 2010, http://english.chosun.com/site/data/html_dir/2010/03/24/2010032400889.html; Lee Sung-jin, "Execution Confirmed by Capitol Source," Daily NK, April 5, 2010, http:// www.dailynk.com/english/read.php?cataId=nk01500&num=6204; and "N. Korea Purges Party, Military," Chosun Ilbo, February 5, 2010, http://english.chosun.com/ site/data/html_dir/2010/02/05/2010020500764.html.

145. "Kim Jong-il's Bloody Purges," Chosun Ilbo, June 9, 2010, http://english.chosun.com/ site/data/html_dir/2010/06/09/2010060900794.html.

146. Michael Sheridan, "Kim Jong-il's Stand-in Outdoes Master," The Times, January 11, 2009, http://www.timesonline.co.uk/tol/news/world/asia/article5489149.ece?print =yes&randnum=1231682952312.

147. Alex Martin, "Escapee Gives Glimpse of North Korean Prison Camps," Japan Times, November 5, 2008, http://search.japantimes.co.jp/cgi-bin/nn20081105f1.html.

148. Luis Ramirez, "North Korean Defectors Risk Lives in Perilous Journey," Voice of America, April 15, 2008, http://www.voanews.com/english/archive/2008-04/2008-04 -15-voa42.cfm?cfid =89183038&cftoken=46335126.

149. "N. Korean Army in Propaganda Leaflet Sweep," Chosun Ilbo, December 3, 2008, http://english.chosun.com/site/data/html_dir/2008/12/03/2008120361011.html.

150. "N. Korea Threatens to Sever Ties with the South," KBS World, October 23, 2008, http://world.kbs.co.kr/english/event/nkorea_nuclear/now_02_detail.htm?no=335.

151. See "N Korea Threatens 'Consequences' for Anti-Communist Leaflets," Yonhap News, October 21, 2008, http://english.yonhapnews.co.kr/northkorea/2008/10/23/25/04010 00000AEN20081022002500325F.HTML]; and "NK Threatens to Strike on South for Leaflets," KBS World, October 28, 2008, http://english.kbs.co.kr/news/newsview_sub .php?menu=8&key=2008102828.

152. Choe Sang-hun, "North Korea Hardens Stance on Reconciliation," New York Times, November 25, 2008, http://www.nytimes.com/2008/11/25/world/asia/25korea.html ?_r=1&partner=rss&emc =rss.

153. For an analysis of the details surrounding the politics in both North and South Korea involving the Kaesong Industrial Complex, see Andrei Lankov, "Pyongyang Puts Poli-tics above Dollars," Asia Times, November 26, 2008, http://www.atimes.com/atimes/ korea/jk26dg01.html.

154. Rhee So-eui, "South Korea Stands Firm as Tension Rises with the North," Reuters, November 23, 2008, http://www.reuters.com/article/worldnews/idustre4am-0mq20081123.

155. "N. Korea Lays out Detailed Border Restrictions," *Asia Pulse*, November 27, 2008, http://www.accessmylibrary.com/coms2/summary_0286-35952723_ITM.

156. Kim Junghyun, "Interview—North Korea Has Dark Plot for South's 'Sunshine,'" Reuters, November 28, 2008, http://uk.reuters.com/assets/print?aid=UKTRE4AR0ZX 20081128.

157. Jung Ha-won, "North-Bound Border Crossings Slow to a Trickle," *Joongang Ilbo*, December 1, 2008, http://joongangdaily.joins.com/article/view.asp?aid=2898003.

158. "N. Korea Cuts S. Korean Staff at Kaesong," *Chosun Ilbo*, December 2, 2008, http://english.chosun.com/site/data/html_dir/2008/12/02/2008120261018.html.

159. Chae Byeong-geon and Jung Ha-won, "Kaesong Complex Teetering," *Joongang Ilbo*, January 8, 2009, http://joongangdaily.joins.com/article/view.asp?aid=2899573.

160. Jung Ha-won and Chae Byung-gun, "North's Military May Be Taking a Grip on Power," *Joongang Ilbo*, January 20, 2009, http://joongangdaily.joins.com/article/view .asp?aid=2900058.

161. Ser Myo-ja and Kim Min-seok, "Seoul Goes on Alert after Sharp Attack by Pyongyang," *Joongang Ilbo*, January 19, 2009, http://joongangdaily.joins.com/article/view .asp?aid=2900020.

162. Kim Hyun and Sam Kim, "Tensions Rise over N. Korea's Renewed Sea Border Claim," *Yonhap News*, January 17, 2009, http://english.yonhapnews.co.kr/news/2009/01/17/ 0200000000aen20090117002600315.html.

163. Sam Kim, "Chinese Boats Vanish as Tension Rises in Waters between Koreas," *Yonhap News*, Feb 10, 2009, http://english.yonhapnews.co.kr/national/2009/02/10/97/030100 0000aen200902100 06900315f.html.

164. "Restriction Announcement," Yantai Shandong Marine Fishing and Production Management Station [in Chinese], January 23, 2009.

165. "Public Announcement," Weihai Economic and Technological Development Zone [in Chinese], February 4, 2009, http://www.e-weihai.gov.cn/cn/news/index_show .jsp?id=7614.

166. Kim So-hyun, "Waters along NLL Cleared of Fishing Boats," *Korea Herald*, June 5, 2009, http://www.koreaherald.co.kr/newkhsite/data/html_dir/2009/06/05/2009 06050042.asp.

167. David Eimer, "North and South Stand on 'the Brink of War,'" *Daily Telegraph*, January 30, 2009, http://www.telegraph.co.uk/news/worldnews/asia/northkorea/4397720/ north-and-south-korea-stand-on-the-brink-of-war.html.

168. Sam Kim, "Top US Commander in S. Korea Urges N. Korea to Stop Raising Tension," *Yonhap News*, February 14, 2009, http://english.yonhapnews.co.kr/national/2009/02/ 04/68/0301000000aen 20090204003600315f.html.

169. See Kim Hyun, "Pyongyang's Bellicose Rhetoric May Suggest Internal Jitters: Analysts," *Yonhap News*, January 19, 2009, http://english.yonhapnews.co.kr/northkorea/ 2009/01/19/45/0401000000AEN20090119006500315F.HTML

170. "N. Korea Lambasts S. Korea's Defense White Paper," *Yonhap News*, March 7, 2009, http:// english.yonhapnews.co.kr/northkorea/2009/03/07/47/0401000000aen20090307 001900315f.html.

171. See Christian Oliver and Kang Buseong, "N. Korea Hardliners to Handle Policy on South," *Financial Times*, March 11, 2009, http://www.ft.com/cms/s/0/90297caa-0dc8-11de-8ea3-0000779fd2ac.html?nclick_check=1; "N. Korea Noncommittal to Seoul's Urge to Reopen Border," *Korea Times*, March 15, 2009, http://www.koreatimes.co.kr/

www/news/nation/2009/03/113_41284.html; Jeong Yong-soo and Ser Myo-ja, "Kaesong Crossing Again Shut with No Explanation," *Joongang Ilbo*, March 14, 2009, http://joongangdaily.joins.com/article/view.asp?aid=2902237; and "N. Korea Fully Reopens Border for S. Koreans Visiting Joint Industrial Complex," *Yonhap News*, March 17, 2009, http://english.yonhapnews.co.kr/news/2009/03/17/0200000000a en200903170028 00315.html.

172. "Will North Korea Give up Its Cash Cow at Kaesong?" *Dong-a Ilbo*, March 16, 2009, http://english.donga.com/srv/service.php3?biid=2009031643698.

173. See "N.Korea Wants Answer to Demands Soon," *Chosun Ilbo*, May 7, 2009, http://english.chosun.com/site/data/html_dir/2009/05/07/2009050700708.html.

174. "North Korea Threatens Military Response after S. Korea Joins PSI," *Yonhap News*, May 27, 2009, http://english.yonhapnews.co.kr/news/2009/05/27/0200000000a en20090527010000315.html.

175. Vijay Joshi, "NKorea Demands 4-Fold Raise in Wages from South," Associated Press, June 11, 2009, http://abcnews.go.com/International/wireStory?id=7810257.

176. See Sam Kim, "N. Korea Bolsters Combat Drills amid Tension with S. Korea: Source," *Yonhap News*, May 27, 2009, http://english.yonhapnews.co.kr/northkorea/2009/05/27/ 68/0401000000AEN20090527003600315F.HTML; and "ROK Ministry Spokesman Says DPRK Air Force Training Increased," AFP, May 27, 2009, http://www.afp.com/afpcom/en.

177. "North Korea Makes Overtures to Normalize Kaesong Project," *Hankyoreh Ilbo*, September 13, 2009, http://english.hani.co.kr/arti/english_edition/e_northkorea/ 376365.html.

178. See Tony Chang, "Koreas to Normalize Traffic Flow at Joint Industrial Park," *Yonhap News*, August 31, 2009, http://english.yonhapnews.co.kr/northkorea/2009/08/ 31/90/0401000000AEN20090831 003000315F.HTML; and "Curbs on Overland Travel at Inter-Korean Border Lifted," *Chosun Ilbo*, August 25, 2009, http://english .chosun.com/site/data/html_dir/2009/08/25/2009082500629.html.

179. Kim Hyun, "Koreas Normalize Border Traffic as Ties Improve," *Yonhap News*, September 1, 2009, http://english.yonhapnews.co.kr/northkorea/2009/09/01/21/04010000 00AEN20090901001700315F.HTML.

180. "DPRK Lifts Cross-Border Restrictions, Signaling Thaw in Inter-Korean Ties," *Xinhua*, August 21, 2009, http://big5.cri.cn/gate/big5/english.cri.cn/6966/2009/ 08/21/1821s510454.htm#.

181. Kim Hyun, "Koreas Normalize Military Hotline," *Yonhap News*, September 2, 2009, http://english. yonhapnews.co.kr/northkorea/2009/09/02/27/0401000000AEN200909 02007900315F.HTML.

182. See "N. Korea Shuts Down S. Korean Assets at Resort, Expels Staff," AFP, April 13, 2010, http://www.ibtimes.com/articles/21597/20100430/north-korea-to-expel-south-korean-workers-from-resort.htm.]; and "S. Korea Rejects N. Korea's Demand over Asset Freeze at Mountain Resort," *Yonhap News*, April 11, 2010, http://english .yonhapnews.co.kr/northkorea/2010/04/11/82/0401000000AEN201004110014003 15F.HTML.

183. See "Kaesong Companies Told to Keep Staff to Minimum," *Donga Ilbo*, May 24, 2010, http://english.donga.com/srv/service.php3?biid=2010052435598; "Kaesong Closure Would Cost $500 Million," *Chosun Ilbo*, May 24, 2010, http://english.chosun.com/ site/data/html_dir/2010/05/24/2010052400654.html; Chang Jae-soon, "S. Korea Unveils Slew of Anti-N. Korea Steps Over Sunken Ship," *Yonhap News*, May 24, 2010, http://english.yonhapnews.co.kr/national/2010/05/24/61/0301000000AEN201005240 09700315F.html; Lee Chi-dong, "Lee Says Seoul Ready to Take Self-Defense Mea-

sures Against Future N. Korean Provocations," *Yonhap News*, May 24, 2010, http://
english.yonhapnews.co.kr/national/2010/05/24/25/0301000000AEN20100524002500
315F.html; Sam Kim, "N. Korea Expels S. Korean Officials from Joint Factory Park,"
Yonhap News, May 26, 2010, http://english.yonhapnews.co.kr/national/2010/05/26/
36/0301000000AEN20100526007200315F.html; Sam Kim, "N. Korea Says it is Re-
tracting all Military Safeguards with S. Korea," *Yonhap News*, May 27, 2010, http://
english.yonhapnews.co.kr/northkorea/2010/05/27/40/0401000000AEN201005270080
00315F.html.

184. "Seoul Gave N. Korea $7 Billion Since '98," *Chosun Ilbo*, June 3, 2009, http://english
.chosun.com/site/data/html_dir/2009/06/03/2009060300718.html.

185. Tarek El-Tablawy, "Orascom to Launch 3G Service in N Korea," Associated Press,
December 14, 2008, http://www.google.com/hostednews/ap/article/aleqm5iyxuhb
vshmoxvimkugkw2ll5 e3rgd952gkvo0.

186. Kelly Olsen, "Impoverished NKorea Gets New Mobile Network," Associated Press,
December 15, 2008, http://seattletimes.nwsource.com/html/businesstechnology/2008
519025_apasnkoreamobilephones.html.

187. Shim Sun-ah, "N. Korea Takes Risk to Enter Information Age," *Yonhap News*, December 16, 2008, http://english.yonhapnews.co.kr/northkorea/2008/12/16/24/0401000000
AEN20081216004800315F.HTML.

188. Shoji Nishioka, "North Korea Takes Half a Year for Developing 'Wiretapping' System—before the Launch of Mobile Phone Service," *Mainichi Shimbun* [in Japanese],
December 26, 2008, http://www.mainichi.co.jp/.

189. See "Cell Phones Providing Valuable Peek into North Korea," *Dong-a Ilbo*, January 13,
2010, http://english.donga.com/srv/service.php3?biid=2010011313298; Jung Kwon-
ho, "Border Cell Phone Crackdown Intensified," *Daily NK*, April 5, 2010, http://
www.dailynk.com/english/read.php?catald=nk01500&num=6205; and Choe Sang-
hun, "North Koreans Use Cellphones to Bare Secrets," *New York Times*, March 28,
2010, http://www.nytimes.com/2010/03/29/world/asia/29news.html?ref=world&page
wanted=print.

190. Jung Kwon-ho, "Special Police Squads Organized Under PSM," *Daily NK*, May 25,
2010, http://www.dailynk.com/english/read.php?catald=nk01500&num=6411.

191. See Christian Caryl and B. J. Lee, "North Korea's Dictator May Be Ailing, but Don't
Hope for Change Soon," *Newsweek*, December 8, 2008, http://www.newsweek.com/
id/171307.

192. See Michael Ha, "[58 Anniversary] Major Changes Are Coming to N. Korea,"
Korea Times, October 29, 2008, http://www.koreatimes.co.kr/www/news/nation/
2008/10/116_33510.html.

193. For yet another example of analysis that predicts a collective leadership following the
demise of Kim Chong-il, see Rudiger Frank, "Has the Next Great Leader of North Korea Been Announced?" *Nautilus Institute Policy Forum Online* 08-080A, October 21,
2008, http://www.nautilus.org/fora/security/08080Frank.html.

194. See "Kim Jong Nam: Leadership Succession," GlobalSecurity.org, April 4, 2005,
http://www.globalsecurity.org/military/world/dprk/kim-jong-nam.htm; and "Son of
Kim Jong-il Living in Macao," *United Press International*, February 2, 2007, http://
www.upi.com/Top_News/2007/02/02/Son-of-Kim-Jong-il-living-in-Macao/UPI
-61091170397705/.

195. Andrei Lankov, "Who Will Lead North Korea after Kim Jong-il?" *Korea Times*, July
30, 2008, http://www.koreatimes.co.kr/www/news/nation/2008/07/120_28467.html.

196. Merrily Baird, e-mail interview by author, February 13, 2009.

197. For more analysis on Yi-chol's associations with Kim Chong-nam, see Lee Kwang-ho,

"Speculation on Kim Jong-il's Successor," *Vantage Point* 32, no. 2 (February 2009): 13–15.

198. Norio Sakurai, "Favorite to Be Successor the 'Morning Star General,' Eldest Son? Or the Mysterious Third Son? Fierce Information War Going on over Succession Issue," *Sankei Shimbun* [in Japanese], January 17, 2009, http://www.sankei.co.jp/.

199. See "Kim Jong-chol: Guitar Playing Heir to the Dynasty?" *Korean Unification Studies*, November 25, 2007, http://koreanunification.net/2007/11/25/kim-jong-chol-guitar-playing-heir-to-communist-dynasty/.

200. Cheong Seong-chang, "Outlook for the Situation in North Korea and North-South Relations in 2009," *Situation and Policy* [in Korean], January 2009, http://www.sejong.org/.

201. "Report: Kim Jong-il Grooming Middle Son as Successor," Associated Press, May 20, 2009, http://www.foxnews.com/story/0,2933,520757,00.html?test=latestnews.

202. See Yang Jung-a, "Kim Jong Woon, Suffering from High-Blood Pressure, Diabetes," *Daily NK*, September 18, 2008, http://www.dailynk.com/english/read.php?cataid=nk00100&num=4087.

203. Choi Byung-muk, "Who Is the Dear Leader's Rumored Successor Kim Jong-un?" *Chosun Ilbo*, February 20, 2009, http://english.chosun.com/site/data/html_dir/news/2009/02/2009022061034.html.

204. Jack Kim, "North Korea Leader Picks 3rd Son as Heir: Media," Reuters, January 15, 2009, http://www.reuters.com/article/topnews/idustre50e2hf20090115?feedtype=rss&feedname=topnews.

205. "N. Korean Leader Names Third Son as Successor: Sources," *Yonhap News*, January 15, 2009, http://english.yonhapnews.co.kr/northkorea/2009/01/15/63/0401000000AEN20090115005100315F.HTML.

206. Kim Sue-young and Michael Ha, "Kim Jong-il's 3rd Son Emerges as Successor," *Korea Times*, January 15, 2009, http://www.koreatimes.co.kr/www/news/nation/2009/01/117_37961.html.

207. Ibid.

208. "Report: NK Not to See Father-to-Son Power Transfer," *Dong-a Ilbo*, February 20, 2009, http://english.donga.com/srv/service.php3?biid=2009022069468.

209. Ibid.

210. "Memo Reportedly Names Kim Jong-il's Third Son as Successor," *Mainichi Daily News*, February 17, 2009, http://mdn.mainichi.jp/mdnnews/news/20090217p2a00m0na019000c.html.

211. See Alex Martin, "Signs in North Point to Kim's Third Son Being Heir," *Japan Times*, May 21, 2009, http://search.japantimes.co.jp/cgi-bin/nn20090521f1.html.

212. "Kim's Brother-in-Law Said to Mastermind N. Korea's Leadership Succession," *Yonhap News*, February 15, 2009, http://english.yonhapnews.co.kr/northkorea/2009/02/15/0401000000AEN20090215001900315.HTML.

213. "'Bloodline Inheritance' Highlighted in N. Korean Editorial for Leader's Birthday," *Yonhap News*, February 17, 2009, http://english.yonhapnews.co.kr/northkorea/2009/02/17/16/0401000000AEN20090217003200315F.HTML.

214. Kim Hyun, "N.K. Military Vows Loyalty to Leader's Bloodline Ahead of Election," *Yonhap News*, February 18, 2009, http://english.yonhapnews.co.kr/northkorea/2009/02/18/0401000000AEN20090218010000315.HTML.

215. James Rosen, "U.S. Intelligence Confirms Kim Jong-il's Son to Inherit North Korean Dictatorship," FOXNews.com, June 12, 2009, http://www.foxnews.com/politics/2009/06/12/intelligence-confirms-kim-jong-ils-son-inherit-north-korean-dictatorship/.

216. "S. Korean Spy Agency Confirms N. Korea Leader's Third Son as Successor," Kuwait News Agency, June 2, 2009, http://www.kuna.net.kw/newsagenciespublicsite/article details.aspx?id=2002622&language=en.

217. "NK Leader Gives Son Control of Secret Police," *Dong-a Ilbo*, June 24, 2009, http://english.donga.com/srv/service.php3?biid=2009062447518.

218. See Yang Jung-a, "Focus on Jang Sung Taek, Charismatic Jang Sung Taek—part II," *Daily NK*, January 9, 2009, http://dailynk.com/english/read.php?cataid=nk00400&num=4433.

219. Sarah Jackson-Han, "Who Will Succeed Kim Jong-il?" *Radio Free Asia*, September 15, 2008, http://www.rfa.org/english/news/korea/succeed-09152008160605.html.

220. Sin Sok-ho, "Signs of a Secret Feud in North Korean Leadership Due to Chang Song Taek's Go-It-Alone [Style]," *Dong-a Ilbo* [in Korean], January 8, 2009, http://www.donga.com/.

221. Masanori Yamaguch, "List of Deputies Elected to Supreme People's Assembly Announced; General Secretary Kim's Three Sons Not Included," *Nihon Keizai Shimbun* [in Japanese], March 10, 2009, http://www.nikkei.co.jp/.

222. "Kim Jong-il Sends Wreath to Bier of Jang Song U," *KCNA*, August 25, 2009, http://www. kcna.co.jp.

223. "NK Assembly to Convene on April 9," *Korea Times*, March 20, 2009, http://www.koreatimes.co.kr/www/news/nation/2009/03/113_41643.html.

224. For an analysis of Chang's relationship with the North Korean military, see Cheong Seong-chang, "Kim Jong-il's Illness and Prospects for Post-Kim Leadership," *East Asian Review* 20, no. 4 (Winter 2008): 16–19.

225. See Lee Kwang-ho, "Endorsing a New Five-Year Term for Kim Jong-il," *Vantage Point* 32, no. 5 (May 2009): 2–7.

226. For details of members appointed to key positions in the government, Kim Chong-il's presence, and possible regime succession ramifications from the Twelfth Supreme People's Assembly, see Yoo Jee-ho, "North Removes Symbolic Agency," *Joongang Ilbo*, April 11, 2009, http://joongangdaily. joins.com/article/view.asp?aid=2903448; "DPRK Radio Lists Leaders, Members of DPRK NDC, Spa Presidium, Cabinet," *KCNA*, April 9, 2009, http://www.kcna.co.jp/index-e.htm; and "NKorea's Kim Strengthens Grip on Power, Prepares for Succession," AFP, April 10, 2009, http://www.spacewar.com/reports/nkoreas_kim_strengthens_grip_on_power_prepares_for_succession_999 .html.

227. Kim Yong-hyun, "[Kim Jong-il's Third Term: Politics] North Korea Strengthens Foundations for a 'Post-Kim System,'" *Hankyoreh Ilbo*, April 14, 2009, http://english.hani .co.kr/arti/english_edition/learningenglish/349668.html.

228. See Jeong Yong-soo, "North's Military Strengthens Its Grip," *Joongang Ilbo*, April 21, 2009, http://joongangdaily.joins.com/article/view.asp?aid=2903832.

229. See "N. Korean Leader's Son Appointed to Post in Top Military Body: Source," *Yonhap News*, April 26, 2009, http://english.yonhapnews.co.kr/northkorea/2009/04/26/17/0401000000AEN20090426 000900315F.HTML; and Hyung-Jin Kim, "Report: Son of NKorea's Kim Given Defense Post," Associated Press, April 26, 2009, http://www.gmanews.tv/story/158651/son-of-nkorea39s-kim-given-defense-post.

230. Lee Young-jong, "Path of Succession in North Growing Clearer by the Day," *Joongang Ilbo*, October 6, 2009, http://joongangdaily.joins.com/article/view.asp?aid=2910930.

231. See Chong Nok-yong, "[In the] North, O Kuk-yol and Kim Kyong-hee Are Emerging—Two Pillars Who Lead Succession by Kim Chong-un Appear on the Rostrum for the First Time—Kim Kyong-hee's Husband Chang Sang-taek Not Included in the Order," *Hankook Ilbo* [in Korean], October 14, 2009, http://news.hankooki.com/; and

Namgung Min, "Three New Faces alongside Kim Jong-il," *Daily NK*, October 14, 2009, http://www.dailynk.com/english/read.php?catald=nk00100&num=5529.

232. See Bill Gertz, "N. Korea General Tied to Forged $100 Bills," *Washington Times*, June 2, 2009, http://www.washingtontimes.com/news/2009/jun/02/n-korea-general-tied-to-forged-100-bills/ print/; Yu Yong-won, "Dangerous Man O Kuk-ryol," *Chosun Ilbo* [in Korean] June 8, 2009, http:// www.chosun.com/; and "Men of Kim Chong-un Taking up Important Positions in the Party and the Military," *Dong-a Ilbo* [in Korean], June 22, 2009, http://www.donga.com/.

233. Toshu Noguchi, "Impossible to Have Discord within North Korean Military," *Sankei Shimbun* [in Japanese], June 27, 2009, http://sankei.jp.msn.com/.

234. "Close Aide to Kim Jong-il Dies," *Chosun Ilbo*, April 27, 2010, http://english.chosun .com/site/data/html_dir/2010/04/27/2010042701086.html.

235. Shin Ju-hyun and Min Cho-hee, "Surprise Public Removal of Core Military Man," *Daily NK*, May 14, 2010, http://www.dailynk.com/english/read .php?catald=nk00400&num=6371

236. "N. Korean Eminence Grise Dead in Mysterious Circumstances," *Chosun Ilbo*, June 4, 2010, http://english.chosun.com/site/data/html_dir/2010/06/04/2010060400549.html

237. See Kim So-yeol, "Jang Sung-taek Emerges on Post-Kim Stage," *Daily NK*, June 8, 2010, http://www.dailynk.com/english/read.php?catald=nk00400&num=6468; "N. Korea Remains an Unpredictable Neighbor," *Chosun Ilbo*, June 9, 2010, http://english .chosun.com/site/data/html_dir/2010/06/09/2010060901335.html; Lim Chang-won, "Kim's Son Seems Certain to Inherit Power: Analysts," AFP, June 8, 2010, http:// ca.news.yahoo.com/s/afp/100608/world/nkorea_politics_succession; "Kim Jong-il's Brother in Law Cements Favored Position," *Chosun Ilbo*, June 8, 2010, http://english .chosun.com/site/data/html_dir/2010/06/08/2010060801344.html.

238. "N. Korea's Rule of 4," *Chosun Ilbo*, June 9, 2010, http://english.chosun.com/site/data/ html_dir/2010/06/09/2010060901340.html.

239. See Yang Jung-a, "Organizing Secretary Successor to Kim Jong-il," *Daily NK*, August 21, 2008, http://www.dailynk.com/english/read.php?cataid=nk00100&num=3992.

240. Andrei Lankov, "Pyongyang Defies All Odds," *Asia Times*, September 18, 2008, http:// www.atimes.com/atimes/korea/ji18dg01.html.

241. "Seoul Says North Korean Leader May Be Succeeded by His Son," *Channel News Asia*, February 26, 2009, http://www.channelnewsasia.com/stories/afp_asiapacific/ view/411441/1/.html.

242. Ser Myo-ja, "Kim Jong-il's Heir Not Seen on List of New Lawmakers," *Joongang Ilbo*, March 11, 2009, http://joongangdaily.joins.com/article/view.asp?aid=2902097.

243. "Why Does Kim Jong-il Promise Great Things for 2012?" *Chosun Ilbo*, January 1, 2009, http://english.chosun.com/w21data/html/news/200901/200901010001.html.

244. Kim Deok-hyun, "N. Korea Likely to Complete Power Succession in 2012: Expert," *Yonhap News*, June 8, 2010, http://english.yonhapnews.co.kr/national/2010/06/08/030 1000000AEN20100608004400315.HTML.

245. For more details on succession and the year 2012, see Spencer, "Kim Jong-il's Women Banned from Planning Succession,"

246. "Says DPRK Sent out Notification Implying No Power Transfer until 2012," Tokyo Broadcasting System Television [in Japanese], December 8, 2009, http://www.tbs .co.jp/.

247. "Seoul Think Tank Forecasts Possible Absence of Kim in N.K. after 2012," *Yonhap News*, January 19, 2010, http://english.yonhapnews.co.kr/northkorea/2010/01/20/59/ 0401000000AEN20100120004300325F.HTML.

248. "North Korean Poster Seems to Confirm Succession," *Chosun Ilbo*, September 25, 2009, http://english.chosun.com/site/data/html_dir/2009/09/25/2009092500912.html.

249. "Seoul Corrects Korean Spelling of North's Heir Apparent," *Yonhap News*, October 6, 2009, http://english.yonhapnews.co.kr/northkorea/2009/10/06/58/0401000000AEN2 0091006006600315F.HTML.

250. See "Report: NKoreans Mark Birthday of Leader's Son," Associated Press, January 8, 2010, http://abcnews.go.com/International/wireStory?id=9509714.; and "Birthday of Kim Jong-il Heir 'to Become National Holiday,'" *Chosun Ilbo*, January 6, 2010, http://english.chosun.com/site/data/html_dir/2010/01/06/2010010602263.html.

251. Jung Kwon-ho, "Kim Jong Eun Succession Document Unveiled," *Daily NK*, March 23, 2010, http://www.dailynk.com/english/read.php?cataid=nk01500&num=6157.

252. "Experts Ponder N. Korea after Kim Jong-il," *Chosun Ilbo*, September 26, 2008, http://english.chosun.com/site/data/html_dir/ 2008/09/26/200809261009.html.

253. Bruce E. Bechtol, Jr., *Red Rogue: The Persistent Challenge of North Korea* (Dulles, VA: Potomac Books, 2007), 126–27.

254. See Alex Martin, "Pyongyang Purge Seen Speeding Helm Change," *Japan Times*, June 4, 2009, http://search.japantimes.co.jp/cgi-bin/nn20090604a3.html; "Purges Expected in N. Korea's Succession Process," *Dong-a Ilbo*, June 5, 2009, http://english.donga .com/srv/service.php3?bicode=050000&biid=2009060571528; and "N. Korean Heir Linked to Assassination Plot," *Chosun Ilbo*, June 16, 2009, http://english.chosun.com/site/data/html_dir/2009/06/16/2009061600816.html.

255. See "Kim Jong-il Asserts Control," *Chosun Ilbo*, September 11, 2009, http://english .chosun.com/site/data/html_dir/2009/09/11/2009091100774.html; and Kurt Achin, "S. Korean Scholar: North Experiencing Discord among Kim Family Members," *Voice of America*, October 22, 2009, http://www.ascfusa.org/content_pages/view/north-korea -experiencing-discord-among-kim-family.

256. Jon Herskovitz, "Analysis: North Korea Heir to Be Puppet of Old Guard Clique," Reuters, June 26, 2009, http://www.reuters.com/article/idUSSEO240801.

257. Bechtol, *Red Rogue*, 128.

258. For analysis and reporting regarding the 2010 meeting of the KWP political bureau and Kim Chong-il's hastening of the succession process due to worries about his health, see "N. Korea's Ruling Party to Meet in September Amid Speculation of Power Transfer," *Yonhap News*, June 26, 2010, http://english.yonhapnews.co.kr/northkorea/2010/06/26/ 64/0401000000AEN20100626002800315F.HTML; Park Chan-Kyong, "North Korea to Pick New Leaders: Official Media," AFP, June 26, 2010, http://news.yahoo.com/s/ afp/20100626/wl_asia_afp/nkoreapoliticssuccession; "North Korea Hastens Power Succession: Spy Chief," *Yonhap News*, June 24, 2010, http://english.yonhapnews .co.kr/northkorea/2010/06/24/0401000000AEN20100624008700320.HTMl.

259. See David Shambaugh, "China and the Korean Peninsula: Playing for the Long Term," *Washington Quarterly* 26, no. 2 (Spring 2003), http://www.twq.com/03spring/ docs/03spring_shambaugh.pdf.

260. Paul B. Stares and Joel S. Wit, "Preparing for Sudden Change in North Korea," Council Special Report no. 42 (Washington, DC: Council on Foreign Relations, January 2009), http://www.cfr.org/content/publications/attachments/North_Korea_CSR42.pdf.

261. See James Clay Moltz, "Russian Policy on the North Korean Nuclear Crisis" (Monterey, CA: Center for Non-Proliferation Studies, Monterey Institute of International Studies, May 5, 2003), http://cns.miis.edu/research/korea/ruspol.htm.

262. For details on the economic burden that will be put on the government in Seoul in a post-unification scenario, see Marcus Noland, "Some Unpleasant Arithmetic Concerning Unification," Peterson Institute for International Economics, Working Paper 96-13, October 23, 1996, http://www.iie.com/publications/wp/wp.cfm?researchid=169.

263. Adm. Mike Mullen, "Remarks by Adm. Mike Mullen, Chairman of the Joint Chiefs of

Staff," Pew Memorial Lecture, Grove City College, Pennsylvania, February 2, 2009, http://www.jcs.mil/chairman/speeches/03feb09_cjcs_grove_city_college.pdf.

264. Bechtol, *Red Rogue*, 129.

SIX. Preparing for the North Korean Threat: The ROK-U.S. Military Alliance and the Lee Myung-bak Presidency

1. Parts of this chapter were earlier published as Bruce E. Bechtol, Jr., "Preparing for Future Threats and Regional Challenges: The ROK-U.S. Military Alliance in 2008–2009," *Korea Economic Institute, Joint U.S.-Korea Academic Studies* 19 (2009): 75–99. The author would like to thank the editors and staff at the Korea Economic Institute. Parts of this chapter were also published in the *International Journal of Korean Studies*, Fall–Winter 2009. The author would like to thank the editor, Dr. Hugo Kim.

2. Norimitsu Onishi, "Conservative Wins Vote in South Korea," *New York Times*, November 20, 2007, http://www.nytimes.com/2007/12/20/world/asia/20korea.html?pagewanted=1&_r=1.

3. Nicholas Eberstadt, "A Chance to Rein In North Korea," *Washington Post*, December 26, 2007, http://www.washingtonpost.com/wp-dyn/content/article/2007/12/25/ar2007122500864.html.

4. See David I. Steinberg, "Elections in the Republic of Korea: Foreign Policy Alternatives under New Leadership," paper presented at the conference Elections, Political Transitions, and Foreign Policy in East Asia, sponsored by the Foreign Policy Research Institute, Philadelphia, April 14, 2008, http://www.fpri.org/enotes/200806.steinberg.electionskorea.html.

5. For examples of criticism of Lee's North Korea policies from left-of-center analysts and politicians, see Georgy Toloraya, "North Korea Now: Will the Clock Be Turned Back?" Brookings Institution Paper (Washington, DC: Brookings, February 11, 2008), http://www.brookings.edu/articles/2008/0211_north_korea_toloraya.aspx; and Shim Jae Hoon, "Korea in Crisis: For the Left, US Beef Imports Become an Issue to Push Back Lee's Reforms," *Asia Sentinel*, June 11, 2008, http://www.asiasentinel.com/index.php?option=com_content&task=view&id=1251&itemid=31.

6. See Junn Sung-chull, "President Lee's Beef Blunder," *Far Eastern Economic Review*, July 11, 2008, http://www.feer.com/international-relations/2008/july/President-Lees-Beef-Blunder.

7. Victor Cha, "Commentary: Destructive Domestic Politics," *Chosun Ilbo*, July 21, 2008, http://english.chosun.com/site/data/html_dir/2008/07/21/2008072161013.html.

8. See Kang In-sik, "Papers Disclose Secrets behind Street Protests," *Joongang Ilbo*, July 12, 2008, http://joongangdaily.joins.com/article/view.asp?aid=2892225.

9. See Kim Sue-young, "Seoul Seeks Unification under Liberal Democracy," *Korea Times*, August 3, 2008, http://www.koreatimes.co.kr/www/news/nation/2008/08/116_28672.html.

10. See Jin Dae-woong, "Military Arms Buildup to Cost W164tr over Next Five Years," *Korea Herald*, July 19, 2007, http://www.koreaherald.co.kr/site/data/html_dir/2007/07/19/200707190038.asp.

11. Jung Sung-ki, "S. Korea-US Joint Drill Begins," *Korea Times*, August 17, 2008, http://www.koreatimes.co.kr/www/news/nation/2008/08/113_29513.html.

12. Sam Kim, "S. Korea, U.S. Pushing to Test New War Plan against N. Korea," *Yonhap News*, February 11, 2009, http://www.koreancenter.or.kr/news/news_foreign_view.aspx?menucode=02001000& news_id=aen20090211004100315; and Kim Min-seok, "U.S. Eighth Army to Remain Stationed in Korea," *Joongang Ilbo*, November 6, 2009, http://joongangdaily.joins.com/article/view.asp?aid=2912218.

13. Kim Min-seok and Ser Myo-ja, "U.S. will command military exercise," *Joongang Ilbo*, June 17, 2010, http://joongangdaily.joins.com/article/view.asp?aid=2921962.

14. Jung Sung-ki, "Timeline for Defense Reform Likely to Be Readjusted," *Korea Times*, July 6, 2008, http://www.koreatimes.co.kr/www/news/nation/2008/07/113_27123.html.

15. For current analysis on the North Korean military threat, see Scobell and Sanford, *North Korea's Military Threat*.

16. See Bruce Klingner, "Supporting Our South Korean Ally and Enhancing Defense Co-operation," Heritage Foundation Web Memo no. 1859, March 18, 2008, http://www.heritage.org/research/asiaandthepacific/wm1859.cfm.

17. For details on this definition, see Applegate, *Preparing for Asymmetry*.

18. For analysis of the impact the lack of readily available fuel has had on North Korean conventional military forces training trends, see Von Hippel, "Estimated DPRK Military Energy Use."

19. For information on how North Korea has increased its sophistication and numbers of missiles, see Gen. B. B. Bell, commander, United Nations Command; commander, Republic of Korea–United States Combined Forces Command; and commander, United States Forces Korea, testimony for the record before the House Armed Services Committee, March 2007, http://www.shaps.hawaii.edu/security/us/2007/bell_testimony030707.html. For analysis of how North Korea has increased its capabilities in command and control of missile forces by forming a missile corps, see Bermudez, "Moving Missiles.".

20. For an excellent analysis of increases in numbers of long-range systems deployed along the DMZ beginning in the late 1990s, see Schwartz, statement to the Senate Armed Services Committee, March 7, 2000. For specific estimates on the number of long-range artillery systems North Korea has forward deployed on or near the DMZ, see Bermudez, "North Korea's Long Reach in Profile." For information regarding the number of long-range artillery systems along the DMZ that can specifically target Seoul, see Donald Macintyre, "Kim's War Machine," *Time Asia* (February 17, 2003), http://www.time.com/time/asia/covers/501030224/army.html.

21. See Jon Herskovitz, "North Korean Guns, Clear and Present Danger to South," Reuters, June 27, 2006, http://www.boston.com/news/world/asia/articles/2006/06/27/north_korean_guns_clear_ and_present_danger_to_south/.

22. Jim Garamone, "North Korean 'Bolt from the Blue' Attack Remains a Concern," American Forces Press Service, October 26, 2006, http://www.defenselink.mil/news/newsarticle.aspx?id=1865.

23. For more analysis of numbers, strategy, tactics, and capabilities of North Korean Special Operations Forces, see Kaplan, "When North Korea Falls"; "North Korea: Special Operations Forces," GlobalSecurity.Org, 1996, http://www.globalsecurity.org/wmd/library/news/dprk/1996/kpa-guide/part03.htm; and Ministry of National Defense, "Defense White Paper" (2008).

24. For analysis of the numbers and capabilities of North Korean Scud and KN-02 missiles, see Jung Sung-ki, "S. Korea Vulnerable to NK Chemical Warheads," *Korea Times*, October 17, 2007, http://www.koreatimes.co.kr/www/news/nation/2010/05/205_12072.html.

25. "Defense Ministry Seeks 20% Hike in Purchases," *Korea Herald*, May 30, 2007, https://www.koreaherald.co.kr/site/data/html_dir/2007/05/30/200705300037.asp.

26. Jung Sung-ki, "Seoul Begins Deploying Patriot Missile Interceptors," *Korea Times*, September 16, 2008, http://www.koreatimes.co.kr/www/news/nation/2008/09/205_31122.html.

27. Brian Lee, "South Korea's Missile Shortage a Concern," *Joonganag Ilbo*, March 10, 2009, http://joongangdaily.joins.com/article/view.asp?aid=2902014.

28. "Raytheon Begins SAM-X/Patriot Missile Work in South Korea," *Defense Industry Daily*, December 1, 2008, http://www.defenseindustrydaily.com/raytheon-begins -sam-xpatriot-missile-work-in-south-korea-04772/.

29. Jung Sung-ki, "Israeli Radar Chosen for Missile Defense," *Korea Times*, September 17, 2009, http://www.koreatimes.co.kr/www/news/nation/2009/09/113_52006.html.

30. See "U.S. to Withdraw Patriot Missiles from Gwangju," *Chosun Ilbo*, August 24, 2006, http://english.chosun.com/w21data/html/news/200608/200608240011.html.

31. See "What Japan's Test Means for Korea's Missile Defense," *Chosun Ilbo*, December 19, 2007, http://english.chosun.com/site/data/html_dir/news/2007/12/19/2007121961008 .html.

32. "Japanese Ballistic Missile Defense," MissileThreat.com, Claremont Institute, August 24, 2008, http://www.missilethreat.com/missiledefensesystems/id.30/system_detail .asp.

33. See "South Korea Plans Affordable Missile Defense Shield," *Chosun Ilbo*, December 21, 2007, http://english.chosun.com/site/data/html_dir/ 2006/12/21/2006122161015 .html.

34. "Most US BMD Warships Positioned in the Pacific," *KBS World*, January 9, 2009, http://world.kbs.co.kr/english/news/news_in_detail.htm?no=60466.

35. See Office of the Spokesman, United States Department of State, "Joint Statement of the U.S.-Japan Security Consultative Committee," May 1, 2007, http://tokyo.us embassy.gov/e/p/tp-20070502-77.html.; and Vince Little, "Control Hub Used to Direct Exercise," *Stars and Stripes*, November 17, 2007, http://www.stripes.com/article.asp ?section=104&article=57805&archive=true.

36. See Wade Boese, "News Analysis: Missile Defense Role Questioned," *Arms Control Today*, July–August 2008, http://www.armscontrol.org/act/2008_07-08/NewsAnalysis.

37. Gen. B. B. Bell, commander, United Nations Command; commander, Republic of Ko-rea–United States Combined Forces Command; and commander, United States Forces Korea, statement before the Senate Armed Services Committee, April 24, 2007, http:// armed-services.senate.gov/statemnt/2007/april/bell%2004-24-07.pdf.

38. Jung Sung-ki, "N. Korea Blasts US Missile Shield," *Korea Times*, April 28, 2008, http://www.koreatimes.co.kr/www/news/nation/2008/08/120_22042.html.

39. Jung Sung-ki, "USFK Chief Urges Seoul to Join US BMD," *Korea Times*, February 25, 2009, http://www.koreatimes.co.kr/www/news/nation/2009/02/205_40279.html.

40. "Lee MB Policies: Lee Seeks to Strengthen U.S. Alliance," *Korea Herald Special Edition*, December 2007, http://www.koreaherald.com/.

41. Kim, "N.K. Threats Rekindle Missile Defense Debate."

42. Kim Ji-hyun, "Seoul Developing Anti-Missile Base," *Korea Herald*, February 16, 2009, http://www.koreaherald.co.kr/newkhsite/data/html_dir/2009/02/16/200902160042 .asp.

43. Kim Min-seok and Yoo Jee-ho, "Korean Navy Will Join U.S. Ballistic Missile Drills," *Joongang Ilbo*, July 22, 2009, http://joongangdaily.joins.com/article/view .asp?aid=2907749.

44. Jung Sung-ki, "Korea to Take over 10th, Last Security Mission from US," *Korea Times*, August 16, 2008, http://www.koreatimes.co.kr/www/news/nation/2008/08/205_25999 .html.

45. Kim Min-seok and Brian Lee, "Key Defense Mission to Go to Korean Military," *Joongang Ilbo*, April 11, 2005, http://joongangdaily.joins.com/200504/10/2005041022534 45679900090309031.html.

46. Jung Sung-ki, "[Exclusive] South Korean Military to Triple Artillery against N. Korea," *Korea Times*, June 21, 2009, http://www.koreatimes.co.kr/www/news/nation/2009/06/205_47204.html.

47. Sang-ho Yun, "1,000 Guided Missiles to Be Introduced to Counter North Korean Artillery," *Dong-a Ilbo*, April 10, 2005, http://english.donga.com/srv/service.php3?biid=2005041158378.

48. Sam Kim, "S. Korean Defense Flawed against N. Korean Artillery: Lawmaker," *Yonhap News*, October 12, 2009, http://english.yonhapnews.co.kr/national/2009/10/12/63/0301000000aen20091012005100315f.html.

49. "Lee MB Policies."

50. See "U.S. to Sell Restricted Spy Aircraft to Korea," *Chosun Ilbo*, August 11, 2008, http://english.chosun.com/site/data/html_dir/2008/08/11/2008081161007.html; and "Buying the Best Eyes on North Korea," StrategyPage.com, August 12, 2008, http://www.strategypage.com/htmw/htintel/articles/20080812.aspx.

51. Jung Sung-ki, "[Exclusive] 1st Early Warning Aircraft Arrives in South Korea," *Korea Times*, February 9, 2010, http://www.koreatimes.co.kr/www/news/nation/2010/02/205_60556.html.

52. Jung Sung-ki, "S. Korea Seeks Recon Planes by 2014," *Defense News*, June 14, 2010, http://www.defensenews.com/story.php?i=4669127&c=ASI&s=AIR.

53. "S. Korea Plans to Develop Unmanned Spy Aircraft by 2014," *Yonhap News*, April 28, 2010, http://english.yonhapnews.co.kr/national/2010/04/28/0301000000AEN20100428010100315.HTML.

54. Sam Kim, "Army Plans to Develop Drones to Step up Vigilance over N. Korea," *Yonhap News*, August 19, 2009, http://english.yonhapnews.co.kr/news/2009/08/19/0200000000aen20090819008300315.html.

55. "Korean Satellite Launch Is a Success," *Dong-a Ilbo*, August 23, 2006, http://english.donga.com/srv/service.php3?biid=2006082373498.

56. Lee Joon-seung, "Military to Operate 'Experimental' Unit to Test-Drive Restructuring," *Yonhap News*, June 28, 2009, http://english.yonhapnews.co.kr/national/2009/06/28/30/0301000000aen20090628001000320f.html.

57. "S. Korea Beefs up Defense against N. Korean Nukes," *Chosun Ilbo*, June 24, 2009, http://english.chosun.com/site/data/html_dir/2009/06/24/2009062400303.html.

58. For details of specific U.S. systems on which South Korea is dependent for providing both strategic and tactical battlefield and potential battlefield information and for filling the current gaps in South Korea's military information systems, see Sang-ho Yun, "Korea Depends on US for Data on North," *Dong-a Ilbo*, June 22, 2006, http://english.donga.com/srv/service.php3?bicode=050000&biid=2006062283888.

59. For specific details of how ROK and U.S. systems integrate and collaborate in order to provide battlefield information, see Kim Min-Seok, "In Spy Versus Spy, Seoul Holds High-Tech Edge," *Joongang Ilbo*, May 19, 2008, http://joongangdaily.joins.com/article/view.asp?aid=2889968.

60. "Q&A: Brigadier General Simeon G. Trombitas," *Special Operations Technology* 5, no. 7 (October 15, 2007), http://www.special-operations-technology.com/sotech-archives/180-sotech-2008-volume-5-issue-7/1670-qaa-brigadier-general-simeon-g-trombitas.html.

61. Lt. Gen. So Chin Tae, "Recasting the Viability of a Small Ally's Airpower: South Korea in Focus," *Air and Space Power Journal: Chronicles Online Journal,* October 1, 2002, http://www.airpower.maxwell.af.mil/airchronicles/cc/tae.html.

62. See Ben-David, "Iran Acquires Ballistic Missiles from DPRK"; and "Iran Bought 18 North Korean Missiles."

63. See "Iran Develops Missile with 4,000-KM Range," *Middle East Newsline*, March 2, 2006, http://www.menewsline.com/stories/2006/march/03_02_1.html; Vick, "Has the No-Dong B/Shahab-4 Finally Been Tested"; and Uzi Rubin, "The Global Range of Iran's Ballistic Missile Program," *Jerusalem Issue Brief* (Jerusalem Center for Public Affairs) 5, no. 26 (June 20, 2006), http://www.jcpa.org/brief/brief005-26.htm.

64. For another analysis of missiles Iran has acquired from North Korea, see House of Representatives, "Recognizing Iran as a Strategic Threat."

65. For more analysis on South Korea's role in the Proliferation Security Initiative, see Kim, "South Korea–North Korea Relations."

66. "Roh Counsels against Stress on Alliance with U.S.," *Chosun Ilbo*, October 2, 2008, http://english.chosun.com/site/data/html_dir/2008/10/02/2008100261002.html.

67. "Lee MB Policies."

68. See Jack Kim, "North Korea to Suspend Nuclear Disablement," Reuters, August 26, 2008, http://www.reuters.com/article/topnews/idusseo2172420080826?feedtype=rss &feedname=topnews; Blaine Harden, "N. Korea, Angry over Terror List, Threatens to Rebuild Nuclear Program," *Washington Post*, August 27, 2008, http://www.washington post.com/wp-dyn/content/article/2008/08/26/AR2008082600300.html; Office of the Director of National Intelligence, "Background Briefing with Senior U.S. Officials on Syria's Covert Nuclear Reactor and North Korea's Involvement"; and Ed Henry, "White House: Syria Reactor Not for 'Peaceful' Purposes," CNNPolitics.com, April 25, 2008, http://www.cnn.com/2008/POLITICS/04/24/syria.nuclear/index.html.

69. See "U.S. Urges S. Korea to Join PSI," *Chosun Ilbo*, May 29, 2008, http://english .chosun.com/site/data/html_dir/2008/05/29/2008052961017.html.

70. Lee Chi-dong, "S. Korea Urged to Step up Support of Anti-Proliferation Drive," *Yonhap News*, January 15, 2009, http://english.yonhapnews.co.kr/northkorea/2009/01/15/ 99/0401000000AEN20090115002300315F.HTML.

71. Kim, "N.K. Threats Rekindle Missile Defense Debate."

72. "Gov't Mulls Fully Joining PSI," *KBS World*, March 23, 2009, http://world.kbs.co.kr/ english/news/news_po_detail.htm?no=62205&id=po.

73. Yoo Jee-ho, "Seoul to Join Proliferation Security Initiative," *Joongang Ilbo*, April 14, 2009, http://joongangdaily.joins.com/article/view.asp?aid=2903557.

74. Hwang Doo-hyong, "U.S. Welcomes S. Korea's Move to Fully Join PSI: State Dept.," *Yonhap News*, April 9, 2009, http://english.yonhapnews.co.kr/news/2009/04/09/02000 00000AEN20090409000300315.HTML.

75. Lee Chi-dong, "S. Korea Joins PSI after N. Korea's Nuke Test," *Yonhap News*, May 26, 2009, http://english.yonhapnews.co.kr/northkorea/2009/05/26/55/0401000000AE N20090526003500315F.HTML.

76. See Evan Ramstad, "North Korea Warns on Ship Searches," *Wall Street Journal*, May 27, 2009, http://online.wsj.com/article/SB124330920945753575.html?KEYWORDS =north+korea+warns+on+ship+searches.

77. Lee Chi-dong, "S. Korea Begins Activity as PSI Member," *Yonhap News*, June 22, 2009, http://english.yonhapnews.co.kr/northkorea/2009/06/22/68/0401000000AEN2 0090622003600315F.HTML.

78. Kang Hyun-kyung, "Nation Faces Tough Times: Lee," *Korea Times*, July 15, 2008, http://www.koreatimes.co.kr/www/news/nation/2008/08/116_27621.html.

79. Jung Sung-ki, "Military Will Reduce Drills to Save Energy," *Korea Times*, July 7, 2008, http://www.koreatimes.co.kr/www/news/nation/2008/08/205_27175.html.

80. Jung Sung-ki, "Defense Reform Faces Overhaul," *Korea Times*, August 27, 2008, http://www.koreatimes.co.kr/www/news/nation/2008/08/116_30141.html.

81. See Lee Chi-dong, "S. Korea May Drop Defense Reform Plan 2020," *Yonhap News*,

May 13, 2010, http://english.yonhapnews.co.kr/news/2010/05/13/0200000000A
EN20100513007400315.HTML; Jung Sung-ki, "Seoul Seeking to Counter NK's
Asymmetrical Warfare," *Korea Times*, May 16, 2010, http://www.koreatimes.co.kr/
www/news/nation/2010/05/205_65967.html.

82. Jung Sung-ki, "S. Korean Military to Slow Troop Cuts," *Korea Times*, November 24,
2008, http://www.koreatimes.co.kr/www/news/nation/2008/11/205_34989.html.

83. Jung Sung-ki, "Service Period Cuts Will Fan Manpower Shortage in Military," *Korea Times*, October 9, 2008, http://www.koreatimes.co.kr/www/news/
nation/2008/10/113_32457.html.

84. For details of requested ROK Defense Ministry changes to its projected budget plans,
see Jung Sung-ki, "Less Spending for Military Modernization," *Korea Times*, April 7,
2009, http://www.koreatimes.co.kr/www/news/nation/2009/04/113_42785.html.

85. Jung Sung-ki, "Fighter, Attack Helicopter Plans Delayed," *Korea Times*, September
28, 2009, http://www.koreatimes.co.kr/www/news/nation/2009/09/113_52640.html.

86. See Na Jeong-ju, "Top Defense Officials Clash over Budget Plan," *Korea Times*, August 26, 2009, http://www.koreatimes.co.kr/www/news/nation/2009/08/113_50746
.html; and Yoo Jee-ho, "Minister Says Defense Budget Cuts Unwise," *Joongang Ilbo*,
August 27, 2009, http://joongangdaily.joins.com/article/view.asp?aid=2909307.

87. Jung Sung-ki, "US Base Relocation Cost Likely to Increase," *Korea Times*, June 8,
2008, http://www.koreatimes.co.kr/www/news/nation/2008/08/205_25512.html.

88. Bell, statement to Senate Armed Services Committee, April 24, 2007.

89. See "Korea, U.S. to Use Shared Funds for U.S. Troop Relocation," *Korea Herald*, April
5, 2007, http://www.koreaherald.co.kr/site/data/html_dir/2007/06/03/200706030002
.asp; "U.S. to Review Relocation Program Unless South Korea Pays More," *Dong-
a Ilbo*, April 26, 2007, http://english.donga.com/srv/service.php3?bicode=050000&
biid=2007042667138; and Brian Lee, "U.S. General Worries that North Poised for
Trouble," *Joongang Ilbo*, April 26, 2007, http://joongangdaily.joins.com/.

90. "S. Korea, U.S. to Negotiate over Military Cooperation," *Xinhua*, July 21, 2008, http://
news.xinhuanet.com/english/2008-07/21/content_8741695.htm.

91. Jung Sung-ki, "Washington Urges Seoul to Pay More for Troops," *Korea Times*, July
22, 2008, http://www.koreatimes.co.kr/www/news/nation/2008/07/205_27990.html.

92. "S Korea, U.S. to Discuss Defense Cost-Sharing," *Xinhua*, August 27, 2008, http://
news.xinhuanet.com/english/2008-08/27/content_9723947.htm.

93. "S. Korea–U.S. Defense Cost Sharing Talks Fail to Bring Breakthrough," *Yonhap
News*, August 29, 2008, http://english.yonhapnews.co.kr/national/2008/08/29/15/
0301000000AEN20080829005500315F.HTML.

94. "U.S. Wants up to 15% More for Forces Upkeep in Korea," *Chosun Ilbo*, April 29,
2008, http://english.chosun.com/site/data/html_dir/2008/08/29/2008082961016.html.

95. Jin Dae-woong, "Seoul, Washington Resume Talks on Troop Funding," *Korea Herald*,
September 25, 2009, http://www.koreaherald.co.kr/.

96. "U.S. Pledges Prompt Military Aid to S. Korea," *Dong-a Ilbo*, October 18, 2008,
http://english.donga.com/srv/service.php3?biid=2008101844358.

97. Jung Sung-ki, "Defense Cost-Sharing Talks End Fruitlessly," *Korea Times*, October
30, 2008, http://www.koreatimes.co.kr/www/news/nation/2008/10/116_33600.html.

98. Lee Chi-dong, "S. Korea to Pay 760 Billion Won for U.S. Troops in 2009," *Yonhap
News*, December 23, 2008, http://english.yonhapnews.co.kr/news/2008/12/23/020000
0000AEN20081223007900315.HTML.

99. "Allies to Seal Deal on Defense Cost Sharing," *Yonhap News*, January 14, 2009,
http://www.koreancenter.or.kr/news/news_foreign_view.aspx?menu_code
=02001000&news_id=aen20090114003000315.

100. Jung Sung-ki, "South Korea, US Sign Defense Cost Sharing Plan," *Korea Times*, January 15, 2009, http://www.koreatimes.co.kr/www/news/nation/2009/01/113_37947 .html.

101. Department of State, "U.S. and Republic of Korea Conclude New Special Measures Agreement," *Media Note,* January 15, 2009, http://www.state.gov/r/pa/prs/ ps/2009/01/113988.htm.

102. Lee Chi-dong, "Stephens Says Seoul's Defense Cost Sharing Is 'Investment' in Alliance," *Yonhap News*, January 15, 2009, http://english.yonhapnews.co.kr/national/2009/ 01/15/53/0301000000AEN20090115008100315F.HTML.

103. See Emma Chanlett-Avery, Mark E. Manyin, and William H. Cooper, "Japan-US Relations: Issues for Congress" (Washington, DC: Congressional Research Service, Library of Congress, October 5, 2006), http://fpc.state.gov/documents/organization/76933.pdf.

104. Richard Halloran, "The New Line in the Pacific," airforce-magazine.com 90, no. 12 (December 2007), http://www.afa.org/magazine/dec2007/1207pacific.asp.

105. Department of State, "United States–Japan Roadmap for Realignment Implementation" (Washington, DC: Department of State, May 1, 2006), http://www.usfj.mil/ Documents/UnitedStates-JapanRoadmapforRealignmentImplementation.pdf.

106. See Jung Sung-ki, "South Korea-U.S. Alliance Enters New Era," *Korea Times*, December 31, 2007, http://www.koreatimes.co.kr/www/news/special/2008/08/180_16501.html.

107. Jung Sung-ki, "Timeline for U.S. Base Relocation May Be Readjusted," *Korea Times*, August 27, 2008, http://www.koreatimes.co.kr/www/news/nation/2008/08/116_30127 .html.

108. "Seoul Set to Alter Plans for U.S. Base Relocation, Causing Delays," *Yonhap News*, July 21, 2008, http://english.yonhapnews.co.kr/.

109. Lee Young-jong, "Citing Budgetary Issues, U.S. Seeks Base Move Delay," *Joongang Ilbo*, October 22, 2008, http://joongangdaily.joins.com/article/view.asp?aid=2896447.

110. "U.S. Forces in Korea to Complete Relocation by 2016," *Dong-a Ilbo*, January 5, 2009, http://english.donga.com/srv/service.php3?bicode=050000&biid =2009010586508.

111. For details on discussions regarding the movement of bases, see "S. Korea, U.S. Hold Talks on U.S. Military Base Relocation," *Xinhua*, April 23, 2009, http://news.xinhua net.com/english/2009-04/23/content_11243835.htm; Jung Sung-ki, "USFK Wants S. Korea to Guarantee Housing Project in Pyeongtaek," *Korea Times*, April 26, 2009, http://www.koreatimes.co.kr/www/news/nation/2009/04/116_43872.html; Jung Sung-ki, "S. Korea, U.S. Near Base Relocation Agreement," *Korea Times*, April 29, 2009, http://www.koreatimes.co.kr/www/news/nation/2009/04/116_44093.html; and Kim Ji-hyun, "Seoul, Washington Nearing Relocation Deal," *Korea Herald*, March 10, 2010, http://www.koreaherald.co.kr/newkhsite/data/html_dir/2009/04/24/20090424 0015.asp.

112. Jung Sung-ki, "USFK Chief Sees Base Relocation to End in 2015," *Korea Times*, March 21, 2010, http://www.koreatimes.co.kr/www/news/nation/2010/03/205_62757.html.

113. For details of the signed agreement between Secretary Gates and Minister Kim, see "Secretary Gates Holds Consultations with ROK Minister of National Defense," *Defense Link*, February 23, 2007, http://www.defenselink.mil/news/feb2007/d20070223s- drok.pdf.

114. "Former Generals Criticize Seoul-Washington Deal on Wartime Control Transfer," *Yonhap News*, February 26, 2007, http://english.yonhapnews.co.kr/engnews/200702 26/610000000020070226140348e0.html.

115. Cheon Seong-whun, "[Korea-U.S. Relations under Obama (2)] Transfer of Troop Control: A Bush Legacy," *Korea Herald*, January 23, 2009, http://www.koreaherald.co.kr/ NEWKHSITE/data/html_dir/2009/01/23/200901230070.asp.

116. "South Korea Increasing Defense Budget, Advancing toward Assumption of Military Control," *Geostrategy-Direct*, April 30, 2008, http://www.geostrategy-direct.com/geostrategy-direct/.

117. Kim Ji-Hyun, "GNP Head Urges OPCON Transfer Review," *Korea Herald*, February 4, 2010, http://www.koreaherald.co.kr/national/Detail.jsp?newsMLId=20100205000079.

118. See "S. Korea Says Redeployment of U.S. Forces a 'Long-Term Discussion,'" *Yonhap News*, February 2, 2010, http://english.yonhapnews.co.kr/national/2010/02/02/89/0301000000AEN2010020200 5300315F.HTML; and Tony Chang, "Seoul Looking into Concerns about Wartime OPCON Transfer: Defense Chief," *Yonhap News*, April 8, 2010, http://english.yonhapnews.co.kr/news/2010/04/08/0200000000A EN20100408004600315.HTML.

119. Ibid.

120. Lee Chi-dong, "U.S. Envoy Hints at Gap between Bush, Lee over OPCON Transfer Time," *Yonhap News*, December 21, 2007, http://english.yonhapnews.co.kr/national/2007/12/21/77/0301000000AEN200712210029 00315F.HTML.

121. Hwang Doo-hyong, "Scheduled 2012 Transfer of OPCON on Track: U.S. Commander," *Yonhap News*, October 7, 2009, http://english.yonhapnews.co.kr/news/2009/10/08/0200000000AEN20091 008000900315.HTML.

122. "Delaying Troop Control Transfer 'Sends Wrong Message,'" *Chosun Ilbo*, March 29, 2010, http://english.chosun.com/site/data/html_dir/2010/03/29/2010032900337.html.

123. "Lee Links Troop Control Issue to N. Korea Nukes," *Korea Herald Special*, December 2007, http://www.koreaherald.com/.

124. Jung Ha-won, "Hot Topics Await Lee-Bush Summit," *Joongang Ilbo*, August 4, 2008, http://joongangdaily.joins.com/article/view.asp?aid=2893206.

125. Chang Jae-soon, "Nearly Half of S. Koreans Want Delay in Command Transfer: Survey," *Yonhap News*, April 29, 2010, http://english.yonhapnews.co.kr/news/2010/04/29/0200000000AEN20100429007100315.HTML.

126. See "Personal History Web Page," Kim Hak-song Profile [in Korean], http://www.jinhaesarang.co.kr/profile/history.php.

127. For more analysis on the political and military dangers of initiating an early OPCON transfer, see Bruce Klingner, "Transforming the U.S.–South Korean Alliance," Heritage Foundation Backgrounder no. 2155, June 30, 2008, http://www.heritage.org/Research/Reports/2008/06/Transforming-the-US-South-Korean-Alliance.

128. For an example of obvious impatience with the current transition in the alliance and perhaps misinformed perceptions about ROK military capabilities from Senators Levin and Warner, see reported statements from Senate confirmation hearings held on April 3, 2008, in: "US Congress Says, Make OPCON Transferred Earlier," *Yonhap News* [in Korean], April 6, 2008, http://english.yonhapnews.co.kr/.

129. Jung Sung-ki, "USFK Chief Pledges Naval, Air-Centric Reinforcement," *Korea Times*, February 1, 2009, http://www.koreatimes.co.kr/www/news/nation/2009/02/116_38782.html.

130. "Korea, U.S. to Combine Air Force Command," *Chosun Ilbo*, February 5, 2009, http://english.chosun.com/site/data/html_dir/2009/02/05/2009020561009.html.

131. Jung Sung-ki, "[Exclusive] Korea, US Devise Broader Air Operations Command," *Korea Times*, September 27, 2009, http://www.koreatimes.co.kr/www/news/nation/2009/09/205_52552.html.

132. "USFK to Continue Major Operations after OPCON Transfer," *KBS News*, October 31, 2009, http://rki.kbs.co.kr/english/news/news_po_detail.htm?no=67770.

133. Kim Ji-hyun, "Construction Starts for JCS Headquarters," *Korea Herald*, March 26, 2010, http://www.koreaherald.com/national/Detail.jsp?newsMLId=20100326000416.

134. See Ministry of National Defense, Republic of Korea, "Entire Military Working toward Transfer under Joint Chiefs of Staff," February 16, 2009, http://www.mnd.go.kr/mndeng/whatsnew/recentnews/.
135. Kim, "U.S. Eighth Army to Remain Stationed in Korea."
136. Gen. Walter L. Sharp, "Transformation Conference Commander's Welcome," speech given at the Renaissance Seoul Hotel, Seoul, Republic of Korea, April 5, 2010, http://www.usfk.mil/usfk/(A(rAJooFALywEkAAAAZmEyM2JkYjctNDIz ZC00OTdjLTg3MjAtYTNjMzk2YWNhOGQ1frCPo_59szFdRl5YFY4bC2nxIco1) S(r5axazfubj2nrr453fneye55))/Uploads/110/transform.pdf.
137. For more details about how the ROK and U.S. forces will launch their separate warfighting commands, see Jung Sung-ki, "South Korea to Launch Theater Command by '09," *Defense News*, March 13, 2008, http://www.defensenews.com/story.php?i=3424 008&c=asi&s=top.
138. Yoo Jee-ho, "Korea, U.S. Could Delay Wartime Control Transfer," *Joongang Ilbo*, March 24, 2010, http://joongangdaily.joins.com/article/view.asp?aid=2918257.
139. "Transfer of Wartime Command Should Be Delayed," *Dong-a Ilbo*, May 27, 2009, http://english.donga.com/srv/service.php3?biid=2009052732988.
140. See Jung Sung-ki, "Calls Grow to Reschedule Command Transfer," *Korea Times*, May 27, 2009, http://www.koreatimes.co.kr/www/news/nation/2009/05/116_45798.html; and Sam Kim and Byun Duk-kun, "N. Korean Nuclear Test Renews Concerns over U.S.–S. Korean Alliance," *Yonhap News*, May 28, 2009, http://english.yonhapnews.co.kr/national/2009/05/28/93/0301000000AEN20090528006100315F.HTML.
141. "Lee Gov't Lacks Its Own Contingency Manual," *Dong-a Ilbo*, September 29, 2008, http://english.donga.com/srv/service.php3?bicode=050000&biid=2008092946248.
142. Jong-Koo Yoon, "CONPLAN 5029 Not to Be Elevated to Status of OPLAN," *Dong-a Ilbo*, June 6, 2005, http://english.donga.com/srv/service.php3?biid=2005060609528.
143. Kim Min-seok and Ser Myo-ja, "Seoul Halts Joing Plan for North Collapse," *Joongang Ilbo*, April 16, 2005, http://joongangdaily.joins.com/200504/15/20050415220313093 9900090309031.html.
144. "Korea, U.S. Close to Agreeing N.K. Contingency Plan," *Chosun Ilbo*, March 6, 2006, http://english.chosun.com/w21data/html/news/200603/200603060012.html.
145. "S. Korea, U.S. Prepare for Post-Kim Jong-il Era," *Dong-a Ilbo*, September 13, 2008, http://english.donga.com/srv/service.php3?bicode=050000& biid=2008091336218.
146. "Is Seoul Ready for Contingencies in North Korea?" *Chosun Ilbo*, September 12, 2008, http://english.chosun.com/site/data/html_dir/2008/09/12/2008091261014.html.
147. "Contingency Plans," *My Sinchew*, September 20, 2008, http://www.mysinchew.com/node/16458.
148. Butaro Kuroi, "U.S. Military's Operational Plans for Seizing North Korean Nuclear Facilities and Nuclear Weapons Already Set in Motion," *Tokyo Shukan Gendai* [in Japanese], October 25, 2008.
149. "USFK to Continue Major Operations."
150. "U.S. Renews Calls for N. Korea Military Action Plan," *Chosun Ilbo*, October 29, 2008, http://english.chosun.com/site/data/html_dir/2008/10/29/2008102961003.html.
151. "U.S. Offers Action Plan in Case of N. Korea Collapse," Newsmax.com, October 29, 2008, http://www.newsmax.com/international/us_korea_collapse/2008/10/29/145288.html.
152. "U.S., Japan Review Joint Emergency Plan for Korea," *Chosun Ilbo*, November 12, 2008, http://english.chosun.com/site/data/html_dir/2008/11/12/2008111261005.html.
153. Kim Ji-hyun, "Sharp Ups Ante against N. Korea," *Korea Herald*, February 10, 2009, http://www.koreaherald.co.kr/newkhsite/data/html_dir/2009/02/10/200902100050.asp.

154. Jung Sung-ki, "S. Korea, U.S. Chart Contingency Plans on N. Korea," *Korea Times*, April 22, 2009, http://www.koreatimes.co.kr/www/news/nation/2009/04/205_43632 .html.

155. "S. Korea, U.S. Set up Contingency Plan on N. Korea: RFA," *Yonhap News*, Oct 2, 2009, http://english.yonhapnews.co.kr/national/2009/10/02/56/0301000000AEN2009 1002001200320F.HTML.

156. "Seoul, Washington Round out Plans to Handle N. Korean Regime Collapse: Source," *Yonhap News*, November 1, 2009, http://enews.mcot.net/view.php?id=12578.

157. "Seoul Overhauls N. Korea Contingency Plan," *Chosun Ilbo*, January 14, 2010, http:// english.chosun.com/site/data/html_dir/2010/01/14/2010011400307.html.

158. See Moshit Joshi, "U.S. China Holding Talks in Case North Korea Collapses," *TopNews*, September 12, 2008, http://www.topnews.in/us-china-holding-talks-case -north-korea-collapses-266574; and Wendell Goler, "U.S., China Laying Plans in Case North Korea Collapses," FoxNews.com, September 11, 2008, http://www.foxnews .com/story/0,2933,421201,00.html.

159. Jay Solomon and Jason Leow, "Beijing Spurns U.S. Effort to Prepare in Event of Ko- rean Leader's Demise," *Wall Street Journal*, November 7, 2008, http://online.wsj.com/ article/SB122599607084505499.html?KEYWORDS=beijing+spurns+us+effort+to +prepare+in+event+of+korean+leader%27s+demise.

160. "Key Points Memo: CSIS U.S.-China Dialogue on North Korean Contingencies and Responses" (POC: Bonnie Glaser) (Washington, DC: Center For Strategic and Inter- national Studies, 2009).

161. Larry M. Wortzel, "PLA 'Joint' Operational Contingencies in South Asia, Central Asia, and Korea," in *Beyond the Strait: PLA Missions Other Than Taiwan*, eds. Roy Kamphausen, David Lai, and Andrew Scobell (Carlisle, PA: U.S. Army War College Strategic Studies Institute, 2009), http://www.strategicstudiesinstitute.army.mil/pubs/ display.cfm?pubid=910.

162. The four basic pillars of military cooperation were previously addressed in Bruce E. Bechtol Jr., "Forging a Common Approach on Strength: Challenges and Opportunities for the Lee Myung-bak Presidency and the ROK-US Alliance," in *Understanding New Political Realities in Seoul: Working toward a Common Approach to Strengthen U.S.- Korean Relations,* eds. L. Gordon Flake and Park Ro-byug (Washington, DC: Maureen and Mike Mansfield Foundation, 2008), http://www.mansfieldfdn.org/pubs/pub_pdfs/ us-rok_final_x.pdf.

163. See "Issue Brief: U.S.–Korea Free Trade Agreement (FTA): Strengthens Relations with a Key Strategic Partner," *Business Roundtable*, 2006, http://trade.business roundtable .org/trade_2006/korea/Korea_FTA4.pdf.

164. For details of the agreement between the two presidents on wartime OPCON, reac- tion from military and policy experts, and the predictable reaction from the Left in South Korea, see Lee Chi-dong, "S. Korea, U.S. Reschedule OPCON Transfer After N. Korea's Provocation," *Yonhap News*, June 27, 2010, http://english.yonhapnews.co.kr/ northkorea/2010/06/27/82/0401000000AEN20100627001400315F.HTML; Kim Deok- hyun, "S. Korea, U.S. to Complete Details for Delay of Command Transfer in Octo- ber," *Yonhap News*, June 28, 2010, http://english.yonhapnews.co.kr/national/2010/06/ 28/15/0301000000AEN20100628005500315F.HTML; Seo Seung-wook and Christine Kim, "Delay in Transfer of Troop Control Angers Liberals," *Joongang Ilbo*, June 28, 2010, http://joongangdaily.joins.com/article/view.asp?aid=2922393; "Delay of War- time Command Transfer to Deter North Korea: U.S. General," *Yonhap News*, June 30, 2010, http://english.yonhapnews.co.kr/national/2010/06/30/59/0301000000AEN2

0100630004300315F.HTML. "Delay of Wartime Command Draws Mixed Responses from Political Parties," *Yonhap News*, June 27, 2010, http://english.yonhapnews.co.kr/national/2010/06/27/0301000000AEN20100627003800315.HTML

165. "U.S. Military Bills N. Korea 'Potential Threat,' Calls for More Info," Japan Economic Newswire, July 15, 2008, http://www.breitbart.com/article.php?id=d91u4qrg0&show_article=1.

SEVEN. **Conclusion: North Korea's Threats to the United States and Its Allies**

1. For analysis on North Korean brinkmanship during the early Clinton administration years, see Patrick E. Tyler, "The World: Living with North Korea's Bomb," *New York Times*, January 23, 1994, http://www.nytimes.com/1994/01/23/weekinreview/the-world-living-with-north-korea-s-bomb.html.

2. For analysis on North Korea's belligerent nation-state behavior, despite having to open up to the West because of desperate economic conditions, see Andrei Lankov, "The Natural Death of North Korean Stalinism," *Asia Policy* 1 (January 2006), http://www.nbr.org/publications/Preview/AP1_NorthKorea_preview.pdf.

3. For a rundown of just some of the many acts of brinkmanship and provocation the North Koreans conducted over a period of several years and how U.S. politicians running for president assessed them, see Council on Foreign Relations, "The Candidates on North Korea Policy," *Issue Tracker,* October 23, 2008, http://www.cfr.org/publication/14757/candidates_on_north_korea_policy.html?breadcrumb=%2fcampaign2008%2ftracker

4. For an analysis of the foreign and domestic policies of Kim Dae-jung and Roh Moo-hyun, see Hoon Jaung, "Foreign Policy and South Korean Democracy: The Failure of Party Politics," *Taiwan Journal of Democracy* 1, no. 2 (December 2005): 49–68, http://www.tfd.org.tw/docs/dj0102/049-068.pdf.

5. For more analysis of how Lee Myung-bak planned to alter the policies of his predecessors and set out on the MB Doctrine, even before he assumed office, see Shaw-Lin Chaw, "Democratic Consolidation and Foreign Relations under Lee Myung-bak," in *SAIS U.S.-Korea Yearbook: 2007, U.S.-Korea Institute at SAIS: 2007* (Washington, DC: Korea Institute at SAIS, 2007), http://uskoreainstitute.org/pdf/yb07/SAIS_Yearbook_Rev072007.pdf.

6. For a detailed description of the policy shift toward North Korea made by the Bush administration in February 2007, see Curtis H. Martin, "U.S. Policy toward North Korea under G. W. Bush: A Critical Perspective," paper presented at the Forty-Eighth Annual Convention of the International Studies Association, Chicago, Illinois, February 28–March 3, 2007, http://www.allacademic.com//meta/p_mla_apa_research_citation/1/8/0/5/2/pages180525/p180525-1.php.

7. For complete details of how the issue of the abduction of Japanese citizens ruined what were looking to be improved relations between Tokyo and Pyongyang, see Secretariat, Headquarters for the Abduction Issue, government of Japan, "The Abduction of Japanese Citizens by North Korea," 2007, http://www.kantei.go.jp/foreign/abduction/index.html.

8. Moon Soon-ho, "Pyongyang's Coercive Diplomacy & U.S. Reaction," *Vantage Point* 32, no. 4 (April 2009): 13–15.

9. For details on how North Korea went through various stages of working with NGOs and other issues related to controlling its populace, see Chaibong Hahm, "Nuclear North Korea and the New Administration," speech given to the Los Angeles World Affairs Council, January 22, 2009, http://www.lawac.org/speech/2008-09/HAHM,%20hCaibong2008.pdf.

10. For an excellent analysis of many of the roadblocks NGOs have run into while carrying out their missions in North Korea, see Scott Snyder, "Lessons of the NGO Experience in North Korea," in Flake and Snyder, *Paved with Good Intentions*, 119–23.

11. Lee Sang Yong, "Defectors Radio Highly Effective Tool: Interview with the Director of Free North Korea Broadcasting," *Daily NK*, March 31, 2009, http://www.dailynk.com/english/read.php?catald=nk02500&num=4755.

12. Joseph S. Bermudez, Jr., "Information and the DPRK's Military and Power-Holding Elite," in *North Korean Policy Elites*, eds. Kongdan Oh Hassig and others, IDA Paper P-3903 (Alexandria, VA: Institute For Defense Analyses, June, 2004), http://www.dtic.mil/cgi-bin/GetTRDoc?AD=ADA427588&Location=U2&doc=GetTRDoc.pdf.

13. See Committee to Protect Journalists, "10 Most Censored Countries: North Korea Tops CPJ's List of 10 Most Censored Countries," *Special Reports,* May 2, 2006, http://cpj.org/reports/2006/05/10-most-censored-countries.php.

14. Andrei Lankov, "Why Pyongyang Clings to Its Weapons," *Asia Times*, April 24, 2009, http://www.atimes.com/atimes/korea/kd24dg02.html.

15. For an example of the DPRK's reaction, see "NKorea Threatens to Turn SKorea into 'Debris.'"

16. For a review of events that occurred during the fall of 2008 in the six-party talks and the lack of transparency that was exhibited by the North Koreans, see Leonor Tomero and Adam Ptacin, "Will Ill Kim Jong-Il Derail Disarmament?" (Washington, DC: Center for Arms Control and Non-Proliferation, October 6, 2008), http://www.armscontrolcenter.org/policy/northkorea/articles/061008_ill_jong-il_derail_disarmament/.

17. See Larry Niksch, "U.S.–North Korean Relations: From the Agreed Framework to the Six-party Talks," *International Journal of Korean Studies* 9, no. 1 (Fall–Winter 2005), http://www.icks.org/publication/pdf_2005_s/1_Niksch.pdf; and Yuan Jing-Dong, "The North Korean Nuclear Impasse: A Long Road to Denuclearisation," *Opinion Asia*, April 7, 2008, http://www.opinionasia.org/alongroadtodenuclearisation.

18. For an example of analysis that assesses the North Korean military threat as having declined compared to the capabilities of South Korea, see John Feffer, "Ploughshares into Swords: Economic Implications of South Korean Military Spending," Academic Paper Series 4, no. 2 (Washington, DC: Korean Economic Institute, February 2009), http://www.keia.org/Publications/AcademicPaperSeries/2009/APS-Feffer.pdf.

19. See Lee Youkyung and Kim Eun-jung, "U.S. Commander Raises Concerns over N. Korean Artillery Threat," *Yonhap News*, April 22, 2009, http://english.yonhapnews.co.kr/northkorea/2009/04/22/1/0401000000AEN20090422007700315F.HTML.

20. For an example of this, see Shanker, "South Korean Says North Still a Threat."

21. Human Rights Watch, "Universal Periodic Review of North Korea: Human Rights Watch's Submission to the Human Rights Council, April 2009," April 18, 2009, http://www.hrw.org/en/news/2009/04/18/universal-periodic-review-north-korea.

22. See Choe Sang-hun, "Embattled North Korea Celebrates Its Military," *New York Times*, April 25, 2007, http://www.nytimes.com/2007/04/25/world/asia/25cnd-korea.html?_r=1.

23. See Don Kirk, "North Korea Has Ransom on Its Mind," *Asia Times*, April 25, 2009, http://www.atimes.com/atimes/korea/kd25dg01.html.

24. For details regarding food aid to North Korea from both South Korea and China, see Stephan Haggard and Marcus Noland, "North Korea in 2008: Twilight of the God?" (Washington, DC: Peterson Institute for International Economics, January 2009), http://www.iie.com/publications/papers/noland0109.pdf.

25. See "North Korea Not Eager to Return to Talks: UN Envoy," Reuters, February 12, 2010, http://www.alertnet.org/thenews/newsdesk/TOE61B05W.htm.

26. George Russell, "U.N. Plans More Cash for North Korea's Dictatorial Regime," FOX News, June 2, 2010.

27. Details of food and energy aid donated by the United States, China, and South Korea can by found in Mark E. Manyin and Mary Beth Nikitin, "Foreign Assistance to North Korea" (Washington, DC: CRS Report for Congress, December 24, 2008), http://www.fas.org/sgp/crs/row/R40095.pdf.

28. See David L. Asher, "The North Korean Criminal State, Its Ties to Organized Crime, and the Possibility of WMD Proliferation," *Nautilus Institute Policy Forum Online* 05-92A, November 15, 2005, http://www.nautilus.org/fora/security/0592asher.html.

SELECTED BIBLIOGRAPHY

Applegate, Melissa. *Preparing for Asymmetry: As Seen through the Lens of Joint Vision 2020.* Carlisle, PA: Strategic Studies Institute, 2001. http://www.au.af.mil/au/awc/awcgate/ssi/preparng.pdf.

Asher, David L. "The North Korean Criminal State, Its Ties to Organized Crime, and the Possibility of WMD Proliferation." *Nautilus Institute Policy Forum Online* 05-92A, November 15, 2005. http://www.nautilus.org/fora/security/0592Asher.html.

Association of Former Intelligence Officers. "North Korean Ship Sunk." *Weekly Intelligence Notes*, 50-01, December 24, 2001. http://www.afio.com/sections/wins/2001/2001-50.html.

Bach, William. Office of African, Asian, and European Affairs, Bureau for International Narcotics and Law Enforcement Affairs, Department of State, Testimony. Hearing on Drugs Counterfeiting and Arms Trade, Senate Subcommittee on Financial Management, the Budget, and International Security, May 20, 2003. http://usinfo.org/wf-archive/2003/030521/epf310.htm.

Baird, Merrily. E-mail interview by author, February 13, 2009.

Bajoria, Jayshree, and Carin Zissis. "The Six-Party Talks on North Korea's Nuclear Program." Council on Foreign Relations, October 14, 2008. http://www.cfr.org/publication/13593/.

Banville, Lee. "North Korea: Nuclear Standoff." *PBS Online NewsHour*, October 19, 2006. http://www.pbs.org/newshour/indepth_coverage/asia/northkorea/nuclear.html.

Bechtol, Bruce E., Jr. "Forging a Common Approach on Strength: Challenges and Opportunities for the Lee Myung-bak Presidency and the ROK-US Alliance." In *Understanding New Political Realities in Seoul: Working toward a Common Approach to Strengthen U.S.-Korean Relations,* edited by L. Gordon Flake and Park Ro-byug. Washington, DC: Maureen and Mike Mansfield Foundation, 2008. http://www.mansfieldfdn.org/pubs/pub_pdfs/US-ROK_final_x.pdf.

———. "The Northern Limit Line of 2002: Motivations and Implications." *Pacific Focus* 19, no. 2 (Fall 2004).

———. *Red Rogue: The Persistent Challenge of North Korea.* Dulles, VA: Potomac Books, 2007.

Bell, Gen. B. B., commander, United Nations Command; commander, Republic of Korea–United States Combined Forces Command; and commander, United States Forces

Korea. Statement. Senate Armed Services Committee, March 7, 2006. http://www
.senate.gov/~armed_services/statemnt/2006/March/Bell%2003-07-06.pdf.
————. Statement. Senate Armed Services Committee, April 24, 2007. http://armed-services
.senate.gov/statemnt/2007/April/Bell%2004-24-07.pdf.
————. Testimony. House Armed Services Committee, March 2007. http://www.shaps
.hawaii.edu/security/us/2007/Bell_Testimony030707.html.
————. Testimony. House Armed Services Committee, March 12, 2008. http://www.shaps
.hawaii.edu/security/us/2008/bell_031208.html.
Ben-David, Alon. "Iran Acquires Ballistic Missiles from DPRK." *Jane's Defence Weekly*,
December 29, 2005. http://www.janes.com/security/international_security/news/jdw/
jdw051229_1_n.shtml.
Bermudez, Joseph S., Jr. *A History of Ballistic Missile Development in the DPRK*. CNS Oc-
casional Papers: #2. Monterey, CA: Center for Nonproliferation Studies, Monterey In-
stitute of International Studies, 1999. http://cns.miis.edu/pubs/opapers/op2/index.htm.
————. "Information and the DPRK's Military and Power-Holding Elite." In *North Korean
Policy Elites*, Kongdan Oh Hassig, Joseph S. Bermudez, Jr.; Kenneth E. Gause; Ralph
C. Hassig; Alexandre Y. Mansourov; and David J. Smith. IDA Paper P-3903. Alexan-
dria, VA: Institute For Defense Analyses, June, 2004. http://www.dtic.mil/cgi-bin/GetT
RDoc?AD=ADA427588&Location=U2&doc=GetTRDoc.pdf.
————. "Launch Failure Frustrates North Korea's Missile Aspirations." *Jane's Defence
Weekly*, April 7, 2009. http://search.janes.com/Search/documentView.do?docId=/
content1/janesdata/mags/jdw/history/jdw2009/jdw39507.htm@current&pageSelec
ted=allJanes&keyword=joseph%20bermudez&backPath=http://search.janes.com/
Search&Prod_Name=JDW&.
————. "Moving Missiles." *Jane's Defence Weekly*, July 27, 2005. http://www.janes.com/
defence/land_forces/news/jdw/jdw050727_1_n.shtml.
————. "North Korea Deploys New Missiles." *Jane's Defence Weekly*, August 2, 2004.
http://www.janes.com/defence/news/jdw/jdw040802_1_n.shtml.
————. "North Korea's Long Reach in Profile." *Jane's Intelligence Review*, November 11,
2003. http://www.janes.com/defence/land_forces/news/idr/idr031111_1_n.shtml.
————. "North Korea's Strategic Culture." Defense Threat Reduction Agency, Advanced
Systems and Concepts Office, Fort Belvoir, VA, October 31, 2006. http://www.dtra
.mil/documents/asco/publications/comparitive_strategic_cultures_curriculum/
case%20studies/North%20Korea%20(Bermudez)%20final%201%20Nov%2006.pdf.
————. "SIGINT, EW, and EIW in the Korean People's Army: An Overview of Develop-
ment and Organization." In *Bytes and Bullets: Information Technology, Revolution,
and National Security on the Korean Peninsula*, edited by Alexandre Y. Monsourov.
Honolulu HI: Asia Pacific Center for Security Studies, 2005. http://www.apcss.org/
Publications/Edited%20Volumes/BytesAndBullets/CH13.pdf.
Bleiker, Roland. *Divided Korea: Toward a Culture of Reconciliation*. Minneapolis: Univer-
sity of Minnesota Press, 2005.
Boese, Wade. "News Analysis: Missile Defense Role Questioned." *Arms Control Today*,
July–August 2008. http://www.armscontrol.org/act/2008_07-08/NewsAnalysis.
Boose, Donald W., Jr.; Balbina Y. Hwang; Patrick Morgan; and Andrew Scobell, eds. *Reca-
librating the U.S.–Republic of Korea Alliance*. Carlisle, PA: Strategic Studies Institute,
2003. http://www.strategicstudiesinstitute.army.mil/pdffiles/pub53.pdf.
Brookes, Peter. "Korean Nukes: Don't Get Giddy." *New York Post,* June 27, 2008. http://
www.nypost.com/seven/06272008/postopinion/opedcolumnists/korean_nukes__dont
_get_giddy_117426.htm.

"Burma: Junta Said Building Armament Factory in Pinlaung with North Korean Help." *Democratic Voice of Burma* (in Burmese), January 20, 2009. http://www.dvb.no/.

"Buying the Best Eyes on North Korea." *StrategyPage.com*, August 12, 2008. http://www.strategypage.com/htmw/htintel/articles/20080812.aspx.

Carpenter, Ted Galen, and Doug Bandow. *The Korean Conundrum: America's Troubled Relationship with North and South Korea*. New York: Palgrave Macmillan, 2004.

Caryl, Christian, and B. J. Lee. "North Korea's Dictator May Be Ailing, but Don't Hope for Change Soon." *Newsweek*, December 8, 2008. http://www.newsweek.com/id/171307.

Center for Nonproliferation Studies (CNS). *Chronology of North Korea's Missile Trade and Developments: 1980–1989*. Center for Nonproliferation Studies (online), Monterey Institute of International Studies, 1999. http://cns.miis.edu/archive/country_north_korea/chr8089.htm.

———. "CNS Special Report on North Korean Ballistic Missile Capabilities." Monterey, CA: Center for Nonproliferation Studies, Monterey Institute of International Studies, March 22, 2006. http://cns.miis.edu/stories/pdfs/060321.pdf.

Central Intelligence Agency. "Untitled CIA Estimate Provided to Congress on November 19, 2002, (UNCLASSIFIED)." November 19, 2002. http://www.fas.org/nuke/guide/dprk/nuke/cia111902.html.

Cha, Victor D., and David C. Kang. *Nuclear North Korea: A Debate for Engagement Strategies*. New York: Columbia University Press, 2003.

Chang, Gordon C. *Nuclear Showdown: North Korea Takes on the World*. New York: Random House, 2006.

———. "What's Going on in Pyongyang? North Korea Responds to Sticks, Not Carrots." *Weekly Standard*, September 21, 2009. http://www.weeklystandard.com/Content/Public/Articles/000/000/016/946ocfak.asp.

Chanlett-Avery, Emma, Mark E. Manyin, and William H. Cooper. "Japan-US Relations: Issues for Congress." Washington, DC: Congressional Research Service (CRS), Library of Congress, October 5, 2006. http://fpc.state.gov/documents/organization/76933.pdf.

Chaw, Shaw-Lin. "Democratic Consolidation and Foreign Relations under Lee Myung-bak," 177–88. In *SAIS U.S.-Korea Yearbook: 2007*. Washington, DC: U.S.-Korea Institute at SAIS, 2007. http://uskoreainstitute.org/pdf/YB07/SAIS_Yearbook_Rev072007.pdf.

Cheney, Richard. "Vice President Speaks at China's Fudan University, April 15." Speech at Fudan University, China, April 15, 2004. http://helsinki.usembassy.gov/servlet/PageServer?Page=today2.html.

Cheon, Seong-whun. "[Korea-U.S. Relations under Obama (2)] Transfer of Troop Control: A Bush Legacy." *Korea Herald*, January 23, 2009. http://www.koreaherald.co.kr/NEWKHSITE/data/html_dir/2009/01/23/200901230070.asp.

Cheong, Seong-chang. "Kim Jong-il's Illness and Prospects for Post-Kim Leadership." *East Asian Review* 20, no. 4, (Winter 2008).

———. "Outlook for the Situation in North Korea and North-South Relations in 2009." *Situation and Policy* (in Korean, Sejong Institute), January 2009. http://www.sejong.org/.

Chestnut, Sheena E. "The 'Sopranos State'? North Korean Involvement in Criminal Activity and Implications for International Security." Center for International Security and Cooperation, Stanford University, May 20, 2005. http://www.nautilus.org/napsnet/sr/2006/0605Chestnut.pdf.

Choe, Julia. "Problems of Enforcement: Iran, North Korea, and the NPT." Harvard International Review: Academy and Policy 28, no. 2 (Summer 2006). http://hir.harvard.edu/index.php?page=article&id=1550&p=2.

Choi, Choel-hee. "The Relationship between the Party and the Army under the Military-First Policy." *Daily NK*, October 21, 2008. http://www.dailynk.com/english/read.php?cataId=nk00400&num=4199.

Choi, Sung-chol, ed. *Understanding Human Rights in North Korea*. Seoul, Korea: Center for the Advancement of North Korean Human Rights, 1997.

Committee to Protect Journalists. "10 Most Censored Countries: North Korea Tops CPJ's List of 10 Most Censored Countries." *Special Reports,* May 2, 2006. http://cpj.org/reports/2006/05/10-most-censored-countries.php.

"Concerns Raised over Possible North Korean Scud Derivative." Jane's Information Group, March 10, 2005. http://www.janes.com/security/international_security/news/jmr/jmr050310_1_n.shtml.

Cordesman, Anthony. *Iran's Military Forces in Transition: Conventional Threats and Weapons of Mass Destruction*. Westport, CT: Praeger, 1999.

Council on Foreign Relations. "The Candidates on North Korea Policy." *Issue Tracker,* October 23, 2008. http://www.cfr.org/publication/14757/candidates_on_north_korea_policy.html?breadcrumb=%2Fcampaign2008%2Ftrackers.

Daalder, Ivo H., and James M. Lindsay. *America Unbound: The Bush Revolution in Foreign Policy*. Washington DC: Brookings Institution Press, 2003.

Davies, Roger. "Sea Tigers, Stealth Technology, and the North Korean Connection." *Jane's Intelligence Review*, March 2001. http://www.lankalibrary.com/pol/korea.htm.

Defense Intelligence Agency. *North Korea: The Foundations of Military Strength, Defense Intelligence Agency–Update 1995*. Washington, DC: Defense Intelligence Agency, 1995. http://www.nautilus.org/DPRKBriefingBook/military/DPRKMilitaryHandbook-MarinesUpdate1995.pdf.

Dies, Harry P., Jr. "North Korean Special Operations Forces: 1996 Kangnung Submarine Infiltration." *Military Intelligence Professional Bulletin*, October–December 2004. http://findarticles.com/p/articles/mi_m0IBS/is_4_30/ai_n13822276.

Downs, Chuck. *Over the Line: North Korea's Negotiating Strategy*. Washington, DC: AEI Press, 1999.

———. "Right Where He Wants Us." *Wall Street Journal,* June 21, 2006.

"DPRK Permanent Representative Sends Letter to President of UNSC." *KCNA*, September 4, 2009. http://www.kcna.co.jp/item/2009/200909/news04/20090904-04ee.html.

Dunnigan, James. "North Korea's SS-21 Missiles." *StrategyPage.com*, May 12, 2005. http://www.strategypage.com/dls/articles/2005512213718.asp.

Eberstadt, Nicholas. *The North Korean Economy: Between Crisis and Catastrophe*. Piscataway, NJ: Transaction Publishers, 2007.

———. "What Went Wrong? The Bush Administration's Failed North Korea Policy." *Weekly Standard*, January 26, 2009. http://www.weeklystandard.com/Content/Public/Articles/000/000/016/024opizu.asp.

Eshel, David. "Iran's Long-Range Missile Program: NATO's Next Challenge." *Defense Update—News Analysis*. January 19, 2005. http://www.defense-update.com/2005/01/irans-long-range-missile-program-natos.html.

"The Failed States Index 2008." *Foreign Policy*, July–August 2008. http://www.foreignpolicy.com/story/cms.php?story_id=4350.

Federation of American Scientists. "Korean People's Air Force." *Nuclear Forces Guide,* 2008. http://www.fas.org/nuke/guide/dprk/agency/af.htm.

Feffer, John. "Ploughshares into Swords: Economic Implications of South Korean Military Spending.", Academic Paper Series, 4, no. 2. Washington, DC: Korean Economic Institute, February 2009. http://www.keia.org/Publications/AcademicPaperSeries/2009/APS-Feffer.pdf.

Flake, L. Gordon, and Scott Snyder, eds. *Paved with Good Intentions: The NGO Experience in North Korea.* Santa Barbara, CA: Praeger, 1999.

Foreign Affairs Committee, National Council of Resistance of Iran. "Nuclear Pyongyang Is Helping Iran." September 23, 2008. http://ncr-iran.org/content/view/5632/107/.

Frank, Rudiger. "Has the Next Great Leader of North Korea Been Announced?" *Nautilus Institute Policy Forum Online* 08-080A, October 21, 2008. http://www.nautilus.org/fora/security/08080Frank.html.

Funabashi, Yoichi. *The Peninsula Question: A Chronicle of the Second Korean Nuclear Crisis.* Washington, DC: Brookings Institution Press, 2007.

Fund for Peace. "Failed States Index Scores 2008." 2008. http://www.fundforpeace.org/web/index.php?option=com_content&task=view&id=292&Itemid=452.

Gallucci, Robert L. "North Korean Nuclear Crisis: An Online Question and Answer Session." *Washingtonpost.com,* June 23, 2004. http://discuss.washingtonpost.com/wp-srv/zforum/04/world_gallucci062304.htm.

Gates, Robert M. "A Balanced Strategy: Reprogramming the Pentagon for a New Age." *Foreign Affairs*, January–February 2009. http://www.foreignaffairs.org/articles/63717/robert-m-gates/a-balanced-strategy.

Gause, Ken E. *North Korean Civil-Military Trends: Military-First Politics to a Point.* Strategic Studies Institute Monograph. Carlisle, PA: U.S. Army War College, September 2006. http://www.strategicstudiesinstitute.army.mil/pdffiles/PUB728.pdf.

Gjelten, Tim. "North Korean Leader's Absence Spurs Stroke Rumors." *National Public Radio*, September 9, 2008. http://www.npr.org/templates/story/story.php?storyId=94428411.

Green, Michael, and Derek Mitchell. "Asia's Forgotten Crisis: A New Approach to Burma." *Foreign Affairs*, November–December 2007. http://www.foreignaffairs.org/20071101faessay86610/michael-green-derek-mitchell/asia-s-forgotten-crisis.html.

Green, Nick. "Dealing Drugs: North Korean Narcotics Trafficking." *Harvard International Review* 26, no. 1 (Spring 2004). http://hir.harvard.edu/articles/1201.

Haggard, Stephan, and Marcus Noland. "North Korea in 2008: Twilight of the God?" Washington, DC: Peterson Institute for International Economics, January 2009. http://www.iie.com/publications/papers/noland0109.pdf.

Hahm, Chaibong. "Nuclear North Korea and the New Administration." Speech given to the Los Angeles World Affairs Council, January 22, 2009. http://www.lawac.org/speech/2008-09/HAHM,%20Chaibong2008.pdf.

Halloran, Richard. "The New Line in the Pacific," *airforce-magazine.com* 90, no. 12 (December 2007). http://www.afa.org/magazine/dec2007/1207pacific.asp.

Harrison, Selig S. "Did North Korea Cheat?" *Foreign Affairs,* January–February 2005. http://www.foreignaffairs.org/20050101faessay84109/selig-s-harrison/did-north-korea-cheat.html.

———. Testimony: "Smart Power: Remaking US Foreign Policy in North Korea." Hearing before the House Foreign Affairs Subcommittee, February 13, 2009. http://royce.house.gov/Multimedia/Default.aspx?MediaID=539.

———. Testimony. U.S. Congress, House Committee on Foreign Affairs, June 17, 2009. http://foreignaffairs.house.gov/111/har061709.pdf.

Hayden, Michael V, director, Central Intelligence Agency. "The CIA's Counterproliferation Efforts." Address given to the Los Angeles World Affairs Council, September 16, 2008. http://www.lawac.org/speech/2008-09/hayden,michael2008.pdf.

Hayes, Peter. "The Multilateral Mantra and North Korea." *DPRK Briefing Book,* Nautilus Institute Online, February 20, 2004,. http://www.nautilus.org/DPRKBriefingBook/multilateralTalks/PHMultilateralMantra.html.

Hecker, Siegfried S. "Report on North Korean Nuclear Program." Center for International Security and Cooperation, Stanford University, November 15, 2006. http://iis-db .stanford.edu/pubs/21266/dprk-report-hecker06.pdf.

————. "Technical Summary of DPRK Nuclear Program." Paper presented at the 2005 Carnegie International Non-Proliferation Conference, Washington, DC, November 8, 2005. http://www.carnegieendowment.org/static/npp/2005conference/presentations/ hecker.pdf.

Henry, Terrence. "After Kim Jong Il," *Atlantic Monthly*, May 2005. http://www.theatlantic .com/doc/200505/henry.

"Hezbollah a North Korea-Type Guerilla Force, " *Intelligence Online*, no. 529 (August 25– September 7, 2006). http://www.oss.net/dynamaster/file_archive/060902/26241feaf47 66b4d441a3a78917cd55c/Intelligence%20Online%20on%20Hezbolllah.pdf.

Hollis, Patrecia Slayden. "The Korean Theater—One-of-a-Kind: Interview with General Robert W. RisCassi." *Field Artillery*, February 1993. http://sill-www.army.mil/ famag/1993/FEB_1993/FEB_1993_PAGES_7_10.pdf.

Hong, Kyudok. "Strengthening the ROK-U.S. Alliance: New Approaches and Obstacles." A position paper submitted to the special seminar North Korea Policy of the Lee Myung-Bak Administration and Prospect for Future: Development of the ROK-US Relationship. Korean Association of International Studies, Best Western Premier Hotel Kukdo, Seoul, Korea, November 3, 2008. www.kaisnet.or.kr/board09/download.asp?idx=380.

Hosenball, Mark. "Nukes: Too Deep to Hit." *Newsweek*, November 3, 2008. http://www .newsweek.com/id/165667.

Hosenball, Mark, and Christian Caryl. "North Korea Arms Deal Intercepted." *Newsweek*, November 22, 2008. http://www.newsweek.com/id/170322?tid=relatedcl.

Human Rights Watch. "Universal Periodic Review of North Korea: Human Rights Watch's Submission to the Human Rights Council, April 2009." April 18, 2009. http://www .hrw.org/en/news/2009/04/18/universal-periodic-review-north-korea.

"Important Political Change in North Korea: Kim Jong-il's Brother-in-Law Comes into Power—Military Hardliners Said to Have Been Dismissed." *Zakzak* (in Japanese), October 21, 2008. http://www.zakzak.co.jp/.

"Initial Actions for the Implementation of the Joint Statement: Joint Statement from the Third Session of the Fifth Round of the Six-Party Talks." *Nautilus Institute Policy Forum Online Special Report* 07-013A, February 13, 2007. http://www.nautilus.org/fora/ security/07013Statement.html.

Institute for Foreign Policy Analysis. "Independent Working Group on Missile Defense, the Space Relationship, and the Twenty-First Century." Cambridge, MA: Institute for Foreign Policy Analysis, 2009. http://www.ifpa.org/pdf/IWG2009.pdf.

International Atomic Energy Agency. "Agreement of 30 January 1992 between the Government of the Democratic People's Republic of Korea and the International Atomic Energy Agency for the Application of Safeguards in Connection with the Treaty on the Non-Proliferation of Nuclear Weapons." *Information Circular,* May 1992. http://www .iaea.org/Publications/Documents/Infcircs/Others/inf403.shtml.

International Civil Aviation Organization. "ICAO Officially Advised of DPRK Plans for Rocket Launch." News release, March 12, 2009. http://www.icao.int/icao/en/nr/2009/ pio200902_e.pdf.

"Issue Brief: U.S.–Korea Free Trade Agreement (FTA): Strengthens Relations with a Key Strategic Partner." *Business Roundtable*, 2006. http://trade.businessroundtable.org/ trade_2006/korea/Korea_FTA4.pdf.

"Japanese Ballistic Missile Defense." *MissileThreat.com*, Claremont Institute, August 24, 2008. http://www.missilethreat.com/missiledefensesystems/id.30/system_detail.asp.

Jaung, Hoon. "Foreign Policy and South Korean Democracy: The Failure of Party Politics."

Taiwan Journal of Democracy 1, no. 2 (December 2005): 49–68. http://www.tfd.org
.tw/docs/dj0102/049-068.pdf.

Joint Doctrine Division. *Joint Pub 1-02: DOD Dictionary of Military and Associated Terms.*
Joint Electronic Library, Department of Defense, October 17, 2008. http://www.dtic
.mil/doctrine/dod_dictionary/.

Jun, Bong-Geun. "Scenarios of North Korea's Power Shift." Korean Institute of Foreign Affairs and National Security, Policy Brief no. 2008/7, November 2008.

Jung, Kwon Ho. "Dare Not Be Curious about Dear Leader's Health." *Daily NK*, November
4, 2008. http://www.dailynk.com/english/read.php?cataId=nk01500&num=4247.

Junn, Sung-chull. "President Lee's Beef Blunder." *Far Eastern Economic Review*, July
11, 2008. http://www.feer.com/international-relations/2008/july/President-Lees-Beef-
Blunder.

Kamphausen, Roy, David Lai, and Andrew Scobell, eds. *Beyond the Strait: PLA Missions
Other Than Taiwan.* Carlisle, PA: U.S. Army War College Strategic Studies Institute,
2009. http://www.strategicstudiesinstitute.army.mil/pdffiles/PUB910.pdf.

Kane, Kevin. "Iran and North Korea's Military Relations: Trading with Terrorists?" *Daily
NK*, February 5, 2007. http://www.dailynk.com/english/read.php?cataId=nk00300
&num=1638.

Kaplan, Robert D. "When North Korea Falls." *Atlantic Monthly*, October 2006. http://www
.theatlantic.com/doc/200610/kaplan-korea.

Karon, Tony. "SCUD Seizure Raises Tricky Questions." *Time,* December 11, 2002. http://
www.time.com/time/world/article/0,8599,398592,00.html.

Kerr, Paul. "North Korea Increasing Weapons Capabilities." *Arms Control Today*, December 2005. http://www.armscontrol.org/act/2005_12/Dec-NKweapons.asp.

Kihl, Young Whan, and Hong Nack Kim, eds. *North Korea: The Politics of Regime Survival.*
Armonk, NY: M. E. Sharp, 2006.

"Kim Jong-chol: Guitar Playing Heir to the Dynasty?" *Korean Unification Studies*, November 27, 2008. http://koreanunification.net/2007/11/25/kim-jong-chol-guitar-playing-
heir-to-communist-dynasty/.

"Kim Jong Nam: Leadership Succession." *GlobalSecurity.org*, April 4, 2005. http://www
.globalsecurity.org/military/world/dprk/kim-jong-nam.htm.

Kim, Myung Jin. "South Korea–North Korea Relations: Influence of the PSI on North
Korea." *Strategic Insights* 5, no. 7 (September 2006). http://www.nps.edu/Academics/
centers/ccc/publications/OnlineJournal/2006/Sep/kimSep06.html.

Kim, Sung Chull. *North Korea under Kim Jong Il: From Consolidation to Systemic Dissonance.* New York: State University of New York Press, 2006.

Kim, Sung-jin. "North Korea's New Launch Site for Missiles." *Vantage Point* 31, no. 10
(October 2008).

Kimball, Daryl, and Peter Crail. "Chronology of U.S.–North Korean Nuclear and Missile
Diplomacy." *Arms Control Association Factsheet*, June 2008. http://www.armscontrol
.org/factsheets/dprkchron.[

Kirk, Donald. "N. Korea's Test Threat Launches Uproar." *Christian Science Monitor*, June
22, 2006. http://www.csmonitor.com/2006/0622/p06s02-woap.html.

Klingner, Bruce. "New North Korean Missile Unit Reflects Growing Missile Threat."
Heritage Foundation Report, March 11, 2010. http://www.heritage.org/Research/
Reports/2010/03/New-North-Korean-Missile-Unit-Reflects-Growing-Missile-Threat.

———. "North Korea Nuclear Verification: Has the U.S. Blinked?" *Heritage Foundation
Web Memo no. 2120*, October 31, 2008. http://www.heritage.org/research/asiaand-
thepacific/wm2120.cfm.

———. "Supporting Our South Korean Ally and Enhancing Defense Cooperation." *Heri-

tage Foundation Web Memo no. 1859, March 18, 2008. http://www.heritage.org/ Research/Asiaandthepacific/wm1859.cfm.

———. "Transforming the U.S.–South Korean Alliance." *Heritage Foundation Backgrounder no. 2155,* June 30, 2008. http://www.heritage.org/Research/Reports/2008/06/ Transforming-the-US-South-Korean-Alliance.

Ko, Jae-hung. "The Status and Role of North Korea's National Defense Commission." *Vantage Point* 32, no. 2 (February 2009).

"Korean People's Army: Introduction." *GlobalSecurity.org,* April 27, 2005. http://www .globalsecurity.org/military/world/dprk/army.htm.

"Korean Peoples' Army Navy." *GlobalSecurity.org,* April 27, 2005. http://www.global security.org/military/world/dprk/navy.htm.

Kotler, Mindy L. "Toward an 'Asian' North Korea." *Nautilus Institute Policy Forum Online* PFO 03-28, April 8, 2003. http://www.nautilus.org/fora/security/0328_Kotler.html.

Kwak, Tae-hwan, and Seung-ho Joo, eds. *The United States and the Korean Peninsula in the 21st Century.* Aldershot, Hampshire, UK: Ashgate, 2006.

Kwon, Ho-Youn, ed. *Divided Korea: Longing for Reunification.* Chicago, IL: North Park University Press, 2004.

Kwon, Soyoung, and Glyn Ford. "Reading North Korean Ruins." *Nautilus Institute Policy Forum Online* PFO 05-18A, February 24, 2005. http://www.nautilus.org/fora/ security/0518A_Ford_Kwon.html.

Lam, Willy. "Chinese Media Go Dark on Events in N. Korea as CCP Cultivates Ties with Key Generals." *East-Asia-Intel.com,* September 17, 2008. http://www.east-asia-intel .com/eai/WL.html.

Lankov, Andrei. "The Natural Death of North Korean Stalinism." *Asia Policy* 1 (January 2006). http://www.nbr.org/publications/asia_policy/Preview/AP1_NorthKorea_preview .pdf.

Lee, Kwang-ho. "Endorsing a New Five-Year Term for Kim Jong-il." *Vantage Point* 32, no. 5 (May 2009).

———. "Speculation on Kim Jong-il's Successor," *Vantage Point* 32, no. 2 (February 2009).

Lee, Sang Yong. "Defectors Radio Highly Effective Tool: Interview with the Director of Free North Korea Broadcasting." *Daily NK,* March 31, 2009. http://www.dailynk.com/ english/read.php?cataId=nk02500&num=4755.

Lee, Suk Bok. *The Impact of U.S. Forces in Korea.* Washington, DC: National Defense University Press, 1987.

Lerner, Mitchell B. *The Pueblo Incident: A Spy Ship and the Failure of American Foreign Policy.* Lawrence: University Press of Kansas, 2003.

Levey, Stuart A. Prepared Remarks by Undersecretary for Terrorism and Financial Intelligence before the American Bar Association's 22nd Annual National Institute on White Collar Crime. Press room, U.S. Department of the Treasury, March 6, 2008. http:// www.ustreas.gov/press/releases/hp863.htm.

Lim, Jae-Hyoung. "The Power Hierarchy: North Korean Foreign Policy Making Process." *East Asian Review* 14, no. 2 (Summer 2002). http://www.ieas.or.kr/vol14_2/14_2_5 .pdf.

Lin, Christina Y. "The King from the East: DPRK-Syria-Iran Nuclear Nexus and Strategic Implications for Israel and the ROK." Korea Economic Institute, Academic Paper Series 3, no. 7 (October 2008). http://www.keia.org/Publications/AcademicPaper Series/2008/APS-Lin.pdf.

Lintner, Bertil. "Burma's Nuclear Temptation." *Yale Global,* December 3, 2008. http:// antidictatorship.wordpress.com/2008/12/19/analysis-burma's-nuclear-temptation- bertil-lintner/.

————. "North Korea: Coming in from the Cold." *Far Eastern Economic Review*, October 25, 2001. http://www.asiapacificms.com/articles/northkorea/.

————. "North Korea's Missile Trade Helps Fund Its Nuclear Program." *Yale Global*, May 5, 2003. http://yaleglobal.yale.edu/content/north-koreas-missile-trade-helps-fund-its-nuclear-program.

————. "Tunnels, Guns, and Kimchi: North Korea's Quest for Dollars—Part I." *Yale Global*, June 9, 2009. http://yaleglobal.yale.edu/content/NK-quest-for-dollars-part1.

Loeffler, Rachel L. "Bank Shots: How the Financial System Can Isolate Rogues." *Foreign Affairs* 88, no. 2 (March–April 2009). http://www.foreignaffairs.com/articles/64822/rachel-l-loeffler/bank-shots.

"M-1978 / M1989 (KOKSAN) 170mm Self Propelled (SP) Gun." *GlobalSecurity.org*, March 2005. http://www.globalsecurity.org/military/world/dprk/m-1978-170.htm.

Macintyre, Donald. "Kim's War Machine." *Time Asia,* February 17, 2003. http://www.time.com/time/asia/covers/501030224/army.html.

Manyin, Mark E., Emma Chanlett-Avery, and Helene Marchart. "North Korea: A Chronology of Events, October 2002–December 2004." Washington, DC: CRS, Library of Congress, January 24, 2005. http://www.fas.org/man/crs/RL32743.pdf.

Manyin, Mark E., and Mary Beth Nikitin. "Foreign Assistance to North Korea." Washington, DC: CRS Report for Congress, September 2009. http://www.fas.org/sgp/crs/row/R40095.pdf.

Martin, Curtis H. "U.S. Policy toward North Korea under G. W. Bush: A Critical Perspective," paper presented at the 48th Annual Convention of the International Studies Association, Chicago, Illinois, February 28–March 3, 2007. http://www.allacademic.com//meta/p_mla_apa_research_citation/1/8/0/5/2/pages180525/p180525-1.php.

McCormack, Gavan. "North Korea and the US 'Strategic Decision.'" *The Asia-Pacific Journal: Japan Focus*, December 2005. http://www.japanfocus.org/-Gavan-McCormack/1925.

McCreary, John. "Nightwatch: For the Night of 11 Feburary 2009." *AFCEA Intelligence*, February 11, 2009. http://nightwatch.afcea.org/NightWatch_20090211.htm.

McGlynn, John. "The U.S. Declaration of War on Iran." *The Asia-Pacific Journal: Japan Focus*, March 22, 2008. http://www.japanfocus.org/products/details/2707.

McQueary, Charles E. "Ballistic Missile Defense Systems," *FY 2008 Annual Report*. Washington, DC: Operational Test and Evaluation, Department of Defense, December 2008. http://www.cdi.org/pdfs/FY08DOTEAnnualReport.pdf.

"Media Release: Extra 75kg of heroin linked to 'Pong Su.'" *Australian Federal Police*, May 27, 2003. http://www.afp.gov.au/afp/page/Media/2003/0527pongsu.htm.

Ministry of Foreign Affairs of Japan. "Initial Actions for the Implementation of the Joint Statement." February 13, 2007. http://www.mofa.go.jp/region/asia-paci/n_korea/6party/action0702.html.

Ministry of National Defense, Republic of Korea. "Defense White Paper" [in Korean]. 2006. http://www.mnd.go.kr/.

————. "Defense White Paper" [in Korean]. 2008. http://www.mnd.go.kr/.

————. "Entire Military Working toward Transfer under Joint Chiefs of Staff." February 16, 2009. http://www.mnd.go.kr/mndEng/WhatsNew/RecentNews/.

————. "The Naval Clash on the Yellow Sea on 29 June 2002 between South and North Korea: The Situation and ROK's Position," *GlobalSecurity.org*, July 1, 2002. http://www.globalsecurity.org/wmd/library/news/rok/2002/0020704-naval.htm.

Minnich, James M. *The Denuclearization of North Korea: The Agreed Framework and Alternative Options Analyzed*. Bloomington, IN: 1st Books Library, 2002.

Moltz, James Clay. "Russian Policy on the North Korean Nuclear Crisis." Monterey, CA:

Center for Non-Proliferation Studies, Monterey Institute of International Studies, May 5, 2003. http://cns.miis.edu/research/korea/ruspol.htm.

Moodie, Amanda. "Syria: Coming in from the Cold?" WMD Insights, October 2008. http://www.wmdinsights.org/I27/I27_ME2_Syria.htm.

Moon, Soon-ho. "Pyongyang's Coercive Diplomacy & U.S. Reaction." *Vantage Point* 32, no. 4 (April 2009): 13–15.

Mullen, Adm. Mike. "Remarks by Adm. Mike Mullen, Chairman of the Joint Chiefs of Staff." Pew Memorial Lecture, Grove City College, Pennsylvania, February 2, 2009. http://www.jcs.mil/chairman/speeches/03FEB09_CJCS_Grove_City_College.pdf.

Myat, Ahunt Phone. "Democratic Voice of Burma: North Korean National Dies in Meikhtila." *BurmaNet News*, January 16, 2009. http://www.burmanet.org/news/2009/01/16/democratic-voice-of-burma-north-korean-national-dies-in-meikhtila-%e2%80%93-ahunt-phone-myat/.

National Intelligence Council. "Strategic Implications of Global Health." Intelligence Community Assessment 2008-10D, December 2008. http://www.dni.gov/nic/PDF_GIF_otherprod/ICA_Global_Health_2008.pdf.

Niksch, Larry A. E-mail interview by the author, July 20, 2009.

———. "North Korea: Terrorism List Removal." Washington, DC: CRS Report for Congress, July 10, 2008. http://www.fas.org/sgp/crs/row/RL30613.pdf.

———. "North Korea's Nuclear Weapons Development and Diplomacy." Washington, DC: CRS Report for Congress, March 30, 2009. http://italy.usembassy.gov/pdf/other/RL33590.pdf.

———. "U.S.–North Korean Relations: From the Agreed Framework to the Six-party Talks." *International Journal of Korean Studies* 9, no. 1 (Fall–Winter 2005). http://www.icks.org/publication/pdf_2005_s/1_Niksch.pdf.

"1983: The Year in Review." Headquarters, United States Forces Korea/Eighth United States Army, 1984. http://www.nautilus.org/foia/foiachrons/ahr_eightythree.pdf.

"N. Korea Lays Out Detailed Border Restrictions." *Asia Pulse*, November 27, 2008. http://www.accessmylibrary.com/coms2/summary_0286-35952723_ITM.

Noland, Marcus. "North Korea: Present Status and Prospects for Survival in the Year 2000." Testimony before the Subcommittee on East Asian and Pacific Affairs, United States Senate, Washington, DC, July 8, 1997. http://www.iie.com/publications/papers/paper.cfm?ResearchID=283.

———. "North Korean Missile Test: Remedial Action." *Asia Pacific Bulletin* 33 (April 6, 2009). http://www.eastwestcenter.org/fileadmin/stored/pdfs/apb033_1.pdf.

———. "Some Unpleasant Arithmetic Concerning Unification." Peterson Institute for International Economics, Working Paper 96-13, October 23, 1996. http://www.iie.com/publications/wp/wp.cfm?researchid=169.

"North Korea Profile: Nuclear Overview." *The Nuclear Threat Initiative*, September 2005. http://www.nti.org/e_research/profiles/NK/Nuclear/.

"North Korea, Iran, Rank One, Two on U.S. Enemies List Wednesday." *Rasmussen Reports*, August 12, 2009. http://www.rasmussenreports.com/public_content/politics/current_events/ally_enemy/north_korea_iran_rank_one_two_on_u_s_enemies_list.

North Korean Affairs Research Institute. "North Korea's Eighth Special Army Corps." *Seoul NK Focus* (in Japanese), April 18, 2008. http://www.nkfocus.jp.

"North Korean Officials Share Thoughts with KEI Staff." Korea Economic Institute, May 2008. http://www.keia.org/.

"North Korea's Nuclear Challenge." 2002 Carnegie International Non-Proliferation Conference, Washington, DC, November 14, 2002. http://www.ceip.org/files/projects/npp/resources/conference2002/northkorea.htm.

Oberdorfer, Don. *The Two Koreas: A Contemporary History*. New York: Basic Books, 2001.

Office of the Director of National Intelligence. "Background Briefing with Senior Intelligence Officials on Syria's Covert Nuclear Reactor and North Korea's Involvement." April 24, 2008. http://www.dni.gov/interviews/20080424_interview.pdf.

———. "The National Intelligence Strategy of the United States of America." August 2009. http://www.dni.gov/reports/2009_NIS.pdf.

———. "Statement by the Office of the Director of National Intelligence on North Korea's Declared Nuclear Test on May 25, 2009." Public Affairs Office news release, Washington, DC, June 15, 2009. http://www.dni.gov/press_releases/20090615_release.pdf.

O'Hanlon, Michael, and Mike Mochizuki. *Crisis on the Korean Peninsula: How to Deal with a Nuclear North Korea*. Washington, DC: Brookings Institution Press, 2003.

Olsen, Edward A. "If the United States Had 'No' Policy toward North Korea." *Strategic Insights* 4, no. 10 (October 2005). http://www.nps.edu/Academics/centers/ccc/publications/OnlineJournal/2005/Oct/olsenOct05.html.

———. *Korea: The Divided Nation*. Wesport, CT: Praeger, 2005.

Paek, Sung-chu. "Characteristics of the North Korean Succession System in the Post–Kim Jong-il Era and Prospects for the Adjustment of Its Policy." Seoul: Korea Institute for Defense Analyses, April 1, 2008.

Pan, Esther. "North Korea's Capitalist Experiment." *Backgrounder,* Council on Foreign Relations, June 8, 2006. http://www.cfr.org/publication/10858/.

Park, Hwee Rhak. "The Self-Entrapment of Rationality in Dealing with North Korea." *Korean Journal of Defense Analysis* 20, no. 4 (December 2008).

Park, Hyeong Jung. "Divergent Threat Perceptions on North Korea." *Mansfield Foundation Commentary*, 2007. http://www.mansfieldfdn.org/programs/program_pdfs/rok_us_park.pdf.

Park, Syung-je, board member, Military Analyst Association of the Republic of Korea, Seoul, Republic of Korea. E-mail interview by author, January 22, 2006.

"Personal History Web Page." Kim Hak-song Profile (in Korean). http://www.jinhaesarang.co.kr/profile/history.php.

Pinkston, Daniel A. "Domestic Politics and Stakeholders in the North Korean Missile Development Program." *Nonproliferation Review*, Summer 2003. http://cns.miis.edu/npr/pdfs/102pink.pdf.

———. "North Korea Conducts Nuclear Test." Monterey, CA: Center for Nonproliferation Studies, Monterey Institute of International Studies, October 10, 2006. http://cns.miis.edu/stories/pdfs/061010_dprktest.pdf.

———. *The North Korean Ballistic Missile Program*, Strategic Studies Institute Monograph. Carlisle, PA: U.S. Army War College, February 2008. http://www.strategicstudiesinstitute.army.mil/pdffiles/PUB842.pdf.

Prahar, Peter A. director, Office of African, Asia and Europe/NIS Programs, Bureau for International Narcotics and Law Enforcement Affairs, Department of State. Statement for hearing North Korea: Illicit Activity Funding the Regime. Federal Financial Management, Government Information, and International Security Subcommittee. Committee on Homeland Security and Governmental Affairs. U.S. Senate, 109th Cong., 2nd sess., April 25, 2006. http://hsgac.senate.gov/_files/042506Prahar.pdf.

Pritchard, Charles L., president, Korea Economic Institute. "Smart Power: Remaking U.S. Foreign Policy in North Korea," statement before the House Committee on Foreign Affairs, Subcommittee on Asia, the Pacific and the Global Environment, February 12, 2009. http://www.internationalrelations.house.gov/111/pri021209.pdf.

"Public Announcement." *Weihai Economic and Technological Development Zone* [in Chinese], February 4, 2009. http://www.e-weihai.gov.cn/cn/news/index_show.jsp?id=7614.

"Q&A: Brigadier General Simeon G. Trombitas." *Special Operations Technology* 5, no. 7 (October 15, 2007). http://www.special-operations-technology.com/sotech-archives/180-sotech-2008-volume-5-issue-7/1670-qaa-brigadier-general-simeon-g-trombitas.html.

"Raytheon Begins SAM-X/Patriot Missile Work in South Korea." *Defense Industry Daily*, December 1, 2008. http://www.defenseindustrydaily.com/Raytheon-Begins-SAM-XPatriot-Missile-Work-in-South-Korea-04772/.

Reiss, Mitchell B., and Robert L. Gallucci. "Red-Handed," *Foreign AffairsOnline*, March–April 2005. http://www.foreignaffairs.org/20050301faresponse84214/mitchell-b-reiss-robert-gallucci/red-handed.html.

"Restriction Announcement." Yantai Shandong Marine Fishing and Production Management Station [in Chinese], January 23, 2009.

Rice, Condoleezza. "Diplomacy Is Working on North Korea," Op-Ed, *Wall Street Journal*, June 26, 2008. http://online.wsj.com/article/SB121443815539505367.html?mod=opinion_main_commentaries.

Robertson, Colin, and Rear Adm. Stephen H. Baker (Ret). "Stand-Off with North Korea: War Scenarios and Consequences." Washington, DC: Center for Defense Information, 2003. http://www.cdi.org/north-korea/north-korea-crisis.pdf.

Robertson, Jeffrey. "After Iraq: A Military Solution in North Korea?" *Research Note* no. 29. Department of the Parliamentary Library, March 24, 2003. http://www.aph.gov.au/library/pubs/rn/2002-03/03rn29.pdf.

Rogin, Josh. "Emerging Asian Power: A Diplomatic Challenge." *Congressional Quarterly: CQ Politics*, October 19, 2008. http://www.cqpolitics.com/wmspage.cfm?docID=weeklyreport-000002976585.

Rosen, James. "U.S. Intelligence Confirms Kim Jong-il's Son to Inherit North Korean Dictatorship." *FOXNews.com*, June 12, 2009. http://www.foxnews.com/politics/2009/06/12/intelligence-confirms-kim-jong-ils-son-inherit-north-korean-dictatorship/.

Royce, Congressman Ed. "Gangster Regime: How North Korea Counterfeits United States Currency." *Staff Report.* United States House of Representatives, March 12, 2007. http://www.royce.house.gov/uploadedfiles/report.3.12.07.FINAL.GansterRegime.pdf.

Rubin, Uzi. "The Global Range of Iran's Ballistic Missile Program." *Jerusalem Issue Brief* (Jerusalem Center for Public Affairs) 5, no. 26 (June 20, 2006). http://www.jcpa.org/brief/brief005-26.htm.

Samore, Gary, and Bernard Gwertzman. "Samore: A Syria–North Korea Nuclear Relationship?" *Interview,* Council on Foreign Relations, September 2007. http://www.cfr.org/publication/14250/.

Samson, Victoria. "Missile Defense: North Korea's Missile Flight Tests." Center for Defense Information, November 20, 2003. http://www.cdi.org/friendlyversion/printversion.cfm?documentID=1677.

Schwartz, Gen. Thomas A., commander, United Nations Command/Combined Forces Command; and commander, United States Forces Korea. Statement for the Record to the Senate Armed Services Committee, March 7, 2000. http://armed-services.senate.gov/statemnt/2000/000307ts.pdf.

———. Statement for the Record to the Senate Armed Services Committee, March 5, 2002. http://www.shaps.hawaii.edu/security/us/schwartz_2002.html.

Scobell, Andrew, and John M. Sanford. *North Korea's Military Threat: Pyongyang's Conventional Forces, Weapons of Mass Destruction, and Ballistic Missiles.* Strategic Studies Institute Monograph. Carlisle, PA: U.S. Army War College, April 2007. http://www.strategicstudiesinstitute.army.mil/pdffiles/PUB771.pdf.

Secretariat, Headquarters for the Abduction Issue, Government of Japan. "The Abduction of Japanese Citizens by North Korea," 2007. http://www.kantei.go.jp/foreign/abduction/index.html.

"Secretary Gates Holds Consultations with ROK Minister of National Defense." *Defense Link*, February 23, 2007. http://www.defenselink.mil/news/Feb2007/d20070223sdrok.pdf.

Shambaugh, David. "China and the Korean Peninsula: Playing for the Long Term." *Washington Quarterly* 26, no. 2 (Spring 2003). http://www.twq.com/03spring/docs/03spring_shambaugh.pdf.

Sharp, Gen. Walter L. "Transformation Conference Commander's Welcome." Speech given at the Renaissance Seoul Hotel, Seoul, Republic of Korea, April 5, 2010. http://www.usfk.mil/usfk/(A(rAJooFALywEkAAAAZmEyM2JkYjctNDIzZC00OTdjLTg3MjAtYTNjMzk2YWNhOGQ1frCPo_59szFdRl5YFY4bC2nxIco1)S(r5axazfubj2nrr453fneye55))/Uploads/110/transform.pdf.

Smith, W. Thomas, Jr. "Kim, His Nukes, and His Army: North Korea's Kim Jong Il Tests Nukes; Threatens War with the United States." *World Defense Review*, October 16, 2006. http://worlddefensereview.com/wts101606.shtml.

So, Lt. Gen. Chin Tae. "Recasting the Viability of a Small Ally's Airpower: South Korea in Focus." *Air and Space Power Journal: Chronicles Online Journal,* October 1, 2002. http://www.airpower.maxwell.af.mil/airchronicles/cc/tae.html.

Sokolski, Henry. "Hide and Seek with Kim Chong-il." *Nautilus Institute Policy Forum Online* 05-80A, September 29, 2005. http://www.nautilus.org/fora/security/0580Sokolski.html.

Spaeth, Anthony. "Kim's Rackets: To Fund His Lifestyle—and His Nukes—Kim Jong Il Helms a Vast Criminal Network." *Time Asia,* June 2, 2003. http://www.time.com/time/asia/covers/501030609/story.html.

Squassoni, Sharon A., and Andrew Feickert. "Disarming Libya: Weapons of Mass Destruction." Washington, DC: CRS Report for Congress, April 22, 2004. http://www.au.af.mil/au/awc/awcgate/crs/rs21823.pdf.

Stares, Paul B., and Joel S. Wit. *Preparing for Sudden Change in North Korea.* Council Special Report no. 42. Washington, DC: Council on Foreign Relations, January 2009. http://www.cfr.org/content/publications/attachments/North_Korea_CSR42.pdf.

Stein, Jeff. "U.S. Claim that Iran Attended Launch Would Be Explosive—if True." *Congressional Quarterly*, July 28, 2006. http://public.cq.com/public/20060728_homeland.html.

Steinberg, David I. "Elections in the Republic of Korea: Foreign Policy Alternatives under New Leadership." Paper presented at the conference Elections, Political Transitions, and Foreign Policy in East Asia, sponsored by the Foreign Policy Research Institute, Philadelphia, April 14, 2008. http://www.fpri.org/enotes/200806.steinberg.electionskorea.html.

———, ed. *Korean Attitudes Toward the United States: Changing Dynamics.* Armonk, NY: M. E. Sharpe, 2004.

"Syria: Chemical Weapons." *GlobalSecurity.org*, April 24, 2004. http://www.globalsecurity.org/wmd/world/syria/cw.htm.

"Syria Improves Its SCUD D Missile with Help from North Korea." *Geostrategy-Direct*, February 22, 2006. http://www.geostrategy-direct.com/geostrategy%2Ddirect/.

"Syria Profile: Missile Capabilities: Scud C (Hwasong-6)." *Nuclear Threat Initiative*, August 2004. http://www.nti.org/e_research/profiles/Syria/Missile/4126_4337.html.

"Syria Profile: Missile Capabilities: Scud D (No-dong 1)." *Nuclear Threat Initiative*, August 2004. http://www.nti.org/e_research/profiles/Syria/Missile/4126_4338.html.

"10 Years of DPRK with SONGUN Policy." *Peoples's Korea*, 2004. http://www1.korea-np.co.jp/pk/207th_issue/2004071702.htm.

Toloraya, Georgy. "North Korea Now: Will the Clock Be Turned Back?" *Brookings Institution Paper*. Washington, DC: Brookings, February 11, 2008. http://www.brookings.edu/articles/2008/0211_north_korea_toloraya.aspx.

Tomero, Leonor, and Adam Ptacin. "Will Ill Kim Jong-Il Derail Disarmament?" Washington, DC: Center for Arms Control and Non-Proliferation, October 6, 2008. http://www.armscontrolcenter.org/policy/northkorea/articles/061008_ill_jong-il_derail_disarmament/.

"Transcript: Update on the Six-Party Talks with Christopher R. Hill." Proceedings of Brookings Institution Center for Northeast Asian Policy Studies, Washington, DC, February 22, 2007. http://www.brook.edu/comm/events/20070228hill.pdf.

United States Joint Forces Command. "Joint Forces Command Glossary," 2006. http://www.jfcom.mil/about/glossary.htm#ONA.

U.S. Congress. Senate. "Iran's Ballistic Missile and Weapons of Mass Destruction Programs." Hearing before the International Security, Proliferation, and Federal Services Subcommittee of the Committee on Governmental Affairs. 106th Cong., 2nd sess., September 21, 2000. http://www.fas.org/irp/congress/2000_hr/hr_092100.html.

U.S. Department of State. "Actions Taken by the United Nations Security Council 1718 Sanctions Committee to Implement Resolution 1874." Bureau of Public Affairs, Office of the Spokesman, July 16, 2009. http://www.state.gov/r/pa/prs/ps/2009/july/126148.htm.

————. "Afternoon Walkthrough with Reporters at Six-Party Talks." October 30, 2007. http://www.state.gov/p/eap/rls/rm/2007/94373.htm.

————. "Briefing on the Agreement Reached at the Six-Party Talks in Beijing." February 13, 2007. http://seoul.usembassy.gov/420_021407b.html.

————. "Joint Statement of the U.S.-Japan Security Consultative Committee." Office of the Spokesman, United States Department of State, May 1, 2007. http://tokyo.usembassy.gov/e/p/tp-20070502-77.html.

————. "North Korea—Denuclearization Action Plan: Initial Actions for the Implementation of the Joint Statement." Beijing, People's Republic of China, February 13, 2007. http://www.acronym.org.uk/docs/0702/doc01.htm.

————. "North Korea: Presidential Action on State Sponsor of Terrorism (SST) and the Trading with the Enemy Act (TWEA)." *Nautilus Institute Policy Forum* Online 08-050A, June 30, 2008. http://www.nautilus.org/fora/security/08050DoS.html.

————. "North Korea Sanctions: Resolution 1718 Versus Resolution 1874." Bureau of Public Affairs, Office of the Spokesman, June 12, 2009. http://www.state.gov/r/pa/prs/ps/2009/06a/124709.htm.

————. "U.S. and Republic of Korea Conclude New Special Measures Agreement." *Media Note*, January 15, 2009. http://www.state.gov/r/pa/prs/ps/2009/01/113988.htm.

————. "United States–Japan Roadmap for Realignment Implementation." May 1, 2006. http://www.usfj.mil/Documents/UnitedStates-JapanRoadmapforRealignmentImplementation.pdf.

U.S. Department of the Treasury. "North Korea Government Agencies' and Front Companies' Involvement in Illicit Financial Activities." *Financial Crimes Enforcement Network Advisory*, FIN-2009-A002, June 18, 2009. http://www.fincen.gov/statutes_regs/guidance/html/fin-2009-a002.html.

————. "Treasury Designates Banco Delta Asia as Primary Money Laundering Concern under USA PATRIOT Act." Press release, September 15, 2005. http://www.treas.gov/press/releases/js2720.htm.

———. "Treasury Designates Financial Institution Tied to North Korea's WMD Proliferation." Press release, August 11, 2009. http://www.ustreas.gov/press/releases/tg260.htm.

U.S. House of Representatives, Permanent Select Committee on Intelligence. "Recognizing Iran as a Strategic Threat: An Intelligence Challenge for the United States." Staff Report. Washington, DC: House Permanent Select Committee on Intelligence, Subcommittee on Intelligence Policy, August 23, 2006. http://intelligence.house.gov/Media/PDFS/IranReport082206v2.pdf#search=%22Recognizing%20Iran%20as%20a%20Strategic%20Threat%3A%20An%20Intelligence%20Challenge%20for%20the%20United%20States%22.

"US Will Sell Global Hawks—Will South Korea Buy?" *Defense Industry Daily*, December 8, 2008. http://www.defenseindustrydaily.com/Report-US-Agrees-to-Sell-Global-Hawks-to-South-Korea-05032/.

Vick, Charles P. "Has the No-Dong B/Shahab-4 Finally Been Tested in Iran for North Korea?" *GlobalSecurity.Org*, May 2, 2006. http://www.globalsecurity.org/wmd/library/report/2006/cpvick-no-dong-b_2006.htm.

Von Hippel, David F. "Estimated DPRK Military Energy Use: Analytical Approach and Draft Updated Results." Paper presented at the DPRK Energy Expert Study Group Meeting, Stanford University, California, June 26–27, 2006. http://nautilus.org/DPRKEnergy-Meeting/papers/DvH_DPRK_Military.ppt#270,1,Estimated DPRK Military Energy Use: Analytical Approach and Draft Updated Results.

Wagner, Alex. "Bush Puts N. Korea Negotiations on Hold, Stresses Verification." *Arms Control Today*, April 2001. http://www.armscontrol.org/act/2001_04/korea.

Wallace, Robert Daniel. *Sustaining the Regime: North Korea's Quest for Financial Support*. Lanham, MD: University Press of America, 2007.

Wishnick, Elizabeth. "Nuclear Tension Between China, N Korea." *International Relations and Security Network*, August 11, 2006. http://www.isn.ethz.ch/isn/Current-Affairs/Security-Watch/Detail/?id=52292&lng=en.

Wisconsin Project on Nuclear Arms Control. "North Korea Chemical and Biological Weapon Update—2005." *The Risk Report* 11, no. 4 (July–August 2005). http://www.wisconsinproject.org/countries/nkorea/north-korea-chem-bioupdate2005.html.

———. "North Korean Missile Exports." *The Risk Report* 2, no. 6 (November–December 1996). http://www.wisconsinproject.org/countries/nkorea/north-korea-missile-exports.html.

———. "North Korea Missile Milestones." *The Risk Report* 6, no. 5 (September–October 2000). http://www.wisconsinproject.org/countries/nkorea/missile-miles.htm.

———. "North Korea's Nuclear-Capable Missiles." *The Risk Report* 2, no. 6 (November–December 1996). http://www.wisconsinproject.org/countries/nkorea/nukemiss.html.

Wit, Joel, Dan Poneman, and Robert Gallucci. "Lessons Learned: The Road Ahead from Going Critical: The First North Korean Nuclear Crisis." *Nautilus Institute Policy Forum Online* PFO 04-24, June 24, 2004. http://www.nautilus.org/fora/security/0424A_Wit.html.

Wood, Lt. Gen. Stephen G., USAF, and Maj. Christopher A. Johnson, DM, USAF. "The Transformation of Air Forces on the Korean Peninsula." *Air and Space Power Journal* 22, no. 3 (Fall 2008). http://www.airpower.maxwell.af.mil/airchronicles/apj/apj08/fal08/wood.html.

Wright, David C. "An Analysis of the North Korean Missile Program." In *Report of the Commission to Assess the Ballistic Missile Threat to the United States*, edited by Donald Rumsfeld and others. Washington, DC: Federation of American Scientists, July 15, 1998. http://www.fas.org/irp/threat/missile/rumsfeld/pt2_wright.htm.

Wright, David C., and Timur Kadyshev. "An Analysis of the North Korean Nodong Missile." *Science & Global Security* 4, no. 2 (1994). http://www.princeton.edu/~globsec/publications/pdf/4_2wright.pdf.

Zhang, Hui. "North Korea's Oct. 9 Nuclear Test: Successful or Failed?" Paper presented at the Institute for Nuclear Materials Management 48th Annual Meeting, Tucson, Arizona, July 8–12, 2007. http://belfercenter.ksg.harvard.edu/files/NKtest_INMM07_Hui.pdf.

INDEX

ABOUT THE AUTHOR

Bruce E. Bechtol, Jr., is a former intelligence officer with the Defense Intelligence Agency and a retired Marine who has lived and worked in Korea and continues to visit there frequently. He received his Ph.D. from the Union Institute in Cincinnati, Ohio, and currently serves as an associate professor of political science at Angelo State University. He previously served on the faculty at both the U.S. Marine Corps Command and Staff College and the Air Command and Staff College. He also served as a visiting adjunct professor at the Korea University Graduate School of International Studies in Seoul, Korea, during 2006–7. In addition to being author of *Red Rogue: The Persistent Challenge of North Korea* (Potomac Books, 2007), he is a contributing author to several books on North Korea and has written nearly two dozen articles dealing with Korean security issues in peer-reviewed journals. Bechtol is the former editor of the *Defense Intelligence Journal* (2004–5) and served on the Editorial Advisory Board of the *East Asian Review* (2005–9). Bechtol sits on the Board of Directors of the International Council on Korean Studies and the Board of Directors of the Council on U.S.-Korean Security Studies, and he is a Fellow at the Institute for Corean-American Studies. He lives in San Angelo, Texas.